DATE DUE

# TOBACCO

A Reference Handbook

Other Titles in ABC-CLIO's
# CONTEMPORARY
# WORLD ISSUES
Series

Books in the Contemporary World Issues series address vital issues in today's society such as genetic engineering, pollution, and biodiversity. Written by professional writers, scholars, and nonacademic experts, these books are authoritative, clearly written, up-to-date, and objective. They provide a good starting point for research by high school and college students, scholars, and general readers as well as by legislators, businesspeople, activists, and others.

Each book, carefully organized and easy to use, contains an overview of the subject, a detailed chronology, biographical sketches, facts and data and/or documents and other primary-source material, a directory of organizations and agencies, annotated lists of print and nonprint resources, and an index.

Readers of books in the Contemporary World Issues series will find the information they need in order to have a better understanding of the social, political, environmental, and economic issues facing the world today.

# TOBACCO

## A Reference Handbook

Harold V. Cordry

**CONTEMPORARY WORLD ISSUES**

**ABC-CLIO**

Santa Barbara, California
Denver, Colorado
Oxford, England

Library of Congress Cataloging-in-Publication Data

Cordry, Harold V.
    Tobacco : a reference handbook / Harold V. Cordry.
       p. ; cm.—(ABC-CLIO's contemporary world issues series)
    Includes bibliographical references and index.
    ISBN 0-87436-967-3 (hardcover; alk. paper); 1-57607-541-9 (e-book)
1. Tobacco habit—Information resources. 2. Antismoking
movement—Information resources. 3. Trials (Products liability—United
States—Information resources. 4. Products liability—Tobacco—United
States—Information resources. 5. Tobacco industry —Law and
legislation—United States—Information resources.
    [DNLM: 1. Tobacco Industry—history 2. Smoking—adverse
effects—Resource Guides. 3. Tobacco—adverse effects—Resource
Guides. HD 9130.5 C796t 2001] I. Title. II. Contemporary world issues
    HV5735 .C67 2001
    362.29'6—dc21

                                                              2001004555


07  06  05  04  03  02  01  10 9 8 7 6 5 4 3 2 1

This book is also available on the World Wide Web as an e-book.
Visit abc-clio.com for details.

ABC-CLIO, Inc.
130 Cremona Drive, P.O. Box 1911
Santa Barbara, California 93116-1911

This book is printed on acid-free paper ∞

Manufactured in the United States of America

# Contents

# Acknowledgments

As I worked on this book, I thought often of my mother and father and my grandmother, who smoked all their lives. I thought about my wife, Janice, who quit, and about my nieces and nephews, Steven and Jenny, and Brian, Britt, and Bailey—nonsmokers. I dedicate this book to all of them—to the one who quit, to those who did not, and to those who chose at some point not to start—thoughts of whom inspired me to do my best to make a book that I hoped would be informative, accurate, objective, and useful.

I am deeply indebted to Janice, as always, for her help and for her ability to tolerate a filing system that engulfed our dining room table and turned the living room into an amusement park for the cats, George, Gracie, and Spot. I am grateful to my editor at ABC-CLIO, Kevin Downing, for his near-saintly patience and his sensitivity to my feelings after I suffered a stroke that left me partially paralyzed, having only one index finger with which to type, and I am grateful also to Deborah Lynes and Melanie Stafford, my project editors, who labored painstakingly to ensure the accuracy and coherence of the book. I am also indebted to the American Cancer Society, the American Heart Association, and the American Lung Association; to Tac Tacelosky, webmaster of Smokescreen; to Anne Landman, regional program coordinator of the American Lung Association of Colorado; to Gene Borio of Tobacco BBS; to Valerie Wheat, archivist, Special Collections, Library and Center for Knowledge Management, University of California, San Francisco; to the World Health Organization; to the Office of Graduate Studies and Research, University of Nebraska, Kearney, which generously gave me a grant to pay the wages of research assistants (though I was only "passing through" as a visiting lecturer); to Keith Terry and Judy Spivey of UNK's Department of Communications, who helped facilitate my writing and solve computer problems I encountered while working in Kearney; to Tim and Suzanne Doyle, who dealt with my computer problems after my return to Kansas; to tobacco researcher Larry Breed; to the Centers for Disease Control and the Office on Smoking and Health; to the National Cancer Institute; to COHIS, Boston University School of Medicine; to Mark Gottlieb and Jacqueline Salcedo, Tobacco Control Resource Center, Inc., Northeastern University School of Law, Boston, Massachusetts; to the National Women's Health Information Center; to Bottary and Partners Public Relations, Jacksonville, Florida; to the U.S. Department of Health and Human Services; to the Institute for Social Research, University of Michigan; to Karl Brookes, ASH UK; and to Jeffrey Wigand for his courage and his example.

*Harold V. Cordry*

# 1

# Overview

There was a time when tobacco was considered a wonder drug, comparable to antibiotics and Jonas Salk's polio vaccine but superior because it could be used to treat virtually any ailment, from mental illness and cancer to constipation and flatulence. American Indians valued its medicinal qualities, not only smoking it but also applying it to burns, wounds, and frostbite and using it as a suppository.

Old World physicians were similarly enthusiastic. A treatise by the Spanish physician Nicholas Monardes described tobacco as a successful treatment for "griefs" of the head, breast, stomach, and joints as well as for toothache, snakebite, and scaly scalp. A Dr. Johannes Vittich wrote that tobacco could "cleanse all impurities and disperse every gross and viscous humour," and he recommended it in cases of breast cancer, sores, goiter, and broken bones. Some believed it to be effective against bubonic plague. A doctor treating plague victims reported feeling the plague invading his own system but being saved from death, he said, because he had the presence of mind to race home and smoke six pipefuls of tobacco. William Byrd hoped to promote the general well-being of his countrymen by persuading them to follow his example and hang tobacco leaves "about [their] clothes" and to "place . . . bundles . . . round [their] beds." Indeed, so widespread was the belief in tobacco's healthful qualities that a student at an exclusive English prep school was reportedly flogged for *not* smoking.

Among tobacco's detractors was King James I of England. In his often-quoted *A Counterblaste to Tobacco*, published in 1604, he not only scoffed at stories of tobacco's supposed medical uses but also berated smokers for having adopted "so vile and stinking a custome." Worse, it produced "a generall sluggishnesse," as he called it, which made its users "wallow in all sorts of idle delights." He also expressed concern that tobacco would undermine the health of the nation, pointing to the "ryotous and disordered Persons of meane and base Condition"—but not "Persons of good Callinge and Qualitye"—who used tobacco immoderately and had consequently become weakened and unfit for labor. Sounding like some of the critics of today, James complained about smoking in public places, where nonsmokers found it necessary to eat garlic as a means of counteracting the odors of smoke and smokers.

> Have you not reason . . . to bee ashamed, and to forbeare this filthie noveltie, so basely grounded, so foolishly received and so grossely mistaken in the right use thereof? In your abuse thereof sinning against God, harming your selves both in persons and goods, and raking also thereby the markes and notes of vanitie upon you: by the custome thereof making your selves to be wondered at by all forraine civil Nations, and by all strangers that come among you, to be scorned and contemned. A custome lothsome to the eye, hateful! to the braine, dangerous to the Lungs, and in the blacke stinking fume thereof, neerest resembling the horrible Stigian smoke of the pit that is bottomelesse. (James I 1604)

Elsewhere in Europe and the East, rulers experienced frustration similar to that of King James. Even in countries like Russia, where smokers were exiled to Siberia, and in China and Turkey, where some were executed, tobacco use nevertheless became widely popular. In England, James's disapproval stopped short of exile and execution. He sought to discourage smoking by raising the import duty on tobacco 4,000 percent. But the custom spread unchecked, with much of the tobacco originating in England's own Virginia Colony, and smuggling flourished. After James gave up trying to put an end to smoking and instead merely taxed imports, tobacco became his government's richest source of revenue and the American colonies' most lucrative export (Deford 1997, H1).

# The Rise of Tobacco in America

At first the colonists cultivated the indigenous variety of *Nicotiana rustica* grown by the local Indians. But the leaf was found to be "poore and weake and of a byting tast," according to William Strachey, first recorder and secretary to the Virginia Colony (quoted in Corina 1975, 32). John Rolfe's arrival in Jamestown led to important changes. Already a confirmed pipe smoker, accustomed to the sweeter, more flavorful tobacco imported to Europe from Trinidad and Venezuela , Rolfe obtained some seeds for this variety and blended them into new plantings in Jamestown, producing a dark leaf comparable in quality to its Latin American progenitor (Kluger 1996, 11).

During the early years of settlement and exploration, the most popular form of tobacco use in America was pipe-smoking. But snuffing into the nose had been developed into an elaborate ritual by the French, and by the first half of the eighteenth century, the snuffbox had become the mark of a gentleman in both London and Virginia. Although snuff was associated with an aristocratic way of life many Americans hated, several snuff mills were set up in America, one by French Huguenot emigre Pierre Lorillard in New York City. Susan Wagner has noted that as the nineteenth century progressed, it began to be known as the cigar age. "The pipe [also] held its grip, as did chewing tobacco. Snuff went into eclipse. By the end of the 1800s, the cigarette would begin to make inroads" (Wagner 1971, 26–27).

The cigarette had originated as the *cigarito* in the Spanish colonies of the New World, and it had become became popular in the first half of the nineteenth century, first in Spain, then in France, and finally in Russia. English soldiers returning from the Crimean War (1854–1856) helped make cigarettes acceptable in England, where they had previously been regarded as suitable mainly for the poor and "so weak-tasting as to invite the suspicion that those smokers who preferred . . . [them] were effeminate" (Kluger 1996, 13).

But popularity developed slowly, both in England and the United States. Boxing legend John L. Sullivan spoke for many Americans in the late nineteenth century when he condemned the cigarette as a smoke fit only for "dudes and college misfits" (Kluger 1996, 62).

Indeed, cigarettes' popularity was largely a phenomenon of

the twentieth century, born of a habit formed by soldiers during World War I in the trenches of Western Europe. Gen. George Pershing had in fact appealed to the War Department to keep U.S. troops adequately supplied with cigarettes, which he said were "no less important than bullets." (In consequence, production topped 36 billion cigarettes in 1917, when the United States entered the war, more than double that of 1914.) After the Armistice was declared and American soldiers returned home, still puffing on their Camels and Luckies, cigarette smoking spread through the middle class, opening a vast new market for the tobacco industry.

At about the same time, women were beginning to smoke in public, making cigarettes more respectable. The industry had begun to woo women before the war, at first almost shyly. A 1912 ad for Velvet pipe tobacco depicted a young woman staring dreamily at a male pipe smoker and thinking, "I wish I were a man!" In another ad, a woman tells a man who is smoking, "Blow some my way." Before long women themselves were told to "reach for a Lucky instead of a sweet," rather than relying on men for an occasional whiff of secondhand smoke.

In 1930 per capita consumption of cigarettes was more than double the level of 1925 (see Table 1.1), owing in part to the growing number of women smokers, enjoying the fruits of emancipation and the loosening of moral standards. The market was dominated at that time by four premium brands—Lucky Strike, Camel, Chesterfield, and Old Gold—which accounted for 9 out of every 10 packs sold in the United States.

**Table 1.1**
**Cigarettes Sold in 1925 and 1930**

| Leading Brands | Cigarettes Sold (Billions*) |
|---|---|
| 1925 | |
| Camel | 34.2 |
| Lucky Strike | 13.7 |
| Chesterfield | 19.7 |
| 1930 | |
| Lucky Strike | 43.2 |
| Camel | 35.3 |
| Chesterfield | 26.4 |

*Source:* Tobacco BBS, http://www.tobacco.org, accessed 1999.

* Unless otherwise stated, number of cigarettes refers to number of packs of cigarettes.

The continuing growth of cigarettes' popularity through the first half of the century was influenced by increasingly pervasive print advertising that depicted pleasant-looking people in comfortable surroundings either smoking or holding cigarettes. Endorsements were common, too, with physicians and opera singers attesting to the smoothness of one brand or another. But it was Hollywood films that probably did the most to encourage the spread of smoking in those years. Although "bad guys" invariably smoked, so did the private eyes who tracked them down, and even more important, so did handsome leading men—Clark Gable, Leslie Howard, John Wayne, William Powell, and Cesar Romero—and glamorous actresses such as Gloria Swanson, Bette Davis, Barbara Stanwyck, and Carole Lombard. From the point of view of the tobacco companies, which are currently besieged by personal-injury lawyers, angry health authorities, and abusive antismoking activists, those were indisputably "the good old days."

Even when smoking seemed nearly universal, however, some always opposed tobacco use, though never with such devastating effect as today. In July 1942, *Reader's Digest* published an article by Robert Littell reporting the results of tests to determine the validity of advertising claims that certain brands contained fewer irritants than others. Littell said that only minute differences had been found in levels of irritants and that the smoker "need no longer worry as to which cigarette can most effectively nail down his coffin" (Littell, quoted in Kluger 1996, 130).

The tests led the Federal Trade Commission (FTC) to file complaints the following month against the nation's four biggest cigarette makers, charging that their advertising claims came too close to being warranties that their products were harmless. Ultimately, however, only Philip Morris was found to have made claims based on insufficient evidence.

Meanwhile, the cigarette makers were facing another threat, far greater than a mere challenge to the veracity of their advertising. Accumulated research findings linked smoking to cancer and to shortened life span. Among the studies were the following:

- 1938—Dr. Raymond Pearl of Johns Hopkins University reported that of 6,813 men whose medical histories he studied, only 45 percent of smokers lived until age 60, compared with 65 percent of nonsmokers (Pearl 1938).

- 1950—After interviewing over 600 lung cancer patients, Drs. Ernst Wynder and Evarts Graham reported in the *Journal of the American Medical Association* that 96.5 percent of the patients had been smokers (Wynder and Graham 1950).
- 1952—After comparing lung cancer patients to a sample of other patients of the same age, sex, and general background, Richard Doll and Bradford Hill, two British physicians, reported that a high percentage of the lung cancer patients had been heavy cigarette smokers (Doll and Hill 1952).
- 1952—Drs. E. Cuyler Hammond and Daniel Horn reported on a major prospective study in which they tracked 187,000 men between the ages of 50 and 69. They found that the death rate from cancer for men who smoked a pack a day or more was 2.5 times as great as that of nonsmokers, and that smokers were 5 times more likely to die of lung cancer and twice as likely to die of heart disease. Even light smokers, who smoked less than half a pack a day, were considerably more likely to die before nonsmokers.
- 1953—Drs. Wynder and Graham carried out experiments on mice, painting their backs with condensate (i.e., tar) from cigarette smoke. Fifty-eight percent of the mice that survived after a year into the experiment developed cancerous tumors. The experiment "shows conclusively," Dr. Graham said, "that there is something in cigarette smoke which can produce cancer" (Wynder, Graham, and Croninger 1953).
- 1954—Drs. Doll and Hill reported on a four-and-one-half-year study during which they gathered information from 40,000 British physicians aged 35 or older. They concluded that "[m]ild smokers are seven times as likely to die of lung cancer as nonsmokers, [and] immoderate smokers are 24 times as likely to die of lung cancer . . . [as] nonsmokers" (Doll and Hill 1954).
- 1954—Researchers also called attention to the fact that in 1950 more women were being diagnosed with lung cancer, and they suggested a relationship to their having begun to smoke in the 1920s and 1930s.

The various studies disturbed smokers. And perhaps they were most disturbed when *Reader's Digest,* an established enemy of the tobacco industry, published an article in December 1952 titled "Cancer by the Carton," in which Roy Norr, the editor of the little-known newsletter "Smoking and Health News," bluntly summarized the case against smoking. Norr's indictment of cigarettes stated the risks as he saw them in terms that readers could not ignore. Other articles—notably in *Ladies Home Journal, The New Republic, Consumer Reports,* and *The Nation*—were similarly hard-hitting.

The industry was disturbed, too—by the sharp decline in cigarette consumption. After a peak of 416 billion cigarettes per year in 1952, the number had fallen in less than two years to 388 billion. Forty percent of the public believed that smoking caused lung cancer. Some in the industry thought the end was in sight.

In this atmosphere of impending disaster, the chief executive officers (CEOs) of the leading tobacco companies came together on December 15, 1953, for a secret summit meeting at the Plaza Hotel in New York City—Parker McComas of Philip Morris, Paul D. Hahn of American Tobacco, Joseph F. Cullman of Benson & Hedges (B&H), and J. Whitney Peterson of the U.S. Tobacco Company. Also present was John Hill of Hill & Knowlton (H&K), a public relations (PR) firm in New York. His presence made it clear that the CEOs perceived not a health crisis but a PR crisis, a crisis of image that the tobacco industry could survive only if it could change public perception.

Thus, in response to published evidence that people were dying as a consequence of using tobacco products, the tobacco industry undertook what has been called the largest, longest-running, most expensive issue campaign in the history of American advertising. Significantly, notes of an H&K employee who took minutes of the meeting reveal that the tobacco executives assured Hill of their confidence in their ability to supply H&K with "comprehensive and authoritative scientific material which completely refutes the health charges." Hill warned the executives that if the dangers of smoking proved real, the industry could not continue on a course of denial (quoted in Hilts 1996, 6).

As a first step in their PR campaign, the CEOs agreed to establish an organization called the Tobacco Industry Research Committee (TIRC). The first name proposed for the unit, by Hahn, was "The Committee of Public Information," but Hill said using the word "research" would imbue the organization with more authority. So it became "Tobacco Industry Research Committee." The committee's principal function would be to develop a campaign attacking scientists and researchers who published reports of a link between smoking and cancer. The name was later changed to "Council for Tobacco Research"(CTR), omitting mention of the committee's connection with the tobacco industry.

The conspiracy of which plaintiffs' attorneys would later accuse the tobacco industry is clearly traceable to that meeting at the Plaza Hotel in 1953, when four tobacco executives sat down with a PR adviser and outlined measures for continuing business as usual in circumstances that seemed to demand an altogether different response. "Money was at the center of [the tobacco industry conspiracy]," says Phil Hilts, a former *New York Times* reporter, "and public relations forestalled any serious look at the issue or any conscience-searching at the time. The plan was to spend large amounts of money every year in the future to prevent, not sworn adversaries, but *scientists and public health officials,* from warning people of a potential hazard. . . . There is no case like it in the annals of business or health"(emphasis in the original) (Hilts 1996, 6–7).

The decisions made at that meeting in 1953 have had far-reaching implications for both the tobacco industry and those who have used its products. In 1976, years after the Plaza meeting, a Brown & Williamson (B&W) vice president, Ernest Pepples, wrote about four steps on which the CEOs decided at that meeting (Pepples 1976, 2205.01.1/.6).

1.   "Produce more filter brands and brands with lower tar delivery." In other words, the industry should produce cigarettes that would convey the impression of being less harmful. Pepples noted that the industry "moved strongly" toward filter cigarettes, "which . . . increased from .5 percent [of the market] in 1950 to 87 percent in 1975." In 1951, he said, "nine out of 20 brands on the market accounted for as much as 1 percent of market share. By 1964, 17 of 41 brands had more than 1 percent share. . . . of market." "There was an urgent effort to highlight and differentiate one brand from the others already on the market. It was important to have the most filter traps," he said. However, although some brands claimed to possess the least amount of tar, "in

most cases . . . the smoker of a filter cigarette was getting as much or more nicotine and tar as he would have gotten from a regular cigarette." Pepples noted that the FTC put an end to what had become known as the "tar derby" by prohibiting tar and nicotine claims in advertising on the grounds that there was no reliable, uniform test for measuring tar and nicotine intake levels in smokers and no proof that one type of cigarette was less harmful than another. The Consumers' Union suggested that the FTC action was probably welcomed by the tobacco industry, which was in effect ordered to extricate itself from a potentially endless war of words and numbers.

2.  "Support scientific research to refute unfavorable findings or at a minimum to keep the scientific question open." According to Pepples, by 1974 the TIRC had disbursed more than $28 million , while the industry as a whole spent more than $50 million on research over approximately the same time period. "The focal point for criticism of [unfavorable] research," Pepples said, was an organization called the Tobacco Institute (TI), founded in 1958. He summarizes TI's functions as generally "attempt[ing] to keep the opposition honest." Various other internal TIRC documents mention paying "whitecoats" (scientists, researchers, etc.) to criticize or dispute unfavorable findings.

3.  "Conduct information campaigns against claims by the antismoking lobby."

4.   Diversify tobacco industry corporations "to minimize the potential adverse financial consequences of the controversy [over] cigarette sales." Corporate diversification was considered a protective measure in 1953, even though tobacco companies were not yet contemplating the possibility of huge settlements and punitive-damages awards.

In 1976, the year of Pepples's reflections on the results of the Plaza meeting, it still seemed possible to defend the tobacco industry's interests by maintaining a solid united front—continuing to insist, even in the face of mounting evidence, that unfavorable research findings were "inconclusive" or "not proven."

# Filter Cigarettes and the Tar Derby

By 1952, annual cigarette consumption in the United States had reached 416 billion. However, total consumption for 1953 and 1954 declined sharply—to 408 billion cigarettes in 1953 and 388 billion in 1954. This decline in consumption was not an earth-shaking setback for the tobacco industry, but it sent a clear signal that smokers were genuinely concerned about the adverse effects of smoking. Many more smokers might have quit had the tobacco industry not responded with measures to suggest, if not to state outright, that cigarettes could be made less hazardous.

Among the tobacco companies, Lorillard was the first to see opportunity in the crisis threatening the industry. Lorillard's response was to introduce a new brand of cigarette called Kent. Kents were equipped with a "micronite" filter, made of crocidolite, a form of asbestos. Other cigarette makers quickly followed suit with filters of their own, all of them designed to trap some of the nasty brown sludge produced by the combustion of tobacco. Of course, advertising companies did not talk about cancer and strokes and emphysema, and they certainly did not claim that one brand of cigarette was "safe" or "safer" than another—only that their brand was "smoother" or "milder." But smokers were predisposed to interpret the ads generously (e.g., a "mild," filtered cigarette is less dangerous), and they crowded aboard the industry's bandwagon with all the enthusiasm of newly saved sinners.

To Lorillard's disappointment, the micronite filter worked too well: Kent smokers complained that the "kick" was gone. So Lorillard quietly substituted a looser filter that drew more easily but at the same time provided less protection against tar and nicotine. In addition, many smokers opted for one of the new brands of longer "king-size" cigarettes that appeared on the market. Because of their length, they were advertised as providing "natural" filtration. The consumer was meant to presume that some of the harmful components of smoke would be absorbed as the smoke passed through the extra millimeters of unburned tobacco, before it could be drawn into the lungs.

An alluring alternative presented itself in 1955, at a time when 20 percent of cigarettes sold in the United States were filtered. (By 1957, filter-tipped cigarettes would account for 50 percent of the U.S. market.) The new product was an old product—the Marlboro brand, which had made its first appearance in the

1920s as a "woman's cigarette" that was "mild as May." But now it was to be marketed as having a rich, full-bodied flavor that could be appreciated only by the most masculine smokers. As for the Marlboro's Selectrate filter, the true "Marlboro man" was a risk-taker who probably would just as soon do without it. The Marlboro became known as a strong, more "virile" cigarette.

Millions of confirmed smokers found a measure of comfort in smoking some brand of filtered or king-size cigarettes, significantly changing the ranking of the country's leading brands (see Table 1.2). In general, however, smokers really were not convinced that less tar and nicotine made cigarettes any less hazardous. Their doubts were reinforced in 1957, when a subcommittee of the House Government

**Table 1.2**
**Top Ten Cigarette Brands and Sales, 1941 and 1961**

| Brand | Unit Sales* (Billions) |
|-------|------------------------|
| **1941** | |
| Lucky Strike | 49.5 |
| Camel | 48.5 |
| Chesterfield | 37.5 |
| Philip Morris | 17.5 |
| Raleigh | 11.0 |
| Old Gold | 6.0 |
| Pall Mall | 4.8 |
| Sensation/Beechnut | 5.5 |
| Marvel | 4.0 |
| Avalon | 4.0 |
| **1961** | |
| Pall Mall | 71.2 |
| Camel | 66.5 |
| Winston | 58.8 |
| Lucky Strike | 41.6 |
| Salem | 41.5 |
| Kent | 38.4 |
| Chesterfield | 25.9 |
| L & M | 25.5 |
| Marlboro | 24.1 |
| Viceroy | 19.9 |

*Source: Printer's Ink,* February 6, 1942, and December 1961. Cited by Gene Borio on Tobacco BBS web site (http://www.tobacco.org/).

*Unit is one cigarette.

Operations Committee held hearings on cigarette advertising. The subcommittee issued a report concluding that cigarette manufacturers had deceived the American public through their advertising, and in 1959 the FTC told manufacturers that statements concerning low or reduced tar or nicotine, whether by filtration or otherwise, would be prohibited. The FTC said its purpose was to eliminate from cigarette advertising all representations that might in any way imply health benefits. The FTC ruling meant that industry advertising could no longer provide the reassurance smokers wanted, except by portraying smokers as happy, healthy, fun-loving people whose use of tobacco contributed in some indefinable way to their high spirits and popularity.

## Surgeon General's Report of 1964

It was January 11, 1964. The body of President John F. Kennedy had lain in its grave only a little more than a month. Kennedy's vice president, Lyndon Baines Johnson, now occupied the Oval Office. On television two new series, "The Beverly Hillbillies" and "My Favorite Martian," would enter their second season in a few months, and "The Munsters" would begin its first. Later in the year the Cardinals would beat the Yankees four games to three in the World Series. The first Super Bowl was still three years in the future.

Despite the warnings issued by researchers and the FTC in the preceding decade, in 1964 tobacco companies were still thriving. Forty-six percent of Americans smoked—more than half of adult males and one-third of adult women. But the industry was about to face a heavy blow, the aftershocks of which would still be felt at the close of the century.

The approximately 200 accredited reporters who gathered outside the State Department auditorium on a cold Saturday morning at the invitation of the surgeon general knew that they were going to hear something important. Not only was the news conference on a Saturday (the purpose being to avert a panic on Wall Street), but it also was being conducted under tightened security, unprecedented for a surgeon general's conference. At 9 A.M., after guards had checked the credentials of the reporters, they were admitted and the doors were locked. Surgeon General Luther L. Terry took a seat on the platform, along with the 10 members of his Advisory Committee on Smoking and Health. As the reporters fidgeted, aides rolled in dollies bearing softbound copies of the committee's 387-page report. Copies had been hand-delivered to the West Wing of the White House only two hours earlier. Apparently even a president was not to be trusted for long with news of this magnitude. The reporters were given 90 minutes to skim the report, after which Dr. Terry and the committee members answered their questions. At last the doors were unlocked and the reporters hurried away. Releasing them, someone said later, was "like flushing ducks off a pond." For most of them it would be the biggest story of their lives (Whelan 1984, 101–102).

The 1964 report, *Smoking and Health: Report of the Advisory Committee to the Surgeon General of the Public Health Service* (for short, *Smoking and Health*) shook the ground under the tobacco industry. Having reviewed more than 7,000 articles about the relationship between smoking and disease, Terry's Advisory Committee on Smoking and Health had concluded that cigarette smoking was indeed a cause of lung cancer and laryngeal cancer in men, a probable cause of lung cancer in women, and the most important cause of chronic bronchitis (Advisory Committee on Smoking and Health 1964).

The committee also said that "smoking is a health hazard of sufficient importance in the United States to warrant appropriate remedial action." The committee left "appropriate remedial action" undefined, but its report was a clear indictment of the tobacco industry as a destroyer of health on a scale comparable to a major war (Advisory Committee on Smoking and Health 1964).

Terry was jubilant. He believed that smokers only had to be made aware of the dangers of smoking to give it up. But of course he was to be disappointed. What was called "the Great Forswearing" of January and February 1964, when many smokers tried to quit, was followed by "the Great Relapse" of March, when good intentions gave way to the unrelenting pull of nicotine. "Within a few months," *Consumer Reports* magazine noted, "cigarette consumption was back almost to pre-1964 levels" (Brecher et al. 1972).

Within hours of the end of Terry's news conference, officials of the Federal Trade Commission were writing the text of warning labels that they believed ought to be required on cigarette packages. In the following year Congress enacted the Federal Cigarette Labeling and Advertising Act of 1965. The act required that the warning "Caution: Cigarette Smoking May Be Hazardous to Your

Health" appear on one of the side panels of each pack of cigarettes but prohibited, for a four-year period, any additional federal, state, or local labeling requirements—a provision pleasing to the tobacco industry, though the wording of the label itself was not. The industry had preferred "excessive use of this product [may be hazardous to your health]," which shifted responsibility for adverse effects to the smokers themselves. The manufacturers had successfully opposed efforts to substitute "*is* hazardous" for "*may be* hazardous." However, in 1969 Congress approved a slightly stronger version—"Warning: The Surgeon General Has Determined That Cigarette Smoking Is Dangerous to Your Health"—and at the same time prohibited cigarette advertising on television and radio. After the FTC reported in 1981 that the labels apparently were not having much effect, Congress enacted yet another label law, the Comprehensive Smoking Education Act of 1984, which instituted the rotating warnings now found on cigarette packages and cigarette advertisements. The four established warnings change periodically, or are "rotated" in and out of use.

Broadly speaking, tobacco manufacturers were not quite as opposed to the warnings as they seemed to be—perhaps because they knew that warnings of some type were probably inevitable and because prescient industry lawyers believed that warnings might become useful in a legal defense based on a smoker's assumption of risk (i.e., individuals chose to smoke even though they had been warned of potential ill effects). Among other immediate consequences of the report *Smoking and Health,* the U.S. Public Health Service (PHS) established the National Clearinghouse for Smoking and Health, later called the Office on Smoking and Health (OSH). Surgeon General Terry also announced that his report would be followed by subsequent reports on smoking and health to be produced and published annually by his successors.

## Other Surgeon General and PHS Reports Relating to Tobacco

After the surgeon general's groundbreaking report in 1964, reports on the links between smoking and ill health were produced almost annually, including the following:

- 1967—*Smoking and Health: Report of the Advisory Committee to the Surgeon General of the Public Health Service*

- 1968—*The Health Consequences of Smoking: A Public Health Service Review*
- 1969—*The Health Consequences of Smoking: 1969 Supplement to the 1967 Public Health Service Review*
- 1971—*The Health Consequences of Smoking: A Report of the Surgeon General*
- 1972—*The Health Consequences of Smoking: A Report of the Surgeon General*
- 1973—*The Health Consequences of Smoking, 1973*
- 1974—*The Health Consequences of Smoking, 1974*
- 1975—*The Health Consequences of Smoking, 1975*
- 1976—*The Health Consequences of Smoking: Selected Chapters from 1971 through 1975 Reports*
- 1978—*The Health Consequences of Smoking, 1977–1978*
- 1979—*Smoking and Health: A Report of the Surgeon General*
- 1980—*The Health Consequences of Smoking for Women: A Report of the Surgeon General*
- 1981—*The Health Consequences of Smoking—the Changing Cigarette: A Report of the Surgeon General*
- 1982—*The Health Consequences of Smoking—Cancer: A Report of the Surgeon General*
- 1983—*The Health Consequences of Smoking—Cardiovascular Disease: A Report of the Surgeon General*
- 1984—*The Health Consequences of Smoking—Chronic Obstructive Lung Disease: A Report of the Surgeon General*
- 1985—*The Health Consequences of Smoking—Cancer and Chronic Lung Disease: A Report of the Surgeon General*
- 1986—*The Health Consequences of Involuntary Smoking: A Report of the Surgeon General*
- 1989—*Reducing the Health Consequences of Smoking—25 Years of Progress: A Report of the Surgeon General*
- 1990—*The Health Benefits of Smoking Cessation: A Report of the Surgeon General*
- 1992—*Smoking in the Americas: A Report of the Surgeon General*
- 1994—*Preventing Tobacco Use among Young People: A Report of the Surgeon General*
- 1998—*Tobacco Use among U.S. Racial/Ethnic Minority Groups, 1998*
- 2000—*Treating Tobacco Use and Dependence: A Clinical Practice Guideline*

The tobacco industry had known months in advance that Surgeon General Terry was assembling a panel of experts to review the many studies relating to tobacco's adverse effects on health and to present to the public a full report of its findings. To avoid possible allegations of bias, Terry had given the tobacco companies a list of prospective panel members and invited them to reject anyone whose objectivity they doubted. None of the candidates had ever taken a position on the issue of smoking and health, and when one of them made the mistake of remarking to reporters before the review had begun that the preponderance of evidence seemed to be against tobacco, he was summarily disqualified. However, no one in the tobacco industry or the public health sector doubted what the panel's results would be.

On February 18, a week after release of the report, Helmut Wakeman, research director of Philip Morris, sent a memo to his superiors saying, "The industry must come forward with evidence of how . . . its products, present and prospective, are not harmful." Later Wakeman recalled that the Philip Morris attorneys scorned his suggestion. Their advice was to plead ignorance, based on the rationale that the company could not be held responsible for health risks if it had not known about them. Given the outcome of subsequent lawsuits, the attorneys were partly right: the "hear no evil" strategy worked, for a time. However, Phillip Morris attorneys could not foresee how tobacco litigation would evolve in the decades ahead or that millions of the industry's own internal documents would be used to prove what it had known and when.

## The Tobacco Industry Besieged

The revelations of the early 1950s, resulting from the studies of Wynder, Graham, and others, together with Roy Norr's article in *Reader's Digest*, did more than simply frighten American smokers, they produced what lawyers call the "first wave" of lawsuits against the tobacco industry, beginning in 1954. Typically the first-wave suits were brought by a single lawyer on behalf of a single plaintiff claiming negligence and breach of warranty. The largest tobacco companies were the first to be the target of lawsuits (see Table 1.3). The principal tactic of the tobacco lawyers was to prolong the proceedings, using the tobacco industry's

**Table 1.3**
**Cigarette Companies by Market Shares, 1961 and 1971**

| Company | Share (%) |
|---|---|
| 1961 | |
| Reynolds | 32.7 |
| American | 25.6 |
| Liggett & Myers | 10.7 |
| Lorillard | 10.4 |
| Brown & Williamson | 9.8 |
| Philip Morris | 9.4 |
| Others | 1.4 |
| | |
| 1971 | |
| Reynolds | 32.3 |
| Philip Morris | 18.0 |
| American | 17.5 |
| Brown & Williamson | 16.7 |
| Lorillard | 9.0 |
| Liggett & Myers | 6.4 |
| Others | 0.1 |

*Source:* Data from *Printer's Ink,* December 1961, and *Business Week,* November 29, 1971. Table from Office of the Attorney General of Washington n.d.

"deep pockets" to force the plaintiff to back down as the cost of the suit soared beyond his or her means.

In those cases that progressed beyond the pretrial stage, industry lawyers argued that companies could not be held liable for breach of warranty because they had not known, at the time the plaintiff developed cancer, that smoking might cause harm. Among the first of those product-liability suits was *Cooper v. R. J. Reynolds,* filed by Eva Cooper on behalf of her late husband, Joseph Cooper, a longtime Camel smoker who had died of lung cancer. She claimed that smoking had caused his cancer and that R. J. Reynolds (RJR) was guilty of negligence and breach of warranty. Cooper's attorney cited RJR advertising that claimed that 20,000 physicians believed Camel cigarettes were "healthful." The court ruled, however, that Cooper had failed to prove causation—i.e., that RJR's advertising had actually influenced her husband to continue smoking—and the case was dismissed.

Many legal experts of the time believed that Eva Cooper would win her case and that her victory would open the door to hundreds of successful suits against big tobacco, eventually bringing the industry to its knees. But other first-wave cases also failed, typically because the plaintiffs could not prove their claims or because the tobacco companies forced them to spend beyond their means. Indeed, after Cooper, the industry was to enjoy an unbroken string of more than 300 courtroom victories.

One of these cases, *Latrigue v. R. J. Reynolds* (1963), significantly influenced the interpretation of tort law as it applied to the liability of tobacco companies. (A "tort" is a wrongful act, other than a breach of contract, for which relief may be obtained in the form of damages.) In *Latrigue* the court held that the cigarette manufacturer could not be an "insurer of the unknowable." Subsequently, the *Latrigue* judge's rationale became the standard for similar claims of liability, in effect nullifying actions against the tobacco industry under existing law (Player 1998). Thus, *Latrigue* marked the end of the first wave of lawsuits and the beginning of a long hiatus in tobacco litigation.

During this lull between the first and second waves, Player observed, several significant events changed the legal terrain. The first was *Smoking and Health,* followed by the 1965 Federal Cigarette Labeling and Advertising Act and the Public Health Cigarette Smoking Act of 1969 (passed in 1970), which banned cigarette advertising on radio and television and required stronger warning labels (Player 1998).

It was not until the second-wave case of *Cipollone v. Liggett Group, Inc., et al.* that a tobacco company experienced its first loss. Rose Cipollone (pronounced CHIP-uh-lohn), the smoker-plaintiff, filed the suit in August 1983. She died in October 1984, after which her husband, Antonio Cipollone continued the case on her behalf. Mrs. Cipollone had begun smoking Chesterfields in 1942, when she was in her mid-teens, and she continued to smoke for more than 40 years, even after the right lobe of her lung was removed because of cancer. Her suit alleged that the tobacco companies had failed to warn her adequately of the risks associated with smoking cigarettes and of their addictiveness. A court held Liggett liable for negligence—on the grounds that it failed to warn smokers prior to 1966, when warning labels were required on cigarette packages, and that it produced advertisements that could be interpreted as a warranty for the safety of smoking cigarettes. (Philip Morris and Lorillard, also named as defendants, were found not culpable because Mrs. Cipollone had not started smoking their brands until after 1966.) Liggett was ordered to pay Mrs. Cipollone's husband $400,000, but the ruling was overturned on appeal. The plaintiff's law firm, having spent $5 million on the case, finally gave up.

In October 1991 the husband-and-wife legal team of Stanley and Susan Rosenblatt filed a $5 billion class-action suit on behalf of Norma Broin, an American Airlines flight attendant, and thousands of other current and former nonsmoking flight attendants. The plaintiffs claimed that they had contracted various heart and lung ailments as a result of exposure to environmental tobacco smoke in the cabins of the commercial airliners on which they worked. The plaintiffs also alleged that the tobacco companies were guilty of fraud, because they had withheld information about the dangers of environmental tobacco smoke (ETS).

Without admitting that ETS posed a health risk to nonsmokers, the companies named in the suit—Brown & Williamson, Philip Morris, R. J. Reynolds, and Lorillard—agreed to a $349 million settlement: $300 million to fund a research center for the study of smoking-related diseases and $49 million for payment of the Rosenblatts' fees. The manner in which *Broin* was resolved allowed plaintiffs to pursue their cases individually but without the possibility of receiving any punitive damages.

In February 1995 the tobacco industry found itself facing the largest product liability lawsuit in U.S. history, *Castano et al. v. the American Tobacco Co. et al.* Certified as a class-action suit, *Castano* had the potential of representing more than 90 million current and future addicted smokers and the potential of resulting in total damages of $40 billion. The suit claimed the industry had conspired to deceive the public about nicotine's addictive properties.

The Liggett Group, the smallest of the nation's five major cigarette manufacturers, announced on March 16, 1996, that it would settle. Liggett agreed to the following provisions:

- To pay 5 percent of its annual pretax income for 25 years to fund smoker cessation programs.
- To withdraw its objections to regulations proposed by the FDA intended to reduce underage smoking.
- To negotiate the release of research records.
- To discontinue use of cartoon characters in advertising.
- To run black-and-white, text-only ads in magazines having more than 15 percent youth readership.

The *Castano* suit ended prematurely in May 1996, when a federal appeals panel in New Orleans dismissed the case, agreeing with the defendants' arguments that the number of plaintiffs made it too unwieldy to manage. A Liggett representative said at the time that the suit's decertification as a class action did not invalidate its settlement agreement.

The first trial in which a tobacco company's internal documents were used by a plaintiff's attorney was *Carter v. Brown & Williamson Tobacco Corp.* in 1995. Attorney Norbert Wilner entered as evidence 21 documents showing plainly that B&W's top executives had known for some time about the addictiveness of nicotine. Wilner's client was Grady Carter, a sixty-five-year-old former air-traffic controller who had smoked for 43 years, mainly Lucky Strikes. He stopped after being diagnosed with lung cancer in 1991. Surgeons removed one of his lungs, after which his cancer went into remission. Carter accepted some of the blame for his illness, acknowledging that he had freely chosen to smoke. However, alluding to the testimony of the six CEOs of big tobacco before the House Energy and Commerce Subcommittee on Health and the Environment that they did not believe tobacco to be addictive, he said, "[T]hese guys lied and lied and lied and withheld evidence that might have helped me quit."

Brown & Williamson's attorneys argued that because the internal documents had been stolen, their use was itself a criminal act. But Judge Brian Davis ruled that the documents were admissible because they showed evidence of criminal conduct. The jury found that cigarettes were a "defective product" and that Brown & Williamson was negligent for not warning of their danger. Finding for the plaintiff, it set damages at $750,000. The ruling was overturned on appeal two years later but was reinstated in November 2000 by the Florida Supreme Court.

Each successive wave of litigation expanded on earlier efforts to make the tobacco industry pay for its sins. In general, it had been impossible to counter the industry's argument that (1) smokers' lawsuits were without merit because there was no conclusive proof that smoking caused the plaintiffs' illnesses, and (2) even if judges and juries believed the plaintiffs, there was still the "assumption of risk" factor: The plaintiffs had freely chosen to smoke a product known for decades to be dangerous. The *Carter v. B&W* case showed, however, that a tobacco company's internal documents could be used to show that the tobacco industry knew, prior to *Smoking and Health,* of cigarettes' ill effects.

The principal way to beat the tobacco industry became to eliminate the individual smoker-plaintiff and substitute the state as the injured party. Mississippi's attorney general, Michael

Moore, did just this, in what has been called the first case of the third wave of tobacco litigation. Moore sought reparation for the financial harm Mississippi had suffered by providing money for treating sick smokers. His legal team had amassed a vast collection of internal documents supporting the state's claim that tobacco companies had known for years that smoking was dangerous and had conspired in an industrywide cover-up, which included destruction of potentially incriminating documents (Tursi, White, and McQuilkin 2000).

After a year's research, reading and rereading the internal documents of various tobacco companies, Moore filed his lawsuit in May 1994. Not only did Moore take a novel approach (i.e., suing big tobacco on behalf of a state), but also he decided to file in chancery court, which ordinarily handles divorce and custody cases. He reasoned that the chancery court offered him an advantage because its cases were decided by a judge only; no jury was involved.

Moore encountered strong opposition within the Mississippi state government. The governor sued him to try to block the lawsuit, and the legislature, which included a number of tobacco supporters, refused to provide the necessary funding. But the governor's suit failed, and Moore found fellow lawyers who were willing to contribute to his war chest.

In August 1994, three months after Moore filed his case, Minnesota's attorney general, Hubert Humphrey III, followed Moore's example by filing the nation's second state suit, but with a twist—it was a joint suit with Minnesota Blue Cross/Blue Shield as coplaintiff. A third lawsuit was filed on September 20, 1994, by West Virginia. It was the first to include U.S. Tobacco, manufacturer of 90 percent of the smokeless tobacco sold in the United States, among the defendants. In February 1995 Florida's attorney general filed the fourth state suit, which was aided by a unique state law, the Medicaid Third-Party Liability Act, passed by the Florida legislature in the final minutes of the 1994 legislative session. The law prohibited the tobacco lawyers' stock defense of blaming smokers for their health problems and left them with little to do except to sit and observe the proceedings (Tursi, White, and McQuilkin 2000). The tobacco companies eventually settled in all four cases.

By the end of 1996, following the lead of the attorneys general of Mississippi, Minnesota, West Virginia, and Florida, similar suits were filed in 18 other states, and negotiations were under way to consolidate the state suits into a single settlement with big tobacco. By the time the Master Settlement Agreement (MSA; sometimes also referred to as the Multistate Settlement Agreement) was presented to the public in June 1997, the total number of states that had filed suits against the tobacco industry stood at 41. Because the MSA had been conceived, written, and negotiated on the assumption that it would be binding for all pending class-action suits and all pending actions against the tobacco industry brought by states and other governmental entities, it was necessary that the agreement be presented as a bill and approved by Congress. Sen. John McCain (R-Arizona) was asked to draft a bill embodying the provisions of the MSA. The McCain bill was introduced in the Senate on November 5, 1997.

The bill encountered more opposition than had been expected. In mid-June 1998 it was defeated after a grueling four-week debate. This outcome was seen as a major setback for President Clinton and members of Congress who had championed it, and a huge victory for big tobacco. The industry had spent $40 million on an eight-week ad campaign on television and radio, more millions lobbying against the bill, and still more in the form of hefty contributions to Republican senators. Even before the bill failed, the CEO of RJR, Steven Goldstone, announced that his company was withdrawing its support of congressional efforts to develop comprehensive tobacco legislation, complaining that the McCain bill ranged too far from the MSA of 1997.

In June 1998 the tobacco companies resumed negotiations with a group of nine states. Despite the withdrawal of one attorney general to pursue a potential settlement in state court, the negotiations resulted in a deal that would settle all 37 pending state cases and quiet potential claims in the remaining states (Hermer 1999, 5–6).

The eight attorneys general announced their settlement proposal on November 16, 1998, calling it "[a] historic settlement proposal that mandates the most significant legal reform in the tobacco industry and the largest financial recovery in the nation's history." Among the provisions of this revised MSA are the following:

- Prohibits youth targeting.
- Bans cartoon characters.
- Opens industry records and research.
- Opens tobacco documents to public access.
- Creates user-friendly web site for industry documents.

- Stops conspiracy to hide research regarding smoking and health.
- Restricts sponsorships by brand names.
- Bans outdoor advertising.
- Bans prominent placement of tobacco products in stores, an advantage previously paid for by tobacco companies.
- Bans sale of merchandise bearing tobacco brand names.
- Bans youth access to free samples.
- Bans proof-of-purchase gifts.
- Sets minimum pack size at 20 cigarettes.
- Requires corporate commitments to reduce youth access to and consumption of tobacco. "Companies must develop and regularly communicate corporate principles that commit to complying with the Master Settlement Agreement and reducing youth smoking; designate executive level manager to identify ways to reduce youth access and consumption of tobacco; and encourage employees to identify additional methods to reduce youth access and youth consumption."
- Disbands the Council for Tobacco Research (CTR), the Tobacco Institute (TI), and the Council for Indoor Air Research (CIAR).
- Restricts industry lobbying. Quoting the MSA, "After state-specific finality, tobacco companies will be prohibited from opposing proposed state or local laws or administrative rules which are intended to limit youth access to, and consumption of, tobacco products. The industry must require its lobbyists to certify in writing they have reviewed and will fully comply with settlement terms including disclosure of financial contributions regarding lobbying activities and new corporate culture principles; in states without laws regarding financial disclosure of lobbying, requires disclosure of lobbying costs to the state Attorney General. Prohibits lobbyists from supporting or opposing state, federal, or local laws or actions without authorization of the companies. Prohibits the industry from lobbying for the diversion of settlement money to non-tobacco or non-health related uses or legislation which would eliminate or diminish state rights under the settlement."

- Dismisses lawsuits against state laws.
- Changes the corporate culture. Specifically, beginning 180 days after the Master Settlement Agreement execution date, companies must develop and regularly communicate corporate principles that commit to complying with the Master Settlement Agreement and reducing youth smoking; must designate executive-level managers to identify ways to reduce youth access and consumption of tobacco; and must encourage employees to identify additional methods to reduce youth access and youth consumption (Gregoire 1999).

Meanwhile, Dr. David Kessler, commissioner of the Food and Drug Administration (FDA), was attacking big tobacco on another front, attempting to assert regulatory authority over tobacco. The tobacco industry had sued to block the FDA's advances— specifically, new FDA rules that would ban billboard advertising of cigarettes near schools. U.S. District Judge William L. Osteen Sr. ruled in April 1997 that the FDA did have authority to regulate the distribution, sale, and use of tobacco products. He accepted Kessler's argument that nicotine ought to be considered a drug and that under law cigarettes and smokeless tobacco products should be considered "drug-delivery devices." But advertising, he said, lay outside the FDA's purview.

Subsequently, a federal appeals panel reversed Osteen's ruling, and the case went to the Supreme Court. On March 21, 2000, the Court ruled that although the Food, Drug, and Cosmetic Act (FDCA) grants the FDA the authority to regulate drugs and devices, Congress had not intended that the FDA have authority to regulate tobacco products. President Clinton called for Congress to pass legislation granting the necessary regulatory power. Sen. John McCain responded: "Having encountered the influence of the special interests, especially the tobacco companies . . . in a $50 million campaign, I'm not optimistic that we will be able to get that done" (Garrett 2000). As of spring 2001, Senator McCain's prediction has been correct.

While Congress was debating the McCain bill in 1997 and the state attorneys general were negotiating with big tobacco, another legal battle of epic proportions was being fought in Dade County, Florida. Filed in 1994, *Howard A. Engle, M.D., et al. v. R. J. Reynolds Tobacco et al.*, known as "the *Engle* case," was the first class-action suit against big tobacco to go to trial and the longest civil action in the history of tobacco litigation. The plaintiffs were Florida citizens and residents, and their survivors, who had suffered or died from diseases and medical problems caused by their addiction to cigarettes that contain nicotine.

As in the *Broin* case, the plaintiffs' attorneys were Stanley and Susan Rosenblatt. In July 2000, after finding the tobacco companies liable for marketing products that were "defective and unreasonably dangerous"; for engaging in "extreme and outrageous conduct . . . with the intent to inflict emotional harm"; and for conspiring "to misrepresent information relating to health effects of cigarette smoking, or the addictive nature of smoking cigarettes, with the intention that smokers and members of the public rely to their detriment," the jury awarded the plaintiffs $145 billion in punitive damages—by far the largest punitive-damages award in U.S. history. (Previously, the largest award had been $5 billion, which Exxon Corp. had been ordered to pay as a result of the Exxon *Valdez* oil spill in Alaska's Prince William Sound in 1989.)

Judge Robert P. Kaye, who presided over the lengthy trial, defended the damages award. "[K]eep in mind the enormity of the 70 years of behavior and the almost incomprehensible damage that was done to such a huge number of people," he said in a 68-page final judgment order. "From the early years of advertising up until July of 1969, defendants engaged in concerted advertising campaigns extolling the virtues of smoking and making references to the lack of health risks and stressing the alleged benefits of smoking. All the while the defendants knew by their own research and the work of others, that cigarettes . . . caused cancer and other deadly diseases"(quoted in Douglas 2000, 1135).

Plans for a third and final phase of the *Engle* trial called for individual factual trials for each of the half-million plaintiffs. If this happens, said Jacqueline Salcedo, a staff attorney for the Tobacco Control Resource Center (TCRC) at Northeastern University, it could take years to complete the third phase (Salcedo 1999). Mark Gottlieb, another TCRC attorney, said that after the judgment is appealed, the case will move to the Florida Supreme Court and possibly to the U.S. Supreme Court. He said these step themselves would probably take three years (Gottlieb 2001).

Following is a breakdown of the $145 billion punitive damage award in the *Engle* trial, along with each company's market share and net worth (TCRC 2000):

- *Philip Morris*
  —Amount sought: $75 billion to $118.5 billion
  —Jury verdict: $73.96 billion
  —Market share: 49 percent
  —Net worth: $6.4 billion
  —Major brands: Marlboro, Benson & Hedges, Virginia
    Slims, Merit, Basic
- *R. J. Reynolds Tobacco Co.*
  —Amount sought: $19.6 billion to $37.5 billion
  —Jury verdict: $36.28 billion
  —Market share: 24 percent
  —Net worth: $7.1 billion
  —Major brands: Winston, Salem, Camel, Doral,
    Vantage
- *Brown & Williamson Tobacco Corp.*
  —Amount sought: $15 billion to $22 billion
  —Jury verdict: $17.59 billion
  —Market share: 14 percent
  —Net worth: $894 million
  —Major brands: Kent, Lucky Strike, Kool, Carlton,
    GPC
- *Lorillard Tobacco Co.*
  —Amount sought: $17 billion
  —Jury verdict: $16.25 billion
  —Market share: 11 percent
  —Net worth: $921 million
  —Major brands: Newport, Kent, True, Maverick,
    Old Gold
- *Liggett Group Inc.*
  —Amount sought: $1.8 billion
  —Jury verdict: $790 million
  —Market share: 1 percent
  —Net worth: $34 million
  —Major brands: Eagle, Eve, Pyramid

## Health Risks

According to the Centers for Disease Control (CDC), a branch of
the U.S. Department of Health and Human Services, tobacco use
causes more than 430,000 deaths annually in the United States
today. "Of the estimated 47 million adult smokers," the CDC said,

"more than half will die or become disabled as a result of smoking. It is now well documented that smoking can cause chronic lung disease, coronary heart disease and stroke, as well as cancer of the lung, larynx, esophagus, mouth, and bladder. Smoking is also known to contribute to cancer of the cervix, pancreas, and kidney" (CDC TIPS 1999e).

According to the American Lung Association (ALA), "smoking is the direct cause of 87 percent of lung cancer cases and of most cases of emphysema and chronic bronchitis." It is also a major factor, the ALA says, in coronary heart disease and stroke. It "may be causally related to malignancies in other parts of the body; and has been linked to a variety of other conditions and disorders, including slowed healing of wounds, infertility, and peptic ulcer disease" (ALA, 1998).

A study published in June 1998 by the American Council on Science and Health (ACSH) states its conclusion bluntly: Smoking causes "irreversible damage to virtually every organ in the human body" (ACSH 1998). "We don't want to dishearten or depress smokers," said Dr. Elizabeth Whelan, president of ACSH. "What we do want to do, particularly, is to show young people—teenagers wondering whether they should light up for the first time—the dangers that lie ahead. The deleterious effects of smoking start with the very first cigarette—and never go away."

## Environmental Tobacco Smoke (ETS)

It is not necessary to be a smoker to suffer the effects of cigarette smoke. A nonsmoker who happens to be in a room or some other enclosed area with a smoker becomes a smoker simply by breathing—not an active smoker but a passive one. Breathing environmental tobacco smoke produced by a smoker is "passive smoking," which amounts to very much the same thing as smoking, even if the smoke is secondhand.

In fact, according to the Mayo Clinic, secondhand smoke may be even more dangerous in some ways than the mainstream smoke drawn directly into a smoker's lungs. "It [ETS] contains twice as much tar and nicotine per unit volume as does smoke inhaled from a cigarette. It contains three times as much of a cancer-causing compound called 3,4 benzpyrene, five times as much carbon monoxide and possibly 50 times as much ammonia. Secondhand smoke from pipes and cigars is equally harmful if not more so" (Mayo Clinic 1997).

## Exposure to ETS

When so many people smoke, it seems inevitable that a great many nonsmokers will be exposed to ETS. And so they are. The American Heart Association (AHA) says that nearly half of all Americans aged 17 or older are exposed to ETS at home or at work (AHA 1997). A survey conducted by the CDC found that 88 percent of adults who did not use tobacco—almost 9 out of 10— were passive smokers (CDC TIPS 1999a).

According to the American Lung Association, 9 to 12 million children under the age of 5 in the United States are exposed to secondhand smoke in the home, and 43 percent of children aged 2 months to 11 years live in a home with at least one smoker (ALA 1999b). The World Health Organization (WHO) has said that half of all the children in the world—700 million—live in homes where at least one person smokes (WHO 1999).

By measuring the levels of cotinine, a chemical in the body that indicates exposure to nicotine, researchers are able to determine which nonsmokers have inhaled the largest amounts of secondhand smoke. These nonsmokers turned out to be people who lived with more than one smoker in their household and people who were exposed to smoke at their workplace. The data also revealed that cotinine levels (and ETS exposure) were highest in three categories: children, non-Hispanic blacks, and men in general (CDC TIPS 1999a).

## Health Risks of ETS

"Each year, exposure to ETS causes an estimated 3,000 non-smoking Americans to die of lung cancer" (CDC TIPS 1999e). Among nonsmoking adults in the United States, ETS causes an estimated 3,000 lung cancer deaths each year, 12,000 deaths from other forms of cancer, and 35,000 to 40,000 deaths from cardiovascular disease (Mayo Clinic 1997). It also causes coughing, buildup of phlegm, chest discomfort, and reduced lung function (American Cancer Society [ACS] 1999a).

Other findings related to the health risks of ETS include:

- A woman who has never smoked has an estimated 24 percent greater risk of lung cancer if she lives with a smoker (Law et al. 1997, 973–980).
- Women who never smoke, who live with a smoker, and who lack a specific gene (the GSTM1 gene) are six

times more likely to develop lung cancer. The GSTM1 gene is known to inactivate carcinogens found in tobacco smoke. It is missing in 50 percent of Caucasians (Bennett et al. 1999).

- Secondhand smoke speeds the process of atherosclerosis (thickening or hardening of the arteries) by 20 percent (Howard et al. 1998, 2374–2379).
- Regular exposure to ETS at home or at work almost doubles the risk of heart disease (Kawachi et al. 1997, 2374–2379).

According to the Indiana Tobacco Control Center, exposure to ETS may kill as many as 50,000 Americans yearly. Several studies, including the recently released report from the U.S. Environmental Protection Agency (EPA), estimate that about 3,000 lung cancer deaths from ETS occur each year. Another analysis estimates 35,000 coronary deaths and more than 10,000 deaths from other kinds of cancer annually resulting from ETS exposure (Indiana Tobacco Control Center 1999).

## Children and ETS

Babies born to women who smoked during pregnancy are more likely to be premature, to weigh less at birth, and to have decreased lung function. Babies exposed to ETS have a higher risk of dying of sudden infant death syndrome (SIDS). Children exposed to ETS during the first 18 months of life are 60 percent more likely to develop lower respiratory illnesses such as croup, bronchitis, bronchiolitis, and pneumonia—the annual incidence of such illnesses ranging from 150,000 to 300,000. ETS can also cause ear infections, coughing, wheezing, and increased mucus production in children less than 18 months old. According to the EPA, secondhand smoke can lead to the buildup of fluid in the middle ear, the most common reason for hospitalization of children for an operation (ALA 1999a).

Physicians believe that smoking during pregnancy accounts for 20 to 30 percent of low-birth-weight babies, up to 14 percent of preterm deliveries, and at least 10 percent of all infant deaths (ALA 1998). "Even apparently healthy, full-term babies of smokers," the ALA has said, "have been found to be born with narrowed airways and curtailed lung function. Only about 30 percent of women . . . [smokers] stop smoking when they find they are pregnant" (ALA 1998). Children who are exposed to ETS are more likely to develop asthma, the leading serious chronic childhood disease in the United States, and continued exposure to ETS will trigger asthma attacks and make them more severe (WHO 1999). According to a study published in 1998, about 160,000 cases of asthma and 79,000 cases of chronic bronchitis among children nationally are directly attributable each year to ETS exposure (Gergen et al. 1998, 8). Children are especially susceptible because their lungs are still developing. Childhood exposure to secondhand smoke results in decreased lung function (ALA 1999b).

## Smokeless Tobacco

If the dangers associated with using tobacco were merely a result of smoking, then smokeless tobacco might be a safe substitute. However, components of tobacco that is chewed or kept between the cheek and gum are absorbed directly through the skin, rather than inhaled. This direct absorption creates dangers of its own.

According to the National Cancer Institute (NCI), smokeless tobacco contains 28 carcinogens (i.e., cancer-causing agents), among them formaldehyde, arsenic, cadmium, nickel, polonium, and—most dangerous of all—tobacco-specific nitrosamines (TSNAs), which are present at high levels (NCI 1998, 1). Users of smokeless tobacco face increased risks of cancers of the mouth, pharynx (throat), larynx (voice box), and esophagus. Oral cancer can also include cancer of the lip, tongue, cheeks, gums, and the floor and roof of the mouth (NCI 1998, 2).

"Oral cancer has been shown to occur several times more frequently among snuff dippers than among nontobacco users," the California Dental Association (CDA) has said, "and the excess risk of cancers of the cheek and gum may reach nearly *fifty-fold* among long-term snuff user" (CDA 1998, 1). One can of snuff per day delivers as much nicotine as 60 cigarettes (CDA 1994). Surgery to treat oral cancer resulting from using smokeless tobacco is often extensive and disfiguring and may require removing parts of the face, tongue, cheek, or lip. "Difficulty chewing, swallowing, talking, and even breathing can result. . . . Oral cancer can spread to other parts of the body quickly. On average, half of oral cancer victims are dead within five years of diagnosis" (National Institute of Dental Research 1997).

Animal studies suggest that smokeless tobacco may also cause lung cancer and cancer of the pancreas, even though the cancer-causing agents are not inhaled (CDC TIPS 1999c). "Some of the other effects of smokeless tobacco include addiction to nicotine, oral leukoplakia (white mouth lesions that can become cancerous), gum disease, gum recession (when the gum pulls away from the teeth), loss of bone in the jaw, tooth decay, tooth loss, tooth abrasion (worn spots on the teeth), yellowing of teeth, chronic bad breath, high blood pressure, and increased risk for cardiovascular (heart) disease" (NCI 1998, 2).

## Cigars and Pipes

In terms of health risks, the main difference between smoking cigarettes and smoking cigars is in the location of the resulting cancers. The former tends to produce lung cancer, whereas cigar smokers tend to suffer from cancer of the head and neck, according to Dr. David Myssiorek, director of the division of head and neck surgery at Long Island Jewish Medical Center in New Hyde Park, New York (Siegel 1998). Otherwise, health risk differences are expressed in terms of probability. The risk of developing lung cancer is 3 times higher for cigar smokers than for nonsmokers. The risk of oral cancer is 4 to 10 times higher for cigar smokers. Even a small cigar, as Jeffrey Cowley reported in *Newsweek,* delivers 7 times as much tar as a cigarette, 11 times as much carbon monoxide, and 4 times as much nicotine. And because cigar smoke is highly alkaline, much of its content is absorbed directly into the bloodstream (Cowley 1997).

Mortality rates for cancer of the oral cavity, larynx, pharynx, and esophagus are approximately equal among users of pipes, cigars, and cigarettes. "Outside of it [cigar smoking] being a disgusting habit," said Dr. David Myssiorek, "it's a dangerous one—every bit as dangerous and harmful as chewing tobacco." When cigarette smokers switch to cigars or pipes, thinking they are safe alternatives to cigarettes, they usually continue to inhale in the way they were accustomed to when they smoked cigarettes, thereby increasing their health risks. "[N]o health benefits should be anticipated from switching" (Smoking Control Advocacy Resource Center [SCARC] 1996).

## Filtered and Light Cigarettes

Adenocarcinoma, a variety of lung cancer that was once rare, is now more common than any other. Scientists believe that it is caused chiefly by filtered and light cigarettes, because smokers draw more strongly through filters and lights to get a jolt of nicotine, causing the carcinogens in the smoke to penetrate deeply into the fine branches and air sacs of the lung, where adenocarcinomas tend to develop. The increased incidence of adenocarcinomas may be attributed in part to the recent use of blended, reconstituted tobacco that releases greater amounts of carcinogenic nitrosamines.

## Bidis

Bidis may be colorful and more attractive than regular cigarettes, and they do smell better, but they are far more dangerous than conventional cigarettes. Although they contain less tobacco than cigarettes, unfiltered bidis release as much as three times more tar and nicotine, according to Samira Asthma, a CDC epidemiologist (Johnson 1999). The risk of getting cancer of the mouth, throat, and lung is higher in bidi smokers than in cigarette smokers. Bidis are more harmful for a number of reasons. The bidi has no filter and is made from unprocessed, sun-cured tobacco in unregulated cottage industries in India. In addition, the bidi is not porous and requires a lot of pulmonary effort to keep lit. Bidis also deliver a higher concentration of other harmful substances, including hydrogen cyanide, carbon monoxide, and ammonia (Johnson 1999).

# Nicotine and Pharmacology

## What's in Cigarettes?

According to the Indiana Prevention Resource Center, industry documents list 599 additives that have been identified in tobacco products: acetanisole, acetic acid, acetone, acetophenone, 6-acetoxydihydrotheaspirane, 2-acetyl-3-ethylpyrazine, 2-acetyl-5-methylfuran, etc.—a list too long for inclusion here (Indiana Prevention Resource Center 1999). Another source noted that the contents of one cigarette include the following: "carbon monoxide (the dangerous gas emitted from automobiles), formaldehyde (used to preserve dead bodies), ammonia (kitchen and bathroom cleaner), carbon dioxide (which contributes to global warming)," and then mentions aluminum, copper, lead, mercury, and zinc as well (Community Outreach Health Information System, Boston University, 1999).

One good general-purpose source (informative and available online) is a British article titled "Tobacco Additives," by Clive Bates, Martin Jarvis, and Gregory Connolly (Bates, Jarvis, and Connolly 1999). The authors draw heavily on tobacco industry documents in explaining how cigarettes "work" and the effects of the various additives. Bates et al. believe that additives are used by manufacturers to boost the pharmacological effects of nicotine, to improve taste and make it more appealing to young and "aspirational" smokers, and to mask the unpleasant aspects of smoke.

The fundamental fact about the cigarette is that it is a delivery device for "doses" of an addictive drug—nicotine, which enters the smoker's lungs in a mixture of smoke particles and gases. Nicotine is then "rapidly absorbed into the blood through the large surface of the lungs (and mouth and throat) and reaches the brain within ten seconds" (Bates, Jarvis, and Connolly 1999).

## What's in Smoke?

The visible part of tobacco smoke (the particulate phase) represents only 5 to 8 percent of what is generated by the burning of tobacco; the rest assumes the form of vapors or gases (Ginzel 1990). In all, some 4,000 compounds are formed during combustion. At least 43 are known carcinogens, causing cancer in humans and animals (CDC TIPS 2000b).

Among the most dangerous carcinogens, says Dr. K. H. Ginzel, a professor of pharmacology and toxicology at the University of Arkansas, are the nitrosamines. Strictly regulated by federal agencies, concentrations of nitrosamines in beer, bacon, and baby bottle nipples must not exceed 5 to 10 parts per billion. A typical person ingests about 1 microgram a day, but a smoker's intake exceeds this level by 17 times for each pack of cigarettes smoked (Ginzel 1990).

## Sidestream and Mainstream Smoke

There are two distinct kinds of smoke: (1) "sidestream smoke," which comes from the burning tip of the cigarette, and (2) "mainstream smoke," from the filter, or mouth, end. In general, about 85 percent of the smoke in a room where someone is smoking results from sidestream smoke and only about 15 percent results from the smoker's exhalations. Many of the toxins and carcinogens contained in smoke are found at higher concentrations in sidestream smoke (Action for Smoking and Health, UK [ASH UK] 1998).

## Nicotine

Nicotine is an alkaloid, like caffeine, morphine, and strychnine. It is highly toxic. As little as 60 milligrams placed on a person's tongue will result in death within minutes (ASH UK 1998). Of the chemical compounds found in the smoke of burning tobacco and in smokeless tobacco as well, nicotine is the primary component that acts on the brain (National Institute on Drug Abuse [NIDA] 1999). A colorless liquid that turns brown when burned, it attaches itself to minute droplets in the smoke (ASH UK 1998). It is absorbed through the skin and mucosal lining of the mouth and nose or through the lining of the lungs after it is inhaled. Depending on how tobacco is taken, nicotine can reach peak levels in the bloodstream and brain within ten seconds (NIDA 1999).

In November 2000 researchers at the University of Minnesota Cancer Center reported that nicotine itself may cause cancer. Studies showed that nicotine metabolism produces a lung carcinogen called NNK and that a substance produced by the metabolism of nicotine, pseudooxynicotine, could be converted outside the body to NNK [4-(methylnitrosamino)-1-(3-pyridyl)-1-butanone]. The researchers suspect the conversion takes place within the body as well. The lead researcher in the Minnesota study, Stephen Hecht, raised the question of whether the findings suggest that smokers trying to quit should seek an alternative to nicotine replacement therapy. "Without question," he said, "nicotine replacement therapy is clearly preferable to continued use of tobacco products. Our research provides scientific evidence, however, that nicotine products designed for long-term use, such as the so-called 'safe' cigarettes, may not be safe" (University of Minnesota Cancer Center, Information Services, 2000). Indeed, many health authorities, among them Dr. Koop, surgeon general of the United States from 1981 to 1989, and Dr. Elizabeth Whelan, insist that there can be no safe cigarette.

## Nicotine Addiction

The National Institute on Drug Abuse (NIDA) has issued a research report that describes what happens after nicotine enters the bloodstream and the brain. Its findings are detailed in the following passage.

> Of primary importance to its addictive nature are findings that nicotine activates the brain circuitry that regulates feelings of pleasure, the so-called reward pathways. A key brain chemical involved in mediating the desire to consume drugs is the neurotransmitter dopamine, and research has shown that nicotine increases the levels of dopamine in the reward circuits. Nicotine's pharmacokinetic properties have been found also to enhance its abuse potential. Cigarette smoking produces a rapid distribution of nicotine to the brain, with drug levels peaking within 10 seconds of inhalation. The acute effects of nicotine dissipate in a few minutes, causing the smoker to continue dosing frequently throughout the day to maintain the drug's pleasurable effects and prevent withdrawal.
>
> What people frequently do not realize is that the cigarette is a very efficient and highly engineered drug-delivery system. By inhaling, the smoker can get nicotine to the brain very rapidly with every puff. A typical smoker will take 10 puffs on a cigarette over a period of five minutes that the cigarette is lit. Thus, a person who smokes about one and one-half packs (30 cigarettes) daily, gets 300 "hits" of nicotine to the brain each day. These factors contribute considerably to nicotine's highly addictive nature. (NIDA 1999)

The risk of becoming addicted to nicotine, according to the American Cancer Society, is between one in three and one in two, while the risk of becoming dependent on crack or cocaine used intravenously is one in four. Some adolescents find themselves addicted within a few days of having smoked their first cigarette, even if they do not smoke every day. On the other hand, symptoms of addiction have also been found among eleven- and twelve-year-olds who smoke no more than one cigarette a month (Hall 2000).

## Tar

Among the hundreds of damaging chemical substances that tobacco smoke contains is a brown, sticky mass called cigarette tar. Smoke from an unfiltered cigarette contains about 5 billion particles per cubic millimeter, which, when condensed, form tobacco tar. Chemicals in tobacco tar are linked to the development of cancer. Some, such as benzopyrene and vinyl chloride, are carcinogens (i.e., they directly cause cancer), while others, such as formaldehyde and phenol, are cocarcinogens (i.e., they combine with other chemicals to stimulate the growth of certain cancers).

Tobacco also contains poisonous substances, including arsenic. In addition to being an addictive psychoactive drug, nicotine is a poison that can be fatal in high doses (Columbia University Health Education Program, Alice, 1999).

## Nicotine Content and Yield

The nicotine "content" of a cigarette is the amount of nicotine in tobacco before it is smoked (ACS 2000). Nicotine "yield" refers to the amount of nicotine that a smoker actually inhales. This amount varies depending on the smoker's manner of smoking. Factors that increase nicotine yield include:

- How deeply one inhales (puff volume)
- How frequently one inhales (puff interval)
- How long one inhales (puff duration)
- How much of the cigarette is smoked
- How many of the filter vents are blocked by the smoker's lips

## Low-Tar Cigarettes and "Compensation"

Various surveys have found that a high percentage of smokers have switched to low-tar cigarettes because they believe they are less dangerous. However, as noted previously, people smoke them differently. Needing the hit of nicotine, they smoke them in a way that enables them to obtain the needed hit. This adopting of a different smoking manner is called "compensation." One method by which smokers of low-tar cigarettes compensate is to use their lips to cover some of the ventilation holes. These holes are intended to dilute the tar intake by making the smoker draw in more air. But a study at Penn State University, for example, found that 53 percent of the butts of "light" brand cigarettes gathered from ashtrays showed evidence that smokers had blocked the vent holes around the filter when they smoked the cigarettes (Sweeney, Kozlowski, and Parsa 1999, 167–173). So in various ways—taking more puffs, inhaling more deeply, blocking the vents—smokers increase a cigarette's nicotine yield, but in doing so they increase the tar yield as well. A smoker's lungs collect from one-fourth to one and one-half pounds of tar for every year of smoking, whether the cigarettes are low-tar or not (Ginzel 1990).

Moreover, according to a study published by the *Journal of the National Cancer Institute*, the tar and nicotine yields listed on packages of low- and medium-yield cigarettes apparently understate by about half the amounts actually taken in by the smoker. The authors of the *Journal* article believe this discrepancy is a result of inadequate test procedures (Djordjevic, Stellman, and Zang 2000, 106–111).

Do smokers realize that they are getting as much tar from low-tar cigarettes as they would get from regular cigarettes? Apparently not. Although they may be aware that they take more puffs or smoke more of each cigarette, many smokers continue to believe that low-tar cigarettes are safer—despite studies showing that low-tar cigarettes do not decrease the incidence of lung cancer. Young smokers in particular are inclined to believe that low-tar cigarettes are safer (British Broadcasting Corporation [BBC] 1999b).

In a sense, low-tar cigarettes pose a special hazard. Dr. Martin Jarvis, of the Behavior Unit of the Imperial Cancer Research Fund, has said: "Because of compensation for nicotine, smokers can and do get as much tar from these low-yielding cigarettes as from standard ones. It is clear that the numbers on cigarette packs are worse than useless and as consumer information they are dangerous and misleading. And it is worrying that people may be switching to these products rather than quitting" (BBC 1999b).

## Testing for Tar and Nicotine

Concerned that the results of tests for tar and nicotine yields were unrealistically low, the Federal Trade Commission announced in December 1996 that it would require tobacco companies to refine their test procedures (National Drug Strategy Network [NDSN] 1996). The FTC also proposed that companies be required to state in advertising and on cigarette packages not just a single figure resulting from their tests but also the range of tar and nicotine that could actually be inhaled, depending on individual smoking techniques. A Philip Morris spokesman argued that the numbers on cigarette packages and in advertising were never intended to tell smokers precisely how much tar and nicotine they might inhale; instead, they were meant to provide an index by which consumers could compare one brand with others (NDSN 1996).

Meanwhile, one state government established its own standards. Massachusetts passed a law requiring tobacco companies to adhere to their requirements in testing their cigarettes and to submit the results to the Massachusetts Department of Public Health. The American Cancer Society posted the companies' 1996 figures on the Internet (ACS 1997).

In keeping with the FTC's insistence on the necessity of new testing standards, a study by researchers at the American Health Foundation, published in the January 19, 2000, issue of the *Journal of the National Cancer Institute,* reported that smokers of low-nicotine cigarettes inhale 2.5 times more nicotine and 2.6 times more tar than current package numbers would indicate. Smokers of medium-nicotine cigarettes, they found, inhale 2.2 times more nicotine and 1.9 times more tar (*Washington Post* 2000, A8).]

Measurements of nicotine and tar levels can be distorted in other ways as well. Adding ammonia compounds to tobacco raises its alkalinity and speeds delivery of nicotine to a smoker's brain. Adding other chemicals, such as acetaldehyde and pyridine, enhances the effects of nicotine on the brain and nervous system. Moreover, the same ammonia compounds that boost nicotine's effects can distort the measurement of tar, causing readings to be low (BBC 1999a).

## Prevalence of and Trends in Tobacco Use

Globally, tobacco use has reached epidemic proportions, the World Health Organization reported. Although prevalence has peaked among men in most developed countries, it is now increasing among men in developing countries and among women in all countries. WHO estimated in 1998 that the total number of smokers in the world was 1.1 billion—about one-third of the global population age 15 years and over. Of these, it said, 800 million smokers were in developing countries (WHO 1998b). Overall, WHO reported, about 47 percent of men and 12 percent of women smoked. In developing countries, the figures were 48

**Table 1.4**
**Percentages of Men and Women Smokers by Race and Ethnicity**

|  | *Men* | *Women* |
|---|---|---|
| Non-Hispanic American whites | 27.3 | 23.9 |
| Non-Hispanic American blacks | 32.3 | 22.3 |
| Hispanic Americans | 25.4 | 13.9 |
| Asian Americans / Pacific islanders | 20.0 | 11.7 |
| Amerindians / Alaska natives | 41.0 | 29.8 |

*Note:* Percentages age-adjusted (2000 standard) by AHA for age 18 and older.

*Source:* CDC 1997.

percent of men and 7 percent of women, and in developed countries, 42 percent of men and 24 percent of women (WHO 1998b).

In the United States the number of smokers remains high but is lower than a few years ago. The American Heart Association, in its *2000 Heart and Stroke Statistical Update,* put the number of adult smokers at 48.6 million—of whom 25.8 million (27.1 percent) were men and 22.8 million (22.2 percent) were women. The AHA also estimated that 4.1 million adolescents—ages 12 through 17—were smokers, bringing the total to 52.5 million (AHA 1999).

Overall consumption of cigarettes stood at 470 billion in 1998, down 2 percent from 1997. The United States Department of Agriculture (USDA) attributed the decline to price increases, higher state taxes, increased regulation, and consumer awareness of links between smoking and disease, and it predicted a continued decline in 1999 (USDA 1999). Based on virtually unchanged figures from 1996 and 1998, it appears that on the whole the decline in tobacco use may be leveling off (AHA 1999).

The percentages of men and women smokers vary somewhat by race and ethnicity. Table 1.4 shows the percentages of men and women who smoke in each of the subgroups on the left. With regard to the four minorities listed in the table, the 1998 surgeon general's report, *Tobacco Use among U.S. Racial and Ethnic Minority Groups,* provides some valuable information (Satcher 1998):

- Estimates of smoking prevalence among Southeast Asian American men vary considerably—ranging from 34 percent to 43 percent.
- Smoking rates among Mexican-American adults tend to increase as they adopt the values and norms of American culture.

- Very little progress has been made since 1983 in reducing tobacco use among American Indian and Alaska natives. The prevalence rate for American Indian and Alaska native women of reproductive age, in particular, has remained disturbingly high.
- Cigarette smoking is a major cause of disease and death in all four of these population groups, but especially for African Americans.

A study of smokers age 25 and older (see Table 1.5) shows dramatic differences linked to education.

Additional facts relating to prevalence of and trends in tobacco use include the following:

- In 1998 the median percentage for smoking prevalence among adults (18 and older) in all 50 states and the District of Columbia was 22.9 percent—25.3 percent for men and 21.0 percent for women (CDC TIPS 1999d).
- Adult smoking prevalence has decreased steadily in recent decades—from 42.4 percent in 1965 to 30.1 percent in 1985 to 23.5 percent in 1995 (CDC TIPS 1996).
- States with the highest smoking prevalence among adults: Kentucky, 30.8 percent; Nevada, 30.4 percent; West Virginia, 27.9 percent; Michigan, 27.4 percent; South Dakota, 27.3 percent (CDC TIPS 1999d).
- States with the lowest smoking prevalence among adults: Utah, 14.2 percent; Minnesota, 18.0 percent; California, 19.2 percent; New Jersey, 19.2 percent; Hawaii, 19.5 percent (CDC TIPS 1999d).

**Table 1.5**
**Percentages of Men and Women Who Smoke, by Education***

| Highest Level of Education | Percentage of Men Who Smoke | Percentage of Women Who Smoke |
|---|---|---|
| 8th grade or less | 28.4 | 17.8 |
| 9th–11th grade | 41.9 | 33.7 |
| 12th grade | 33.7 | 26.2 |
| 1–3 years beyond high school | 25 | 22.5 |
| 4 years or more beyond high school | 14.3 | 13.7 |

*Source:* AHA 1999.

*Study surveyed people 25 years or older.

- Although smoking among both men and women has decreased over the years, women—who once smoked at half the rate of men—are now almost as likely to smoke (Campaign for Tobacco-Free Kids 1997).
- Male smoking prevalence in the United States decreased by 24 percentage points between 1965 and 1993, but the prevalence of female smoking dropped only 11 percentage points during the same period (CDC TIPS 1996).
- Recent increases in smoking by high school girls (CDC 1998) suggest that the problem of increased prevalence among women may worsen. "Gender differences in the cultural and social influences on smoking, consumption patterns, health effects, and responses to tobacco marketing and promotion require that tobacco use among women be considered separately from general discussions on the topic" (Campaign for Tobacco-Free Kids 1997).

## Underage Tobacco Use

The best source of information on underage smoking is the *Monitoring the Future* study conducted at the University of Michigan Institute for Social Research (ISR) under grants from the National Institute on Drug Abuse. A report published in December 1999 noted a continuing decline in underage smoking (Johnston, O'Malley, and Buchanan 1999). (Smoking peaked in 1996 among eighth- and tenth-graders.) The ISR study found that 17.5 percent of eighth-graders were "current smokers" (having smoked one or more cigarettes in the preceding 30 days), down from 21 percent in 1996. The percentage of tenth-graders who were current smokers in 1999 was 25.7. Among twelfth-graders the decline was quite small, from a peak of 36.5 percent in 1997 to 34.6 percent in 1999.

Lloyd D. Johnson, the study's principal investigator and an ISR research scientist, had this to say about the results: "Despite these recent improvements, over one-third of today's young people are active smokers by the time they leave high school. In fact, more than one in every six is an active smoker as early as eighth grade. These rates are still well above smoking rates in the early '90s, when teen smoking began to increase substantially" (Johnston, O'Malley, and Buchanan 1999). Another trend evident in the 1990s was the increased use of Indian cigarettes, bidis, and kreteks (clove cigarettes), which are popular with teens, apparently because they are available in a variety of flavors and are rather exotic in appearance.

## Do Cigarette Companies Want Kids to Smoke?

The tobacco industry's standard response to this question has always been an unequivocal "no." The Tobacco Institute maintains that smoking is an adult activity and that young people are not equipped to make an "informed decision" about whether to begin smoking (RJR n.d.).

However, the truth about big tobacco's view of children smoking is presented clearly in numerous internal documents that are now available on the Internet and at various repositories across the country. A Philip Morris document, for example, said this: "Today's teenagers are tomorrow's potential regular customers, and the overwhelming majority of smokers first begin to smoke while still in their teens. In addition, the ten years following the teenage years is the period during which average daily consumption per smoker increases to the average adult level. . . . Furthermore, it is during the teenage years that the initial brand choices are made" (Johnston 1999). A Lorillard memo stated outright: "[T]he base of our business is the high school student" (Achey 1978).

Of course TI knows that almost all smokers begin to smoke when they are underage—too young to make informed decisions—and that many of them continue to smoke after they become adults, despite their increased ability to make informed decisions. The central point, however, is that tobacco companies must have new smokers—1.6 million every year, according to the American Lung Association, to replace smokers who have quit or died (ALA 1999a).

Tobacco companies are not permitted to give free samples to children, but according to Anne Landman of the American Lung Association of Colorado (ALAC), they circumvent this restriction by encouraging young people to steal cigarettes. Landman has researched the placement of tobacco products in convenience stores and found that some tobacco companies pay retailers to display cigarettes and smokeless tobacco in locations where they are manifestly vulnerable to theft. Landman explains:

> Big tobacco compensates retailers generously for lost products through payments called variously "placement," or "rack" fees. Actually, big Tobacco MORE than compensates them. Two retailers have told us that they can easily make $10,000 per year PER STORE in placement fees alone for tobacco. These fees alter the normal marketing principles that usually make retailers keep merchandise from being shoplifted. The tobacco industry, through these fees, makes it more profitable for retailers to LET THEIR PRODUCTS BE STOLEN [emphasis in original]. (Landman 1999)

## Targeting Youth

Ninety percent of new smokers are under 18 years old. Tobacco companies must recruit minors if they are to replace the customers who quit smoking or die. This is a fundamental truth about the tobacco business, and it is routinely discussed in the various industry documents that have come to light in the past few years.

After reviewing RJR internal documents spanning the years 1973 to 1990, two *Washington Post* reporters concluded that RJR "sought for decades to reverse the declining sales of its brands by developing aggressive marketing proposals to reach adolescents as young as 14 years old" (Mintz and Torry 1998, A1). Similar findings were reported by Toronto *Globe and Mail* reporters who read internal documents made public by Canadian tobacco companies: "Despite repeated denials, . . . Canadian cigarette manufacturers spent much of the past 25 years trying to persuade young people to take up smoking" (MacKinnon 2000). The *Washington Post* team also found a 1984 RJR document in which twelve-year-olds are included in a discussion of "younger adult smokers" (Mintz and Torry 1998, A1). On March 12, 1986, the codeveloper of the Joe Camel campaign, Rick T. Caulfield, wrote a memo to RJR marketing officials saying that the planned Joe Camel campaign would use "peer acceptance/influence" to "motivate the target audience to take up cigarettes." The goal, he said, was "[to convince] target smokers that by selecting Camel as their usual brand they will project an image that will enhance their acceptance among their peers" (Mintz and Torry 1998, A1).

A study in Missouri found that almost one-third (32 percent) of tobacco advertisements in retail stores were located at a small child's eye level—below three feet and next to a candy display (Missouri Department of Health, ASSIST, 1997). The targeting of underage prospects is clearly evident, as kickbutt.org pointed out, in the amount of advertising dollars going toward "promotional activities that appeal to young people, such as sponsorship of public entertainment, distribution of specialty items bearing product names, and the issuing of coupons and premiums" (Washington DOC 1999). Such investments, now largely prohibited, produced healthy dividends for the tobacco industry, which until very recently netted more than $1 billion a year on illegal sales to youth (Washington DOC 1999).

## Smoking Initiation (First Use)

Each day, more than 6,000 teenagers under 18 try their first cigarette. More than half of them become daily smokers (CDC TIPS 2000a, 1). This amounts to more than 1 million new smokers every year, all of them underage but all of whom nevertheless manage to obtain cigarettes. Although tobacco companies are prohibited from directing their advertising at persons under 18, most underage smokers—86 percent according to one study—prefer the three most heavily advertised brands: Marlboro, Camel, and Newport (Grace 1999, Z28). Whether, or to what extent, advertising influences youngsters who become regular smokers may be a matter for research and debate, but the larger question—Why do young people decide to smoke in the first place?—remains largely a matter of speculation.

## Starting: Why?

The teenage years are a bridge from childhood to adulthood, a difficult period of transition during which a child grows—physically, emotionally, intellectually—and emerges from the ordeal more or less an adult. Some of the most important decisions in life are made in this period, decisions that shape personality and character and values and that may very well determine the quality and length of one's life.

It is in this period of learning about oneself, shaping one's identity, especially in relation to others, that some 80 percent of tobacco users smoke their first cigarette or begin using chewing tobacco or snuff. And unlike some of the other decisions made during these years—decisions regarding hair color, body piercing, clothing style, etc.—the decision to smoke or use smokeless tobacco will probably have long-term consequences. This is why efforts to prevent tobacco use focus almost exclusively on the young. It is also why young people ought to try to understand the reasons underlying their decision to begin using tobacco—or even to experiment with it.

What follows is a list of ideas, suggestions, and facts having to do with teenagers' decisions to start using tobacco. Some of the points are drawn from surveys and research studies. Some are opinions, educated guesses—of teachers, health professionals, and prevention specialists—based not on research findings but on common sense. And perhaps there are other reasons for starting that might be added to the list (Dichter 1947).

- Tobacco use may be a statement or a form of self-definition, signifying rebelliousness, independence, maturity, sophistication, and disregard for "the rules."
- Some teenagers believe that self-destructive behavior (such as tobacco use) is glamorous.
- A British American Tobacco (BAT) document dated December 15, 1977, cited a study of boys aged 10 to 15 that identified four main influences that led them to smoking: (1) the number of friends who smoke; (2) anticipation of adulthood; (3) parents' permissiveness toward smoking; and (4) whether they were put off by the danger of lung cancer.
- Some children are seduced by advertising and marketing. A study in England of 37,000 children aged 9 through 16 found that 71 percent of those who smoked said they were influenced by advertising. A researcher noted that of those teenagers who begin by smoking more than one cigarette, only 15 percent avoid becoming regular dependent smokers (O'Neill 1998).
- According to a 1994 survey, the three most popular brands among teenagers in the United States were the three brands most heavily advertised—Marlboro, Camel, and Newport. Interestingly, only about one-third of adult smokers smoked those brands. Do

teenagers pay more attention to advertising than adults do (CDC 1994a)?

- A more recent study showed that Marlboro, Camel, and Newport continue to be the favorites among teenagers, with nearly two-thirds preferring Marlboros (Swanbrow 1999).

- Joe Camel proved to be a huge attraction. Between 1988, when Joe Camel made his first appearance, and 1996, the number of Americans under the age of 18 who were smoking cigarettes every day increased by 73 percent, according to the CDC. The CDC said part of the increase could be attributed to ads that included merchandise giveaways (Rubin 1998 and Rosenbaum 1998).

- "Movies are a big problem," said Stanton Glantz, professor of medicine at the University of California–San Francisco's Institute of Health Policy Studies. "There's been a radical increase in cigar and cigarette use in the movies. And the people who are doing the smoking in movies are never the losers" (Walliser, 1998).

- Peer pressure is, of course, an important factor. English and Canadian teenagers who smoke told researchers that role models had nothing to do with their decision to smoke and that it was all about peer pressure (Irwin 1998).

- Researchers concluded from the English-Canadian study cited earlier that girls smoked in order stay thin or to lose weight (so that they would be more attractive to boys), while boys smoked to look more mature (Irwin 1998).

- Teenagers are told that smoking is dangerous, but "[w]hen kids see people smoking, they don't see them dropping over dead," stated Steve Sussman, associate professor of preventive medicine at the University of Southern California. Consequently, "young people typically don't pay attention to the links between smoking and adverse health effects" (Weiss and Reyes 1999).

- A teenager who is warned that smoking may have bad consequences "in 30 or 40 years" is inclined not to be alarmed. Teenagers' sense of time is to some extent distorted. If current trends continue, however, "about

250 million children alive in the world today will eventually be killed by tobacco" (WHO 1998a). In the United States, according to the CDC, "[m]ore than 5 million children under age 18 alive today will eventually die from smoking-related disease, unless current rates are reversed" (CDC 1996).

- Teenagers have argued that if smoking were really as dangerous as people say it is, the government would have prohibited the sale of cigarettes.
- An experiment with smoking easily develops into a positive experience, as the smoker perfects the skills involved in handling the cigarette, lighting it, and exhaling smoke. It becomes an accomplishment (Weiss and Reyes 1999).
- Once a person has learned to smoke, there are physiological rewards. The bodies of smokers give up warning signs like coughing and nausea" (Weiss and Reyes 1999).
- Young people aged 16 through 24 said it was often a member of their family who led them to begin smoking (Weiss and Reyes 1999).
- Young people are sensitive to signals that smoking is the norm. These signals include visible public smoking, the availability of cigarettes to minors, and the widespread promotion and advertising of tobacco products (Surgeon General 1994).

The World Health Organization has spoken of "the pervasive pressures" for young people to use tobacco. "People everywhere seem to be smoking. Attractive advertisements and exciting tobacco promotions are difficult to resist" (WHO 1998b). Remember, the Marlboro Man and Joe Camel are not prohibited forms of advertising in much of the world. Additionally, WHO pointed out that "[a]dults who smoke, such as family members, film stars and sports heroes, influence children and, especially, adolescents a great deal. In many countries, very high numbers of teachers, medical professionals and politicians [and] government officials smoke" (WHO 1998c).

Statistics show that teenagers with low grades and poor self-images are more likely to begin using tobacco. This may explain why some young people are more vulnerable to advertising or peer pressure, for example.

Statistics indicate that young people from low-income families who have fewer than two adults living in their homes are
especially at risk. Again, the question is, Why?

Cigarettes are still relatively easy to get, despite recently
implemented regulations intended to make it more difficult for
minors to obtain them.

Tobacco products are still fairly affordable. The American
Cancer Society favors higher taxes on cigarettes reporting that
every 10 percent increase in the price of cigarettes results in a 7
percent decrease in the number of kids who start smoking.
According to Linda Crawford, ACS vice president, "[p]rice is a
deterrent" (Walliser 1998).

In general, not much of an effort is made to keep young
people from smoking in schools. Less than half of students surveyed by the American Academy of Pediatrics said that teachers
and administrators vigorously attempted to prevent smoking,
while more than half said the consequences for smoking in school
are either mild or nonexistent (American Academy of Pediatrics
1997).

Young people vastly underestimate the addictiveness of
nicotine, according to the CDC. Of teenage smokers interviewed
in the *Monitoring the Future* project, 59 percent said they "definitely" would *not* continue to smoke (American Academy of
Pediatrics 1997). In another study, only 5 percent of high school
seniors said they "definitely" *would* continue to smoke. However,
the CDC found, 70 percent of high school seniors who intended
to stop were still smoking five years later (CDC 1994c).

The increase in cigar smoking in recent years, especially
among teenagers, is partly based on the mistaken assumption
that cigars are not as dangerous as cigarettes, because cigar smokers in general do not inhale. However, according to Dr. Krystyna
Kiel, a radiation oncologist at Northwestern University Medical
Center in Chicago, that only means that cigar smokers get cancers
in the mouth and neck rather than in the lungs (Siegel 1998).

Imagery helps to make cigars popular. "Movie stars and athletes smoke stogies on the cover of magazines," said Jeff Siegel.
"Bars and liquor stores sell fine cigars the way they do fine
brandies. It's a symbol of the good life, '90s style" (Siegel 1998).

Chewing tobacco and snuff, along with smoking bidis and
kreteks, are also popular as "safe" alternatives to cigarettes.
Chewing tobacco and snuff, however, are more dangerous than
cigars, and bidis and kreteks are more dangerous than cigarettes.

An article on former surgeon general Koop's web site alleged that tobacco companies "are trying to replace the income they have lost from cigarettes with profits from smokeless tobacco, and they have even promoted dip and chewing tobaccos as 'a safe alternative' to smoking. As with cigarettes, the tobacco companies have targeted children. 'Dips' (not containing tobacco) in similar containers as snuff tins are sold in convenience stores so that children can practice the behavior of using dip and have a can ring on the back pocket of their jeans. Such promotional items have been successful because half of smokeless tobacco users started before they were 13 years old!" (Orrick 1999).

Bidis come in a variety of flavors, they're less expensive than cigarettes, and in some areas they are more easily obtainable. Some teenagers find them appealing because they look like marijuana "joints," others because they're "cute," "hip," "cool," "trendy," "exotic," and "more natural." In some states they are available in health-food stores, which suggests that they are not harmful. A survey in 1998 found that 58 percent of students at four San Francisco high schools had tried bidis (Johnson 1999, 1).

## Prevention

Most of the thousands of young people who begin to smoke each day start to do so, the CDC has said, "not fully understanding that nicotine in tobacco is as addictive as heroin, cocaine, or alcohol." Most of them also underestimate the health consequences. The CDC advocates school-based prevention programs, which it believes can greatly reduce the number of young people who become daily smokers.

CDC guidelines for school-based prevention programs include the following:

1. *Policy:* Develop and enforce a school policy on tobacco use. The policy—developed in collaboration with students, parents, school staff, health professionals, and school boards—should

- Prohibit students, staff, and visitors from using tobacco on school premises, in school vehicles, and at school functions.
- Prohibit tobacco advertising (e.g., on signs, T-shirts, or caps or through sponsorship of school events) in school buildings, at school functions, and in school publications.

- Require that all students receive instruction on avoiding tobacco use.
- Provide access and referral to cessation programs for students and staff.

2. *Instruction:* Provide instruction about the short- and long-term negative physiological and social consequences of tobacco use, social influences on tobacco use, peer norms regarding tobacco use, and refusal skills. This instruction should

- Decrease the social acceptability of tobacco use and show that most young people do not smoke.
- Help students understand why young people start to use tobacco and identify more positive activities to meet their goals.
- Develop students' skills in assertiveness, goal setting, problem solving, and resisting pressure from the media and peers to use tobacco.
- Make clear that programs that only discuss tobacco's harmful effects or attempt to instill fear do not prevent tobacco use.

3. *Curriculum:* Provide tobacco-use prevention education in grades K–12.

- This instruction should be introduced in elementary school and intensified in middle/junior high school, when students are exposed to older students who typically use tobacco at higher rates.
- Reinforcement throughout high school is essential to ensure that successes in preventing tobacco use do not dissipate over time.

4. *Training:* Provide program-specific training for teachers. The training should include reviewing the curriculum, modeling instructional activities, and providing opportunities to practice implementing the lessons. Well-trained peer leaders can be an important adjunct to teacher-led instruction.

5. *Family Involvement:* Involve parents or families in support of school-based programs to prevent tobacco use. Schools should

- Promote discussions at home about tobacco use by

assigning homework and projects that involve families.
* Encourage parents to participate in community efforts to prevent tobacco use and addiction.

6. *Tobacco Cessation Efforts:* Support cessation efforts among students and school staff who use tobacco. Schools should provide access to cessation programs that help students and staff stop using tobacco rather than punishing them for violating tobacco-use policies.

7. *Evaluation:* Assess the tobacco-use prevention program at regular intervals. Schools can use the CDC's "Guidelines for School Health Programs to Prevent Tobacco Use and Addiction" to assess whether they are providing effective policies, curricula, training, and cessation programs (CDC 1994b).

Unfortunately, despite conscientious adherence to the "best practices" guidelines promoted by the CDC, some prevention programs fall short of their goals. In December 2000, for example, the man in charge of the massive antismoking program in Washington State, Arthur V. Peterson Jr., declared the project a failure. It had been hailed as a model for the rest of the world to follow, employing the latest theories and based on the best research. Yet after 14 years and expenditures totaling $15 million, more than one-fourth of the young people who went through the program subsequently became regular smokers—a prevalence percentage approximately equal to that among those who were not in the program.

## Quitting

Eighty percent of American smokers, according to one survey, "wish they had never started." So presumably, by conservative estimate, there are upward of 40 million potential quitters.

But the same survey found that 78 percent of smokers said they "could quit if they wanted to." If this figure is viewed as a glass half-empty, 78 percent of smokers do not want to quit, even though many of them must be among the 80 percent who wish they had never started. What is going on?

Mark Twain once commented that "Quitting smoking is easy. I've done it a thousand times." Well, there's "quitting"—and there's quitting. Mark Twain's was of the first variety, stopping for a while, perhaps a few days or weeks, and then starting again. The second type, quitting permanently, poses more of a challenge—a challenge that many smokers may feel is too much for them. Even among those who say they could quit if they "decided to," some probably have in mind a level of commitment—a degree of determination—that is beyond their capacity.

Still, there are about as many former smokers in America as there are current smokers. And with advances in nicotine-replacement therapy, quitting has become easier than ever. Nicotine gum and patches make it possible for smokers to continue their daily dosings of nicotine after they quit smoking. According to Jacob Sullum, the fact that about a quarter of the adult population continues to smoke "suggests that there's something more to smoking than chemical dependence (Cato Institute 1999). Indeed, it seems that smokers simply like to smoke, and that for many of them it is as much a pleasurable habit as an addiction.

## Why Quitting Is Difficult

A smoker who quits smoking cuts off the supply of nicotine to the brain. Without it, the smoker begins to experience symptoms of withdrawal, which may include any or all of the following: depression, anger, frustration, irritability, difficulty sleeping, difficulty concentrating, restlessness, headache, fatigue, and increased appetite. Women and girls are especially vulnerable to slight weight gain (ACS 1999b). For someone who is highly addicted, the experience is similar to withdrawal from heroin or cocaine. Women and girls are significantly more likely than men and boys to feel dependent on cigarettes, and some apparently find it unusually difficult to quit (Office on Women's Health, HHS, 1999).

Withdrawal is psychological as well—a reaction to a sharp alteration in habit. Some smokers become accustomed to smoking while talking on the phone, some miss cigarettes with their coffee, others feel uncomfortable having nothing to do with their hands. Interestingly, a number of former smokers mention that cigarettes were a measure of time, especially among those who took cigarette breaks that were one cigarette in duration.

Quitting may be especially difficult if one's friends and acquaintances are smokers. In fact, the most effective programs for young smokers include the development of refusal skills. For some young smokers it is easier to smoke a cigarette than to say no to it.

The American Cancer Society says withdrawal symptoms

usually peak about 48 to 72 hours after quitting and can last for a few days or several weeks. For some smokers the desire for a cigarette never goes away—one more good argument for not starting in the first place.

## How to Quit

The CDC recommends three methods for quitting. They are most effective when used in combination.

- Using the nicotine patch or gum.
- Getting support and encouragement.
- Learning how to handle stress and the urge to smoke (CDC TIPS 1999b).

In general, it seems advisable to talk with a physician or other health professional to work out precisely what strategy to follow when trying to quit. This approach is especially important for persons who think that switching to smokeless tobacco is a good way to taper off. As the National Cancer Institute has explained, users of smokeless tobacco absorb two to three times the amount of nicotine delivered by a cigarette, so a person who consumes 8 to 10 dips or chews per day receives the same amount of nicotine as a smoker who smokes 30 to 40 cigarettes a day (NCI 2000). A physician or other health professional can help the smoker develop a realistic, workable program to quit smoking and overcome the addiction to nicotine.

## Help for Quitting

Searching the Internet for more information is not necessarily a bad idea, but some of the information out there is of dubious value, and the selection, of course, is virtually unlimited. The best advice is to search only sources that are unquestionably reliable, such as those on the following list:

- American Cancer Society, 1-800-ACS-2345
- American Heart Association, 1-800-AHA-USA1
- American Lung Association, 1-800-LUNG-USA
- Centers for Disease Control, 1-800-358-9295
- National Cancer Institute,1-800-4-CANCER
- Office of Smoking and Health,1-800-CDC-1311

## The Benefits of Quitting

The body begins to recover—to repair itself—almost immediately after a smoker stubs out his or her last cigarette. The American Cancer Society and other research foundations have developed a schedule showing how much time the body needs to do its work.

- *20 minutes after quitting*—The (former) smoker's blood pressure drops to a level close to that before the last cigarette.
- *In 8 hours*—The carbon monoxide level in the blood drops to normal.
- *In 24 hours*—The risk of heart attack begins to decrease.
- *In a few days*—The sense of taste and smell return; breathing becomes increasingly easier. (NCI 2000).
- *In 2 weeks to 3 months*—The circulation improves; lung function increases by as much as 30 percent.
- *In 1 to 9 months*—Coughing, sinus congestion, fatigue, and shortness of breath decrease; the cilia on the walls of the lungs regain normal function, enabling them to handle mucus, clean the lungs, and reduce infection.
- *In 1 year*—The risk of coronary heart disease has decreased by 50 percent (WHO 1998a).
- *In 5 to 15 years*—The risk of stroke is reduced to that of a nonsmoker.
- *In 10 years*—The lung cancer death rate has fallen to about half that of a smoker, and there is a decrease in the risk of cancer of the mouth, throat, esophagus, bladder, kidney, cervix, and pancreas.
- *In 15 years*—The risk of coronary heart disease is no higher than that of a nonsmoker.

(Except as indicated, the material in the preceding list is from ACS 1999b.)

## Tobacco Use Worldwide

According to the WHO, the use of tobacco worldwide has reached the proportion of a global epidemic. It is approaching its peak among men in most developed countries and spreading now to men in developing countries and women in all countries (WHO 1998b).

A WHO fact sheet called attention to the following points:

- Today, according to WHO estimates, there are approximately 1.2 billion smokers in the world, constituting about one-third of the global population aged 15 years and over. Of these, 800 million are in developing countries.
- Since the mid-1980s, global cigarette consumption has remained relatively steady at an estimated 1,600 cigarettes per adult per year.
- The distribution of tobacco consumption has shifted in the last two decades. Declining consumption in developed countries has been counterbalanced by increasing consumption in developing countries. This imbalance will increase as lawsuits in the United States force tobacco companies to expand their marketing in other less hostile markets.
- Available data suggest that approximately 47 percent of men and 12 percent of women smoke. In developing countries, 48 percent of men and 7 percent of women smoke, while in developed countries, the percentages are 42 percent of men and 24 percent of women (WHO 1998b).

In the early 1990s, according to WHO estimates, tobacco caused about 3 million deaths a year around the world. Since then the rate of death has been rising steadily. If current trends are not reversed, the toll will top 10 million a year by the 2020s or the early 2030s (when the young smokers of today are in middle age). Seventy percent of those deaths will occur in developing countries (WHO 1996).

On World No Tobacco Day, May 30, 2000, WHO announced that the number of smokers worldwide had reached 1.2 billion, of whom 11,000 die every day as a result of some smoking-related illness. WHO's director-general, Dr. Gro Harlem Brundtland, denounced tobacco advertising and the tobacco industry's efforts to attract young people. "Tobacco advertisements talk to us from our streets, films, radios, television sets, and sports events," she said. "Everywhere our children turn there is something or someone telling you to smoke. What makes all this unacceptable and treacherous is that this dangerous and addictive product is sold to youth and adolescents as an assertion of their freedom to choose." And, of course, it is also attractive to youngsters around the world because they see it as part—almost as a symbol—of the American lifestyle.

## The Future of Tobacco

Tobacco's future can best be understood in the context of the warnings and predictions issued by the World Health Organization. The rising toll of tobacco-related deaths in Asia and the developing nations in coming years will provide a gauge of the tobacco industry's success in penetrating and developing those markets. WHO estimates that there are 1.2 billion smokers in the world—about one-third of the global population aged 11 and over. One-fourth of all smokers are in China, and U.S. tobacco companies are eager to break into that market. Action on Smoking and Health (ASH UK) predicts that the number of smokers worldwide will reach 1.64 billion by 2025, with most of the increase expected in developing countries. Both WHO and ASH (UK) believe that a disproportionate number of the world's new smokers will be women.

Any discussion of the future of tobacco invariably works its way around to the topic of "safe" cigarettes. Star Tobacco Corp., of Petersburg, Virginia, is mentioned occasionally as a developer of safer tobacco, and the tobacco companies themselves are said to be able to manufacture safe products. Antitobacco sources argue, however, that the so-called safe and safer cigarettes are not safe, but are only to some extent less dangerous. Most health authorities adamantly maintain that all tobacco products should be avoided, regardless of manufacturers' claims.

## Issues and Topics for Research

As the debate over tobacco has raged, with tobacco lawyers, smokers, and various industry supporters facing antitobacco groups in courtrooms and sniping at one another in the pages of newspapers and magazines, the issues and questions surrounding tobacco use and marketing have become increasingly clear. The debate has not been simply about whether smoking is harmful. Fundamental issues of freedom and responsibility have been raised—the conflicting rights of smokers and nonsmokers; the ethics of lawyers, business leaders, scientists, and lawmakers; the ethics of inaction, passivity, deception, and the withholding of information; corporate and individual accountability; the rights of advertisers and merchants; and other conflicts arising from contradictory values and interests and differences over which values and which rights should be accorded higher standing than others.

Some questions have been settled to the satisfaction of those involved in the disputes, while others remain open to debate and further investigation:

- To what extent can the blame for encouraging young people to smoke be attributed to celebrities and to movies in which glamorous people are depicted smoking? Some women have become public endorsers of cigar smoking, challenging the concept that only powerful men smoke cigars. Ads by cigar companies portray smoking as a glamorous "woman thing." Cigar smoking (and smoking in general) are common in movies and on television. According to a survey by the American Lung Association of Sacramento, California, of 133 Hollywood films reviewed in 1995, more than half depicted tobacco use and more than one-fourth depicted cigar use (SCARC 1996).

- Researchers at the Dartmouth-Hitchcock Medical Center in Lebanon, New Hampshire, reported that a multiyear study (1988–1997) of new film releases showed that more than 85 percent of the films had scenes in which actors used tobacco and that identifiable brands appear in 28 percent. Among the films that showed identifiable brands were *Ghostbusters II, Home Alone II (Lost in New York), Honey I Shrunk the Kids, Kindergarten Cop, Men in Black, The Nutty Professor,* and *Volcano.* Paid product placement has been banned, but the study suggested that the tobacco industry might pay directly or through in-kind payments for placement of its brands in films (Mulvihill 2001).

- Is it fair to try to discourage smoking by raising the cost of cigarettes? Although the government acknowledges that nicotine is addictive, is it appropriate to increase taxes on tobacco products (thereby raising prices) in order to discourage their use? Who suffers more—tobacco companies or persons who use tobacco products and become addicted to them? Tobacco companies already increase their prices because of lawsuits. When a tobacco company loses a case, smokers wind up paying the penalty.

- Society has to pay a large percentage of the medical bills of people who die of smoking-related illnesses. Is it right that lawsuits force the tobacco industry to pay part of this cost? Jacob Sullum, a senior editor at *Reason* magazine, has argued that it is not. Because smokers tend to die earlier than nonsmokers, he says, the short-term costs of treating tobacco-related illness are balanced, and probably outweighed, by savings on Social Security, nursing home stays, and medical care in old age (Sullum 1999).

- What is the distinction between smoking-related illnesses and illnesses caused by smoking? Drs. Ernst Wynder and Evarts A. Graham conducted a study in which they selected over 600 men with lung cancer and talked with them to determine how many had smoked cigarettes. Graham at first hesitated, arguing that they might just as well ask them if they had ever bought silk stockings, and conclude that there was a relationship, or correlation, between men who bought silk stockings and who later developed lung cancer. His point was that the correlation might have nothing to do with cause and effect (Wynder and Graham 1950).

- Another point having to do with cause and effect: Although smoking cigarettes may cause a specific illness, it does not follow that smoking cigarettes is the sole cause of that illness. Thus, as a Philip Morris (PM) executive has argued, cancer victims suing PM should have to prove that cigarettes, rather than any other possible cause, were the proximate cause of their disease.

- Where should the line be drawn between an individual's legal right to use tobacco and society's obligation to limit the use of a lethal product?

- Where should the line be drawn between the rights of smokers and the rights of nonsmokers?

- Some people argue that advertising does not cause anyone to smoke but that it does influence brand choice. If this is true, should restrictions on tobacco advertising be lifted?
- Would prohibiting cigarettes and allowing only smokeless tobacco benefit public health? This question is debated in a 1995 issue of *Priorities* magazine (Rodu and Tomar 1995).
- To what extent is it appropriate to censure people working in public relations, advertising, and marketing who may have known more about tobacco than the public did but who nevertheless helped to promote smoking?

A survey conducted in 1964 by *Printer's Ink* found that copywriters working on tobacco accounts suspected that smoking was dangerous. Thirty-five percent of the advertising writers said they themselves had stopped smoking and 15 percent said they had cut down. "However," as Elizabeth Whelan reported in *A Smoking Gun,* "not one of the 20 cigarette copywriters interviewed admitted to any pangs of conscience at creating copy for a product reported by the government to be harmful. One writer said, 'Writing cigarette copy doesn't bother me one bit! Why should it? Should an automobile copywriter worry about writing copy for automobiles just because thousands of people die in car accidents every year?' Another writer said, 'It's all a fad. A little while back it was the scare over cholesterol and heart disease.' And a third said, "I write for the man who feeds me'" (Whelan 1984, 111).

A Philip Morris internal memo noted the concern expressed about whether there is a moral obligation to tell the FTC that some cigarette smokers may be getting more tar than the FTC rating of that cigarette would indicate. The author of the memo said he believed "that there need be no such concern, at least from a position of morality. It is obvious that HEW [the Department of Health, Education, and Welfare] knows that smokers can vary their intake. Otherwise they would not urge smokers to take fewer puffs [puffing behavior—puff volume, puff duration, and puff interval—determines the quantity of tar that is inhaled]." In other words, smokers may be getting more tar than FTC ratings indicate, but they could get less by following HEW's advice and changing their puffing behavior (Fagan 1974).

How well have the news media handled reports of studies on

the dangers of smoking? In *A Smoking Gun,* Dr. Elizabeth Whelan contends that the media's efforts to present both sides of the tobacco story resulted in news reports that failed to convey the importance of the findings. Such articles reported the findings of a study and routinely quoted an industry spokesperson denying its accuracy or validity. Many readers, undoubtedly, did not know what to believe.

What about individual accountability and the assumption of risk? "There's no question that smoking involves risk," attorney Robert Heim said in his defense of Philip Morris Inc., in a class-action lawsuit brought on behalf of a half-million sick Florida smokers. "But of all the consumer products that have been manufactured and sold in these United States over the course of the last century, none have had risks that have been better understood and better appreciated by consumers than the health risks of smoking. None" (quoted in Fields 1998). Smoking is legal and people are free to smoke if they choose to do so, just as they are free to eat fatty foods, walk in high-crime areas late at night, sky-dive, drive race cars, and feed the bears in national parks.

As the columnist George Will put it, tobacco lawsuits punish "a legal industry for selling legal products to people supposedly not responsible for the foolish decisions Joe Camel made them make" (Will 1998, A19). A physician responded to George Will's column by arguing that people "don't really realize how dangerous smoking is." Besides, he pointed out, "Most smokers become addicted as minors, when they are too naive to resist the tobacco industry's multibillion-dollar marketing campaigns. Most smokers try to quit and fail." The justice system, he said, is "society's last chance to protect itself." On the other hand, economist W. K. Viscusi has stated, in his book *Smoking: Making the Risky Decision,* that most smokers not only are aware of the risks, but tend to overestimate them (Viscusi quoted in Adams 1999, A18).

Michael Moore, the attorney general of Mississippi, filed the first of the states' Medicaid suits. Speaking of the tobacco companies, he said: "I believe they're the most corrupt and evil corporate animal that has ever been created in this country's history. They make a drug, and they sell it knowing that it's addictive. They market it to our children, who they know will become addicts, and they know that they will die from . . . a tobacco-related disease" (quoted in Tursi, White, and McQuilkin 2000). Consider, among other matters, the question of whether a corporation (versus the individuals who work for it) may be, or should be, considered moral or immoral.

With reference to the early state suits, Charles Blixt, RJR general counsel, had this to say:

> We have never believed, and I still don't believe, that those cases were well founded on the law or the facts. Unfortunately, what happened is the organized plaintiffs' bar, the anti-smoking industry and the political arm of the states' governments all coalesced into this huge assault on the industry. And those three forces combined resulted in the misapplication of the law and in many cases made new law that we've come to characterize as the 'tobacco exception' to the American legal system. There were rulings that I continue to believe were completely egregious. They were unfair and unfounded. They allowed the anti-smoking industry and the organized plaintiffs' contingency-fee lawyers to control the agenda on these things."
> (quoted in Tursi, White, and McQuilkin 2000)

In Nathan Horton's liability suit against American Tobacco Company, the defense argued that Horton had assumed the risk by freely choosing to smoke. This argument shifts responsibility from the product's manufacturer to the consumer. Its underlying assumptions are pertinent to such questions as the following:

- How effective are warning labels in discouraging people from smoking? Critics argue that most people do not know what the labels say until after they have bought the product.
- To what extent should warning labels diminish the responsibility of tobacco companies?
- Should tobacco products include inserts providing more specific and detailed information relating to the various risks?
- Columnists Jack Anderson and Douglas Cohn have argued that the penalties for possession of small amounts of cocaine are out of proportion to the harm inflicted by using the drug. "A far more lethal product is not only legal but heavily promoted," they said, "and that's tobacco. A third of people who smoke will

die prematurely of lung cancer and other smoking-related illnesses. Yet 35 years after the first surgeon general's report warned of its danger, smoking is on the rise among juveniles, the demographic group most likely to get hooked and stay hooked" (Anderson and Cohn 1999, 4B).

- To what extent is it valid to criticize the U.S. Congress for its support for the tobacco industry? Do the correlations between contributions and votes justify Ellen Goodman's characterization of Congress as "a wholly owned subsidiary" of big tobacco?

- To what extent should tobacco advertising be restricted? Robert Peck, a legislative counsel to the American Civil Liberties Union (ACLU), argued in a column published in 1993 that the dangers of tobacco justified regulating tobacco but not speech (Peck 1993).

- Does the tobacco industry target underage smokers? In a 1996 Online Newshour, Brennan Dawson, senior vice president of the Tobacco Institute, had this to say: "[T]he Federal Trade Commission undertook a three-year study of the Joe Camel campaign. At the end of that lengthy, intensive study, they said that . . . the evidence wasn't there to support [claims that the campaign was directed at kids.]. . . . If you look at the studies that have been done on tobacco advertising here in the United States, you find that kids may be aware of tobacco ads, but they also don't like tobacco products, they say that tobacco ads don't make them smoke, and we can then turn to the international experience where many countries have experimented with tobacco advertising bans, and what they've found is that youth smoking continues along the same track that it was on before the advertising was removed" (Public Broadcasting System [PBS] 1996).

- Some smokers complain that they have become addicted to cigarettes and cannot quit. However, the tobacco industry says that in the past 30 years 46 million people have quit smoking for good. How should the blame be divided?

- Some magazines that accept smoking ads have apparently chosen not to publish articles critical of smoking.

- How effective are prevention programs? Some critics have observed that prevention programs (which are aimed primarily at young people) may unintentionally communicate the old concept of smoking as being "for adults," thus making it seem more a part of growing up.
- Documents obtained from tobacco companies reveal that at one time research was under way to produce tobacco that would be even more addictive than regular tobacco—by manipulating nicotine levels. It is also known that the industry has used ammonia to increase the addictiveness of tobacco.
- Should tobacco industry regulations be changed? The main question, with regard to regulation, is how to regulate a product that is deadly when used as intended, but remains legal for most people over 18 years of age. Traditionally, government has sought to protect people from one another. In recent years, however, government has concerned itself more and more with the more difficult task of protecting people from themselves. As Larry White observed, "Cigarettes are the only products on the market (aside from weapons) that kill and injure when used as they are intended to be used" (White 1988, 24).
- Why do people start smoking in the first place? "Many smokers reacted [to the 1964 *Surgeon General's Report*] like the man in the story who had just seen a film on the removal of a cancerous lung: 'After I saw that, I decided to give up going to the movies'" (Whelan 1984, 103).
- How influential is cigarette advertising in leading people, teenagers in particular, to start smoking? Why were teenagers influenced by Joe Camel? Consider the fact that Marlboro was "a woman's cigarette" until a new advertising strategy changed its image. One survey has found that 86 percent of new smokers, aged 11 to 20, prefer the three most heavily advertised brands of cigarettes, even though the advertising for those brands is said to be directed at an older audience.
- Figures issued by the tobacco industry differ from those issued by government agencies. For example, in 1998 R. J. Reynolds stated that Camel cigarettes had been

purchased in 1997 by only 3 percent of underage cigarette buyers, not 13 percent, as FTC staff members had said a week earlier in a news conference (RJR 1998).

- On April 28, 1997, Dr. Elizabeth Whelan, president of the American Council on Science and Health, said that "any deal with the cigarette industry that include[d] shielding it from current and future private-sector litigation would be an unparalleled setback for the cause of public health in America." She said that "the ongoing public debate about future FDA jurisdiction over tobacco products and the current focus on 'state Medicaid suits' [were] principally red herrings that [might] distract the American public from the cigarette industry's primary goal: a Congressionally mandated global deal" (ACSH 1997).

- According to David Satcher, surgeon general in 1999, "The single most promising public health intervention today is not the development of a new drug but the opportunity to invest part of the recent $246 billion settlement with the tobacco companies into public health and proven programs that would prevent our nation's children from smoking" (Satcher 1999, A15).

## References*

Achey, T. L. 1978. "Product Information." Lorillard Tobacco Company document. 03537131/7132. lorillarddocs.com

ACS (American Cancer Society). 1997. "1997 Cigarette Nicotine Disclosure Report." http://www.cancer.org/tobacco/index.html.

ACS. 1999a. "Cancer Facts and Figures 1999. Tobacco Use." *Facts and Figures.* http://www.cancer.org.

ACS. 1999b. "Quitting Smoking." Revised July 20. http://www.cancer.org/.

*A note about Bates numbers: Bates numbers (e.g., 1000123662/3666) are used to identify some documents listed here. A Bates number appears as nine digits followed by a slash and then four more digits. The first nine digits identify the first page of the document. The last four digits, after the slash, indicate the Bates number on the last page of the document, without repeating the first part of the original number. In other words, if the number of the first page is 503969238 and the four-digit number after the slash is 9242, this means the number of the final page is 503969242 and that the document is five pages long.

ACS. 2000. "Study Finds Low-Tar Cigarettes Don't Let You off the Hook." February 11. http://www.cancer.org/.

ACSH (American Council on Science and Health). 1997. "Cigarette Deal Unparalleled Setback for Public Health." News Release. April 28.

ACSH. 1998. "Public Health Scientists Warn about the Irreversible Effects of Smoking." June 17.

Adams, Joseph. 1999. "Smokers Really Don't Get It," *Washington Post,* October 19: A18.

Advisory Committee on Smoking and Health. 1964. *Smoking and Health: Report of the Advisory Committee to the Surgeon General of the Public Health Service.* Washington, D.C.: Government Printing Office.

AHA (American Heart Association). 1997. "Cigarette and Tobacco Smoke." Biostatistical Fact Sheets. http://www.americanheart.org/statistics/biostats/index.html.

AHA. 1999. "Risk Factors." *2000 Heart and Stroke Statistical Update.* http://www.americanheart.org/statistics/08rskfct.html.

ALA (American Lung Association). 1998. "Smoking." Fact Sheet. September.

ALA. 1999a. "Secondhand Smoke." Fact Sheet. September.

ALA. 1999b. "Secondhand Smoke and Children." Fact Sheet. May.

American Academy of Pediatrics. 1997. "First Cigarette in Grade 6 or Below Not Uncommon." Press Release. October 1.

Anderson, Jack, and Douglas Cohn. 1999. "Tobacco Is the Real Killer Drug." *Lawrence Journal-World,* August 31: 4B.

ASH UK (Action on Smoking and Health [UK]). 1998. "The Constituents of Tobacco Smoke." Fact Sheet No. 12. http://www.ash.org/.

Bates, Clive, Martin Jarvis, and Gregory Connolly. 1999. "Tobacco Additives: Cigarette Engineering and Nicotine Addiction." July 14. http://www.ash.org.uk/papers/additives.html.

BBC (British Broadcasting Corporation). 1999a. "Cigarettes: A Complex Cocktail of Chemicals." February 17. http://news.bbc.co.uk/hi/english/world/.

BBC. 1999b. "Low-Tar Cigarettes 'Fool Smokers.'" March 18. http://news.bbc.co.uk/hi/english/world/.

Bennett, W. P., Michael Alavanja, Brunhilde Blomeke, Kirsi H. Vahakangas, Katariina Castren, Judith A. Welsh, Elise D. Bowman, Mohammed A. Khan, Douglas B. Flieder, and Curtis C. Harris. 1999. "Environmental Tobacco Smoke, Genetic Susceptibility, and Risk of Lung Cancer in Never-Smoking Women." *Journal of the National Cancer Institute,* December 1: 2009–2014.

Brecher, Edward M., and the editors of *Consumer Reports Magazine*. 1972. *The Consumers Union Report on Licit and Illicit Drugs*. Online Drug Library (Schaffer Library). http://www.druglibrary.org/schaffer/library/studies/cu/CU26.html.

Campaign for Tobacco-Free Kids. 1997. "Women and Tobacco." Fact Sheet. http://tobaccofreekids.org.

Cato Institute. 1999. "Cutting through the Smoke: The Science and Politics of Tobacco." Seminar. October 3. http://www.cato.org.

CDA (California Dental Association). 1994. "Primer: This Month's Topic: Tobacco." March. http://www.cda.org.

CDA. 1998. "Using Smokeless Tobacco Is Gambling with Your Health!" November. http://www.cda.org.

CDC (Centers for Disease Control). 1994a. "Changes in the Cigarette Brand Preference of Adolescent Smokers, U.S., 1989–1993." *Morbidity and Mortality Weekly Report (MMWR)*. August 19.

CDC. 1994b. "Guidelines for School Health Programs to Prevent Tobacco Use and Addiction." http://www.cdc.gov/mmwr/preview/mmwrhtml/00026213.htm.

CDC. 1994c. Preventing Tobacco Use among Young People." A Report of the Surgeon General AT-A-GLANCE. http://www.cdc.gov/tobacco/sgr/sgr_1994/94oshaag.htm#kidstf.

CDC. 1996. "Youth Risk Behavior Survey." *MMWR*, November 8.

CDC. 1997. "National Health Interview Survey." Public Use Data Release. ftp://ftp.cdc.gov/pub/Health_Statistics/NCHSProgram_Code/NHIS/1995/20/2001.

CDC. 1998. "Youth Risk Behavior Surveillance—United States, 1997." *MMWR*, August 14.

CDC TIPS (Centers for Disease Control, Tobacco Information and Prevention Source). 1996. "Smoking Prevalence among U.S. Adults," TIPS Fact Sheet. July. http://www.cdc.gov/tobacco/research_data/adults_prev/prevali/htm

CDC TIPS. 1999a. "Exposure to Secondhand Smoke Widespread." CDC Tobacco Information and Prevention Source. http://www.cdc.gov/tobacco/research_data/environmental/etsrel.htm.

CDC TIPS. 1999b. "How to Quit: Useful Resources to Quit Smoking." http://www.cdc.gov/tobacco/how2Quit.htm.

CDC TIPS. 1999c. "Smokeless Tobacco: A Dangerous Alternative." Atlanta: CDC.

CDC TIPS. 1999d. "State-Specific Prevalence of Current Cigarette and Cigar Smoking among Adults, United States, 1998." Originally published as a Monitoring the Future Study Press Release, December 18, 1998.

CDC TIPS. 1999e. "Targeting Tobacco Use: The Nation's Leading Cause of Death." TIPS At-a-Glance Fact Sheet. http://www.cdc.gov/tobacco/overview/oshaag98.htm.

CDC TIPS. 2000a. "Incidence of Cigarette Smoking among U.S. Teens." TIPS Fact Sheet. April: 1.

CDC TIPS. 2000b. "Tobacco Use in the United States." http://www.cdc.gov/tobacco/tobus_us.htm. February 3.

Columbia University Health Education Program, Alice. 1999. "Low Tar and Nicotine Cigarettes." http://www.goaskalice.columbia.edu/0508.html.

Community Outreach Health Information System, Boston University. 1999. "What's in That Butt?" http://www.bu.edu/COHIS/smoking/about/butt.htm.

Corina, Maurice. 1975. *Trust in Tobacco: The Anglo-American Struggle for Power.* London: Michael Joseph.

Cowley, Geoffrey. 1997. "Are Stogies Safer Than Cigarettes?" *Newsweek,* July 21.

Deford, Susan. 1997. "Tobacco: The Noxious Weed That Built a Nation." *Washington Post,* May 14.

Dichter, Ernest. 1947. "Why Do We Smoke Cigarettes?" *The Psychology of Everyday Living.* http://www.tobacco.org/. Accessed 1999.

Djordjevic, M. V., S. D. Stellman, and E. Zang. 2000. "Doses of Nicotine and Lung Carcinogens Delivered to Cigarette Smokers." *Journal of the National Cancer Institute,* January.

Doll, Richard, and Bradford A. Hill. 1952. "Study of the Aeliology of Carcinoma of the Lung." *British Medical Journal,* December 15.

Doll, Richard, and Bradford A. Hill. 1954. "The Mortality of Doctors in Relation to Their Smoking Habits." *British Medical Journal,* June 26: 1451–1455.

Douglas, Drew. 2000. "Florida Judge Enters Judgment in 'Engle,' Allows $145 Billion Punitive Damages Award." *Toxics Law Reporter,* Vol. 15, No. 44. November 9.

Fagan, R. 1974. "Moral Issue on FTC Tar." Philip Morris (PM) Internal Memo. PM Document Site. March 7. http://www.pmdocs.com/getallimg.asp? DOCID=1000211075/1076.

Fields, Tracy. 1998. "Florida Smokers Battle on in Court Despite 46-State Tobacco Deal." *Washington Post,* November 29.

Garrett, Major. 2000. "Clinton Calls on Congress to Grant FDA Authority to Regulate Tobacco." March 21. http://www.cnn.com/.

Gergen, Peter J., J. A. Fowler, K. R. Maurer, W. W. Davis, and M. D. Overpeck. 1998. "The Burden of Environmental Tobacco Smoke Exposure on the Respiratory Health of Children 2 Months through 5 Years of Age in the United States." *Pediatrics,* February.

Ginzel, K. H. 1990. "What's in a Cigarette?" *Priorities,* Vol. 2, No. 4. Reprinted by ACSH. http://www.acsh.org/publications/priorities/0102/nicotine.html.

Gottlieb, Mark. 2001. Tobacco Control Resource Center, Inc. (TCRC), Northeastern University School of Law. E-mail to author. January 5.

Grace, Catherine O'Neill. 1999. "How and Why: The Evils of Huffing and Puffing." *Washington Post,* October 12: Z28.

Gregoire, Christine. 1999. "Master Settlement Briefing." http://www.wa.gov/ago/tobacco/ag_summary.htm.

Hall, Celia. 2000. "A Few Cigarettes 'Enough to Make Children Addicts.'" *Daily Telegraph* (London), September 12. http://www.telegraph.co.uk/et?ac=003782091322794&rtmo=LStbG3bo5/20/2001.

Hermer, Laura. 1999. "Executive Summary." *The Multistate Master Settlement and the Future of State and Local Tobacco Control.* Boston: TCRC, Northeastern University School of Law. March 24.

Hilts, Philip J. 1996. *Smokescreen.* Reading, MA: Addison-Wesley Publishing.

Howard, George, Lynne E. Wagenknecht, Gregory L. Burke, Ana Diez-Roux, Gregory W. Evans, Paul McGovern, F. Javier Nieto, and Grethe S. Tell. 1998. "Cigarette Smoking and Progression of Atherosclerosis." *Journal of the American Medical Association,* Vol. 279, No. 2. January 14.

Indiana Prevention Resource Center. 1999. "Additives Found in American Cigarettes." http://www.drugs.indiana.edu/druginfo/additives.html.

Indiana Tobacco Control Center. 1999. "Tobacco Use in America." http://iumeded.med.iupui.edu/tobacco/tobuse.htm.

Irwin, Aisling. 1998. "Girls Say Smoking Is Aid to Staying Slim." *Daily Telegraph* (London), August 4. http://www.telegraph.co.uk/.

James I, King of England. 1604. *A Counterblaste to Tobacco.* London: Robert Barker.

Johnson, Lori. 1999. "Young Smokers Sucked In by Cigarettes with Flavor." *Lawrence Journal-World.* May 11: 1.

Johnston, L. D., P. M. O'Malley, and J. G. Buchanan. 1999. "Cigarette Smoking among American Teens Continues Gradual Decline." Monitoring the Future Study Press Release. December 17. Ann Arbor: University of Michigan, News and Information Services.

Johnston, Myron. 1999. "Young Smokers: Prevalence, Trends, Implications, and Related Demographic Trends." Philip Morris report. May 17. http://tobaccofreedom.globalink.org/issues/documents/landman/youth/emo1.gif.

Kawachi, Ichiro, Graham A. Colditz, Frank E. Pseizer, JoAnn E. Manson, Meir J. Stampfer, Walter C. Willett, and Charles H. Hennekens. 1997. "A Prospective Study of Passive Smoking and Coronary Heart Disease." *Circulation*, May 20.

Kluger, Richard. 1996. *Ashes to Ashes: America's Hundred-Year Cigarette War, the Public Health, and the Unabashed Triumph of Philip Morris.* New York: Alfred A. Knopf.

Landman, Anne. 1999. "Big Tobacco's Seldom Told Plan for Our Children—How Big Tobacco Encourages Shoplifting by Kids." ALAC Shoplifting Project. http://www.smokescreen.org/alac/Index.html.

Law, M. R., J. K. Morris, and N. J. Wald. 1997. "Environmental Tobacco Smoke Exposure and Ischaemic Heart Disease: An Evaluation of the Evidence." *British Medical Journal*, October 18: 973–980.

MacKinnon, Mark. 2000. "Tobacco Sales' Target Was Youth." *Globe and Mail* (Toronto), May 29. http://theglobeandmail.com/gam/National/20000529/UTOBAN.html.

Mayo Clinic. 1997. "Secondhand Smoke: Clearing the Air of a Cloudy Debate." August 11. http://www.mayohealth.org/mayo/9708/htm/2nd_hand.htm.

Mintz, John, and Saundra Torry. 1998. "Internal R. J. Reynolds Documents Detail Cigarette Marketing Aimed at Children." *Washington Post*, January 15: A1.

Missouri Department of Health, ASSIST (American Stop Smoking Intervention Study). 1997. "Operation Storefront: Statewide Results." August 7. http://www.ago.state.mo.us/4799.htm#top.

Mulvihill, Keith. 2001."Cigarettes Get More Leading Roles in Hollywood Films." Reuters, January 4. http://www.heartinfo.com/reuters2001/010105elin017.htm

National Institute of Dental Research. 1997. "Spit Tobacco: Know the Score." Fact Sheet. April.

NCI (National Cancer Institute). 1998. "Cancer Facts: Questions and Answers about Smokeless Tobacco and Cancer." Washington, D.C.: NCI. Revised October 23. http://newscenter.cancer.gov.

NCI. 2000. "Cancer Facts: Questions and Answers About the Benefits of Smoking Cessation." Fact Sheet 8.11. Washington, D.C.: NCI. Revised January 27. http//newscenter.cancer.gov.

NDSN (National Drug Strategy Network). 1996. "FTC Announces Changes in Cigarette Tar Rating System." News Briefs. February. http://www.ndsn.org/TOPICS/tobacco.html.

NIDA (National Institute on Drug Abuse). 1999. "Nicotine Addiction" Research Report Series, NIDA. Revised May 13. http://www.nida.nih.gov/researchreports/nicotine/nicotine2.html#what.

Office of the Attorney General of Washington. 1999. http://www.wa.gov/ago/tobaccosettlement/ag_summary.html.

Office on Women's Health, HHS (U.S. Department of Health and Human Services). 1999. "Young Women and Smoking: The Facts." http://www.4women.gov/owh/pub/smoking/index.htm.

O'Neill, Sean. 1998. "Adverts Do Have Effect, Say Young Smokers." *Daily Telegraph* (London), June 17. http://www.telegraph.co.uk/.

Orrick, Debora J. 1999. "Smokeless Tobacco Not Safer Than Smoking," May 19. http://www.drkoop.com/wellness/tobacco/articles/smokeless.asp.

PBS (Public Broadcasting System). 1996. "Smoke Screening." Online News Hour. August 23. http://www.pbs.org.

Pearl, Raymond. 1938. "Tobacco Smoking and Longevity." *Science,* Vol. 87, No. 2253. March 4: 216–217.

Peck, Robert S. 1993. "Is Cigarette Advertising Protected by the First Amendment? Yes." *Priorities,* Vol. 5, No.3.

Pepples, Ernest. 1976. "Industry Response to Cigarette-Health Controversy." B&W Collection, University of California at San Francisco. Memo. 2205.01.1/.6.

Player, Tucker. 1998. "After the Fall: The Cigarette Papers, the Global Settlement, and the Future of Tobacco Litigation." *South Carolina Law Review,* Vol. 49, No. 2.

RJR (R. J. Reynolds). n.d. "Do Cigarette Companies Want Kids to Smoke?" Online Litigation Archive. www.rjrtdocs.com/rjrtdocs/frames.html.

RJR. 1998. "FTC Staff Misrepresents Camel's Use among Underage Smokers." News Release. October 12.

Rodu, Brad, and Scott L. Tomar. 1995. "Point-Counterpoint: Would a Switch from Cigarettes to Smokeless Tobacco Benefit Public Health?" *Priorities,* Vol. 7, No. 4. http://www.asch.org/publications/priorites/0704/index.html.

Rosenbaum, David E. 1998. "Smoking by College Students Is on the Rise, Research Finds." *New York Times,* November 18: A28.

Rubin, Alissa J. 1998. "28% Jump in College Smokers Raises Alarm." *Los Angeles Times,* November 18: A3.

Salcedo, Jacqueline. 1999. "A Summary of the Engle Verdict." Tobacco Control Resource Center (TCRC), Northeastern University School of Law, Boston. *http://www.tobaccocontrol.neu.edu/*.

Satcher, David. 1999. "Save the Kids, Fight Tobacco." *Washington Post*, May 25: A15.

SCARC (Smoking Control Advocacy Resource Center). 1996. "Cigar Alert." ScarcNet. December 27. http://www.tobacco.org/Misc/cigaralert.html.

Siegel, Jeff. 1998. "Cigars: Coolish or Foolish?" ALA. November 13. http://www.lungusa.org/.

Suchetka, Diane. 1997. "Not Healthful, Just Trendy." *The Charlotte Observer*, January 13.

Sullum, Jacob. 1999. "Top Ten Myths of the Anti-Smoking Movement." *Reason Online*, December 3. http://www.reason.com/.

Surgeon General. 1994. *Preventing Tobacco Use among Young People: Surgeon General's Report.* Washington, D.C.: Government Printing Office.

Surgeon General. 1998. *Tobacco Use among U.S. Racial/Ethnic Minority Groups: Report of the Surgeon General.* Washington, D.C.: Government Printing Office.

Swanbrow, Diana. 1999. "Cigarette Brands Smoked by American Teens: One Brand Predominates; Three Account for Nearly All Teen Smoking." Monitoring the Future Study. News Release. April 14. Ann Arbor: University of Michigan, News and Information Services. http://www.monitoringthefuture.org/pressreleases/cigbrandpr.html.

Sweeney, Christine, Lynn Kozlowski, and Pantea Parsa. 1999. "Effect of Filter Vent Blocking on Carbon Monoxide Exposure from Selected Lower Tar Cigarette Brands." *Pharmacology, Biochemistry and Behavior*, May: 167–173.

TCRC (Tobacco Control Resource Center, Northeastern University Law School). 2000. Personal communication. November 8.

Tursi, Frank V., Susan E. White, and Steve McQuilkin. 2000. *Lost Empire: The Fall of R. J. Reynolds Tobacco Company.* Winston-Salem Journal.

University of Minnesota Cancer Center, Information Services. 2000. "University of Minnesota Research Suggests Nicotine May Be Linked to Lung Carcinogen." November 7. http://www.cancer.umn.edu.

USDA (U.S. Department of Agriculture), Tobacco Division, Agricultural Marketing Service. 1999. "Current Tobacco Situation and Outlook Summary." April 21. http://www.usda.gov.

Wagner, Susan. 1971. *Cigarette Country: Tobacco in American History and Politics.* New York: Praeger Publishers.

Walliser, Tristanne L. 1998. "Teen Tobacco Use: Bad News." ABC News.com. April 9. http://abcnews.go.com/.

Washingon DOC (Doctors Ought to Care). 1999. "Youth and Advertising: Facts." Fact Sheet. kickbutt.org/youth/factguide/51.html.

*Washington Post.* 2000. "Tar, Nicotine Numbers on Packs Belie Reality." *Washington Post,* January 19: A8.

Weiss, Lisa, and David Reyes. 1999. "Smoking among Youths Continues to Rise." *Los Angeles Times,* January 8.

Whelan, Elizabeth M. 1984. *A Smoking Gun: How the Tobacco Industry Gets Away with Murder.* Philadelphia: George F. Stickley.

White, Larry C. 1988. *Merchants of Death.* New York: William Morrow.

WHO (World Health Organization). 1996. "The Tobacco Epidemic: A Global Public Health Emergency." Fact Sheet No. 118. May. http://www.who.int/inf-fs/en/index_n.html.

WHO. 1998a. "Growing up without Tobacco: World No-Tobacco Day 1998." Press release. May 28. http://www.who.int/inf-pr-1998/en/pr98-42.html.

WHO. 1998b. "Tobacco Epidemic: Health Dimensions." Fact Sheet No. 154. Revised May 1998. http:www.who.int/inf-fs/en/index_n.html.

WHO. 1998c. "Tobacco Use by Children: A Paediatric Disease." Fact Sheet No. 197. May. http:www.who.int/inf-fs/en/index_n.html.

WHO. 1999. "Environmental Tobacco Smoke Seriously Endangers Children's Health." June 16. http://www.who.int/inf-pr1999/en/pr99-35.html.

Will, George. 1998. "EPA's Crusaders." *Washington Post,* July 30: A19.

Wynder, Ernst L., and Evarts A. Graham. 1950. "Tobacco Smoking as a Possible Etiologic Factor in Bronchiogenic Carcinoma: A Study of Six Hundred and Eighty-Four Proved Cases." *JAMA,* May 27.

Wynder, Ernst L., Evarts A. Graham, and A. B. Croninger. 1953. *Cancer Research,* Vol. 13: 855–864.

# 2

# Chronology

1492    Sailors with Christopher Columbus obtain tobacco and take it back to Europe.

1526    In his history of the West Indies, Fernandez de Oviedo y Valdes (1478–1557) writes, "Among other evil practices, the Indians have one that is especially harmful, the inhaling of a certain kind of smoke which they call tobacco, in order to produce a state of stupor. . . . I cannot imagine what pleasure they derive from this practice" (quoted in Sullum 1998, 16–17).

1558    Tobacco is introduced in Portugal.

1561    Jean Nicot, French ambassador to Portugal, obtains a specimen of tobacco while in Lisbon and sends seeds and plants to the French court, in particular to the queen mother, Catherine de Medici.

1565    "Tobacco was first brought and made known in England by Sir John Hawkins, about the yeare 1565, but not used by Englishmen in many yeeres after, though at this day commonly used by most men, and many women" (Howes 1631).

Sir Walter Raleigh, tobacco's leading promoter, persuades Queen Elizabeth I to try a pipeful. Reportedly, she becomes nauseated.

1570        Belgium, Spain, Italy, Switzerland, and England are now among the countries in which tobacco is being grown.

1571        In a book on the medicinal plants of the New World, the Spanish physician Nicolò Monardes recommends tobacco as a cure for more than 20 ailments, including asthma, toothache, stomach cramps, intestinal worms, and cancer (Sullum 1998, 17).

1573        "In these daies the taking-in of the smoke of the Indian herbe called 'Tobaco,' by an instrument formed like a litle ladell, whereby it passeth from the mouth into the hed and stomach, is gretlie taken-up and used in England" (Harrison 1573).

1586        Thomas Hariot's "A Briefe and True Report of the New Found Land of Virginia" helps to generate interest in tobacco, especially among potential investors. In it, he claims, "By [using tobacco] the natives keep in excellent health, without many of the grievous diseases which often afflict us in England."

1600        The growing of tobacco has expanded to the Philippines, India, Java, Japan, West Africa, and China.

1603        Students at the English prep school Eton are required to "smoake" every morning.

1604        King James I of England denounces smoking in *A Counterblaste to Tobacco.*

1606        Philip III of Spain issues a decree limiting the cultivation of tobacco in Spain and the Spanish colonies.

            King James I increases the duty on tobacco to discourage smoking but because of opposition from Parliament the measure is not enforced.

1612        In Jamestown, John Rolfe produces the first successful commercial tobacco crop in the American colonies.

Within seven years, it will be Virginia Colony's chief export.

1614      "In Tabacco there is nothing which is not medicine, the root, the stalke, the leaves, the seeds, the smoake, the ashes" (Barclay 1614).

In London 7,000 shops sell tobacco.

1615      Jamestown exports 2,300 pounds of tobacco.

1618      Jamestown exports 20,000 pounds of tobacco.

1620      Jamestown exports 40,000 pounds of tobacco.

To protect colonial revenue, cultivation of tobacco in England is prohibited.

1621      Robert Burton, in *The Anatomy of Melancholy*, declares tobacco "a virtuous herbe, if it be . . . opportunely taken, and medicinally used, but, as it is commonly abused by most men, which take it as Tinkers do Ale, 'tis a plague, a mischief, a vicious purger of goods, lands, health, . . . the ruin and overthrow of body and soul" (Burton 1660).

1622      James I of England grants tobacco companies in Virginia and Bermuda an import monopoly on tobacco.

1628      Jamestown exports 500,000 pounds of tobacco.

1632      Massachusetts prohibits smoking in public.

1633      In Turkey, smoking is declared punishable by death.

1634      In Russia, the punishment for a first violation of the Czar's ban on smoking is a slit nose. Repeat offenders are to be executed.

1635      Tobacco is legally obtainable in France only by prescription.

1637     King Louis XIII develops a fondness for snuff and repeals restrictions on its use.

1638     Jamestown exports 1.4 million pounds of tobacco.

Use of tobacco in China is punishable by death.

1640     "Tobacco engages / Both sexes, all ages, / The poor as well as the wealthy; / From the court to the cottage, / From childhood to dotage, / Both those that are sick and the healthy" (Mennes 1640).

1642     Pope Urban VIII denounces the use of tobacco, threatening to excommunicate priests who "take tobacco in leaf, in powder, in smoke by mouth or nostrils."

1647     Connecticut passes a law prohibiting the use of tobacco in public and restricting private use to persons above the age of 21 who have already acquired the habit or who have obtained a physician's certificate and a court license. (But according to Sullum, "these Puritan laws were not seriously enforced, and they were soon repealed or forgotten" [1998, 19].)

Turkey lifts its ban on tobacco.

1658     "What difference is there between a smoker and a suicide except that the one takes longer to kill himself than the other? Because of this perpetual smoking, the pure oil of the lamp of life dries up and disappears, and the fair flame of life itself flickers out and goes out, all because of this barbarous habit"(Jakob Balde quoted in Sullum 1998, 20).

1665     In England, smoking is thought to serve as protection against the plague. "The American Silver-weed, or Tobacco, is . . . an excellent defence against bad air, being smoked in a pipe, either by itself, or with Nutmegs shred, and Rew Seeds mixed with it, . . . for it cleanseth the air, and choaketh, suppresseth and disperseth any venomous vapour" (Kemp 1665)

1689    The Medical School of Paris issues an official statement that smoking shortens life.

1700    Peter the Great permits smoking in Russia.

1701    Nicholas Andryde Boisregard warns that excessive use of tobacco by young people causes trembling, staggering, and a withering of "their noble parts."

1724    Pope Benedict XIII repeals the papal ban on smoking.

1726    "If once you get into the way of Smoking, there will be extreme hazard, of your becoming a Slave to the Pipe; and ever Insatiably craving for it. People may think what they will; But such a Slavery, is much below the Dignity of a Rational Creature; and much more of a Gracious Christian" (Cotton Mather offering advice to candidates for the ministry, *Rules of Health* [in Thayer 1905] ).

1753    The Swedish botanist Carolus Lennaeus names the tobacco plant "nicotiana," after Jean Nicot, who helped to promote its spread throughout the world.

1760    Pierre Lorillard establishes a plant in New York City for processing tobacco.

1761    In *Cautions against the Immoderate Use of Snuff,* the English physician John Hill declares snuff to be a cause of cancer.

1771    England and Scotland import a total of 102 million pounds of tobacco.

1776    Tobacco is used as collateral for loans to help finance the American Revolution.

1794    Congress passes the first tobacco tax, which applies only to snuff.

1798    Dr. Benjamin Rush condemns tobacco in an essay titled "Observations upon the Influence of the Habitual Use of Tobacco upon Health, Morals, and Property."

| | |
|---|---|
| 1826 | England imports 26 pounds of cigars. Within four years it will be importing 250,000 pounds. |
| | Two students in Heidelberg conduct an extensive study of nicotine, concluding that it is a "dangerous poison." |
| 1839 | A change in the curing process produces Bright leaf tobacco. It has a brilliant golden color and a milder, more appealing taste. |
| 1852 | Washington Duke establishes a business near Durham, North Carolina, which will later become the American Tobacco Company. |
| | Matches are introduced. |
| 1854 | Philip Morris begins making cigarettes in London. |
| | The *Lancet*, a British medical journal, begins a long-running debate on the possible health risks associated with tobacco. |
| 1857 | James Buchanan "Buck" Duke, a leader in the American tobacco industry, is born. |
| 1860 | Lucy Page Gaston, founder of the Anti-Cigarette League of America, is born. |
| | Bull Durham, a granulated version of Bright leaf tobacco, becomes popular for roll-your-own cigarettes. |
| 1868 | Cigarettes are manufactured in the United States for the first time. |
| | The British Parliament passes a bill requiring that some railway cars be smoke-free. |
| 1869 | The first blended cigarettes are created, combining Virginia and Turkish tobaccos. |

1870        Estimated per capita consumption of cigarettes in the United States is 0.4 cigarettes.

1873        Philip Morris dies, and his cousin Leopold takes over the company.

George Smith Myers buys Henry Dausman's interest in the Liggett & Dausman tobacco company in St. Louis, Missouri. The new company is called Liggett & Myers.

1874        Washington Duke and his sons, Benjamin Duke and James Buchanan Duke, known as "Buck," build their first tobacco factory.

1875        R. J. Reynolds Tobacco Co. is established to produce chewing tobacco. Dixie's Delight and Yellow Rose are among the first brands produced.

1876        Liggett & Myers introduces L&M brand plug chewing tobacco.

1878        Cigarette trading cards appear.

1880        The patent for the Bonsack cigarette-making machine, invented by James A. Bonsack, is approved.

United States consumes 1.3 billion cigarettes annually.

1881        The Dukes' factory produces 9.8 million cigarettes.

1884        On January 4, the *New York Times* notes, "[t]he decadence of Spain began when the Spaniards adopted cigarettes, and if this pernicious practice obtains among adult Americans the ruin of the republic is close at hand."

On April 30, the Bonsack cigarette-rolling machines at Dukes's factory operate successfully for a full workday. This date, says Dr. Elizabeth Whelan, marks the birth of the modern cigarette (Whelan 1984, xiii).

| 1884 (cont.) | The Dukes produce 744 million cigarettes this year, more than was produced in the entire country in 1883. |
|---|---|
| 1885 | Liggett & Myers is the world's largest manufacturer of plug chewing tobacco. |
| | The Women's Christian Temperance Union declares that "[s]moking leads to drinking and drinking leads to the devil." |
| 1890 | American Tobacco Co. is formed, combining the five largest cigarette companies in the United States, with Buck Duke as president. |
| | Estimated per capita consumption of cigarettes in the United States is 35.5 |
| 1896 | The founder of the Young Men's Christian Association (YMCA), Sir George Williams, denounces cigarettes as a "growing evil." |
| 1897 | Cigarette production in the United States reaches 4.9 billion. |
| | John Liggett dies. |
| 1899 | Continental Tobacco, headed by Buck Duke, buys Liggett & Myers. L&M cofounder George S. Myers retires. |
| | Lucy Page Gaston founds the Anti-Cigarette League of America. |
| 1900 | The number of cigarettes sold in the United States. reaches 2.5 billion (Whelan 1984, 142). |
| | Cigar sales exceed 5 billion. |
| | R. J. Reynolds's tobacco company is acquired by Duke's American Tobacco trust for $3 million. |

Bull Durham cigarette and pipe tobacco dominates the tobacco market.

1901        The number of cigarettes produced in the United States is 3.5 billion.

Cigar sales exceed 6 billion.

The Anti-Cigarette League of America claims a membership of 300,000.

1901–      Buck Duke combines American Tobacco with Conti-
1902        nental Tobacco, forming Consolidated Tobacco, the largest tobacco company in the world.

1902        Philip Morris incorporates in New York. Among its products is Marlborough, a British cigarette named for the street where the original manufacturer was located.

1903        The National Anti-Cigarette League holds its first convention.

1904        A woman is arrested on Fifth Avenue in New York for smoking a cigarette.

1906        The Food and Drugs Act of 1906, the first federal food and drug law, is passed. It contains no mention of tobacco products.

Cigar sales exceed 7 billion; cigarette sales exceed 5.5 billion.

A group of farmers found Brown & Williamson Tobacco Corp. to produce plug, snuff, and pipe tobacco.

1907        A federal antitrust suit is filed against American Tobacco, which controls 90 percent of the world's tobacco market.

Illinois makes it illegal to manufacture or sell cigarettes.

1907
(cont.)
*Education* magazine reports, "There are in the United States today 500,000 boys and youths who are habitual cigarette smokers. Few of them can be educated beyond the eighth grade, and practically all of them are destined to remain physical and mental dwarfs" (quoted in Whelan 1984, 49).

1908
The Supreme Court finds that Duke's American Tobacco trust violates the Sherman Antitrust Act.

New York City makes it illegal for women to smoke in public.

1910
George S. Myers dies.

The number of cigarettes sold in the United States reaches 8.6 billion (Whelan 1984, 142).

1911
Duke's tobacco trust is dissolved by the Supreme Court. It is succeeded by the American Tobacco Co., R. J. Reynolds, Liggett & Myers, Lorillard, and the British American Tobacco Co.

Cigarette sales reach 11.7 billion.

1912
Liggett introduces Chesterfield cigarettes—20 for 10 cents.

1913
The American Society for the Control of Cancer (later the American Cancer Society [ACS]) is founded.

R. J. Reynolds introduces Camel cigarettes.

1914
A judicial interpretation of the Food and Drugs Act of 1906 advises that tobacco be regulated as a drug only when it is used to cure, treat, or prevent disease.

The U.S. Census Bureau finds the lung cancer mortality rate to be 0.6 per 100,000 Americans. By 1925 it will increase to 1.7.

Henry Ford swears that no cigarette smoker will ever work for the Ford Motor Company. He writes *The Case against the Little White Slaver* (four volumes, 1914–1916), in which he goes into detail.

1915        Chesterfield's slogan is "They Satisfy."

A survey of 115 YMCA associations finds that most do not permit smoking in their facilities and those that allow smoking do not allow cigarettes. But during World War I the YMCA will become one of the largest distributors of tobacco products in the world (Tate 1999, 77).

1917        The United States enters World War I. Duke and the National Cigarette Service Committee distribute millions of free cigarettes to U.S. troops in France.

1918        Given a boost by World War I, cigarette production rises from 18 billion cigarettes in 1914 to 47 billion in 1918.

1919        R. J. Reynolds dies.

Lorillard produces the first advertisement depicting a woman holding a cigarette. She was not shown smoking it, however.

1920        The number of cigarettes sold in the United States. reaches 44.6 billion. Per capita consumption is 665, up from 310 in 1915 (Whelan 1984).

1921        Lucy Page Gaston organizes a new National Anti-Cigarette League, concentrating on women. Her new motto is "Save the Girl."

R. J. Reynolds introduces the slogan "I'd walk a mile for a Camel."

1922        Manufactured cigarettes surpass plug tobacco and cigars in pounds sold.

1922
(cont.)
In *Tobaccoism: How Tobacco Kills,* Dr. John H. Kellogg identifies smoking as a cause of lip, throat, and mouth cancer (Whelan 1984, 67).

1924
Lucy Page Gaston dies.

Cigarette sales exceed 73 billion.

Phillip Morris markets Marlboro (originally spelled "Marlborough") as a woman's cigarette, billing it as being "mild as May."

1925
Buck Duke dies.

The *American Mercury* calls cigarettes "the most democratic commodity in common use."

"Has smoking any more to do with a woman's morals than has the color of her hair?" (Marlboro ad).

1927
British American Tobacco (BAT) Industries buys Brown & Williamson and operates it under its original name.

Lucky Strike captures 38 percent of the U.S. market.

An advertising campaign proclaims that 11,105 physicians have endorsed Lucky Strikes as "less irritating to sensitive or tender throats than any other cigarettes."

Kansas drops its ban on cigarette sales, the last state to do so.

A Philip Morris ad for Marlboro cigarettes states: "Women, when they smoke at all, quickly develop discriminating taste."

1930
Philip Morris buys a factory in Richmond, Virginia, and begins making its own cigarettes.

Researchers in Cologne, Germany, find a statistical correlation between cancer and smoking.

The annual lung cancer death rate for men is 4.9 per 100,000. In 1990 the rate will have increased to 75.6 per 100,000.

The number of cigarettes sold in the United States. reaches 119.3 billion (Whelan 1984, 142).

1932    "There is little real evidence that smoking in moderation has any serious harmful effect upon the average individual" (Johnson 1932).

Dr. William McNally, writing in the *American Journal of Cancer,* calls smoking "an important factor" in the growing number of cases of lung cancer.

1933    Brown & Williamson introduces Kool menthol cigarettes to compete with Spud, another mentholated brand produced by Axton-Fisher.

Ads in the *New York State Journal of Medicine* proclaim Chesterfields to be "[j]ust as pure as the water you drink."

On November 25, the *Journal of the American Medical Association* publishes its first cigarette advertisement.

1934    Eleanor Roosevelt becomes "the first first lady to smoke in public" (Whelan 1984, 61).

1938    The Federal Food, Drug, and Cosmetic Act of 1938 is passed, superseding the Food and Drugs Act of 1906.

Professor Raymond Pearl of Johns Hopkins University tells the New York Academy of Medicine that his research shows a link between smoking and shortened life span.

1939    A German study of 86 lung-cancer patients finds that 83 of them had been smokers. The study, "Tobacco Misuse and Lung Carcinoma," by Franz Hermann

1939      Muller of the University of Cologne, provides the first
(cont.)   major research establishing a strong link between
          smoking and lung cancer (Muller 1939).

          *Fortune* magazine reports that 53 percent of American
          men and 18 percent of adult women smoke cigarettes.
          According to Elizabeth Whelan, in the under-40 age
          group, the percentages are higher: 66 percent of men
          and 26 percent of women (Whelan 1984, 70).

          American Tobacco Company introduces Pall Mall
          cigarettes.

1940      The number of cigarettes sold in the U.S. reaches 181.9
          billion (Whelan 1984, 142).

          The most popular brands of cigarettes in the United
          States are Camel, Lucky Strike, Chesterfield, Philip
          Morris, and Old Gold.

1941      The United States enters World War II. Billions of cig-
          arettes are given away, and they are sold at post
          exchanges and ships' stores for five cents.

1943      In the June issue of the *American Journal of Surgery*, Dr.
          Edwin Grace summarizes his 10 years' experience
          with lung cancer patients in two New York City hos-
          pitals: "first, the patients were almost always men;
          second, they were heavy cigarette smokers and almost
          always inhalers."

          Another physician, writing in an issue from the same
          year, observes, "If you are in good health, and use
          tobacco moderately, you needn't worry much about
          your smoking" (Feldt 1943).

1944      The American Cancer Society begins to issue warn-
          ings about the possible ill effects of smoking.

          Cigarettes cost about 15 cents a pack.

1946      R. J. Reynolds launches an advertising campaign

claiming that "more doctors smoke Camels than any other cigarette."

1947    The song "Smoke! Smoke! Smoke That Cigarette!" is a national hit.

1949    A Camel ad claims that a group of "noted throat specialists" (shown in a photograph) have encountered "not one case of throat irritation due to smoking Camels."

1950    After studying over 600 men with lung cancer, Drs. Ernst L. Wynder and Evarts Graham report in a *JAMA* article that 96.5 percent were moderate to heavy smokers. In a control group of men without cancer only 73.7 percent were smokers (Wynder and Graham 1950).

The annual death rate from lung cancer among men rises to more than 20 per 100,000. In 1930 the death rate was 5 per 100,000. By 1992, according to Dr. John A. Meyer, author of *Lung Cancer Chronicles,* it will rise to more than 70 per 100,000 (Meyer 1992).

Two percent of cigarettes have filters.

The number of cigarettes sold in the United States is 369.8 billion (Whelan 1984, 142).

"A massive potential market still exists among women and young adults," according to industry leaders speaking in the *U.S. Tobacco Journal.* "[R]ecruitment of these millions of prospective smokers comprises the major objective for the immediate future and on a long term basis as well" (quoted in Hilts 1996, 76–77).

*Coronet* magazine publishes "The Facts about Cigarettes and Your Health," an article that compares warnings about the health hazards of smoking to "such scares as Orson Welles' famed broadcast of an Invasion from Mars" (quoted in Whelan, 87).

1952        Drs. Richard Doll and A. Bradford Hill publish a
            study based on interviews with 5,000 male patients in
            British hospitals. Among their findings: Of 1,357 men
            with lung cancer, 99.5 percent were smokers (Doll and
            Hill 1952).

            An Arthur D. Little study finds that smoking
            Chesterfields has no adverse effect on the throat.

            Liggett introduces L&M, its first filtered cigarette.

            Chesterfield becomes the first cigarette to be marketed
            in two sizes—king-size and regular.

            Lorillard introduces Kent cigarettes, which have a
            "micronite" filter. The filter contains asbestos.

            In December, *Reader's Digest* publishes "Cancer by the
            Carton," reporting the dangers of smoking (Norr 1952).

1953        The manufacturer of Fairfax cigarettes claims that
            they prevent respiratory disease. The (Food and Drug
            Administration) FDA asserts jurisdiction and pro-
            hibits Fairfax from making such a claim.

            A study by Drs. Ernst Wynder and Evarts Graham
            shows that painting cigarette tar on the backs of mice
            produces tumors (Wynder, Graham, and Croninger
            1953).

            By the end of 1953, filter-tip cigarettes have captured
            only 3 percent of the market.

            Dr. Alton Ochsner predicts that "[i]n 1970 cancer of
            the lung will represent 18 percent of all cancer, . . . one
            out of every 10 or 12 men." (In fact, by 1970 lung
            cancer accounts for 19.7 percent of all cancers.)

            Cigarette sales decline for the first time.

1954        Marlboro cigarettes have less than .025 percent of the
            cigarette market. With a red paper "beauty tip" to con-

ceal lipstick stains and their "mild as May" slogan, they appeal mainly to women. But 1954 marks the birth of the Marlboro man and a turnaround in Marlboro's fortunes.

R. J. Reynolds introduces filtered Winstons and a new slogan proclaiming: "Winston tastes good—like a cigarette should."

The Tobacco Industry Research Committee issues a "Frank Statement"—a two-page ad—saying that cigarette makers do not believe that their products are harmful.

In the beginning of the first wave of liability suits against the tobacco industry, Eva Cooper sues R. J. Reynolds, claiming that smoking led to the death of her husband. (The suit will be dropped 13 years later.)

After tracking 40,000 physicians aged 35 and older for four-and-a-half years, Drs. Richard Doll and A. Bradford Hill conclude: "Mild smokers are seven times as likely to die of lung cancer as nonsmokers, moderate smokers are 12 times as likely to die of lung cancer as nonsmokers, immoderate smokers are 24 times as likely to die of lung cancer than nonsmokers" (Doll and Hill 1954).

L&M advertises its "alpha cellulose" filter as "[j]ust what the doctor ordered."

By the end of the year, sales of Winston filter-tip cigarettes have surpassed Parliament, Kent, and L&M, second only to Viceroy.

1955    The FTC issues guidelines to eliminate misleading health claims by the tobacco industry.

1956    R. J. Reynolds introduces Salem, the first filter-tipped menthol cigarette.

1957      With regard to advertising strategy, a Philip Morris executive writes that "hitting the youth can be more efficient even though the cost to reach them is higher, because they are willing to experiment, they have more influence over others in their age group than they will later in life, and they are far more loyal to their starting brand" (quoted in Hilts 1996, p. 77).

1960      More than 50 percent of cigarettes have filters.

The FTC prohibits cigarette makers from claiming that filtered cigarettes are less dangerous than nonfiltered.

The number of cigarettes sold in the United States reaches 484.4 billion (Whelan 1984, 142).

1962      Britain's Royal College of Physicians publishes its first report on smoking and health. It recommends restrictions on tobacco advertising, higher taxes on cigarettes, additional restrictions on the sale of cigarettes to children and on smoking in public places, and more information about the tar and nicotine content of cigarettes (UCSF 2001).

1963      L&M introduces the Lark cigarette, which has a charcoal filter.

In a confidential memo, Brown & Williamson's general counsel, Addison Yeaman, says: "Nicotine is addictive. We are, then, in the business of selling nicotine, an addictive drug" (UCSF 2001).

The number of cigarettes sold in the United States is 2.5 billion (Whelan 1984, 142).

1964      Cigarette manufacturers voluntarily establish the Cigarette Advertising Code for radio and television ads.

The American Medical Association declares smoking "a serious health hazard."

State Mutual Life Assurance Company becomes the first company to offer lower rates to nonsmokers.

Surgeon General Luther L. Terry releases the first surgeon general's report on smoking and health. In it, he concludes that cigarette smoking is a cause of lung cancer and other serious diseases. The report also says that the average smoker is 9 to 10 times more likely to get lung cancer than the average nonsmoker (Advisory Committee to the Surgeon General 1964).

It is the end of the cigarette's Golden Age (Whelan 1984, xiii).

1965    The number of cigarettes sold in the United States is 521.1 billion (Whelan 1984, 142).

The prevalence of adult smokers (18 and older) reaches 42.4 percent.

Congress passes the Federal Cigarette Labeling and Advertising Act, requiring the label "Caution: Cigarette Smoking May Be Hazardous to Your Health" on every package of cigarettes.

The Public Health Service establishes the National Clearinghouse for Smoking and Health.

1967    The surgeon general says smoking is the main cause of lung cancer.

The Federal Communications Commission (FCC) rules that stations broadcasting cigarette commercials must donate air time for antismoking messages (i.e., the FCC's "fairness doctrine" applies to cigarette advertising).

The Federal Trade Commission (FTC) releases its first report on tar and nicotine yields in cigarette brands.

1968    Action on Smoking and Health (ASH) is formed in the United Kingdom (UK). Its purpose is to serve as a

| | |
|---|---|
| 1968 (cont.) | legal action arm for antismoking forces in the UK and abroad. |
| | Liggett & Myers Tobacco Co. changes its name to Liggett & Myers Inc. Its nontobacco operations now account for 36 percent of its sales. |
| 1969 | The National Association of Broadcasters endorses the phasing out of cigarette advertising on television and radio. |
| 1970 | The World Health Organization (WHO) takes a public position against cigarette smoking. |
| | Congress enacts the Public Health Cigarette Smoking Act. It prohibits cigarette advertising on radio and television and requires a stronger warning label on cigarette packages: "Warning: The Surgeon General Has Determined that Cigarette Smoking Is Dangerous to Your Health." |
| | Liggett introduces Eve cigarettes, intended to appeal to women. |
| | The number of cigarettes sold in the United States is 534.2 billion (Whelan 1984, 142). |
| 1971 | The surgeon general proposes a ban on smoking in public places. |
| | A voluntary agreement by cigarette manufacturers to list tar and nicotine yields in all advertising takes effect. |
| | All broadcast advertising of tobacco products is banned. |
| | Appearing on the CBS program *Face the Nation,* the chairman of the board of Philip Morris is asked what he thinks of a British study showing that babies of smoking mothers tend to weigh less than babies of nonsmoking mothers. His response: "Some women would prefer having smaller babies." |

1972    The surgeon general identifies secondhand smoking as a health risk.

Six cigarette companies agree to include a "clear and conspicuous" health warning in all advertising.

Marlboro becomes the world's best-selling brand of cigarette.

1973    In April, a table listing tar and nicotine yields for various brands of cigarettes is published in Britain for the first time. Nicotine content for cigarettes sold in Britain ranges from a low of 4 milligrams to a high of 38 milligrams. The average tar yield is 20.6 milligrams.

Congress bans ads for little cigars from radio and television.

The Civil Aeronautics Board requires airlines to provide no-smoking sections on all commercial flights.

Arizona becomes the first state to restrict smoking in public places.

1975    Cigarettes are no longer included in K-rations and C-rations for soldiers and sailors.

The Minnesota Clean Indoor Air Act restricts smoking in most buildings open to the public.

The number of cigarettes sold in the United States is 603.2 billion (Whelan 1984, 142).

1976    On March 15, RJR's research department produces a secret report that is later made public: "Evidence is now available to indicate that the 14- to 18-year-old group is an increasing segment of the smoking population. RJR-T must soon establish a successful new brand in this market if our position in the industry is to be maintained over the long term."

1976
(cont.)
Low-tar cigarettes constitute less than 17 percent of the total sold. By 1981 they account for more than 60 percent.

Thames TV broadcasts *Death in the West*, a British documentary about smoking-related illnesses suffered by American cowboys. The film presents a sharp contrast to the image of Philip Morris's Marlboro Man, prompting PM to seek an injunction to prevent a second showing of the film. The court finds that two PM executives had been fraudulently induced to participate in the making of the film and grants the injunction in the United States and Britain.

In December, Richard Doll and Richard Peto publish the results of a 20-year study of nearly 35,000 doctors' smoking habits. They conclude that one in three doctors died of smoking-related illness (Doll and Peto 1976).

1977
The American Cancer Society sponsors the first Great American Smokeout.

Doctors Ought to Care (DOC) is formed to provide a focal point for physicians' smoking-prevention advocacy, especially through antismoking advertising.

L&M introduces low-tar Decade cigarettes.

1978
The Center for Disease Control's (CDC) National Clearinghouse for Smoking and Health is renamed the Office on Smoking and Health (OSH).

Utah bans tobacco advertisements on billboards, streetcars, and buses.

A B&W memo notes that "[v]ery few consumers are aware . . . that nicotine is a poison."

1979
WHO publishes a major report titled "Controlling the Smoking Epidemic."

Minneapolis and St. Paul ban the distribution of free cigarette samples.

Surgeon General Julius Richmond calls the case against smoking "overwhelming."

In November, Britain reports a sharp increase in women's deaths from lung cancer over the previous 10 years.

1980    The *Surgeon General's Report* highlights the health consequences of smoking for women.

The Public Health Service announces its health objectives for the nation, which include reducing the percentage of adult smokers to less than 25 percent by 1990.

The FTC begins testing cigarettes for carbon monoxide yields.

The September issue of the *Journal of the American Dental Association* reports that as many as one-third of varsity football and baseball players are chewing, dipping, or both (Whelan 1984).

The surgeon general reports that smoking is a major threat to women's health.

The number of cigarettes sold in the United States is 631.5 billion (Whelan 1984, 142).

1981    In February the number of smokers in Britain drops below 50 percent.

Many insurers begin offering discounts on life insurance premiums to nonsmokers.

The *Surgeon General's Report* focuses on "the changing cigarette." It concludes that no cigarette or level of tar or nicotine consumption is safe.

1982    The American Cancer Society (ACS), the American Lung Association (ALA), and the American Heart Association (AHA) form the Coalition on Smoking OR Health.

The *Surgeon General's Report* focuses exclusively on smoking and cancer and warns that secondhand smoke may cause lung cancer.

Congress temporarily doubles the federal excise tax on cigarettes to 16 cents per pack. The first increase in the cigarette tax since 1951, it is to remain effective from January 1, 1983, to October 1, 1985.

In August the British Medical Association asks the government to ban all forms of tobacco advertising.

The National Cancer Institute (NCI) reorganizes its smoking research program. Renamed the Smoking, Tobacco and Cancer Program, its focus is on smoking behavior research and interventions.

1983    San Francisco passes a law to restrict smoking in private workplaces.

Tobacco advertisements urge smokers to "take a pouch instead of a puff."

The *Surgeon General's Report* deals exclusively with smoking and cardiovascular disease.

Beginning the second wave of lawsuits against the tobacco industry, Rose Cipollone sues the tobacco industry.

The increased federal excise tax on cigarettes of 16 cents a pack takes effect.

In October Britain's Independent Scientific Committee on Smoking and Health recommends a progressive reduction of tar levels in cigarettes over the next four years.

1984    The *Surgeon General's Report* deals exclusively with smoking and chronic obstructive lung disease.

The Office of the Surgeon General announces that its goal is a smoke-free society by the year 2000.

San Francisco requires businesses to accommodate nonsmokers.

Nicotine-based chewing gum is approved by the FDA as an aid to quitting smoking.

Rose Cipollone dies. Her family takes up her lawsuit.

The Comprehensive Smoking Education Act requires four rotating warning labels on cigarette packages and advertisements: (1) "Smoking causes lung cancer, heart disease and may complicate pregnancy"; (2) "Quitting smoking now greatly reduces serious risks to your health"; (3) "Smoking by pregnant women may result in fetal injury, premature birth, and low birth weight"; and (4) "Cigarette smoke contains carbon monoxide."

1985    The antismoking group Stop Teenage Addiction to Tobacco is formed.

The AMA urges the government to ban all tobacco advertising.

Philip Morris buys General Foods, and R. J. Reynolds buys Nabisco.

*The Surgeon General's Report* focuses on smoking and exposure to secondhand smoke in the workplace.

Minnesota is the first state to earmark part of its state cigarette excise tax to support a smoking prevention program.

Lung cancer surpasses breast cancer as the number one killer of women.

1986   *The Surgeon General's Report* says secondhand smoke causes lung cancer. A *Special Report of the Surgeon General* documents the health consequences of using spit tobacco.

The National Academy of Sciences releases a report on the health consequences of environmental tobacco smoke.

Congress enacts the Comprehensive Smokeless Tobacco Health Education Act of 1986, which bans smokeless tobacco advertising on radio and television and requires three rotating health warnings on spit tobacco packages and advertisements: (1) "This product may cause mouth cancer"; (2) "This product may cause gum disease and tooth loss"; and (3) "This product is not a safe alternative to cigarettes."

Congress extends permanently the 16 cents per pack federal excise tax on cigarettes.

Californians for Nonsmokers' Rights becomes a national organization—Americans for Nonsmokers' Rights (ANR).

Minnesota is the first state to enact a law banning the free distribution of smokeless ("spit") tobacco samples.

Congress imposes a federal excise tax on smokeless tobacco products.

1987   The U.S. Department of Health and Human Services (HHS) orders that its facilities be smoke-free, affecting 120,000 HHS employees nationwide.

The Minnesota Sports Commission places a ban on tobacco advertising in Metrodome Sports Stadium in Minneapolis, to become effective in 1992. It is the first such action in the United States.

Public Law 100–202 takes effect, banning smoking on domestic airline flights of two hours or less.

1988    The *Surgeon General's Report* says that nicotine is as addictive as heroin.

Finding evidence of a tobacco industry conspiracy in the *Cipollone* case, a jury orders Liggett to pay Cipollone $400,000 in compensatory damages. The award is later overturned on appeal.

California voters pass a referendum raising the state's cigarette excise tax by 25 cents a pack. It is the largest cigarette excise tax increase in U.S. history.

The World Health Organization sponsors the first World No-Tobacco Day.

Joe Camel makes his first appearance, on the 75th anniversary of Camel cigarettes.

L&M introduces Pyramid cigarettes.

U.S. smokers spend $33.3 billion on cigarettes.

The U.S. tobacco industry exports 100 billion cigarettes. (Two years previously the figure was 64 billion.)

1989    Marking the twenty-fifth anniversary of the first "Smoking and Health' report, the *Surgeon General's Report* focuses on progress made in the intervening years.

1990    The *Surgeon General's Report* focuses on the health benefits of smoking cessation.

The Office of the Inspector General of Health and Human Services (HHS) issues a report concluding that laws restricting minors' access to tobacco are being ignored. HHS proposes a model law for states.

A man splashes red paint on a billboard advertising cigarettes on Chicago's South Side. This sets off a grass-roots campaign protesting the targeting of minorities by alcohol and tobacco companies.

| | |
|---|---|
| 1990 (cont.) | The annual lung cancer death rate for men is 75.6 per 100,000. In 1930 the rate was 4.9 per 100,000. |

The secretary of Health and Human Services denounces R. J. Reynolds' plan to test-market Uptown cigarettes to blacks. RJR agrees to drop the plan.

Smoking is banned on interstate buses and all domestic airline flights of six hours or less.

**1991**   The CDC's National Institute for Occupational Safety and Health issues a bulletin recommending that secondhand smoke be reduced to the lowest feasible concentration in the workplace.

The federal excise tax on cigarettes is increased to 20 cents.

The FDA approves a nicotine patch as a prescription drug.

**1992**   A survey finds that 32 percent of high school students have tried smokeless tobacco (CDC TIPS 1999).

The Synar Amendment to the Alcohol, Drug Abuse, and Mental Health Administration (ADAMHA) Reorganization Act requires all states to adopt and enforce restrictions on tobacco sales and distribution to minors.

New York City requires tobacco companies to fund one antismoking ad for every four cigarette ads they display on city property or where there are activities (such as an athletic event or concert) requiring a city license.

The U.S. Supreme Court rules in *Cipollone v. Liggett Group, Inc.* that warning labels on cigarette packages do not shield companies from lawsuits.

Based on Judge Sarokin's opinion in the *Haines* case, Matthew Fishbein and other U.S. attorneys from the

Eastern District of New York open a federal probe into criminal wrongdoing by the tobacco industry. In *Haines*, Sarokin called the industry the "king of concealment."

Wayne McLaren, who portrayed the Marlboro Man, dies of lung cancer.

1993   The Environmental Protection Agency (EPA) releases its final risk assessment of secondhand smoke, classifying it as a "Group A" (i.e., human) carcinogen. The tobacco industry responds by suing the EPA.

The U.S. Postal Service bans smoking in all of its facilities.

The federal cigarette excise tax is increased to 24 cents.

Congress enacts legislation requiring American cigarettes to contain at least 75 percent U.S.-grown tobacco. To help finance the federal tobacco crop subsidy program, Congress also places a tariff on imported tobacco.

A working group of 16 state attorneys general releases recommendations for establishing smoke-free policies in fast-food restaurants.

Vermont bans smoking in indoor public places.

Brown & Williamson sues Jeffrey Wigand for libel, claiming that he said malicious things to another employee about the company president.

The tobacco industry spends a total of $6 billion on advertising and promotions in 1993.

1994   In February FDA Commissioner David Kessler announces plans to consider regulation of tobacco as a drug, saying that tobacco manufacturers use nicotine to satisfy addiction.

1994
(cont.)

On February 28 an ABC news show called "Day One" reports that cigarette companies "spike" cigarettes by increasing nicotine levels. On March 7, the second segment of "Day One" publicizes a list of secret additives in cigarettes. Philip Morris announces on March 24 that it is suing ABC News because of allegations made in the "Day One" program that the company manipulated the amount of nicotine in its cigarettes.

Peter Castano, a former Louisiana attorney who died of lung cancer, becomes the named plaintiff in a class-action suit known as the *Castano* suit, filed on behalf of smokers nationwide.

On March 25 FDA Commissioner David Kessler testifies before a House subcommittee that cigarette companies create and sustain addiction by altering the levels of nicotine in their products.

The chief executives of the seven largest U.S. tobacco companies testify before a House subcommittee on April 14. Under oath, all seven say they believe that nicotine is not addictive.

In May Richard Scruggs delivers B&W internal documents to U.S. Rep. Henry Waxman. These B&W documents reveal that tobacco executives knew about the dangers of smoking before the surgeon general did.

On May 7 the *New York Times* publishes the first of a series of articles based on B&W internal documents. The *Times* says it received these documents from a government official.

On May 12 a package containing 4,000 pages of internal B&W documents is left at the office of Professor Stanton Glantz at the University of California at San Francisco (UCSF). The return address on the package says simply "Mr. Butts."

Beginning the third wave of lawsuits against the

tobacco industry, on May 23 Mississippi Attorney General Michael Moore sues the tobacco industry to recoup $940 million the state of Mississippi paid for smokers' Medicaid bills. Mississippi is the first state to do so.

In May, Amtrak bans smoking on short- and medium-distance trips.

Geoffrey Bible is named president and CEO of Philip Morris in June.

Dr. David Kessler testifies before a House subcommittee on June 21 about evidence gathered by the FDA concerning the tobacco industry's manipulation of nicotine levels. He also testifies about one company's efforts to develop a high-nicotine strain of tobacco and the industry's use of chemical compounds in cigarettes to enhance nicotine delivery.

In July, the Justice Department opens a criminal investigation of possible perjury by tobacco executives testifying before the Waxman subcommittee.

Minnesota Attorney General Hubert Humphrey III files a Medicaid suit against the tobacco industry on August 17.

West Virginia files a Medicaid suit against the tobacco industry on September 20.

In December, the Florida Legislature passes a law making it easier to sue the tobacco industry for Medicaid costs.

On December 14 Rep. Marty Meehan asks U.S. Attorney General Janet Reno to open a criminal investigation against the tobacco industry.

The *Surgeon General's Report* focuses on tobacco use among young people.

1994
*(cont.)*
Congress enacts the Pro-Children Act of 1994, requiring all federally funded children's services to become smoke-free.

The Occupational Safety and Health Administration (OSHA) announces a proposed regulation to prohibit smoking in the workplace, except in separately ventilated smoking rooms.

The Department of Defense (DOD) bans smoking in all DOD workplaces.

The Robert Wood Johnson Foundation and the American Medical Association launch the "SmokeLess States" grant program to fund local initiatives for tobacco use prevention.

BAT Industries agrees to buy American Tobacco from American Brands.

1995
Florida files a Medicaid suit against the tobacco industry on February 21.

In February R. J. Reynolds files suit against ABC News in connection with allegations made on the "Day One" program. (See February 1994.)

On May 25 a San Francisco superior court rules that the Brown & Williamson documents donated to UCSF by "Mr. Butts" may be made public. Brown & Williamson's appeal is rejected on June 23. Stanton Glantz posts the Brown & Williamson documents on the Internet on July 1.

On August 19 Oxford University researchers report that smokers in their thirties and forties are five times as likely to suffer a heart attack as nonsmokers and that switching to low-tar cigarettes has little positive effect.

On August 21 ABC agrees to settle the lawsuits brought by B&W and RJR with a prime-time apology and a promise to cover the companies' legal fees.

In October Steven Goldstone is named CEO of RJR Nabisco Holdings Corp., after having served as president and general counsel.

On November 12 *60 Minutes* broadcasts part of a taped interview with Jeffrey Wigand in which he talks about a cancer-causing flavor additive used in B&W cigarettes.

On November 29 Jeffrey Wigand provides information to plaintiffs' lawyers in Mississippi's Medicaid suit against the tobacco industry.

Philip Morris drops its suit against ABC in November— in exchange for an on-camera apology for suggesting that tobacco manufacturers manipulate nicotine levels in cigarettes. ABC also agrees to pay PM $16 million for the legal fees it incurred during the lawsuit.

In December U.S. Justice Department officials question Wigand in their criminal investigation of the tobacco industry.

On December 19 Massachusetts files a Medicaid suit against the tobacco industry.

President Clinton announces a proposed FDA rule to reduce access to tobacco products by children and adolescents and to reduce the appeal of tobacco products to children and adolescents.

FDA Commissioner David Kessler declares tobacco use a "pediatric disease."

The *Journal of the American Medical Association* publishes articles on Brown & Williamson documents indicating that the company knew for years about the harmful effects of tobacco use and the addictive nature of nicotine.

The American Academy of Pediatrics stages a nationwide school-based event targeting youth, discussing the dangers of using tobacco.

1995
(cont.)
To ensure compliance with the federal ban of tobacco ads on television, the Department of Justice reaches a settlement with Philip Morris under which tobacco advertisements would be removed from the line of sight of TV cameras in sports stadiums.

1996
The Department of Transportation reports that about 80 percent of nonstop international flights on U.S. airlines will be smoke-free by June 1, 1996.

WHO issues a document called "Guidelines for Controlling and Monitoring the Tobacco Epidemic." The purpose of the document is to assist countries in developing a national antismoking action plan, enacting the plan, and collaborating with government, organizations, and businesses.

An alliance of antismoking groups establishes the National Center for Tobacco-Free Kids to focus attention on the importance of reducing tobacco use among youth.

The first annual "Kick Butts Day" promotes youth working with youth to discourage tobacco use.

The FDA approves nicotine gum and two brands of nicotine patches for over-the-counter sale.

R. J. Reynolds begins test-marketing Camel menthols.

The American Medical Association calls for corporations and individuals to divest themselves of all tobacco stocks and mutual funds.

In an effort to head off FDA regulation of tobacco, Philip Morris and the U.S. Tobacco Company offer a proposal for federal legislation that includes a ban on vending machine and partial-pack sales, free samples to kids, and transit advertisements.

On January 26 the *Wall Street Journal* publishes an article containing excerpts of Wigand's leaked deposition from the Mississippi Medicaid suit and posts the entire deposition on the Internet (Freedman 1996).

On February 4 CBS broadcasts the full interview with Wigand.

R. J. Reynolds CEO Steven Goldstone says in March that the industry would consider a settlement.

Louisiana files a Medicaid suit against the tobacco industry on March 13.

Texas files a Medicaid suit against the tobacco industry on March 28.

In March the Liggett Group, the smallest of the major tobacco companies, settles lawsuits with five state attorneys general and promises to help them in their suits against other companies.

In May a federal appeals court dismisses the *Castano* suit, a major win for the tobacco industry.

Liggett launches its first media campaign since 1992, promoting its 120-millimeter version of the Eve cigarette with the slogan "Who says length doesn't matter?"

Maryland files a Medicaid suit against the tobacco industry on May 1.

On June 3 R. J. Reynolds begins test-marketing the Eclipse, a "smokeless" cigarette.

Washington State files a Medicaid suit against the tobacco industry on June 5.

Connecticut files a Medicaid suit against the tobacco industry on July 18.

Kansas files a Medicaid suit against the tobacco industry on August 20.

1996
(cont.)      Michigan and Oklahoma file Medicaid suits against the tobacco industry in August.

In August the FDA assumes regulatory authority over the sale and distribution of cigarettes and smokeless tobacco to children and adolescents.

On August 9 a jury in Jacksonville, Florida, awards $750,000 to Grady Carter in his suit against Brown & Williamson. One juror says that B&W internal documents influenced the verdict. Philip Morris's stock loses $12 billion in value within one hour.

New Jersey and Utah file Medicaid suits against the tobacco industry in September.

In October BAT CEO Martin Broughton says settling antitobacco lawsuits would be "common sense."

Alabama files a Medicaid suit against the tobacco industry on October 17.

Illinois and Iowa file Medicaid suits against the tobacco industry in November.

The U.S. tobacco industry reports that cigarette exports in 1996 total 130 billion. Imports of foreign cigarettes total 2.8 billion.

Teen smoking reaches its highest level in 16 years, according to the CDC.

1997         New York and Hawaii file Medicaid suits against the tobacco industry in January.

In February tobacco attorneys argue in a U.S. district court in Greensboro, North Carolina, that the FDA does not have the power to regulate tobacco.

Wisconsin and Indiana file Medicaid suits against the tobacco industry in February.

On February 28 a new FDA rule takes effect. The rule requires retailers to check the identification of customers buying cigarettes; anyone who appears younger than 27 must prove that they are at least 18. Storeowners who violate the law face fines of $250 per violation.

On March 20 Liggett reaches a settlement with states that protects it from tobacco litigation. In exchange Liggett must admit that cigarettes are addictive and help implicate other tobacco companies. Liggett also agrees to release internal industry documents.

On April 3 Philip Morris CEO Geoffrey Bible, RJR's CEO Steven Goldstone, and their attorneys sit down with state attorneys general to discuss a national settlement.

Alaska files a Medicaid suit against the tobacco industry on April 14.

Pennsylvania files a Medicaid suit against the tobacco industry on April 22.

On April 25 in North Carolina, U.S. District Judge William Osteen rules that the FDA has the authority to regulate tobacco as a drug. The tobacco industry immediately appeals the ruling.

Montana, Arkansas, Ohio, South Carolina, Missouri, Nevada, Vermont, and New Mexico file Medicaid suits against the tobacco industry in May.

On May 5 RJR wins a lawsuit in Jacksonville, Florida, filed by a lawyer representing the estate of a deceased smoker. The estate blamed the cigarette maker for not adequately warning the deceased of the dangers of smoking.

New Hampshire, Colorado, Oregon, Idaho, California, Puerto Rico, Maine, and Rhode Island file Medicaid suits against the tobacco industry in June.

**1997**
*(cont.)*
On June 20 the tobacco companies named in the suits and state attorneys general announce agreement on a landmark $368.5 billion settlement. It will also provide, subject to congressional approval, unprecedented restrictions on the liability of tobacco companies in lawsuits.

In July Congress introduces a new tax bill that includes a $50 billion tobacco-tax credit. If passed, the bill will save the industry billions of dollars by reducing the amount of money companies owe based on the June 20 settlement.

On July 3 Mississippi, the first state to settle with the tobacco industry, agrees to a $3.6 billion deal with industry defendants, including Brown & Williamson, R. J. Reynolds, Philip Morris, and Lorillard.

Florida settles its suit against the tobacco industry on August 25. The tobacco companies agree to pay $11.3 billion.

Georgia files a Medicaid suit against the tobacco industry on August 29.

On September 11 the Senate votes to repeal the $50 billion tax break for the tobacco industry that was slipped into tax cut legislation in July.

The tobacco industry settles a landmark class-action suit over secondhand smoke on October 10, agreeing to pay a total of $349 million.

On October 17 a Philadelphia judge dismisses a *Castano* national class-action lawsuit against the cigarette companies, weeks before the plaintiffs were set to go to trial.

On December 4 Rep. Thomas Bliley subpoenas documents from four tobacco companies named as defendants in the Minnesota Medicaid case. The documents are released to his office and to the public later in the week.

R. J. Reynolds discontinues use of the Joe Camel character in its advertising.

Mississippi and Florida settle their Medicaid suits against the tobacco companies without going to trial.

The smoking prevalence rate for adults (18 and older) drops to 24.7 percent.

1998    On January 7 the Justice Department files charges against a California company, DNA Plant Technology, for participating in research to produce tobacco with an abnormally high level of nicotine and for illegally shipping its tobacco seeds to Brazil.

The state of Texas settles its lawsuit against the tobacco industry for a record $14.5 billion.

On January 23 DNA Plant Technology pleads guilty to attempting to produce high-nicotine tobacco.

Minnesota's Medicaid trial begins on January 26.

On January 29 tobacco executives testify before Congress that nicotine is addictive and that smoking may cause cancer.

The Associated Press reports on February 10 that B&W is still selling cigarettes made with genetically altered, high-nicotine tobacco despite assurances that it had stopped doing so four years earlier.

On February 25 tobacco company executives tell Congress they will not modify their advertising and marketing practices unless Congress first gives the industry substantial protection against lawsuits.

On March 13 the tobacco industry makes public 26 million pages of internal documents that have been collected in connection with the Minnesota suit.

1998
(cont.)

The Senate Commerce Committee passes the McCain bill on April 1. The bill gives the FDA unrestricted control over nicotine and is much tougher than the June 20, 1997, agreement between the state attorneys general and the tobacco industry. It provides no liability protection for the industry, just a cap on potential yearly damages.

On April 8 RJR CEO Steven Goldstone announces that RJR is withdrawing its support for a settlement and complains that the McCain bill will bankrupt his company. Within hours, the rest of the tobacco industry backs away from the national settlement proposed in June 1997.

Dr. Stanton Glantz, professor of medicine at the University of California at San Francisco, observes "[t]here's been a radical increase in cigar and cigarette use in the movies. And the people who are doing the smoking in movies are never the losers" (quoted by ABC News on April 9).

On April 28 Liggett, which had settled with the states in 1997, agrees to serve as an informant in the government's probe to determine whether tobacco companies lie about the health risks of smoking.

On April 30 the New York attorney general files a petition to shut down the Tobacco Institute Inc. and the Council for Tobacco Research USA.

Minnesota and Blue Cross and Blue Shield of Minnesota reach a $6.6 billion settlement with the tobacco industry on May 8.

On May 18 the Senate begins debate on the McCain tobacco bill, which would give the FDA power to regulate nicotine, impose restrictions on tobacco industry advertising, and force companies to meet targets to reduce teen smoking or face up to $3.5 billion in penalties annually. Cigarette prices would increase by $1.10 a pack over five years.

Despite pressure from President Clinton, on May 20 the Senate rejects a proposed $1.50-per-pack tax increase on cigarettes.

Rep. Henry Waxman releases RJR documents revealing that for the past 30 years the company deliberately targeted youth, minorities, and women.

On June 11 the Senate rejects an amendment to the tobacco bill that would limit attorneys' fees in tobacco company settlements.

After lengthy debate, the Senate effectively kills the McCain tobacco bill on June 17. The bill would have cost tobacco companies at least $516 billion over 25 years. It would have levied an additional $7 billion a year in penalties if youth smoking did not drop enough to meet targets.

According to figures released in July by the Public Citizen watchdog group, the tobacco industry spent $43.3 million on congressional lobbying in the first half of 1998, an increase of 174 percent over the same period in 1997.

On October 21 WHO declares war on the tobacco industry, announcing that it hopes to avert a "smoking epidemic" by means of international standards on issues such as tobacco taxes, smuggling, advertising, and commercial sponsorship (BBC News 1998).

On November 18 a study is published revealing that children as young as 3 and 4 think it is "cool" to smoke if their parents do (Reuters 1998).

Forty-six states accept a tobacco settlement of $206 billion on November 20.

U.S. cigarette consumption falls 2 percent, to 470 billion cigarettes.

1999        President Clinton announces in his state of the union address on January 19 that the Justice Department will sue cigarette makers to recover hundreds of billions of dollars the federal government has spent treating sick smokers.

On March 4 WHO says that 4 million people die each year because of tobacco and the annual toll by the late 2020s could be 10 million.

On March 30 a jury in Portland, Oregon, orders Philip Morris to pay a record $81 million to the family of a man who died of lung cancer after smoking Marlboros for four decades.

On April 19 a major study by the International Agency for Research on Cancer (IARC) determines that pipes and cigars are "as lethal" as cigarettes (WHO 1999).

On April 26 the World Health Organization tells international food and drug regulators that tobacco products should be regulated just as other drug delivery devices are.

On April 30 it is reported that B&W is experimenting with a curing process that removes some of the nitrosamines from tobacco. Nitrosamines cause cancer in laboratory animals.

On June 2 the tobacco industry is found not liable for the cancer that killed a Mississippi barber. The barber had claimed that the disease was caused by decades of exposure to secondhand smoke in his barbershop.

On July 7 jurors in Florida's class-action suit against the tobacco industry find that cigarette makers produce a defective product that causes emphysema, lung cancer, and other illnesses.

An appeals court rules on September 3 that damage claims in Florida's huge class-action lawsuit against tobacco must be determined one smoker at a time. However, on October 20, the court abandons this ruling and reopens the door to a lump-sum award.

The Justice Department files a massive lawsuit against the major tobacco companies on September 22. The purpose of the suit is to recover part of the $20 billion the federal government spends each year for the treatment of smoking-related illnesses.

The World Health Organization initiates an investigation on October 12, saying it has evidence that the tobacco industry tried to undermine U.N. efforts to control smoking.

In October Philip Morris launches a $100 million a year television advertising campaign to improve its corporate image.

In October the BBC reports that between 50 and 60 percent of adults in China and Japan are smokers.

On November 14 the head of the World Health Organization warns that Asia faces an epidemic of tobacco use among women and youth.

On December 10 the BBC reports that smoking causes 46,000 cancer deaths per year—30 percent of all cancer deaths in the United Kingdom. It is also responsible for 40,000 heart disease deaths per year—25 percent of all heart disease deaths in Britain.

Canada files suit against RJR on December 21, alleging that the company has defrauded the government and subverted its antismoking campaign by smuggling billions of cigarettes into the country.

On December 27 cigarette makers ask a federal court to dismiss the government's suit against them, saying the suit ignores settlements the industry has already reached with all 50 states.

1999
(cont.)

On December 27 Turkmenistan in Central Asia bans public smoking "in the name of the health of the nation."

The BBC reports that the British tobacco industry's income from the sale of tobacco products in the U.S. exceeds $45 billion.

The World Health Organization announces that worldwide 1.1 billion people are smokers, a third of the world's adult population. Forty-seven percent are men; 12 percent are women. Tobacco use causes about 10,000 deaths per day.

The government of Canada files a lawsuit against R. J. Reynolds Tobacco Holdings U.S. on December 22. Canada alleges that RJR orchestrated an international tobacco-smuggling conspiracy that defrauded Canadian taxpayers of more than $1 billion.

2000

On January 5 a study finds that a gene linked to abnormal cell growth in the lung is more active in women than in men. This finding may explain why female smokers are more than twice as likely as male smokers to develop lung cancer.

Tobacco kills one person every eight seconds, says Gro Harlem Brundtland, director general of WHO, on January 8. She warns that if the nations of the world do not act to control tobacco, the toll by 2030 could be 10 million lives annually, with 70 percent of the deaths occurring in developing countries.

On March 27 Philip Morris and RJR are each ordered to pay $10 million in compensatory damages to a California woman. A 40-year-old mother of four, the woman is dying of lung cancer after having smoked cigarettes for 25 years. This is the first such award to a person who began smoking after warning labels were placed on cigarette packages.

On April 7 a Florida jury orders the tobacco industry

to pay $12.7 million to three former smokers in a class-action suit that may eventually cost the industry billions of dollars.

# References

Advisory Committee to the Surgeon General. 1964. *Smoking and Health: Report of the Advisory Committee to the Surgeon General of the Public Health Service.* Washington, D.C.: Government Printing Office.

Barclay, William. 1614. *Nepenthes; or, The Vertues of Tabacco.* Edinburgh.

BBC News. 1998. "WHO Declares War on Tobacco Firms." October 21. ws.bbc.co.ok/hi/english/health/background_briefings/smoking/newsid_198000/198338.stm.

Burton, Robert. 1660. *The Anatomy of Melancholy.* London.

CDC TIPS (Centers for Disease Control, Tobacco Information and Prevention Source). 1999. "Chronology: Significant Developments Related to Smoking and Health: 1964–1996." http://www.cdc.gov/tobacco/overview/chron96.htm.

Doll, Richard, and Bradford A. Hill. 1952. "Study of the Aeliology of Carcinoma of the Lung." *British Medical Journal* December 15.

Doll, Richard, and Bradford A. Hill. 1954. "The Mortality of Doctors in Relation to Their Smoking Habits." *British Medical Journal* June 26: 1451–1455.

Doll, Richard, and Richard Peto. 1976. "Mortality in Relation to Smoking: 20 Years' Observations on Male British Doctors." *British Medical Journal,* Vol. 4:1525–1536.

Feldt, Robert. 1943. "The Truth about Tobacco." *The American Mercury.*

Freedman, Alix M. 1996. "Cigarette Defector Says CEO Lied to Congress about View of Nicotine." *Wall Street Journal,* January 26.

Hariot, Thomas. 1586. *A Briefe and True Report of the New Found Land of Virginia.*

Harrison, William. 1573. *Chronologie.*

Hilts, Philip J. 1996. *Smokescreen: The Truth behind the Tobacco Industry Cover-Up.* Reading, MA: Addison-Wesley Publishing.

Howes, Edmond. 1631. *Annales; or, A Generall Chronicle of England.* London: Richardi Meighen.

Johnson, Wingate. 1932. *The American Mercury.*

Kemp, William. 1665. *A Brief Treatise of the Nature, Causes, Signes, Preservation from and Cure of the Pestilence.* London.

Mennes, John. 1640. "Wits' Recreations." Reprinted 1874. London: John Camden Hotten.

Muller, Franz Hermann. 1939. "Tobacco Misuse and Lung Carcinoma."

Norr, Roy. 1952. "Cancer by the Carton." *Reader's Digest.*

Reuters. 1998. "Daddies 'Cool' If They Smoke, Say Children." November 18. http://www.nzdr/update/messages/438.htm.

Sullum, Jacob. 1998. *For Your Own Good: The Anti-Smoking Crusade and the Tyranny of Public Health.* New York: The Free Press.

Tate, Cassandra. 1999. *Cigarette Wars.* New York: Oxford University Press.

Thayer William Sydney. 1905. "Cotton Mather's *Rules of Health.*" *Johns Hopkins Bulletin* Vol. 16, No. 174 (September).

UCSF (University of California at San Francisco). 2001. B&W document. http://galen.library.ucsf.edu/tobacco/docs/html/1007.01/1007.01.1html.

Whelan, Elizabeth. 1984. *A Smoking Gun: How the Tobacco Industry Gets Away with Murder.* Philadelphia: George F. Stickley.

WHO (World Health Organization). 1996. "Guidelines for Controlling and Monitoring the Tobacco Epidemic." Geneva: WHO. http://Saturn. who.ch/uhtbin/cgisirsi/Thu+Sep++7+13:17:28+MET+DST+2000/0/497.

WHO. 1999. "Cigars and Pipes as Lethal as Cigarettes, Says New European Study." Press release, April 19. http://www.who.int/ inf-pr-1999/en/pr99-23.html.

Wynder, Ernst L., and Evarts A. Graham. 1950. "Tobacco Smoking as a Possible Etiologic Factor in Bronchogenic Carcinoma: A Study of Six-Hundred-Eighty-Four Proved Cases." *JAMA* May 27.

Wydner, Ernst L., Evarts A. Graham, and A. B. Croninger. 1953. *Cancer Research* Vol. 13: 855–864.

# 3

# Biographical Sketches

## Edward Bernays (1891–1995)

Edward Bernays is known today as the father of public relations. In the 1920s he worked for American Tobacco. It was the Jazz Age, an era of new freedom for women. Many of them—more than ever before—were smoking cigarettes, but American Tobacco executives were not satisfied. Luckies were fairly popular among women, but why did so many women choose other brands? Edward Bernays, one of the company's most gifted advertising men theorized that it was the green package. Green, he said, clashed with the colors women were wearing. Bernays first suggested changing the color of the package, but that was out of the question. The company had spent millions to advertise the package and was not about to change its appearance. So Bernays decided on another approach. Rather than change the package, he would change women. More specifically, he would change their minds about green. First he approached friends in the fashion industry and persuaded them to help. Robert Sobel, in *They Satisfy*, described a "Green Fashion Luncheon" (for which American Tobacco footed the bill), with green menus, green food, and green drinks, and a "Green Charity Ball" (also paid for by American Tobacco) to which women were required to wear green gowns (Sobel 1978). And, of course, fashion designers and clothing manufacturers began to feature lines of green clothes. Green became the color of the year, and a package of Luckies was the perfect accessory.

## James Bonsack and James Buchanan (Buck) Duke (1856–1925)

James Bonsack, the 21-year-old son of a Virginia plantation owner, designed a machine that could reliably roll cigarettes of a consistent quality. Patented in 1880, the machine could do the work of 40 to 50 workers, producing 70,000 cigarettes a day. James Buchanan (Buck) Duke placed Bonsack under contract and began building a cigarette monopoly, the American Tobacco Co., which would eventually control 92 percent of the world's cigarette market.

In an era of mass production, when Americans were being offered a growing assortment of moderately priced factory-made goods—everything from clothing to chewing gum—cigarettes were still being made by hand. In 1876, according to Richard Kluger, the cost-per-thousand for hand-rolled cigarettes was 96 cents, with all but 10 cents going to the rollers for their labor. Machinery existed to roll cigarettes, but it broke down frequently and the cigarettes it produced were of inconsistent quality. Determined to find a solution, the Richmond cigarette manufacturer Allen & Ginter offered a prize of $75,000 to anyone who could come up with a reliable machine. At that time James Bonsack obtained a patent for a design he had worked on for several years, one that could produce tens of thousands of cigarettes a day. (Modern machines produce more than 6 million a day.)

Allen & Ginter tried Bonsack's roller and was impressed. But then, for reasons no one can explain, the company decided to pass on it. Perhaps the $75,000 that would be owed in prize money was a factor in its decision. Kluger has suggested that behind the company's change of heart lay "the managerial timidity and fear of technological advances, with their accompanying risks and dislocations (e.g., the dismissal of unneeded workers), which affected Richmond industrialists of this period." (Kluger 1996, 20) Whatever the reason, Allen & Ginter stood on the threshold of unimagined financial success and chose not to grasp what was within its reach. Buck Duke, however, did not hesitate. He used Bonsack's cigarette-rolling machine to make American Tobacco Co. the largest cigarette monopoly in the world.

## Gene Borio (1944– )

Gene Borio gathers tobacco news and publishes it on his web site, http://www.tobacco.org an essential resource for students, researchers, health professionals, and lawyers. "Sunlight is the best disinfectant," a quote from Justice Brandeis, summarizes Borio's guiding philosophy: Tobacco news and tobacco history should see the light of day, so that consumers and researchers are well informed. The "HOT News" section of his web site contains a variety of categories that compete for the browser's attention (e.g., "Quotes/Alerts," "Summaries," "THIS JUST IN," "Today's News"), all of which are archived and searchable. Other categories include "History," a guide for antitobacco activists; "Latest Health News"; and "Health Info." Borio also provides links to numerous related sites, many of which contain internal tobacco industry documents that companies were forced to make public.

## Abraham Arden Brill (1874–1948)

In the early years of the twentieth century, Edward Bernays of American Tobacco enlisted the help of A. A. Brill, a prominent psychoanalyst, to popularize smoking among young women. Brill articulated what Bernays and other forward-thinking advertising people already knew—that cigarettes were "torches of freedom" and that smoking symbolized women's liberation from the traditional roles of keeping house and having babies. More and more women were taking jobs outside the home, many of which had in the past been men's jobs. Smoking cigarettes distinguished working women from those who remained in the traditional roles of housewife and mother.

Brill also identified a sexual element in smoking. Drawing on the writings of Sigmund Freud, he noted that "[s]moking is a sublimation of oral eroticism; holding a cigarette in the mouth excites the oral zone" (Sobel 1978). The other side of that coin is that smoking could be perceived as sexy. Women smokers were portrayed as more attractive to men, a theme that has remained dominant in tobacco advertising.

## Gro Harlem Brundtland (1939– )

After becoming the first woman director-general of the World Health Organization in 1998, Gro Harlem Brundtland quickly established herself as a force to be reckoned with, declaring war on the world's vast tobacco industry. Brundtland had also served three terms as the prime minister of Norway, the first woman to hold the position. She was known to Norwegians simply as

"Gro," a Norwegian counterpart of conservative British Prime Minister Margaret Thatcher, whom many Americans as well as Britons called "Maggie." Like Thatcher, she was a strong leader, a dominant force on the national scene—so strong that editorial cartoonists depicted her as a giant, drawing only her feet, with the country's other political figures shown as tiny creatures scuttling around them.

Brundtland is also a strong leader of WHO. She argues that "[i]mportant determinants of better health lie outside the health system," determinants such as education, economic well-being, human rights, and the environment. She believes, moreover, that while health is "a moral obligation and a basic human right," it is also "pure and sound economics: Healthy people build healthy economies." Thus, she has campaigned not only for greater emphasis on research, improved health care, and freer access to health care, but also for economic development, sustainable agriculture, protection of the rights of women and children, protection of the environment, reduction of poverty, better and more widely accessible systems of education, alternate energy sources, government control of health care, international cooperation, and population control. She has campaigned vigorously against tobacco and for international opposition to the tobacco industry.

## Joe Camel (1974–1997)

The oldest branch in Joe Camel's family tree links him to a camel known as "Old Joe," a member of the Barnum and Bailey circus (Goodrum and Dalrymple 1990). Old Joe served as a model for the artist whose drawing still appears on the front of R. J. Reynolds's Camel cigarette package. This camel was easily recognizable and became widely known. In Camel advertisements, in print and on television, Joe was steady: he literally just stood there. He never moved, he never wore funny clothes, and he never made controversial statements. Older smokers liked him, but younger people hardly noticed him at all. In the 1980s, as RJR's seventy-fifth anniversary approached, the Camel cigarette's market share was only 3 percent. The ad people decided to put Joe to work. He had appeared in an ad campaign in the early 1970s in France, where human beings were not permitted to appear in cigarette ads. Joe wore a Foreign Legion uniform and presented himself as suave and dashing. Bring him to the United States, someone suggested, and make him the centerpiece of a new advertising campaign (*Mangini v. R. J. Reynolds Tobacco Company* Collection 1999). In 1988, with sharp clothes and shades, Joe was put into action. He became one of the most popular advertising figures of the time—the quintessential party animal, an icon for millions of young people. Even children as young as three knew who Joe Camel was. His popularity rivaled that of Mickey Mouse. But Joe was a smoker, a bad influence. Adults became concerned. They accused R. J. Reynolds of trying to entice children to smoke. In 1991 Janet Mangini, a lawyer, sued RJR, accusing the company of targeting minors (*Mangini v. R. J. Reynolds Tobacco Company* Collection 1999). R. J. Reynolds's attorneys denied everything, insisting that Joe Camel was just a cartoon figure. But RJR was found guilty, and the company reluctantly put Joe out to pasture.

## Grady Carter (1931– ) and Woody Wilner

When Grady Carter's doctor told him to quit smoking, he found another doctor. Eventually, though, he found a lawyer: Woody Wilner. Despite a vague belief that smoking might cause cancer and several attempts to quit, like many smokers, Carter did not smoke that last cigarette until he was told he had cancer. Even then, after half of his left lung was removed, he remained philosophical, accepting his share of the blame. But on the afternoon of April 14, 1994, Grady Carter changed his mind. He was watching the televised hearings of the House Energy and Commerce Subcommittee on Health and the Environment, when Rep. Ron Wyden (D–Oregon) asked the chief executives of the major tobacco companies if they believed that nicotine is addictive. Each of them, one after another, stated under oath that he did not believe nicotine to be addictive. Carter was incensed. "I wasn't a crusader until that very minute," he said later. "Then I became one. I had tried so hard to quit, and there they all were, saying it wasn't addictive. I knew for certain that I wanted to sue these guys" (Mollenkamp et al. 1998).

Carter sued B&W, the maker of Lucky Strikes, the brand Carter had been smoking for years. Acting as Carter's attorney in the case, Woody Wilner used B&W's own internal documents, released to the public in 1995, to show that the company had been aware that nicotine was addictive and that it had known as early as 1927 that research showed that cigarettes caused cancer. A jury in Jacksonville, Florida, found B&W liable for Carter's health problems, and on August 9, 1996, a federal district court awarded Carter $750,000. It was only the second time in 40 years of tobacco litigation that a jury had ordered a company to pay damages to an individual plaintiff in a smoking liability case. However, as in the *Cipollone* case in 1988, the judgment was overturned on appeal. A three-judge panel ruled that Carter's suit was barred by the statute of limitations because the initial complaint was filed more than four years after Grady Carter knew or should have known, with the exercise of "due diligence," that he had a smoking-related disease. In addition, the court found that Carter's claims of misrepresentation were preempted by the Federal Cigarette Labeling Act that went into effect in 1969 (Orey 1999).

In 2000 the Florida state supreme court reinstated the verdict. B&W appealed to the U.S. Supreme Court, but the following year the Court refused to hear the case, sealing Carter's victory. Carter collected his original award of $750,000 plus interest, for a total of nearly $1.1 million from B&W.

## Rose Cipollone (?–1984)

Rose Cipollone's suit against Liggett, first adjudicated in 1988, marked the first time a jury awarded damages in a tobacco lawsuit. In 1955 Cipollone switched from Chesterfields to Liggett's new filtered brand, L&M. Although she noticed a dark stain in the filter, she said later, "I figured, 'Gee, that's good,'"—proof that the filter was doing its job. The advertisements for L&M did not actually say that filtered cigarettes were safer, she said, but "they gave me that impression that they were. . . . They would say 'milder, low tar, low nicotine.'" When the *Surgeon General's Report of 1964* linked smoking to cancer, Cipollone was disturbed, but she said she was sure that "if there was anything that dangerous that the tobacco people wouldn't allow it and the government wouldn't let them. . . . The tobacco companies wouldn't do anything that was going to kill you . . . so I figured until they proved it to me . . . I didn't have to take it seriously" (Kluger 1996).

It was only after cancer developed in her right lung and spread to her liver and her brain that Cipollone sued the companies whose cigarettes she had smoked, alleging that they had failed to warn her of the risks. Rose Cipollone died in 1984, not living to see the end of the trial. In 1988, a jury found Liggett 20 percent responsible for her death, but a minimum of 50 percent responsibility was required for damages to be awarded. Apparently feeling sorry for her husband, Tony Cipollone, the jurors agreed to award him $400,000, which Peter Pringle described as "a sort of consolation prize for being a dutiful and concerned husband" (Pringle 1998). It was the first time a jury had awarded any damages in a tobacco lawsuit. The tobacco companies appealed, however, and the judgment was overturned.

## Christopher Columbus (1451–1506) and Rodrigo de Jerez

When Christopher Columbus first came to the New World, the natives welcomed him with a bunch of dried tobacco leaves, among other gifts. Apparently, Columbus was not impressed by tobacco, not understanding what he was expected to do with it. But within a week Columbus and his crewmen saw natives chewing it and "drinking" the smoke through a Y-shaped pipe that they called *toboca* or *tobaga*. Some of his sailors decided to try it themselves, and Columbus is reported to have remarked later that "it was not within their power to refrain from indulging in the habit."

One of Columbus's sailors, Rodrigo de Jerez, took some tobacco with him when he returned to his hometown of Ayamonte, in Spain. Unfortunately, the townspeople became alarmed when they saw Jerez walking around with smoke coming out of his nose, assuming that Satan had something to do with it. In consequence, Jerez spent several years in prison, during which he presumably succeeded in quitting.

Offering a cigarette as a form of introduction became one of the social rituals of modern society. Although the beginnings of this gesture are traceable to the nineteenth century, one might argue that they can be traced much further back, to Christopher Columbus's first visit to the New World. By the early twentieth century, an offer of tobacco conveyed a broad array of meanings, ranging from sympathy to congratulations to sexual interest. The social uses of tobacco have declined, however, as awareness of its dangers has increased (Goodman 1993).

## Thomas Edison (1847–1931) and Henry Ford (1863–1947)

Although Thomas Edison smoked 10 to 20 cigars a day, as well as using chewing tobacco, he drew the line at cigarettes, and he refused to employ anyone who smoked them. In a letter to Henry

Ford, he explained that acrolein, a compound released by burning cigarette paper, "has a violent action on the nerve centers," causing severe damage to the cells of the brain. "Unlike most narcotics," Edison said, "this degeneration is permanent and uncontrollable. I employ no person who smokes."

Ford, influenced by Edison and Lucy Page Gaston, wrote a four-volume treatise—*The Little White Slaver*—in which he presented his own arguments against tobacco. "If you will study the history of almost any criminal," Ford wrote, "you will find that he is an inveterate cigarette smoker. . . . Boys, through cigarettes, train with bad company. They go with other smokers to the poolrooms and saloons. The cigarette drags them down" (Ford quoted in Tate 1999).

Edison withheld criticism of cigarettes during World War I, during which they became virtually a necessity to the troops, but when it was over he spoke out even more strongly than before. "I think the habit of using tobacco is the most reprehensible to which the human animal is addicted. I do not believe there is a wors[e] form in which tobacco can be used than in the form of a cigaret[te]" (Tate 1999; Sullum 1998).

## Lucy Page Gaston (1860–1924)

As a schoolteacher in Illinois in the late 1800s, Lucy Page Gaston noticed that boys who sneaked out behind the schoolhouse to smoke were invariably her worst students. In her mind there was a clear cause-and-effect relationship. Not only did children who smoke cigarettes experience an intellectual decline, but they also, if not intercepted and set on the right path, eventually turned to drink and finally became irredeemable criminals.

Gaston also claimed to be able to identify a smoker by studying his face. Most killers, rapists, and other degenerates had what she called "cigarette face," a certain look they acquired from smoking cigarettes. She claimed that anyone could be trained to spot them. Where cigarettes were concerned, Gaston was the self-proclaimed "extremist of extremists," tobacco's Carry Nation. Unalterably opposed and uncompromising in her opposition, she wanted nothing less than the total abolition of cigarettes, and she campaigned tirelessly all her life—only to see cigarette consumption in the United States rise from 2 billion to nearly 200 billion.

In her last years Gaston found herself increasingly the object of criticism and even ridicule, largely because of her dependence on pseudoscience and her evangelical excesses—and what Cassandra Tate has called an unfortunate resemblance to a shaven Abraham Lincoln (Tate 1999). But more than anything else, it was the swelling tide of public acceptance of cigarettes that doomed her campaign against smoking. Had she been born in 1960 instead of 1860 and known a bit more about science, most of her ideas—such as government regulation of cigarettes as "a habit-forming drug"—would not have seemed so extreme (Kluger 1996).

## Dr. Stanton Glantz (1946– ) and Mr. Butts

On May 12, 1994, Dr. Stanton Glantz, a professor at the University of California at San Francisco, received a FedEx box containing copies of internal documents of the Brown & Williamson tobacco company. On the return address label there was only a name—"Mr. Butts." Dr. Glantz described his reaction to the package as follows: "When these documents arrived on my doorstep, the thing that sucked me into them was not their potential political or legal import, it was the documents as history, . . . as science. It was just an unbelievable find. As a professor, it would be like an archaeologist finding a new tomb in Egypt."

In the FedEx box were papers stolen from B&W by Merrell Williams and then passed on to Michael Moore, Richard Scruggs, and Don Barrett, the Mississippi lawyers who were preparing a Medicaid suit against big tobacco. "Mr. Butts" was Don Barrett, but all three had been busy copying the documents and distributing them to Rep. Henry Waxman, to the *New York Times,* CBS, and others, including Dr. Glantz. Their purpose was to get the documents into the public domain, to give them to people and organizations who would help to publicize some of the information they contained (Orey 1999).

Stanton Glantz turned out to be a good choice. Along with colleagues at the University of California at San Francisco, he posted all of the Brown & Williamson documents on the Internet at http://www.library.ucsf.edu/tobacco and wrote a book, *The Cigarette Papers* (1996), in which he quoted extensively from the documents and assessed their importance (Frontline 1999).

## Judge Harold Greene (1923–2000)

Harold Greene was the judge who on May 25, 1995, told B&W lawyers that their internal documents could be made public. In

May 1994, B&W's internal documents were in the hands of a U.S. congressman and were being quoted in the *New York Times* and elsewhere. Brown & Williamson attorneys scrambled to block their publication. At B&W's request, the Superior Court of the District of Columbia issued a number of supoenas—to Rep. Henry Waxman, whose subcommittee was investigating big tobacco, and to the *New York Times,* the *Washington Post,* National Public Radio, CBS, and the *National Law Journal.* As Waxman later remarked, "I had never heard of a committee chairman being subpoenaed by the target of its own investigation."

Judge Harold Greene told B&W lawyers that the "speech or debate" clause of the Constitution provided immunity to members of Congress not only for what they might say in connection with congressional business but also in regard to all material they collected for investigative purposes. B&W countered that the documents had been stolen, not merely collected. But they had been stolen by Merrell Williams, Greene said, not by members of Congress. Moreover, Williams's motive in stealing the documents was to make them public out of concern for public health. Greene said that by focusing on the theft of the documents, B&W was obscuring a public health threat. "One may well doubt," he concluded, "that B&W would be mounting a tremendous and costly effort . . . in proceedings against members of a congressional committee and against the mass of the media, if the documents at issue did not represent the proverbial 'smoking gun' evidencing the company's long-held and long-suppressed knowledge that its product constitutes a serious health hazard" (Pringle 1998).

## David Kessler (1951– )

David Kessler, head of the Food and Drug Administration (FDA), did not know the man who spoke to him. He appeared nervous and refused to identify himself except by the code name "Research." Then he began talking about Brown & Williamson cigarettes, and he continued talking about them in a series of meetings with Kessler that extended over several weeks. "Research" was familiar with every one of the thousands of ingredients and additives that went into B&W cigarettes. He could explain the role of each, describe precisely how they interacted, what happened during the burning process, and what was in the smoke.

"Research" turned out to be the whistle-blower Jeffrey Wigand (*see* Wigand). His first visit to Dr. David Kessler's office at the FDA was on May 18, 1994. As head of the FDA, Kessler wanted to know whether the tobacco companies had ways of enhancing the impact of nicotine. If tobacco companies were using nicotine as a drug, manipulating it in such a way as to increase its power to addict, then the FDA would have a good chance of winning the right to regulate tobacco. Did Wigand know anything about this? In fact, he knew quite a lot, and he spelled it out in detail, identifying ammonia-based compounds that companies like B&W added to tobacco to boost the potency of nicotine, making it even more addictive. Using what he had learned from Wigand, Kessler put together the final pages of his case against tobacco, received approval from President Clinton, and began his campaign to take control of tobacco regulation.

## Anne Landman

Like Gene Borio, Anne Landman believes in letting the sun shine in, that is, in letting internal tobacco company documents see the light of day. To some extent, Landman has exposed what had already been exposed—documents that have been made public in the past few years and are available in various document repositories and on a number of web sites. Unfortunately, making the impact of these internal tobacco industry documents clear was not merely a matter of making them available to the public. Of the millions of internal documents, many are of no interest whatever, many are highly technical, many are inscrutable, and some use code words to conceal their subject matter.

Landman's contribution lies in identifying important documents and focusing public attention on them. She maintains a small archive of important documents, at http://tobaccofreedom.globalink.org/issues/documents/landman/, and also produces "Doc-Alert," a daily document Internet newsletter), complete with an introduction to and explanation of the significance of various documents. Doc-Alert is a free update service. Anyone who wants to receive it may do so by going to http://tobaccodocuments.org/, scrolling down to the bottom of the page, and entering his or her e-mail address in the box marked "Daily Document Newsletter."

Once a respiratory therapist, Anne Landman completed degrees in environmental restoration/waste management technology and communications. She is now west region program coordinator for the American Lung Association of Colorado.

## The Marlboro Man (1954– )

Wayne McLaren, the first actor who portrayed the Marlboro Man, died of lung cancer in 1992. Three years later, *Time* magazine reported the death of another Marlboro Man, the actor David McLean, noting that he, too, had died of lung cancer.

How did the Marlboro "Man" come about? Philip Morris initially marketed its Marlboro cigarettes to women. Early advertisements described the Marlboro as "mild as May." Each one had a little red "beauty tip" on the filter to conceal traces of the smoker's lipstick. But not many women liked it. Marlboro's market share was less than .025.

So Philip Morris gave the advertising account to the Leo Burnett agency in Chicago. In 1954, the soft pack was changed to a red and white flip-top box, and the dreamy young woman in a frilly dress was replaced by a male model who had wrinkles around his eyes and was dressed as a cowboy. Also, the little "beauty tip" was removed. It was the same Marlboro cigarette, but with a different image.

Men immediately perceived the quality of the Marlboro, the kind of cigarette only a real man could appreciate. The Marlboro was billed as a masculine cigarette, something to be smoked while riding the range or just sitting around the campfire with the rest of the wranglers. Almost overnight it became one of the three most popular brands in America (Goodrum and Dalrymple 1990).

## Sean Marsee (1965–1984)

When he was 12 years old, Sean Marsee attended a rodeo and was given a free sample of Copenhagen snuff. He tried it and liked it. And he liked carrying the can in his hip pocket, where it wore a whitish circle in the denim, symbolizing his masculinity (White 1988, 90–91). Marsee became involved in track, as a runner, so he stayed away from cigarettes, knowing they would impair his breathing. Besides, cigarette packages carried warning labels, but snuff cans did not, and Sean wanted to stay in peak condition. Training and hard work paid off. In 1983, his senior year at Talihina High School, in Talihina, Oklahoma, he was named outstanding athlete. That same year he noticed a whitish sore on the right side of his tongue, the side where he kept his quid of Copenhagen. His doctor diagnosed it as a precancerous growth known as a leukoplakia (Robinson 1986).

The first specialist who looked at Sean offered no hope. The leukoplakia had already developed into oral cancer. A second specialist, Dr. Carl Hook, in nearby Ada, Oklahoma, said he might be able to excise the growth and stop it from spreading. In February 1984, after daily radiation treatments and three operations to remove sections of his face and tongue and lymph nodes from his neck, leaving him horribly disfigured, wracked by pain, and unable to speak or eat, Sean died.

Partly as a result of Sean's experience, Congress passed the Smokeless Tobacco Health Education Act of 1986, which requires one of the following three warning labels on every package of smokeless tobacco:

- WARNING: THIS PRODUCT IS NOT A SAFE ALTERNATIVE TO CIGARETTES.
- WARNING: THIS PRODUCT MAY CAUSE GUM DISEASE AND TOOTH LOSS.
- WARNING: THIS PRODUCT MAY CAUSE MOUTH CANCER. (White 1988, 114)

## Nicolò Monardes (1493–1588)

In 1571 Nicolò Monardes, the leading physician of Seville and a medical scholar respected throughout Europe and Mexico, published a hugely influential reference work on the medicinal plants of the New World. In it, he explained the several ways of using tobacco.

- First, fresh green leaves, soaked in water or mixed with their own juice and warmed, could be applied to sores, wounds, or areas of pain.
- Second, leaves could be mixed with lime and chewed to alleviate hunger or thirst.
- Third, dried leaves could be smoked to provide relaxation and relief from weariness.

Monardes greatly influenced worldwide acceptance of tobacco's curative qualities. He achieved this in part by determining tobacco's humoral essence, thus establishing its place in the context of the prevailing belief that human health required a balance of four humors (Latin for "moistures"). These humors were known as phlegm, black bile, yellow bile, and blood. Being "hot and dry in the second degree," tobacco would dry the "cold humors" and help the smoker to expel phlegm. Monardes's book, which was translated into the major European languages and published in a number of editions, remained the major reference on tobacco until the nineteenth century.

## Ronald Lee Motley

A nationally famous plaintiff's attorney, Ron Motley first built a reputation with his suits against the asbestos industry. The principal target of his efforts now is the tobacco industry, and his successes so far have made him a multimillionaire. Perhaps Motley is motivated in part by memories of his mother, who smoked two to three packs of Winstons daily and eventually died of emphysema. It is her experience, her unavailing efforts to quit, that Motley remembers when he hears tobacco people claim that nicotine is not addictive. "If she wasn't addicted to cigarettes," he said in a *Frontline* interview, "then there is no such thing as addiction" (Motley 1999).

Motley recalled his mother's death:

> She actually would talk one of her sisters into sneaking her a cigarette. She would take the oxygen away from her and smoke a cigarette—which was, you know, very dangerous because it could have exploded. . . . It is deeply ingrained in my mind. Well, it is. . . . To watch someone that you love very much die a slow miserable death, suffocating day by day, is a very unpleasant thing. . . . And to know exactly what caused it. And then when you hear the denials of the cigarette companies that they had never caused the illness or death of a single American citizen, having sat there and watched my mother suffocating. . . . [I]t made me very angry. And when I get angry, I try to get even. (Motley 1999)

## Jean Nicot (1530–1600)

As French ambassador to the court of Portugal, from 1559 to 1561, Jean Nicot contributed greatly to the early popularity of tobacco. He sent specimens of the plant to the French court—in particular to Catherine de Medici, the Queen Mother, who in turn promoted tobacco's cultivation in France. Having obtained tobacco plants while in Lisbon and having witnessed what he regarded as their remarkable curative powers, Nicot recommended them for the treatment of sores, abrasions, lesions, and headaches, among other ailments. For his efforts, Nicot's name would eventually be used in the name of the tobacco plant's genus, *Nicotiana,* and of the plant's main psychoactive ingredient, nicotine.

## Patrick Reynolds (1940– )

Although he was a direct descendant of the founder of the R. J. Reynolds tobacco empire, Patrick Reynolds was concerned about the health risks apparently linked to tobacco. He had watched members of his own family die of diseases that seemed to him the result of using tobacco products. In the spring of 1986, Reynolds was present as Sen. Bob Packwood chatted with a group of potential contributors. When Packwood mentioned that the Senate would vote later that day on a bill to increase the federal cigarette tax, Reynolds remarked that he favored an increase. Challenged by Packwood to go public, he at first hesitated. Would taking a stand against tobacco alienate his family? What would people think? Tobacco had made him a rich man. How could he speak out against it? But on July 18, 1986, he sat before a House subcommittee on health and the environment and condemned tobacco as a killer. "Am I biting the hand that feeds me?" he asked. "If the hand that once fed me is the tobacco industry, then that same hand has killed millions of people and may kill millions more" (Reynolds and Shachtman 1989, 315–316).

## Richard Reynolds (1850–1918)

Richard Reynolds, the grandson of R. J. Reynolds, took his grandfather's company into new markets and led the cigarette industry into a new era of advertising. Before the dissolution of the American Tobacco trust in 1911, the R. J. Reynolds Company had been a manufacturer of chewing tobacco. But with the renewal of competition among the various tobacco companies, Richard Reynolds decided to go into the cigarette business. First he experimented with new blends, but they generated little interest in test markets. So he turned to the company's popular Prince Albert pipe tobacco. After a series of experiments, tinkering with the Prince Albert formula, researchers produced a blend for cigarettes that they believed tasted better than anything then on the market. Reynolds agreed (Reynolds and Shachtman 1989, 38).

This new brand of cigarettes was named Camel and was sold in packs of 20 for a dime, whereas other companies were selling cigarettes in units of 10 or 5. Reynolds also broke with tradition by refusing to use bonus inserts. A statement on the package explained their absence: "Don't look for Premiums or Coupons, as the cost of the Tobaccos blended in CAMEL cigarettes prohibits the use of them" (Kluger 1996, 56)

Most important was Reynolds's decision to advertise cigarettes as they had never been advertised before. In 1913 RJR's total budget for advertising and promotion was $680,000. In 1914 the budget was $1.3 million. By 1918, when Richard Reynolds died, one of every three cigarettes sold in the United States was a Camel (Kluger 1996, 58).

## Richard Scruggs

Richard Scruggs assisted his friend Michael Moore, the Mississippi attorney general, in filing the nation's first Medicaid lawsuit against big tobacco. In mid-April 1994, only a few weeks before Moore and Scruggs filed suit, Scruggs received the Brown & Williamson internal documents stolen by Merrell Williams. Scruggs and Moore sat among the piles of documents and began to read, hoping they would find information they could use in the Medicaid case (Mollenkamp et al. 1998, 46).

Their first reaction was shock. As the authors of *The People vs. Big Tobacco* put it, the industry documents contained "the hidden story of Big Tobacco from deep inside" and offered " a view of the cigarette companies—their most intimate secrets—that nobody had ever uncovered before" (Mollenkamp et al. 1998, 46). Document after document acknowledged that nicotine was addictive, that smoking was linked to cancer and other diseases. There was also considerable evidence that B&W had abused attorney-client privilege by routing research reports through the B&W legal department so that they could not be used against the company in lawsuits (Orey 1999, 162).

But there were problems. First, the documents had been stolen. Would a judge permit them to be used as evidence? And second, would it be possible to overcome attorney-client privilege? The solution, Moore and Scruggs believed, was to "leak" the documents—anonymously. Scruggs flew to Washington and gave a copy of the documents to Rep. Henry Waxman, tobacco's biggest opponent in Congress. Another set went to Philip Hilts, a *New York Times* reporter covering the tobacco industry, and another was delivered to the office of Dr. Stanton Glantz, a professor at the University of California at San Francisco and an outspoken critic of the tobacco industry (Mollenkamp et al. 1998, 47–48). At this point, the tobacco industry's "secret" internal documents were no longer secret. Scruggs recalled the tobacco company CEOs who had sworn before Waxman's subcommittee that they did not believe nicotine was addictive: "These guys are toast," he said (Pringle 1998, 68).

## Bill Tuttle (1929–1998)

Bill Tuttle was a role model for thousands of youngsters in Kansas City in the 1950s. He was the tough, dependable center fielder for the Kansas City A's baseball team (before it moved to California). Tuttle was the kind of player who came through in clutch situations; his value to the team did not show up in his batting average or his fielding percentage. But he could be counted on to make the game-saving catch or the game-saving throw to the plate or to knock in the winning run in the bottom of the ninth.

Not always, of course. But it seemed that way. Tuttle had class and character. He was neither flashy nor a show-off; he just did his job. He would make a fine play in the outfield and casually touch a finger to the bill of his cap as he jogged across the third-base line. Brushed back by an opposing pitcher, he would simply look at him, with no expression in particular, spit out some tobacco juice, and then step back up to the plate-crowding it just as much as before. The big wad of tobacco was always there, giving Tuttle's face a lopsided look that might have been a little comical if it were not for his eyes and his seriousness of purpose, his character.

When Tuttle developed oral cancer, he began to think about all the young people who had cheered for him throughout his career in baseball. He knew he had been a role model and wondered how many young men were using smokeless tobacco because they had seen him using it. And he began to think that maybe he could still be a role model, of a different kind.

After surgeons removed parts of his face in an effort to prevent the spread of his cancer, Tuttle began a second career as a spokesman against spit tobacco. He talked to players in the minors as well as the majors and to many thousands of teenagers. Although numbers never reflected Tuttle's worth as a ballplayer, it is easier now to judge his success—and the success of a few others who campaigned with him—by the number of athletes who do not chew tobacco.

## Jeffrey Wigand

Other whistle-blowers have emerged from within the tobacco industry, but none so centrally placed or so knowledgeable as Jeffrey Wigand, the subject of the film *The Insider*. His former colleagues at Brown & Williamson hate him passionately. Wigand has said that even strangers approach him in airports and restaurants and abuse him verbally for his "betrayal" of B&W, but such experiences no longer surprise him. He is not the classic "good guy"; not everyone admires him for what he has done. He has caused grave damage to an entire industry, violating a confidentiality agreement and revealing some of B&W's innermost secrets.

Wigand was in charge of research at B&W from December 1980 to March 1993, a top-level executive paid $300,000 plus stock options per year. He drove a Mercedes Benz given him by the company, enjoyed memberships at exclusive golf clubs, and lived in a princely home. But he became increasingly uncomfortable in his job, having discovered, he said later, that B&W was manipulating nicotine levels in cigarettes to make them more addictive, that the company was specifically targeting young people as prospective smokers, and that work on a "safer" cigarette had been shelved. When Wigand objected to the continued use of coumarin in pipe tobacco after it had been shown to cause liver cancer in mice, he was fired. In exchange for a comfortable pension and health benefits to cover his daughter's asthma problems, he signed a confidentiality agreement before he left.

But *60 Minutes* producer Lowell Bergman (played by Al Pacino in the film *The Insider*) continued to pursue him, and eventually he revealed everything—not only on *60 Minutes,* but also in sessions with David Kessler of the FDA, in testimony that helped to decide the states' suit against big tobacco, and in other interviews with journalists. "It was hell," Wigand told a writer for the Edinburgh *Scotsman.* "Brown & Williamson threatened me. They took away my health care. They had people follow me. . . . They broke into my lawyers' offices. . . . These guys are evil, simple and straightforward" (Branson 2000).

## Merrell Williams

When Merrell Williams showed up for his first day of work at the Brown & Williamson building in downtown Louisville, Kentucky, he and his fellow temporary employees must have felt overwhelmed by the task before them. Their job was to sort through hundreds of thousands of B&W documents, which had to be read, classified, and coded for entry into a huge database.

The motive behind the project became clear in their first few days of training. Facing the threat of more lawsuits against the tobacco companies—lawsuits that would require the companies to turn over internal documents in response to subpoenas—B&W's lawyers wanted to know precisely what was in those documents. Just as important, according to Orey, they also wanted to know what documents were "privileged" and would not have to be turned over. Documents involving communication between a lawyer and a client, for example, would be privileged and a client could be any individual employee of a company (Orey 1999).

It was grueling work, but Williams found it interesting. First, he came across a group of documents relating to product placement in movies. There was even a note from Sylvester Stallone in which he agreed to use B&W products in five feature films for a fee of $500,000. Such an agreement was not illegal, but most movies eventually wind up on television, where cigarette advertising is prohibited.

Williams found a document in which a B&W lawyer stated that nicotine is addictive, a fact that B&W denied publicly. One document referred to marketing studies involving sixteen-year-olds. Another revealed how much B&W knew about the effects of nicotine on the central nervous system. Still another contained a list of documents to be shipped out of the country just in case they were ever wanted in connection with a lawsuit.

Alarmed by what he was reading and concerned that such information might never come to light, Williams decided to start making notes about documents that seemed important. Soon he began taking the documents themselves. As he became bolder, he bought a pair of baggy pants in which to conceal them, and casually walked past security guards who apparently never noticed that he was stockier going out than he was going in. Williams began anonymously mailing samples to people in government and elsewhere, apparently hoping to derive some remuneration. Accounts of how the documents stolen by Merrell Williams were eventually obtained by lawyers suing the tobacco industry have been published in several versions, each account based on the writer's unique perspective, each providing details missing from the others. The information that Williams obtained during his temporary job at B&W would eventually be used in lawsuits against big tobacco.

## Dr. Ernst Wynder and Dr. Evarts A. Graham

Dr. Evarts Graham was a professor at Washington University Medical School in St. Louis, and Ernst (later Ernest) Wynder was one of his students. In 1949 the American Cancer Society (ACS) gave Dr. Graham a grant to study the relationship between lung cancer and cigarettes. Their project was simple enough: find men with lung cancer and talk to them, ask them whether they'd ever smoked cigarettes. Wynder was enthusiastic; the professor was less so. Graham, a cigarette smoker, pointed out that they could just as easily establish a relationship between the incidence of lung cancer and the purchase of silk stockings, and then warn men not to buy silk stockings.

In any case, they set to work. Before long they had managed to identify over 600 men with lung cancer. They eventually determined that 96.5 percent of them had been smokers, while only 73.7 percent of men without cancer were smokers (Wynder and Graham 1950). Statistically, this difference was huge, a shocking indictment of smoking—so shocking that Dr. Graham immediately decided to give up smoking. The study was published in the May 27, 1950, issue of the *Journal of the American Medical Association*, and it is now regarded as one of the landmark studies in the history of tobacco research.

## References

Branson, Louise. 2000. "No Smoke . . . Without Fire." *Scotsman* (Edinburgh). February 11. http://www.scotsman.com/.

Frontline. 1999. "Inside the Tobacco Deal." Frontline Online. http://www.pbs.org/wgbh/pages/frontline/shows/settlement/.

Glantz, Stanton A., John Slade, Lisa A. Bero, Peter Hanauer, and Deborah E. Barnes. 1996. *The Cigarette Papers*. Berkeley: University of California Press.

Goodman, Jordan. 1993. *Tobacco in History: The Cultures of Dependence*. London: Routledge.

Goodrum, Charles, and Helen Dalrymple. 1990. *Advertising in America: The First 200 Years.* New York: Harry N. Abrams.

Kluger, Richard. 1996. *Ashes to Ashes: America's Hundred-Year Cigarette War, the Public Health, and the Unabashed Triumph of Philip Morris.* New York: Alfred A. Knopf.

*Mangini v. R. J. Reynolds Tobacco Company* Collection. 1999. University of California at San Francisco Archive. http://galen.library.ucsf.edu/tobacco.

Mollenkamp, Carrick, Adam Levn, Joseph Menn, and Jeffrey Rothfeder. 1998. *The People vs. Big Tobacco.* Princeton, NJ: Bloomberg Press.

Motley, Ron. 1999. "Frontline: Inside the Tobacco Deal." Interview. PBS: WGBH. http://www.pbs.org/wgbh/pages/frontline/shows/settlement.

Orey, Michael. 1999. *Assuming the Risk: The Mavericks, the Lawyers, and the Whistle-Blowers Who Beat Big Tobacco.* Boston: Little, Brown, Inc.

Pringle, Peter. 1998. *Cornered: Big Tobacco at the Bar of Justice.* New York: Holt.

Reynolds, Patrick and Tom Shachtman. 1989. *The Gilded Leaf: Triumph, Tragedy, and Tobacco.* Boston: Little, Brown and Company.

Robinson, Ray. 1986. "Surgeon Blames Sooner's Fatal Oral Cancer." *Oklahoma City Oklahoman,* May 21. http://archives.oklahoman.com/.

Sobel, Robert. 1978. *They Satisfy: The Cigarette in American Life.* Garden City, NJ: Anchor Press.

Sullum, Jacob. 1998. *For Your Own Good: The Anti-Smoking Crusade and the Tyranny of Public Health.* New York: Free Press.

Tate, Cassandra. 1999. *Cigarette Wars: The Triumph of "The Little White Slaver."* New York: Oxford University Press.

White, Larry C. 1988. *Merchants of Death: The American Tobacco Industry.* New York: William Morrow.

Wynder, Ernst L., and Evarts A. Graham. 1950. "Tobacco Smoking as a Possible Etiologic Factor in Bronchogenic Carcinoma: A Study of Six Hundred and Eighty-Four Proved Cases." *Journal of the American Medical Association,* May 27.

# 4

# Documents

## "State-Specific Prevalence of Current Cigarette and Cigar Smoking among Adults—United States, December 18, 1998"

*"State-Specific Prevalence of Current Cigarette and Cigar Smoking among Adults—United States, 1998," from the CDC, reports in part the findings of the 1998 Behavioral Risk Factor Surveillance System. Accompanying the document are two tables. Table 1 shows percentages of cigarette smokers by state and sex, and Table 2 shows percentages of cigar smokers.*

Each year, cigarette smoking causes an estimated 430,000 deaths in the United States (1). In addition, the health risks for smoking cigars, which include mouth, throat, and lung cancers, are well documented (2). This report summarizes the findings from the 1998 Behavioral Risk Factor Surveillance System (BRFSS) on the prevalence of current cigarette and cigar smoking in the 50 states and the District of Columbia. The findings indicate that state-specific cigarette smoking prevalence among adults aged greater than or equal to 18 years varied twofold and having ever smoked a cigar (i.e., ever cigar smoking) varied nearly fourfold.

---

*Source:* CDC. 1999. "State-Specific Prevalence of Current Cigarette and Cigar Smoking among Adults—United States, 1998." (Drawing on Monitoring the Future Study, Press Release, December 18, 1998.) *Morbidity and Mortality Weekly Report,* 48 (45) (November 19, 1999), 1034–1039.

BRFSS is a state-based, random-digit-dialed telephone survey of the civilian, noninstitutionalized U.S. population aged greater than or equal to 18 years. To determine current cigarette smoking, respondents were asked "Have you ever smoked at least 100 cigarettes in your entire life?" and "Do you now smoke cigarettes every day, some days, or not at all?" Current cigarette smokers were defined as persons who reported having smoked at least 100 cigarettes during their lifetime and who currently smoke every day or some days. For cigar smoking (i.e., large cigars, cigarillos, and small cigars), respondents were asked "Have you ever smoked a cigar, even just a few puffs?" and "When was the last time you smoked a cigar?" Ever cigar smoking was defined as ever having smoked a cigar, even just a few puffs. Past month cigar smoking was defined as smoking a cigar within the previous month. Estimates were weighted to represent the populations of each state; because BRFSS data are state-specific, median values, rather than a national average, are reported.

During 1998, the median prevalence of current cigarette smoking was 22.9% (Table 1); state-specific prevalences ranged from 14.2% (Utah) to 30.8% (Kentucky). Range endpoints were higher for men (15.9%–36.5%) than for women (12.5%–28.5%). Median prevalence also was higher for men (25.3%) than for women (21.0%). Current cigarette smoking was highest in Kentucky (30.8%), Nevada (30.4%), West Virginia (27.9%), Michigan (27.4%), and South Dakota (27.3%). Current smoking prevalence was highest for men in South Dakota (36.5%) and for women in Kentucky (28.5%). Current smoking prevalence was lowest for both men (15.9%) and women (12.5%) in Utah.

The median prevalence of ever cigar smoking was 39.0% (Table 2); state-specific prevalences ranged from 14.8% (Arizona) to 52.0% (Alaska). The median prevalence of past month cigar smoking was 5.2%; state-specific prevalences ranged from 1.4% (Arizona) to 7.4% (Nevada). Range endpoints were higher for men than for women for both ever cigar smoking (23.1%–76.7% compared with 6.9%–26.0%) and past month cigar smoking (2.9–13.2% compared with 0.1–2.9%). Median prevalence rates for ever cigar smoking (67.4% compared with 15.8%) and past month cigar smoking (9.7% compared with 1.3%) also were higher for men than for women. Ever cigar smoking rates were highest in Alaska (52.0%), Wisconsin (49.7%), Nevada (48.6%), Michigan (47.9%), and Oregon (46.7). Ever cigar smoking was highest for men in Wisconsin (76.7%) and for women in Alaska (26.0%). Past month cigar smoking was highest in Nevada (7.4%), Indiana (7.3%), Illinois (7.1%), Michigan (6.9%), and New Jersey (6.6%). Past month cigar smoking was highest for men in Indiana (13.2%) and for women in Nevada (2.9%).

Reported by the following BRFSS coordinators: J. Cook, MBA, Alabama; P. Owen, Alaska; B. Bender, MBA, Arizona; T. Clark, Arkansas; B. Davis, PhD, California; M. Leff, MSPH, Colorado; M.

**Table 1**
**Prevalence of Current Cigarette Smoking\* among Adults, by State and Sex—United States, Behavioral Risk Factor Surveillance System, 1998**

| State | Men % | (95% CI) | Women % | (95% CI) | Total % | (95% CI) |
|---|---|---|---|---|---|---|
| Alabama | 27.2 | (±3.5) | 22.3 | (±2.5) | 24.6 | (±2.1) |
| Alaska | 28.3 | (±3.9) | 23.5 | (±3.4) | 26 | (±2.6) |
| Arizona | 24.7 | (±4.0) | 19.2 | (±3.3) | 21.9 | (±2.6) |
| Arkansas | 28.6 | (±3.0) | 23.7 | (±2.2) | 26 | (±1.8) |
| California | 21.9 | (±2.2) | 16.6 | (±1.7) | 19.2 | (±1.4) |
| Colorado | 26.4 | (±3.6) | 19.5 | (±2.6) | 22.8 | (±2.2) |
| Connecticut | 21.7 | (±3.3) | 20.6 | (±2.3) | 21.1 | (±2.0) |
| Delaware | 27.3 | (±4.1) | 21.9 | (±2.8) | 24.5 | (±2.4) |
| District of Columbia | 24.5 | (±4.4) | 19.0 | (±3.1) | 21.6 | (±2.6) |
| Florida | 23.5 | (±2.2) | 20.6 | (±1.6) | 22.0 | (±1.4) |
| Georgia | 28.0 | (±3.4) | 19.7 | (±2.3) | 23.7 | (±2.0) |
| Hawaii | 22.3 | (±3.6) | 16.7 | (±2.7) | 19.5 | (±2.3) |
| Idaho | 21.9 | (±2.2) | 18.8 | (±1.7) | 20.3 | (±1.4) |
| Illinois | 26.0 | (±2.7) | 20.6 | (±2.3) | 23.1 | (±1.8) |
| Indiana | 29.6 | (±3.2) | 22.7 | (±2.4) | 26.0 | (±2.0) |
| Iowa | 25.8 | (±2.7) | 21.1 | (±2.0) | 23.4 | (±1.7) |
| Kansas | 23.0 | (±2.5) | 19.5 | (±1.9) | 21.2 | (±1.5) |
| Kentucky | 33.3 | (±2.8) | 28.5 | (±2.0) | 30.8 | (±1.7) |
| Louisiana | 28.2 | (±3.9) | 23.1 | (±3.0) | 25.5 | (±2.4) |
| Maine | 21.2 | (±3.5) | 23.5 | (±3.2) | 22.4 | (±2.4) |
| Maryland | 24.3 | (±3.2) | 20.6 | (±2.4) | 22.4 | (±2.0) |
| Massachusetts | 22.5 | (±2.5) | 19.5 | (±1.9) | 20.9 | (±1.6) |
| Michigan | 30.3 | (±3.1) | 24.8 | (±2.4) | 27.4 | (±2.0) |
| Minnesota | 19.7 | (±1.9) | 16.4 | (±1.7) | 18 | (±1.3) |
| Mississippi | 26.9 | (±3.4) | 21.7 | (±2.4) | 24.1 | (±2.0) |
| Missouri | 29.4 | (±3.2) | 23.6 | (±2.3) | 26.3 | (±2.0) |
| Montana | 21.5 | (±3.0) | 21.5 | (±2.9) | 21.5 | (±2.1) |
| Nebraska | 25.2 | (±2.8) | 19.1 | (±2.1) | 22.1 | (±1.8) |
| Nevada | 32.6 | (±4.6) | 28.1 | (±4.7) | 30.4 | (±3.2) |
| New Hampshire | 25.7 | (±4.0) | 21.0 | (±3.3) | 23.3 | (±2.5) |
| New Jersey | 20.9 | (±3.0) | 17.6 | (±2.2) | 19.2 | (±1.9) |
| New Mexico | 25.1 | (±2.4) | 20.2 | (±2.0) | 22.6 | (±1.5) |
| New York | 25.9 | (±3.1) | 22.9 | (±2.5) | 24.3 | (±2.0) |
| North Carolina | 27.4 | (±3.6) | 22.3 | (±2.6) | 24.7 | (±2.2) |
| North Dakota | 21.8 | (±3.1) | 18.3 | (±2.6) | 20.0 | (±2.0) |
| Ohio | 29.7 | (±3.6) | 23.0 | (±2.7) | 26.2 | (±2.3) |
| Oklahoma | 26.7 | (±3.2) | 21.1 | (±2.3) | 23.8 | (±2.0) |
| Oregon | 21.6 | (±3.4) | 20.6 | (±2.7) | 21.1 | (±2.2) |
| Pennsylvania | 24.0 | (±2.5) | 23.6 | (±2.1) | 23.8 | (±1.6) |
| Rhode Island | 24.1 | (±2.5) | 21.5 | (±1.9) | 22.7 | (±1.6) |
| South Carolina | 29.8 | (±3.0) | 20.2 | (±2.0) | 24.7 | (±1.8) |
| South Dakota | 36.5 | (±3.6) | 18.5 | (±2.4) | 27.3 | (±2.3) |

*(continues)*

**Table 1 (cont.)**

|  | Men | | Women | | Total | |
|---|---|---|---|---|---|---|
| State | % | (95% CI) | % | (95% CI) | % | (95% CI) |
| Tennessee | 30.3 | (±3.2) | 22.4 | (±2.2) | 26.1 | (±1.9) |
| Texas | 25.3 | (±2.4) | 18.9 | (±1.6) | 22.0 | (±1.4) |
| Utah | 15.9 | (±2.5) | 12.5 | (±2.0) | 14.2 | (±1.6) |
| Vermont | 23.6 | (±2.7) | 21.0 | (±2.3) | 22.3 | (±1.8) |
| Virginia | 25.8 | (±3.1) | 20.2 | (±2.4) | 22.9 | (±1.9) |
| Washington | 22.4 | (±2.4) | 20.3 | (±2.1) | 21.4 | (±1.6) |
| West Virginia | 29.6 | (±3.3) | 26.4 | (±2.5) | 27.9 | (±2.0) |
| Wisconsin | 24.0 | (±3.4) | 22.9 | (±3.2) | 23.4 | (±2.3) |
| Wyoming | 23.9 | (±3.1) | 21.7 | (±2.3) | 22.8 | (±1.9) |
| Range | 15.9–36.5 | | 12.5–28.5 | | 14.2–30.8 | |
| Median | 25.3 | | 21.0 | | 22.9 | |

* Persons aged ≥18 years who reported having smoked ≥100 cigarettes and who reported smoking every day and some days.
CI = Confidence interval.

Adams, MPH, Connecticut; F. Breukelman, Delaware; I. Bullo, District of Columbia; S. Hoecherl, Florida; L. Martin, MS, Georgia; A. Onaka, PhD, Hawaii; J. Aydelotte, MA, Idaho; B. Steiner, MS, Illinois; K. Horvath, Indiana; K. MacIntyre, Iowa; J. Tasheff, Kansas; T. Sparks, Kentucky; B. Bates, MSPH, Louisiana; D. Maines, Maine; A. Weinstein, MA, Maryland; D. Brooks, MPH, Massachusetts; H. McGee, MPH, Michigan; N. Salem, PhD, Minnesota; D. Johnson, MS, Mississippi; T. Murayi, PhD, Missouri; P. Feigley, PhD, Montana; L. Andelt, PhD, Nebraska; E. DeJan, MPH, Nevada; L. Powers, MA, New Hampshire; G. Boeselager, MS, New Jersey; W. Honey, MPH, New Mexico; C. Baker, New York; P. Buescher, PhD, North Carolina; L. Shireley, MPH, North Dakota; P. Pullen, Ohio; N. Hann, MPH, Oklahoma; J. Grant-Worley, MS, Oregon; L. Mann, Pennsylvania; J. Hesser, PhD, Rhode Island; M. Wu, MD, South Carolina; M. Gildemaster, South Dakota; D. Ridings, Tennessee; K. Condon, Texas; K. Marti, Utah; C. Roe, MS, Vermont; K. Carswell, MPH, Virginia; K. Wynkoop-Simmons, PhD, Washington; F. King, West Virginia; P. Imm, MS, Wisconsin; M. Futa, MA, Wyoming. K. Gerlach, PhD, Robert Wood Johnson Foundation, Princeton, New Jersey. Office on Smoking and Health, National Center for Chronic Disease Prevention and Health Promotion, CDC.

*Editorial Note:* In 1996, the prevalence of cigarette smoking was added to the list of nationally notifiable health conditions reported by states to CDC (3). Current cigarette smoking has remained relatively stable during the 1990s in most states; however, smoking has declined

**Table 2**
**Prevalence of Cigar Smoking among Adults, by State and Sex—United States,**
**Behavioral Risk Factor Surveillance System, 1998**

| State | Ever cigar smoking* | | | | | | Past month cigar smoking † | | | | | |
|---|---|---|---|---|---|---|---|---|---|---|---|---|
| | Men | | Women | | Total | | Men | | Women | | Total | |
| | % | (95% CI) | % | (95% CI) | % | (95% CI) | % | (95% CI) | % | (95% CI) | % | (95% CI) |
| Alabama | 65.8 | (±3.9) | 18.4 | (±2.5) | 40.8 | (±2.5) | 11.2 | (±2.6) | 2.0 | (±0.9) | 6.3 | (±1.3) |
| Alaska | 75.4 | (±4.0) | 26.0 | (±3.6) | 52.0 | (±3.1) | 9.9 | (±2.8) | 2.0 | (±1.2) | 6.1 | (±1.6) |
| Arizona | 23.1 | (±3.7) | 6.9 | (±2.1) | 14.8 | (±2.1) | 2.9 | (±1.6) | 0.1 | (±0.1) | 1.4 | (±0.8) |
| Arkansas | 60.9 | (±3.2) | 13.0 | (±1.8) | 35.6 | (±2.0) | 9.8 | (±2.2) | 1.4 | (±0.7) | 5.4 | (±1.1) |
| California | 63.0 | (±2.5) | 20.7 | (±1.8) | 41.7 | (±1.7) | 10.1 | (±1.5) | 1.8 | (±0.6) | 5.9 | (±0.8) |
| Colorado | 66.9 | (±3.8) | 22.4 | (±2.9) | 44.2 | (±2.6) | 8.2 | (±2.0) | 0.9 | (±0.6) | 4.4 | (±1.0) |
| Connecticut | 56.8 | (±3.6) | 13.0 | (±2.0) | 33.8 | (±2.3) | 9.7 | (±2.2) | 1.2 | (±0.6) | 5.2 | (±1.1) |
| Delaware | 52.3 | (±4.4) | 9.0 | (±1.8) | 29.6 | (±2.6) | 9.8 | (±3.3) | 0.5 | (±0.3) | 4.9 | (±1.6) |
| District of Columbia | 32.3 | (±4.8) | 10.5 | (±2.4) | 20.6 | (±2.6) | 7.1 | (±2.5) | 1.0 | (±0.8) | 3.8 | (±1.2) |
| Florida | 59.4 | (±2.6) | 15.8 | (±1.6) | 36.6 | (±1.6) | 10.8 | (±1.7) | 2.1 | (±0.6) | 6.2 | (±0.9) |
| Georgia | 64.7 | (±3.9) | 19.0 | (±2.4) | 40.9 | (±2.4) | 10.5 | (±2.2) | 1.8 | (±1.0) | 5.9 | (±1.2) |
| Hawaii | 53.6 | (±4.3) | 11.6 | (±2.1) | 32.8 | (±2.6) | 6.6 | (±1.9) | 0.8 | (±0.6) | 3.7 | (±1.0) |
| Idaho | 64.5 | (±2.4) | 18.3 | (±1.6) | 40.9 | (±1.6) | 7.2 | (±1.3) | 1.6 | (±0.6) | 4.3 | (±0.7) |
| Illinois | 68.9 | (±4.2) | 18.4 | (±3.1) | 41.8 | (±2.9) | 13.1 | (±2.9) | 2.0 | (±1.6) | 7.1 | (±1.6) |
| Indiana | 72.6 | (±3.1) | 18.3 | (±2.2) | 44.2 | (±2.2) | 13.2 | (±2.4) | 2.0 | (±0.8) | 7.3 | (±1.2) |
| Iowa | 73.5 | (±2.7) | 18.0 | (±1.9) | 44.4 | (±1.9) | 9.7 | (±1.9) | 1.3 | (±0.5) | 5.2 | (±1.0) |
| Kansas | 49.8 | (±2.9) | 12.5 | (±1.6) | 30.5 | (±1.8) | 5.4 | (±1.2) | 0.5 | (±0.3) | 2.8 | (±0.6) |
| Kentucky | 67.5 | (±2.8) | 11.7 | (±1.4) | 38.2 | (±1.9) | 10.4 | (±2.1) | 1.1 | (±0.6) | 5.5 | (±1.1) |
| Louisiana | 57.6 | (±4.4) | 12.4 | (±2.4) | 33.8 | (±2.7) | 7.8 | (±2.2) | 0.8 | (±0.6) | 4.1 | (±1.1) |
| Maine | 56.9 | (±4.3) | 14.2 | (±2.8) | 34.6 | (±2.7) | 7.3 | (±2.4) | 1.3 | (±1.2) | 4.1 | (±1.3) |
| Maryland | 53.7 | (±3.6) | 15.5 | (±2.1) | 33.7 | (±2.2) | 8.8 | (±2.2) | 1.6 | (±1.0) | 5.0 | (±1.2) |
| Massachusetts | 60.8 | (+2.9) | 17.1 | (±2.1) | 37.8 | (±1.9) | 11.2 | (±1.8) | 1.2 | (±0.6) | 5.9 | (±0.9) |
| Michigan | 74.5 | (±3.0) | 23.6 | (±2.4) | 47.9 | (±2.2) | 12.1 | (±2.2) | 2.2 | (±0.8) | 6.9 | (±1.2) |
| Minnesota | 45.3 | (±2.4) | 16.1 | (±1.7) | 30.3 | (±1.5) | 7.5 | (±1.3) | 1.3 | (±0.5) | 4.3 | (±0.7) |
| Mississippi | 66.1 | (±3.6) | 14.3 | (±2.0) | 38.6 | (±2.3) | 9.5 | (±2.4) | 1.0 | (±0.6) | 5.0 | (±1.2) |
| Missouri | 69.0 | (±3.0) | 18.2 | (±2.1) | 42.2 | (±2.2) | 10.9 | (±2.3) | 2.1 | (±1.0) | 6.2 | (±1.2) |
| Montana | 68.7 | (±3.4) | 16.9 | (±2.5) | 42.1 | (±2.5) | 8.2 | (±2.0) | 0.2 | (±0.2) | 4.1 | (±1.0) |
| Nebraska | 70.4 | (±3.5) | 20.0 | (±2.2) | 44.2 | (±2.2) | 9.5 | (±2.0) | 1.3 | (±0.6) | 5.2 | (±1.0) |
| Nevada | 71.1 | (±4.3) | 25.6 | (±4.5) | 48.6 | (±3.3) | 11.9 | (±2.9) | 2.9 | (±1.4) | 7.4 | (±1.6) |
| New Hampshire | 66.8 | (±4.0) | 15.9 | (±3.0) | 40.6 | (±2.9) | 10.7 | (±3.2) | 1.5 | (±1.0) | 5.9 | (±1.6) |
| New Jersey | 54.3 | (±3.7) | 15.1 | (±2.2) | 33.8 | (±2.2) | 12.5 | (±2.4) | 1.3 | (±0.7) | 6.6 | (±1.2) |
| New Mexico | 68.6 | (±2.6) | 20.0 | (±1.9) | 43.6 | (±1.8) | 7.7 | (±1.5) | 0.9 | (±0.4) | 4.2 | (±0.8) |
| New York | 54.4 | (±3.5) | 15.2 | (±2.1) | 33.6 | (±2.2) | 12.1 | (±2.4) | 1.0 | (±0.5) | 6.2 | (±1.2) |
| North Carolina | 61.0 | (±4.3) | 16.2 | (±2.5) | 37.6 | (±2.6) | 7.6 | (±2.2) | 1.6 | (±1.0) | 4.5 | (±1.2) |
| North Dakota | 68.1 | (±3.6) | 15.7 | (±2.6) | 41.5 | (±2.6) | 7.0 | (±1.9) | 1.0 | (±0.8) | 4.0 | (±1.0) |
| Ohio | 65.7 | (±3.7) | 14.8 | (±2.2) | 39.0 | (±2.2) | 10.0 | (±2.5) | 1.8 | (±1.0) | 5.7 | (±1.3) |
| Oklahoma | 35.4 | (±3.4) | 12.7 | (±1.9) | 23.6 | (±2.0) | 3.5 | (±1.4) | 1.2 | (±0.7) | 2.3 | (±0.8) |
| Oregon | 72.5 | (±3.6) | 22.3 | (±2.7) | 46.7 | (±2.6) | 8.8 | (±2.3) | 1.1 | (±0.6) | 4.8 | (±1.2) |
| Pennsylvania | 60.0 | (±2.9) | 14.3 | (±1.7) | 35.8 | (±1.8) | 11.9 | (±2.0) | 1.9 | (±0.7) | 6.5 | (±1.0) |
| Rhode Island | 59.3 | (±2.9) | 15.1 | (±1.7) | 36.0 | (±1.8) | 10.8 | (±1.9) | 1.0 | (±0.5) | 5.5 | (±0.9) |
| South Carolina | 60.6 | (±3.1) | 15.7 | (±2.0) | 37.1 | (±2.0) | 10.0 | (±1.9) | 1.6 | (±0.7) | 5.6 | (±1.0) |
| South Dakota | 66.2 | (±3.5) | 14.2 | (±2.2) | 39.5 | (±2.4) | 9.7 | (±2.3) | 1.0 | (±0.7) | 5.2 | (±1.2) |
| Tennessee | 46.2 | (±3.5) | 11.3 | (±1.7) | 27.8 | (±2.0) | 7.4 | (±1.8) | 0.8 | (±0.4) | 3.9 | (±0.9) |
| Texas | 62.9 | (±2.6) | 16.7 | (±1.4) | 39.2 | (±1.7) | 7.5 | (±1.1) | 1.6 | (±0.6) | 4.5 | (±0.6) |
| Utah | 47.8 | (±3.8) | 13.4 | (±2.0) | 30.2 | (±2.2) | 3.9 | (±1.2) | 1.1 | (±0.7) | 2.5 | (±0.7) |
| Vermont | 66.8 | (±3.0) | 17.4 | (±2.1) | 41.3 | (±2.2) | 9.6 | (±3.1) | 0.9 | (±0.5) | 5.1 | (±1.6) |
| Virginia | 65.4 | (±3.6) | 15.4 | (±2.3) | 39.6 | (±2.5) | 10.5 | (±2.0) | 1.3 | (±0.6) | 5.7 | (±1.0) |
| Washington | 69.7 | (±2.6) | 22.4 | (±2.2) | 45.6 | (±1.9) | 9.0 | (±1.7) | 1.4 | (±0.5) | 5.1 | (±0.9) |
| West Virginia | 65.9 | (±3.3) | 15.0 | (±2.0) | 39.0 | (±2.2) | 7.1 | (±1.8) | 1.0 | (±0.6) | 3.8 | (±0.9) |
| Wisconsin | 76.7 | (±3.1) | 24.6 | (±3.1) | 49.7 | (±2.6) | 11.8 | (±2.5) | 1.6 | (±1.0) | 6.5 | (±1.3) |
| Wyoming | 71.9 | (±3.3) | 21.6 | (±2.3) | 46.5 | (±2.3) | 5.9 | (±1.5) | 1.2 | (±0.8) | 3.5 | (±0.8) |
| Range | 23.1-76.7 | | 6.9-26.0 | | 14.8-52.0 | | 2.9-13.2 | | 0.1-2.9 | | 1.4-7.4 | |
| Median | 64.7 | | 15.8 | | 39.0 | | 9.7 | | 1.3 | | 5.2 | |

* Persons aged ≥18 years who reported having ever smoked a cigar, even just a few puffs.
† Persons aged ≥18 years who reported smoking a cigar within the previous month.
CI = Confidence interval.

significantly in Minnesota since 1997 and increased significantly in South Dakota since 1996 (4). Utah is the only state to have achieved the health objective for 2000 to reduce cigarette smoking to a prevalence of no more than 15.0% among persons aged greater than or equal to 18 years (objective 3.4) (5). The wide variation in current cigarette smoking prevalence across states underscores the potential for prevention and the need for continued efforts aimed at reducing tobacco use.

The findings in this report indicate that cigar smoking prevalences by state vary significantly. Despite the health effects associated with cigar smoking, total cigar consumption in the United States was approximately 5.3 billion cigars in 1998 (6). Overall, cigar consumption in the United States declined during the 1970s and 1980s but began increasing in the 1990s (2); however, a 1998 report suggests that the recent growth in cigar sales may have slowed (7).

National surveys have used various questions to ascertain cigar smoking status (2). This variation, combined with the lack of inclusion of cigar smoking questions on most national surveys after 1992, makes comparison of data among national surveys difficult. Questions about cigar smoking were included on the 1998 National Health Interview Survey and will provide more data on national patterns in adult cigar smoking prevalence.

The findings in this report are subject to at least three limitations. First, data are based on self-reports without biochemical verification. Second, the lack of standardized questions for cigar use among surveys limits comparisons between state-specific estimates and national estimates. Third, these prevalence estimates are only for adults and do not include persons aged less than 18 years. However, to assess adequately the impact of cigarette and cigar smoking, data about the prevalence of youth tobacco use also should be considered. Data on youth cigarette and cigar smoking in 1997 are available through the Youth Risk Behavior Survey (8,9).

Decreases in tobacco use consistent with national health objectives for 2010 are achievable. Given the large differences in current cigarette and cigar smoking rates among states, future state surveys should continue to monitor cigar smoking among adults and youth, and questions should be standardized across surveys. Such information is important to direct policy changes and develop public health initiatives that address the negative health effects of smoking. Monitoring trends of cigarette smoking and the use of other tobacco products also is essential for evaluating state efforts aimed at reducing tobacco-related morbidity and mortality.

CDC recommends that states establish tobacco-control programs that are comprehensive, sustainable, and accountable (10). Guidelines determined by evidence-based analyses of existing comprehensive state tobacco-control programs have been prepared to help states assess options for comprehensive tobacco-control programs and to evaluate local funding priorities. The guidelines provide evidence to support each of nine specific elements of a comprehensive program, including community programs to reduce tobacco use, chronic disease programs to reduce the burden of tobacco-related diseases, school programs, enforcement, statewide programs, counter-marketing, cessation programs, surveillance and evaluation, and administration and management (10).

## References

1. CDC. Smoking-attributable mortality and years of potential life lost—United States, 1984. *MMWR* 1997;46:444–51.

2. National Cancer Institute. *Cigars: health effects and trends. Smoking and Tobacco Control Monograph No. 9.* Rockville, Maryland: US Department of Health and Human Services, National Institutes of Health, National Cancer Institute, 1998. NIH publication no. 98-4302.

3. CDC. Addition of prevalence of cigarette smoking as a nationally notifiable condition—June 1996. *MMWR* 1996;45:537.

4. CDC. *State tobacco control highlights—1999.* Atlanta, Georgia: US Department of Health and Human Services, CDC, National Center for Chronic Disease Prevention and Health Promotion, Office on Smoking and Health, 1999.

5. National Center for Health Statistics. *Healthy people 2000 review, 1989–1999.* Hyattsville, Maryland: US Department of Health and Human Services, Public Health Service, CDC, 1999.

6. US Department of Agriculture. *Tobacco situation and outlook report.* Washington, DC: US Department of Agriculture, Commodity Economics Division, Economics, Research Service, April 1999; document no. TBS-243.

7. Maxwell, J.C. Slowing sales: US cigar boom settles down. *Tobacco Reporter,* August 1999:36–8.

8. CDC. Youth Risk Behavior Surveillance—United States, 1997. *MMWR 1998;* 47 (no. SS-3).

9. CDC. Tobacco use among high school students—United States, 1997. *MMWR* 1998;47:229–33.

10. CDC. *Best practices for comprehensive tobacco control programs—August 1999.* Atlanta, Georgia: US Department of Health and Human Services, CDC, National Center for Chronic Disease Prevention and Health Promotion, Office on Smoking and Health, 1999.

# "Cigarette Smoking among American Teens Continues Gradual Decline": News Release and Data

*The Monitoring the Future Study conducted by the University of Michigan provides reliable and highly specific information relating to tobacco use in grades 8 through 12. This excerpt contains data from the study (Tables 3 and 4 and Figures 1, 2, and 3) and a press release, "Cigarette Smoking among American Teens Continues Gradual Decline," that accompanied the research data made public on December 17, 1999. The press release states that since the peak years of 1996 and 1997, smoking rates among eighth-graders, tenth-graders, and twelfth-graders continued to decline in 1999.*

*Table 3, "Long-term Trends in Prevalence of Cigarettes for Eighth, Tenth, and Twelfth Graders," shows specific findings of the survey. The figures listed under years are percentages. Figures under "Lifetime" are the percentages of students who have "ever" smoked a cigarette. Additional information and survey data may be found at the ISR MTF web site: www.monitoringthefuture.org/.*

*Figure 1, "Trends in Thirty-Day Prevalence of Cigarette Smoking for Eighth, Tenth, and Twelfth Graders," is simply a graphic representation of part of Table 1, showing the relative prevalence of cigarette smoking in the past 30 days.*

*Figure 2, "Trends in Perceived Harmfulness of Smoking for Eighth, Tenth, and Twelfth Graders," shows comparisons of the three groups with regard to the percentage of each group that sees "great risk" in smoking one or more packs per day.*

*Figure 3, "Trends in Perceived Availability of Cigarettes for Eighth and Tenth Graders," shows the percentages of each group that say it is "fairly easy" or "very easy" to obtain cigarettes. The source of the information shown in Figures 2 and 3 is Table 4, "Trends in Availability and Attitudes about Smoking One or More Packs of Cigarettes per Day, for Eighth, Tenth, and Twelfth Graders," which also contains data showing the percentages of students who said they disapproved of people smoking one or more packs per day. Notice that disapproval is highest among eighth graders and lowest among twelfth graders. At the same*

*Source:* Excerpted from: L. D. Johnston, P. M. O'Malley, and J. G. Bachman. 1999. *Drug Trends in 1999 Are Mixed.* (Monitoring the Future Study. Press Release. December 17, 1999.) Ann Arbor, MI: University of Michigan Information Services. Available online www.monitoringthefuture.org.

*time, the percentage of students who believe that people are harming themselves by smoking one or more packs a day is higher among twelfth graders than among eighth graders.*

## News Release

FOR RELEASE AT 1:00 P.M., EST, FRIDAY, DECEMBER 17, 1999

EDITORS: Results of this survey are scheduled to be announced at a news conference in Washington, D.C. Among those participating in the release of results will be Secretary of Health and Human Services Donna E. Shalala, Director of the Office of National Drug Control Policy Barry R. McCaffrey, Director of the National Institute on Drug Abuse Alan I. Leshner, and the principal investigator of the Monitoring the Future Study, Lloyd D. Johnston. For further information on the study, contact Johnston at (734) 763-5043.

ANN ARBOR—The proportion of teens who are current cigarette smokers continued to decline gradually in 1999, according to the 25th national survey of the Monitoring the Future Study, conducted at the University of Michigan Institute for Social Research (ISR) under grants from the National Institute on Drug Abuse [see Figure 1 and Table 3]. Cigarette smoking peaked in 1996 among eighth- and 10th-graders

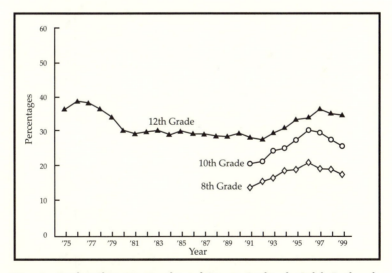

**Figure 1    Trends in Thirty-Day Prevalence of Cigarette Smoking for Eighth, Tenth, and Twelfth Graders**

*Source:* The Monitoring the Future Study, The University of Michigan. See Table 1 for exact numbers for selected years.

**Table [3]**
**Long-Term Trends in Prevalence of Cigarettes for Eighth, Tenth, and Twelfth Graders**

| | 1975 | 1976 | 1977 | 1978 | 1979 | 1980 | 1981 | 1982 | 1983 | 1984 | 1985 | 1986 | 1987 | 1988 | 1989 | 1990 | 1991 | 1992 | 1993 | 1994 | 1995 | 1996 | 1997 | 1998 | 1999 | '98–'99 change |
|---|---|---|---|---|---|---|---|---|---|---|---|---|---|---|---|---|---|---|---|---|---|---|---|---|---|---|
| *Lifetime [percent]* | | | | | | | | | | | | | | | | | | | | | | | | | | |
| 8th Grade | | | | | | | | | | | | | | | | | 44.0 | 45.2 | 45.3 | 46.1 | 46.4 | 49.2 | 47.3 | 45.7 | 44.1 | -1.6 |
| 10th Grade | | | | | | | | | | | | | | | | | 55.1 | 53.5 | 56.3 | 56.9 | 57.6 | 61.2 | 60.2 | 57.7 | 57.6 | -0.1 |
| 12th Grade | 73.6 | 75.4 | 75.7 | 75.3 | 74.0 | 71.0 | 71.0 | 70.1 | 70.6 | 69.7 | 68.8 | 67.6 | 67.2 | 66.4 | 65.7 | 64.4 | 63.1 | 61.8 | 61.9 | 62.0 | 64.2 | 63.5 | 65.4 | 65.3 | 64.6 | -0.7 |
| *Thirty-Day [percent]* | | | | | | | | | | | | | | | | | | | | | | | | | | |
| 8th Grade | | | | | | | | | | | | | | | | | 14.3 | 15.5 | 16.7 | 18.6 | 19.1 | 21.0 | 19.4 | 19.1 | 17.5 | -1.6s |
| 10th Grade | | | | | | | | | | | | | | | | | 20.8 | 21.5 | 24.7 | 25.4 | 27.9 | 30.4 | 29.8 | 27.6 | 25.7 | -1.9 |
| 12th Grade | 36.7 | 38.8 | 38.4 | 36.7 | 34.4 | 30.5 | 29.4 | 30.0 | 30.3 | 29.3 | 30.1 | 29.6 | 29.4 | 28.7 | 28.6 | 29.4 | 28.3 | 27.8 | 29.9 | 31.2 | 33.5 | 34.0 | 36.5 | 35.1 | 34.6 | -0.5 |
| *Daily [percent]* | | | | | | | | | | | | | | | | | | | | | | | | | | |
| 8th Grade | | | | | | | | | | | | | | | | | 7.2 | 7.0 | 8.3 | 8.8 | 9.3 | 10.4 | 9.0 | 8.8 | 8.1 | -0.7 |
| 10th Grade | | | | | | | | | | | | | | | | | 12.6 | 12.3 | 14.2 | 14.6 | 16.3 | 18.3 | 18.0 | 15.8 | 15.9 | -0.1 |
| 12th Grade | 26.9 | 28.8 | 28.8 | 27.5 | 25.4 | 21.3 | 20.3 | 21.1 | 21.2 | 18.7 | 19.5 | 18.7 | 18.7 | 18.1 | 18.9 | 19.1 | 18.5 | 17.2 | 19.0 | 19.4 | 21.6 | 22.2 | 24.6 | 22.4 | 23.4 | +0.7 |
| *1/2 pack+ per day [percent]* | | | | | | | | | | | | | | | | | | | | | | | | | | |
| 8th Grade | | | | | | | | | | | | | | | | | 3.1 | 2.9 | 3.5 | 3.6 | 3.4 | 4.3 | 3.5 | 3.6 | 3.3 | -0.3 |
| 10th Grade | | | | | | | | | | | | | | | | | 6.5 | 6.0 | 7.0 | 7.6 | 8.3 | 9.4 | 8.6 | 7.9 | 7.6 | -0.3 |
| 12th Grade | 17.9 | 19.2 | 19.4 | 18.8 | 16.5 | 14.3 | 13.5 | 14.2 | 13.8 | 12.3 | 12.5 | 11.4 | 11.4 | 10.6 | 11.2 | 11.3 | 10.7 | 10.0 | 10.9 | 11.2 | 12.4 | 13.0 | 14.3 | 12.6 | 13.2 | +0.6 |
| *Approx. Ns* | | | | | | | | | | | | | | | | | | | | | | | | | | |
| 8th Grade | | | | | | | | | | | | | | | | | 17,500 | 18,600 | 18,300 | 17,300 | 17,500 | 17,800 | 18,600 | 18,100 | 16,700 | |
| 10th Grade | | | | | | | | | | | | | | | | | 14,800 | 14,800 | 15,300 | 15,800 | 17,000 | 15,600 | 15,500 | 15,000 | 13,600 | |
| 12th Grade | 9,400 | 15,400 | 17,100 | 17,800 | 15,500 | 15,900 | 17,500 | 17,700 | 16,300 | 15,900 | 16,000 | 15,200 | 16,300 | 16,700 | 15,200 | 15,000 | 15,800 | 16,300 | 15,400 | 15,400 | 15,400 | 14,300 | 15,400 | 15,200 | 13,600 | |

*Note:* Level of significance of difference between the two years indicated: s = .05, ss = .01, sss = .001
*Source:* The Monitoring the Future Study, The University of Michigan.

[Approx. Ns = approximate numbers.]

nationwide, and in 1997 among 12th-graders. Since those peak years, there has been a gradual decline in smoking rates, which continued in 1999. Among eighth-graders, most of whom are 13 or 14 years old, 17.5 percent said they had smoked one or more cigarettes in the past 30 days (defined as "current smoking"), down by one-sixth from a peak of 21 percent in 1996. Among 10th-graders, most of whom are 15 or 16 years old, 25.7 percent reported smoking in the past 30 days, down nearly one-sixth from the peak of 30.4 percent in 1996. Among 12th-graders, most of whom are 17 or 18 years old, the decline has been very modest—from 36.5 percent in the peak year of 1997 to 34.6 percent in 1999. This represents only about a 5 percent drop in their smoking rate from their recent peak. Because these declines are gradual, in 1999 only the one-year decline among eighth-graders reached statistical significance. The one-year decline was just short of significance among 10th-graders, but the three-year declines in both eighth- and 10th-grades are highly significant. "Despite these recent improvements, over one-third of today's young people are active smokers by the time they leave high school. In fact, more than one in every six is an active smoker as early as eighth-grade," observes Lloyd D. Johnston, the study's principal investigator and a research scientist at the U-M Institute for Social Research (ISR). "These rates are still well above smoking rates in the early 90s, when teen smoking began to increase substantially." Rates of daily smoking are also down from their peak levels (in 1996 for eighth- and 10th-graders and in 1997 for 12th-graders) but did not show much improvement in 1999 specifically, according to Johnston and his collaborators, Jerald G. Bachman and Patrick M. O'Malley, both at the ISR. "The great majority of eighth- and 10th-grade students today say that they expect to complete college eventually, and it is in this large college-bound sector that we see most of the decline in smoking so far," reports Johnston. "There has been rather little improvement in the lower grades among the non-college bound, who traditionally have far higher smoking rates." Consistent with this fact, most of the recent improvement in eighth- and 10th-grade smoking has been concentrated among children from more educated families. Traditionally there were large smoking differences associated with social class, as measured by the parents' education level, notes Johnston. But those differences had narrowed considerably by 1990, according to the long-term data for high school seniors. Now those social class differences appear to be re-emerging. At 12th-grade there has been very little decline so far either among the college-bound or the non-college bound, although both groups have current smoking rates below their recent peak levels.

### Attitudes and Beliefs about Smoking
Since 1995 there has been a steady, though gradual, increase in the proportion of students at all three grade levels who see pack-a-day smoking as carrying a "great risk" of harm for the user. [The question

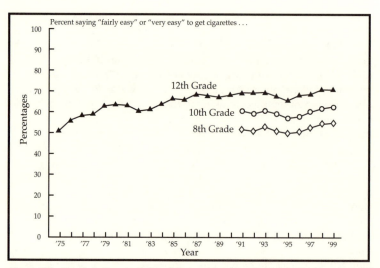

**Figure [2]   Trends in Perceived Harmfulness of Smoking for Eighth, Tenth, and Twelfth Graders**

*Source:* The Monitoring the Future Study. The University of Michigan. See Table 4 for exact numbers for selected years.

asks how much "people risk harming themselves (physically or in other ways) if they smoke one or more packs of cigarettes per day."] . . . [See Figure 2.] "Certainly this is a move in the right direction," Johnston comments, "but among the eighth-graders, even today only 55 percent think there is a great risk of harm associated with pack-a-day smoking." Disapproval of cigarette smoking also has risen a bit since 1996 in the case of the eighth- and 10th-graders, and since 1997 in the case of the 12th-graders. . . . [Table 4.] The researchers believe that the changes in perceived risk and disapproval in recent years may be attributable to the policy debate that has been raging in the country. Also, a number of states have conducted anti-smoking ad campaigns aimed at young people.

### Availability of Cigarettes

While the great majority of young teens feel that they could get cigarettes "fairly easily" or "very easily" if they wanted them (72 percent of eighth-graders and 88 percent of 10th-graders), reported accessibility has been falling since 1996, particularly among the eighth-graders. . . . [Figure 3.] "This suggests that the efforts by federal and state governments are starting to have an effect," comments Johnston. The U.S. Food and Drug Administration has been assisting states in monitoring retailer behavior and levying penalties on retailers who sell to underage buyers.

**Table 4**
**Trends in Availability and Attitudes about Smoking One or More Packs of Cigarettes per Day, for Eighth, Tenth, and Twelfth Graders**

| | 1975 | 1976 | 1977 | 1978 | 1979 | 1980 | 1981 | 1982 | 1983 | 1984 | 1985 | 1986 | 1987 | 1988 | 1989 | 1990 | 1991 | 1992 | 1993 | 1994 | 1995 | 1996 | 1997 | 1998 | 1999 | '98–'99 change |
|---|---|---|---|---|---|---|---|---|---|---|---|---|---|---|---|---|---|---|---|---|---|---|---|---|---|---|
| *Perceived Risk[a] [percent]* | | | | | | | | | | | | | | | | | | | | | | | | | | |
| 8th Grade | | | | | | | | | | | | | | | | | 51.6 | 50.8 | 52.7 | 50.8 | 49.8 | 50.4 | 52.6 | 54.3 | 54.8 | +0.5 |
| 10th Grade | | | | | | | | | | | | | | | | | 60.3 | 59.3 | 60.7 | 59.0 | 57.0 | 57.9 | 59.9 | 61.9 | 62.7 | +0.8 |
| 12th Grade | 51.3 | 56.4 | 58.4 | 59.0 | 63.0 | 63.7 | 63.3 | 60.5 | 61.2 | 63.8 | 66.5 | 66.0 | 68.6 | 68.0 | 67.2 | 68.2 | 69.4 | 69.2 | 69.5 | 67.6 | 65.6 | 68.2 | 68.7 | 70.8 | 70.8 | 0.0 |
| *Disapproval[b] [percent]* | | | | | | | | | | | | | | | | | | | | | | | | | | |
| 8th Grade | | | | | | | | | | | | | | | | | 82.8 | 82.3 | 80.6 | 78.4 | 78.6 | 77.3 | 80.3 | 80.0 | 81.4 | +1.4 |
| 10th Grade | | | | | | | | | | | | | | | | | 79.4 | 77.8 | 76.5 | 73.9 | 73.2 | 71.6 | 73.8 | 75.3 | 76.1 | +0.8 |
| 12th Grade | 67.5 | 65.9 | 66.4 | 67.0 | 70.3 | 70.8 | 69.9 | 69.4 | 70.8 | 73.0 | 72.3 | 75.4 | 74.3 | 73.1 | 72.4 | 72.8 | 71.4 | 73.5 | 70.6 | 69.8 | 68.2 | 67.2 | 67.1 | 68.8 | 69.5 | +0.7 |
| *Availability[c,d] [percent]* | | | | | | | | | | | | | | | | | | | | | | | | | | |
| 8th Grade | | | | | | | | | | | | | | | | | | 77.8 | 75.5 | 76.1 | 76.4 | 76.9 | 76.0 | 73.6 | 71.5 | -2.1ss |
| 10th Grade | | | | | | | | | | | | | | | | | | 89.1 | 89.4 | 90.3 | 90.7 | 91.3 | 89.6 | 88.1 | 88.3 | +0.7 |
| 12th Grade | | | | | | | | | | | | | | | | | | | | | | | | | | |
| *Approx. Ns:* | | | | | | | | | | | | | | | | | | | | | | | | | | |
| 8th Grade | | | | | | | | | | | | | | | | | 17,500 | 18,600 | 18,300 | 17,300 | 17,500 | 17,800 | 18,600 | 18,100 | 16,700 | |
| 10th Grade | | | | | | | | | | | | | | | | | 14,800 | 14,800 | 15,300 | 15,800 | 17,000 | 15,600 | 15,000 | 13,600 | | |
| 12th Grade | 2,800 | 2,900 | 3,100 | 3,800 | 3,300 | 3,300 | 3,600 | 3,600 | 3,300 | 3,300 | 3,300 | 3,000 | 3,300 | 3,300 | 2,800 | 2,600 | 2,500 | 2,700 | 2,800 | 2,600 | 2,600 | 2,400 | 2,600 | 2,500 | 2,300 | |

*Note:* Level of significance of difference between the two years indicated: s = .05, ss = .01, sss = .001
*Source:* The Monitoring the Future Study, The University of Michigan.

[a]The question text was: How much do you think people risk harming themselves (physically or in other ways) if they smoke one or more packs of cigarettes per day? Answer alternatives were: (1) No risk, (2) Slight risk, (3) Moderate risk, (4) Great risk, and (5) Can't say, drug unfamiliar. The percentage saying "great risk" is shown. For 8th and 10th graders: Beginning in 1999, perceived risk data based on two of four forms; N is two-thirds of N indicated.

[b]The question text was: Do you disapprove of people smoking one or more packs of cigarettes per day? For 12th graders, the question asked about people who are "18 or older." Answer alternatives were: (1) Don't disapprove, (2) Disapprove, and (3) Strongly disapprove. For 8th and 10th graders, there was another category—"Can't say, drug unfamiliar"—which was included in the calculation of these percentages. The percentage saying they "disapprove" or "strongly disapprove" is shown. For 8th and 10th graders: Beginning in 1999, disapproval data based on two of four forms; N is two-thirds of N indicated.

[c]The question text was: How difficult do you think it would be for you to get cigarettes, if you wanted some? Answer alternatives were: (1) Probably impossible, (2) Very difficult, (3) Fairly difficult, (4) Fairly easy, (5) Very easy, and (8) Can't say, drug unfamiliar (included in the calculation of these percentages). The percentage saying cigarettes are "fairly easy" or "very easy" to get is shown. In 1992 only, availability data based on one of two forms; N is one-half of N indicated. The question was not asked of the 12th graders.

[d]Data in 1992 based on one of two forms; N is one-half of N indicated.

[Approx. Ns = approximate numbers.]

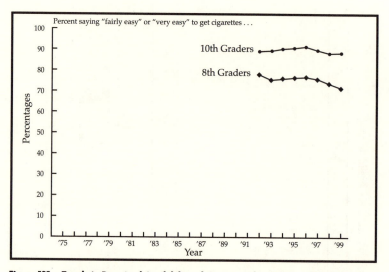

**Figure [3] Trends in Perceived Availability of Cigarettes for Eighth and Tenth Graders**

*Source:* The Monitoring the Future Study, The University of Michigan. See Table 4 for exact numbers for selected years.

The "Monitoring the Future" study is conducted at the University of Michigan's Institute for Social Research and has been supported since its inception under a series of investigator-initiated research grants from the National Institute of Drug Abuse, one of the National Institutes of Health in the U.S. Department of Health and Human Services. Annual surveys of high school seniors began in 1975, and annual surveys of eighth- and 10th-grade students were added, beginning in 1991. At each grade level students are drawn to be representative of all students in public and private schools in the coterminous United States. They complete self-administered, optically-scanned questionnaires given to them in their classrooms in the spring of the year by U-M personnel. In 1999 the sample sizes for eighth-, 10th-, and 12th-grades, respectively, were 17,300, 13,900, and 14,100. In all, about 45,000 students located in 433 secondary schools participated in the study.

# "Health Effects of Smoking among Young People"

*"Health Effects of Smoking among Young People," a CDC fact sheet, lists some of the more common consequences of early tobacco use, including retardation of lung growth and accelerated heart rate.*

Among young people, the short-term health consequences of smoking include respiratory and nonrespiratory damage, addiction to nicotine, and the associated risk of other drug use. Long-term health consequences of youth smoking are reinforced by the fact that most young people who smoke regularly continue to smoke throughout adulthood.[1]

- Cigarette smokers have a lower level of lung function than those persons who have never smoked.[2]
- Smoking reduces the rate of lung growth.[2]
- In adults, cigarette smoking causes heart disease and stroke. Studies have shown that early signs of these diseases can be found in adolescents who smoke.[3]
- Smoking hurts young people's physical fitness in terms of both performance and endurance—even among young people trained in competitive running.[4]
- On average, someone who smokes a pack or more of cigarettes each day lives 6.6 years less than someone who never smokes regularly.[5]
- The resting heart rates of young adult smokers are two to three beats per minute faster than non-smokers'.[4]
- Smoking at an early age increases the risk of lung cancer. For most smoking-related cancers, the risk rises as the individual continues to smoke.[6]
- Teenage smokers suffer from shortness of breath almost three times as often as teens who don't smoke, and produce phlegm more than twice as often as teens who don't smoke.[5]

## [Notes]

1. *SGR (Surgeon General Report), Preventing Tobacco Use Among Young People,* p. 15.
2. *SGR, Preventing Tobacco Use Among Young People,* p. 17.

---

*Source:* CDC, TIPS. 1995. "Health Effects of Smoking among Young People." Fact Sheet. Available online http://www.cdc.gov/tobacco/research_data/youth/stspta5.htm.

3. *SGR, Preventing Tobacco Use Among Young People,* p. 25 to p. 156.
4. *SGR, Preventing Tobacco Use Among Young People,* p. 28.
5. CDC unpublished data, 1993.
6. *SGR, Preventing Tobacco Use Among Young People,* p. 29.

# "Magazines with High Youth Readership in Which Philip Morris Advertises"

*The Master Settlement Agreement prohibits tobacco companies from targeting youth in advertising, but the Campaign for Tobacco-Free Kids reports some apparent violations by Philip Morris in "Magazines with High Youth Readership in Which Philip Morris Advertises." The list includes magazines with youth readership as high as 42 percent.*

Despite its claims that it does not market to kids, Philip Morris has advertised in recent months in the following magazines [see Table 5] with high youth readership. The magazines listed have youth readership totaling either more than two million or more than 15 percent of the magazine's overall readership.

**[Table 5]**
**[Youth Readership of Magazines in Which Philip Morris Has Advertised, 1999]**

| Magazine | Youth Readership (000) | Total Readership (000) | Youth Readership (%) |
|---|---|---|---|
| Sports Illustrated | 7,254 | 32,164 | 22.5 |
| People* | 5,634 | 43,766 | 12.9 |
| Rolling Stone | 3,318 | 11,779 | 28.2 |
| Inside Sports | 3,116 | 9,009 | 34.5 |
| Hot Rod | 2,937 | 9,431 | 31.1 |
| Glamour | 2,882 | 14,547 | 19.8 |
| Vibe | 2,864 | 6,782 | 42.2 |
| Sport | 2,605 | 7,907 | 32.9 |
| Motor Trend | 2,131 | 8,454 | 25.2 |
| Field and Stream | 2,016 | 13,807 | 14.6 |
| Outdoor Life | 1,867 | 9,185 | 20.3 |
| Mademoiselle | 1,540 | 6,509 | 23.6 |
| Spin | 1,316 | 4,109 | 32.0 |
| The Sporting News | 1,190 | 3,965 | 30.0 |

*Source:* Simmons Market Research Bureau.

*\*People* self-reports teen (12–19) readership of 3.8 million, of 17 percent of total readership.

*Source:* Campaign for Tobacco-Free Kids. 2000. "Magazines with High Youth Readership in Which Philip Morris Advertises." Internet posting, February 16, 2000. http://tobaccofreekids.org/reports/doubletalk/readership.shtml.

# When Quitting Seems Hard

*When Quitting Seems Hard, an excerpt from an American Cancer Society essay "Quit Spitting," provides advice for quitting spit tobacco. Recognizing that quitting is not easy, it emphasizes the importance of support and encouragement. For more information, call toll free 1-800-ACS-2345 or visit the ACS web site at: http://www.cancer.org/.*

Quitting spit tobacco is hard enough because changing any habit is tough. But added to that, quitting also means fighting an addiction to nicotine which is scientifically proven to be as strong as that of heroin and cocaine.

One way to help with quitting is nicotine gum, now available over-the-counter to people 18 or older. It will help ease your body's craving for nicotine. Once you've quit spit tobacco you might feel awkward at certain times because you don't have something in your mouth. Nicotine gum can also give you a psychological boost by providing something to chew while it also helps you kick spit tobacco.

You may feel fidgety or grouchy. You may have headaches, feel drowsy, or have trouble sleeping. These side effects are temporary. They will go away. After a week you will feel much better. An addiction to nicotine doesn't take hold of you in one day and you can't let go of it in one day. But every day, your work to get through withdrawal symptoms will get easier.

Here are some helpful tips:

- Tell your friends and family that you are quitting. Their support and encouragement will help.
- Take deep breaths of fresh air.
- Enjoy your favorite exercise.
- Brush your teeth and admire how clean they are.
- If you can, get your teeth professionally cleaned soon after you begin your new life without tobacco.
- Throw away any spit tobacco you have left as well as spitting cups and spittoons.
- Start a money jar to collect money you would have spent on spit tobacco.
- Avoid situations that will tempt you to dip or chew.

Don't give up if you slip up. You will feel some stress during this

*Source:* Excerpted from: American Cancer Society. 1996. "Quit Spitting." Pamphlet. http://www.cancer.org/. Atlanta, GA: American Cancer Society. Copyright 1996, American Cancer Society, Inc. Reprinted with permission.

time. Perhaps the pressures of school, friends, and home will trick you into believing that returning to your old habit isn't as bad as the hassle of quitting. That's not true. Remember, at a time in your life when many new choices are coming your way, this is a perfect opportunity to make a solid decision about your future. You can guarantee that it will be a tobacco-free future which will go a long way toward making it a cancer-free future as well.

# "Don't Let Another Year Go Up in Smoke: Quit Tips"

*"Don't Let Another Year Go Up in Smoke" has some encouraging words for smokers who want to kick the habit. Millions of people—half of all adult smokers—have already succeeded.*

Are you one of most smokers who want to quit? Then try following this advice.

1. Don't smoke any number or any kind of cigarette. Smoking even a few cigarettes a day can hurt your health. If you try to smoke fewer cigarettes, but do not stop completely, soon you'll be smoking the same amount again.

Smoking "low-tar, low-nicotine" cigarettes usually does little good, either. Because nicotine is so addictive, if you switch to lower-nicotine brands you'll likely just puff harder, longer and more often on each cigarette. The only safe choice is to quit completely.

2. Write down why you want to quit. Do you want

- to feel in control of your life?
- to have better health?
- to set a good example for your children?
- to protect your family from breathing other people's smoke?

Really wanting to quit smoking is very important to how much success you will have in quitting. Smokers who live after a heart attack are the most likely to quit for good. They're very motivated. Find a reason for quitting before you have no choice.

3. Know that it will take effort to quit smoking. Nicotine is habit forming. Half of the battle in quitting is knowing you need to quit. This will help you be more able to deal with the withdrawal that can occur, such as bad moods and really wanting to smoke. There are many ways smokers quit, including nicotine replacement products (gum and patches), but there is no easy way. Nearly all smokers have some feelings of nicotine withdrawal when they try to quit. Give yourself a month to get over these feelings. Take quitting one day at a time, even one minute at a time—whatever you need to succeed.

4. Half of all adult smokers have quit so you can, too. That's the good news. There are millions of people alive today who have learned to face life without a cigarette. For staying healthy, quitting smoking is the best step you can take.

5. Get help if you need it. Many groups offer written materials,

---

*Source:* CDC, TIPS. 1998. "Don't Let Another Year Go Up in Smoke: Quit Tips." Date accessed: December 1998. http://www.cdc.gov/tobacco/quit/quittip.htm.

programs, and advice to help smokers quit for good. Your doctor or dentist is also a good source of help and support. The following national groups have toll-free telephone numbers for information and resources:

- Agency for Health Care Policy and Research, Clinical Practice Guidelines on Smoking Cessation, Instant Fax 301-594-2800 [Press 1]; or call 1-800-358-9295 for physician materials and a "You Can Quit Smoking" consumer guide.
- American Cancer Society, 1-800-ACS-2345
- American Heart Association, 1-800-AHA-USA1
- American Lung Association, 1-800-LUNG-USA
- Office on Smoking and Health, 1-800-CDC-1311
- National Cancer Institute, 1-800-4-CANCER

# "Cigarettes Should Be Regulated Like Other Drugs, Says Director-General"

*"A cigarette is a euphemism for a cleverly crafted product that delivers just the right amount of nicotine to keep its user addicted for life before killing the person," says Dr. Gro Harlem Brundtland in "Cigarettes Should Be Regulated," a WHO news release. The director-general of the World Health Organization made the statement in Berlin in a speech to world drug regulators. She argued that the product should be judged "for what it is, not for what it is made out to be by the tobacco industry," making the point that it is not merely an agricultural product like other agricultural products, but "one of the most highly engineered consumer products available."*

The World Health Organization (WHO) today called on international food and drug regulators to bring cigarettes and tobacco industry products under the same ambit of rules that govern the sales and promotion of other nicotine delivery devices.

"A cigarette is a euphemism for a cleverly crafted product that delivers just the right amount of nicotine to keep its user addicted for life before killing the person," WHO Director-General Dr. Gro Harlem Brundtland told a key meeting of international drug regulators in Berlin today. WHO said the product should be judged for what it is, not what it is made out to be by the tobacco industry.

"The tobacco companies will inevitably tell you they are selling a simple agricultural product—chopped up tobacco leaves rolled into a paper tube. This is categorically untrue. Cigarettes are one of the most highly engineered consumer products available . . . the problem is the product itself," Dr. Brundtland told the Ninth International Conference of Drug Regulatory Authorities (ICDRA).

WHO's pitch is significant. This is the first time the world's premier health agency is calling food and drug regulators—whose remit it is to examine everything from chewing gum to pharmaceuticals to ensure public health safety standards—to rationalize rules that govern all forms of nicotine consumption. Tobacco control experts say it does not stand to reason that harmful nicotine from cigarettes is available freely while prescriptions are necessary for therapeutic nicotine sold by pharmaceuticals. As cigarette companies diversify, the incongruity increases. Food sold by tobacco companies is regulated but their cigarette brands are not. At one point, in 1890, tobacco was included in the US Pharmacopia but, after intense lobbying of Congress by tobacco manufacturers, it was excluded from the purview of the US Food and Drug Administration, which was created in 1906 with jurisdiction over those products listed in Pharmacopia.

WHO is now calling on that omission to be rectified.

Dr. Brundtland said the WHO would soon convene a high-level meeting of international regulators to assess the extent to which the tobacco industry had subverted science and used false advertising and promotional tactics to veil nicotine addiction as an act of free choice. She quoted a senior scientist at Philip Morris to show there was nothing innocent about a cigarette. According to the scientist, "The cigarette should not be construed as a product but a package. The product is nicotine. Think of the cigarette pack as a storage container for a day's supply of nicotine. Think of the cigarette as a dispenser for a dose of nicotine. Think of a puff of smoke as a vehicle of nicotine."

Dr. Brundtland also pointed out that the tobacco industry uses the camouflage of "light" cigarettes to fool smokers into believing they are consuming less dangerous products. An industry which does not respect life and works by rules that are its own and barred from scrutiny "shamefully uses this misperception to exploit health concerns as a marketing opportunity," she added.

A cigarette is the only consumer product which, when consumed as indicated, kills. Tobacco kills 4 million people today, over 70% of them in the developing world. In the first quarter of the next century, tobacco industry products will kill 10 million people, many of them in the prime of their lives. The decision to smoke is enhanced by advertising. The addictiveness of tobacco and its sales and promotion tactics severely handicap people's freedom to make informed decisions.

WHO is calling on the regulators, on whom lies the responsibility of ensuring that food and drugs meet public health standards, to turn their attention to tobacco which, in the next century, will emerge as the single most important public health hazard. The high point of WHO's contribution to global tobacco control will come through the Framework Convention on Tobacco Control (FCTC), on which preliminary work has begun. The Convention will address the entire gamut of tobacco related issues ranging from taxes to epidemiology, advertising bans and smuggling. WHO is calling for a synchronization of national plans and international action so that tobacco control takes root and spreads.

"Governments must push for the inclusion of effective tobacco content and design controls in the protocols to the FCTC," Dr. Brundtland said. "The time for meaningful and integrated tobacco control is now."

# "Targeting Tobacco Use: The Nation's Leading Cause of Death"

*"Targeting Tobacco Use: The Nation's Leading Cause of Death" is a fact sheet from the Centers for Disease Control and Prevention. It notes that although the risks of smoking are known, new smokers join the ranks every day, and some 430,000 smokers die every year, generating costs totaling more than $100 billion a year. The document also explains the role of the CDC in supporting prevention efforts.*

Today, nearly 3,000 young people across our country will begin smoking regularly. Of these 3,000 young people, 1,000 will lose that gamble to the diseases caused by smoking. The net effect of this is that among children living in America today, 5 million will die an early, preventable death because of a decision made as a child.—Donna E. Shalala, Ph.D., Secretary, U.S. Department of Health and Human Services.

. . . An estimated 47 million adults in the United States smoke cigarettes, even though this behavior will result in death or disability for half of all regular users. Tobacco use is responsible for more than 430,000 deaths each year, or one in every five deaths. Paralleling this enormous health burden is the economic burden of tobacco use: more than $50 billion in medical expenditures and another $50 billion in indirect costs.

Since the release in 1964 of the first Surgeon General's report on smoking and health, the scientific knowledge about the health consequences of tobacco use has greatly increased. It is now well documented that smoking can cause chronic lung disease, coronary heart disease, and stroke, as well as cancer of the lung, larynx, esophagus, mouth, and bladder. In addition, smoking is known to contribute to cancer of the cervix, pancreas, and kidney. Researchers have identified more than 40 chemicals in tobacco smoke that cause cancer in humans and animals. Smokeless tobacco and cigars also have deadly consequences, including lung, larynx, esophageal, and oral cancer.

The harmful effects of smoking do not end with the smoker. Women who use tobacco during pregnancy are more likely to have adverse birth outcomes, including babies with low birth weight, a

---

*Source:* CDC. 1998. "Targeting Tobacco Use: The Nation's Leading Cause of Death." At-a-Glance Fact Sheet. CDC, TIPS. http://www.cdc.gov/tobacco/overview/oshaag98.htm.

leading cause of death among infants. The health of nonsmokers is adversely affected by environmental tobacco smoke (ETS). Each year, exposure to ETS causes an estimated 3,000 nonsmoking Americans to die of lung cancer and causes up to 300,000 children to suffer from lower respiratory tract infections. Evidence also indicates that exposure to ETS increases the risk of coronary heart disease. . . .

## A Comprehensive, Broad-Based Approach to Tobacco Control

In the past, helping people quit smoking was the primary focus of efforts to reduce tobacco use. This strategy has been a critical one, since smoking cessation at all ages reduces the risk of premature death. In recent years, the focus of tobacco control has expanded to include strategies to prevent individuals from ever starting to smoke— particularly young people, since the decision to use tobacco is nearly always made in the teenage years, and about one-half of young people who take up smoking continue to use tobacco products as adults. This preventive strategy also includes efforts to protect people from exposure to ETS. . . .

A broad-based spectrum of federal, state, and local government agencies, professional and voluntary organizations, and academic institutions have joined together to advance the elements of a comprehensive approach to tobacco use, including:

- Eliminating exposure to ETS.
- Preventing initiation among youth.
- Promoting quitting among adults and youth.
- Eliminating disparities among population groups.

This comprehensive approach will involve

- State and community interventions.
- Countermarketing.
- Policy/Regulation.
- Surveillance/Evaluation.

## CDC's Tobacco Control Framework

With estimated fiscal year 1999 appropriations of approximately $74 million, the Centers for Disease Control and Prevention (CDC) provides national leadership for a comprehensive, broad-based approach to preventing and controlling tobacco use. Through collaboration with the states, with national, professional, and voluntary organizations, with academic institutions, and with other federal agencies, CDC leads and coordinates strategic efforts to prevent tobacco use among young people, promote smoking cessation, and reduce exposure to ETS. Designed to reach multiple populations, these activities target high-risk groups, such as young people, racial and ethnic minority groups, blue-collar workers, persons with low income, and women.

## Building State Capacity

Beginning in fiscal year 1999, CDC is supporting comprehensive programs for preventing and controlling tobacco use in all 50 states, the District of Columbia, and 8 territories (American Samoa, the Commonwealth of Puerto Rico, the Virgin Islands, the Federated States of Micronesia, Guam, the Northern Mariana Islands, the Republic of the Marshall Islands, and the Republic of Palau). CDC provides extensive technical assistance and training through site visits, workshops, and teleconferences on planning, developing, implementing, and evaluating tobacco control programs. Although CDC supports all 50 states with fiscal year 1999 funding, available resources enable only limited support to 33 states and more comprehensive support to 17 states. States funded at the higher level are able to more comprehensively address youth and adult tobacco use, as well as ETS issues, and to fully extend these programs to reach diverse and local communities in all states. To define and implement the best practices in prevention and control, CDC is working with all states receiving substantial additional resources from excise taxes or settlements with the tobacco industry.

CDC supports and actively collaborates with a variety of national organizations (for example, the National Medical Association and the National Association for African-Americans for Positive Imagery) to ensure the participation of diverse community groups, coalitions, and community leaders in tobacco control efforts.

## Reaching Young People through Schools

The key to reducing adult tobacco use is to prevent children from using tobacco. CDC's state-based tobacco control programs are closely linked to its state-based coordinated health education programs in schools.

- CDC has established a national framework to support coordinated school health programs. In addition to fiscal year 1999 tobacco control resources of $74 million, CDC dedicates more than $9.6 million to directly support 15 states to provide coordinated health programs in schools. Such programs are targeting high-risk health behaviors among young people, with a heavy focus on tobacco use. Planned, sequential health education has been found to result in a 37% reduction in the onset of smoking among 7th-grade students. CDC also collaborates with more than 30 professional and voluntary organizations to assist schools and agencies serving youth in developing model policies and guidelines. States are using these to implement effective school health programs.

- Through the Research to Classroom project, CDC works with health and education experts to identify curricula that have credible evidence of reducing health risk behaviors, including tobacco use, among young people. CDC then ensures that curricula found to be effective, together with training, are available to schools nationwide.

## Expanding the Science Base

CDC strengthens and expands the scientific foundation for tobacco-use prevention and control by examining trends, patterns, health effects, and the economic costs associated with tobacco use. For example,

- Since 1964, the Surgeon General's reports on the health consequences of tobacco use have documented comprehensive, scientific findings on cigarette smoking and smokeless tobacco use. Recent reports have addressed tobacco use among adolescents and special populations.
- CDC's *Morbidity and Mortality Weekly Report (MMWR)* serves as a major outlet for surveillance data and research findings on tobacco use. Topics include the enactment and status of state laws on tobacco use and trends in smoking initiation and prevalence among young people.
- CDC's Smoking-Attributable Mortality, Morbidity, and Economic Cost (SAMMEC) software, a computer program designed to estimate deaths, disease impact, and costs related to smoking, provides essential information to state tobacco control programs and for Surgeon General's reports, *MMWR* articles, and responses to public inquiries.
- CDC's State Tobacco Activities Tracking and Evaluation (STATE) System is a state-based comprehensive surveillance system that tracks legislative, programmatic, and epidemiologic data that will be used for reporting on current status and trends of tobacco use. The system will answer state-specific queries and generate reports on topic areas of particular interest to individual states. In 1999, information from the STATE System will be available to states via the Internet. CDC is collaborating with the World Health Organization to create a similar system to support international efforts to reduce tobacco use.
- CDC's air toxicants laboratory is developing and applying

laboratory technology to further public health efforts to prevent death and disease resulting from tobacco use and ETS exposure. Specific areas of interest are tobacco additives, toxic chemicals in cigarette smoke, and biological monitoring to assess exposure to harmful substances in tobacco products.

## Communicating Information to the Public

CDC serves as a primary resource for tobacco and health information. In this role, CDC develops and distributes important information to the public and other interested groups nationwide. For example,

- CDC responds to a diverse audience, including 50,000 personal inquiries and 30,000 automatic voice-operated facsimile requests, through a variety of channels, including brochures, fact sheets, articles, and video products—many available through a toll-free dissemination service. In addition, CDC provides the public with ready access to tobacco use prevention information through a Web site on the Internet. This Web site documented approximately 200,000 visits during 1998.
- Responding to a call from the Secretary of Health and Human Services, CDC developed the Secretarial Initiative: Reduce Tobacco Use Among Teens and Preteens. Through partnerships with other federal, state, and local agencies, key tobacco control messages are being communicated through a variety of avenues, including the media, schools, and communities. The following themes are being highlighted:

    —Promote positive alternatives to tobacco use—through national- and local-level sports activities as well as dance, theater, and art.
    —Empower young people—through educational programs such as Research to Class-rooms, MediaSharp, and MTV Talks Tobacco, and by providing resources to mentors.
    —Deglamorize tobacco use through the entertainment industry—by providing technical assistance to movie and television productions, coordinating with producers, directors, and writers, and establishing partnerships with spokespeople, such as the popular music group Boyz II Men.
    —Involve parents and families—through scientifically grounded interventions while offering support and enhancing skills to reduce tobacco use.

—Implement paid counteradvertising campaigns—for example, through the Media Campaign Resource Center.

• Through the Media Campaign Resource Center, CDC develops, obtains, and distributes high-quality materials to help states and local programs conduct counteradvertising media campaigns to prevent tobacco use. Materials available include television, radio, magazine, newspaper, and billboard advertisements. The resource center also provides direct technical assistance in conducting counteradvertising campaigns. . . .

## Facilitating Action through Partners

CDC works with state health departments, national organizations, other federal agencies, and professional, voluntary, academic, medical, and international organizations to reduce tobacco use. For example:

• CDC supports the Interagency Committee on Smoking and Health and cosponsors the annual Tobacco Use Prevention Summer Institute.
• CDC is the lead agency for the Healthy People 2000/2010 national objectives on tobacco use. This role includes monitoring the nation's progress toward reaching the year 2000 and 2010 goals for reducing tobacco use. The objectives include topics such as youth and adult smoking prevalence, reduction of tobacco-related diseases, cessation treatment, ETS exposure, and state legislation for clean indoor air.
• CDC collaborates with the National Association of County and City Health Officials, the National Association of Local Boards of Health, the National Conference of State Legislators, and the Association of State and Territorial Health Officials in the coordination and promotion of tobacco prevention and control activities.
• Through an agreement with the World Health Organization, CDC serves as the only WHO Collaborating Center for Smoking and Health in the United States [see for example, Table 6] and as the catalyst for communication between all nine international WHO Collaborating Centers and the six WHO Regional Offices. CDC prepares and implements international and regional studies, as well as epidemiologic research, and provides health education and other assistance to help international organizations and other countries reduce tobacco use.

[Table 6]
**Prevalance of Cigarette Smoking among Adults and Youths—United States, 1997**

| State | Adults | Youth | State | Adults | Youth |
|---|---|---|---|---|---|
| Alabama | 24.7 | 35.8 | Montana | 20.5 | 38.1 |
| Alaska | 26.7 | n/a | Nebraska | 22.2 | n/a |
| Arizona | 21.1 | n/a | Nevada | 27.7 | 29.4 |
| Arkansas | 28.5 | 43.2 | New | | |
| California | 18.4 | 26.6 | Hampshire | 24.8 | 39.6* |
| Colorado | 22.6 | 36.6 | New Jersey | 21.5 | 37.9* |
| Connecticut | 21.8 | 35.2 | New Mexico | 22.1 | n/a |
| Delaware | 26.6 | 35.0* | New York | 23.1 | 32.9 |
| District of | | | North Carolina | 25.8 | 35.8* |
| Columbia | 18.8 | 22.7 | North Dakota | 22.2 | 45.0* |
| Florida | 23.6 | 33.6 | Ohio | 25.1 | 34.5 |
| Georgia | 22.4 | n/a | Oklahoma | 24.6 | n/a |
| Hawaii | 18.6 | 29.2 | Oregon | 20.7 | n/a |
| Idaho | 19.9 | n/a | Pennsylvania | 24.3 | n/a |
| Illinois | 23.2 | n/a | Rhode Island | 24.2 | 35.4 |
| Indiana | 26.3 | n/a | South Carolina | 23.4 | 38.6 |
| Iowa | 23.1 | 37.5 | South Dakota | 24.3 | 44.0 |
| Kansas | 22.7 | n/a | Tennessee | 26.9 | 38.6* |
| Kentucky | 30.8 | 47.0 | Texas | 22.6 | n/a |
| Louisiana | 24.6 | 36.4 | Utah | 13.7 | 16.4 |
| Maine | 22.7 | 39.2 | Vermont | 23.2 | 38.3 |
| Maryland | 20.6 | n/a | Virginia | 24.6 | n/a |
| Massachusetts | 20.4 | 34.4 | Washington | 23.9 | n/a |
| Michigan | 26.1 | 38.2 | West Virginia | 27.4 | 41.9 |
| Minnesota | 21.8 | n/a | Wisconsin | 23.2 | 36.0 |
| Mississippi | 23.2 | 31.3 | Wyoming | 24.0 | 37.4 |
| Missouri | 28.7 | 40.3 | United States | 23.2 | 36.4 |

n/a = Data not available.

*Unweighted data apply only to the students participating in the survey. For California, the survey excludes students from the Los Angeles Unified School District.

*Sources:* CDC, Behavioral Risk Factor Surveillance System (data on persons aged 18 years or older who reported having smoked 100 or more cigarettes and who reported currently smoking every day or some day), and CDC, Youth Risk Behavior Surveillance System (data on young people in grades 9–12 who reported smoking cigarettes on one or more of the 30 days preceding the survey).

For more information or additional copies of this document, please contact the Centers for Disease Control and Prevention, National Center for Chronic Disease Prevention and Health Promotion, Mail Stop K-50, 4770 Buford Highway NE, Atlanta, GA 30341-3717, 800-CDC-1311. E-mail: ccdinfo@cdc.gov; [and URL:] http://www.cdc.gov/tobacco.

## Statement by President Clinton (March 21, 2000) in Response to the Supreme Court Ruling That the FDA Does Not Have the Authority to Regulate Tobacco

*The following statement by by President Clinton is his official statement in response to the Supreme Court's 5–4 ruling March 21, 2000, that the Federal Drug Administration does not have authority to regulate tobacco products.*

Since we took office, Vice President Gore and I have worked hard to protect our children from the dangers of tobacco. Five years ago, the FDA put forward an important proposal to protect children from tobacco by eliminating advertising aimed at children and curbing minors' access to tobacco products. Today's Supreme Court opinion, while holding that Congress has not given FDA the authority to regulate tobacco products, does affirm our view that tobacco use by young people "poses perhaps the single most significant threat to public health in the United States."

# Alcohol, Tobacco, and Other Drug Prevention

*This excerpt from a CSAP article on alcohol, tobacco, and other drugs (ATOD) suggests a number of strategies for preventing use of tobacco.*

Several strategies are used effectively, especially in combination:

- *Information Dissemination*—This strategy provides awareness and knowledge of the nature and extent of ATOD use, abuse, and addiction and their effects on individuals, families, and communities, as well as information to increase perceptions of risk associated with ATOD use. It also provides knowledge and awareness of prevention policies, programs, and services. It helps set and reinforce norms (for example, underage drinking and drug dealers will not be tolerated in this neighborhood).
- *Prevention Education*—This strategy aims to affect critical life and social skills, including decision making, refusal skills, critical analysis (for example, of media messages), and systematic and judgmental abilities. Children learn to comprehend and integrate no-use messages.
- *Alternatives*—This strategy provides for the participation of targeted population in activities that exclude ATOD use by youth. Constructive and healthy activities offset the attraction to, or otherwise meet the needs usually filled by, ATOD use.
- *Problem Identification and Referral*—This strategy calls for identification, education, and counseling for those youth who have indulged in age-inappropriate use of tobacco products or alcohol, or who have indulged in the first use of illicit drugs. Activities under this strategy would include screening for tendencies toward substance abuse and referral for preventative treatment for curbing such tendencies.
- *Community-Based Process*—This strategy aims to enhance the ability of the community to provide prevention and treatment services to ATOD disorders more effectively. Activities include organizing, planning, enhancing efficiency and effectiveness of services implementation, interagency

---

*Source:* Excerpted from: Center for Substance Abuse Prevention. 2000 (access date). "Frequently Asked Questions about Preventing Alcohol, Tobacco, and Other Drug Problems." http://www.samhsa.gov/centers/csap/csap.html. For additional information, call or write CSAP's National Clearinghouse for Alcohol and Drug Information at 1-800-729-6686; P.O. Box 2345 Rockville, MD 20852. Free materials will be sent within four to six weeks.

collaboration, coalition building, and networking. Building healthy communities encourages healthy lifestyle choices.

- *Environmental Approach*—This strategy sets up or changes written and unwritten community standards, codes, and attitudes—influencing incidence and prevalence of ATOD problems in the general population. Included are laws to restrict availability and access, price increases, and community-wide actions.

# Directions in Development—*Curbing the Epidemic: Governments and the Economics of Tobacco Control*

*Curbing the Epidemic: Governments and the Economics of Tobacco Control, a report by the World Bank, explains how low- and middle-income nations will be affected as the worldwide tobacco epidemic begins to sweep through developing nations, where smoking is still on the rise, in contrast to high-income nations, where it is already on the decline. The report stresses the potential for reducing smoking-related mortality by means of cost-effective policies.*

## Summary

Smoking already kills one in 10 adults worldwide. By 2030, perhaps a little sooner, the proportion will be one in six, or 10 million deaths per year—more than any other single cause. Whereas until recently this epidemic of chronic disease and premature death mainly affected the rich countries, it is now rapidly shifting to the developing world. By 2020, seven of every 10 people killed by smoking will be in low- and middle-income nations.

## Why This Report?

Few people now dispute that smoking is damaging human health on a global scale. However, many governments have avoided taking action to control smoking—such as higher taxes, comprehensive bans on advertising and promotion, or restrictions on smoking in public places—because of concerns that their interventions might have harmful economic consequences. For example, some policymakers fear that reduced sales of cigarettes would mean the permanent loss of thousands of jobs; that higher tobacco taxes would result in lower government revenues; and that higher prices would encourage massive levels of cigarette smuggling.

This report examines the economic questions that policymakers must address when contemplating tobacco control. It asks whether smokers know the risks and bear the costs of their consumption choices, and explores the options for governments if they decide that intervention is justified. The report assesses the expected consequences of tobacco control for health, for economies, and for individuals. It

---

*Source:* World Bank. 1999. *Curbing the Epidemic: Governments and the Economics of Tobacco Control.* Washington, DC: World Bank. Reprinted with permission.

demonstrates that the economic fears that have deterred policymakers from taking action are largely unfounded. Policies that reduce the demand for tobacco, such as a decision to increase tobacco taxes, would not cause long-term job losses in the vast majority of countries. Nor would higher tobacco taxes reduce tax revenues; rather, revenues would climb in the medium term. Such policies could, in sum, bring unprecedented health benefits without harming economies. . . .

## Current Trends

About 1.1 billion people smoke worldwide. By 2025, the number is expected to rise to more than 1.6 billion. In the high-income countries, smoking has been in overall decline for decades, although it continues to rise in some groups. In low- and middle-income countries, by contrast, cigarette consumption has been increasing. Freer trade in cigarettes has contributed to rising consumption in these countries in recent years.

Most smokers start young. In the high-income countries, about eight out of 10 begin in their teens. While most smokers in low- and middle-income countries start in the early twenties, the peak age of uptake in these countries is falling. In most countries today, the poor are more likely to smoke than the rich.

## The Health Consequences

The health consequences of smoking are twofold. First, the smoker rapidly becomes addicted to nicotine. The addictive properties of nicotine are well documented but are often underestimated by the consumer. In the United States, studies among final-year high school students suggest that fewer than two out of five smokers who believe that they will quit within five years actually do quit. About seven out of 10 adult smokers in high-income countries say they regret starting, and would like to stop. Over decades and as knowledge has increased, the high-income countries have accumulated a substantial number of former smokers who have successfully quit. However, individual attempts to quit have low success rates: of those who try without the assistance of cessation programs, about 98 percent will have started again within a year. In low- and middle-income countries, quitting is rare.

Smoking causes fatal and disabling disease, and, compared with other risky behaviors, the risk of premature death is extremely high. Half of all long-term smokers will eventually be killed by tobacco, and of these, half will die during productive middle age, losing 20 to 25 years of life. The diseases associated with smoking are well documented and include cancers of the lung and other organs, ischemic heart disease and other circulatory diseases, and respiratory diseases such as emphysema. In regions where tuberculosis is prevalent, smokers also face a greater risk than nonsmokers of dying from this disease.

Since the poor are more likely to smoke than the rich, their risk of smoking-related and premature death is also greater. In high- and middle-income countries, men in the lowest socioeconomic groups are up to twice as likely to die in middle age as men in the highest socioeconomic groups, and smoking accounts for at least half their excess risk.

Smoking also affects the health of nonsmokers. Babies born to smoking mothers have lower birth weights, face greater risks of respiratory disease and are more likely to die of sudden infant death syndrome than babies born to nonsmokers. Adult nonsmokers face small but increased risks of fatal and disabling disease from exposure to others' smoke.

## Do Smokers Know Their Risks and Bear Their Costs?

Modern economic theory holds that consumers are usually the best judges of how to spend their money on goods and services. This principle of consumer sovereignty is based on certain assumptions: first, that the consumer makes rational and informed choices after weighing the costs and benefits of purchases, and, second, that the consumer incurs all costs of the choice. When all consumers exercise their sovereignty in this way—knowing their risks and bearing their costs—then society's resources are, in theory, allocated as efficiently as possible. This report examines consumers' incentives to smoke, asks whether their choice to do so is like other consumption choices, and whether it results in an efficient allocation of society's resources, before discussing the implications for governments.

Smokers clearly perceive benefits from smoking, such as pleasure and the avoidance of withdrawal, and weigh these against the private costs of their choice. Defined this way, the perceived benefits outweigh the perceived costs, otherwise smokers would not pay to smoke. However, it appears that the choice to smoke may differ from the choice to buy other consumer goods in three specific ways.

First, there is evidence that many smokers are not fully aware of the high risks of disease and premature death that their choice entails. In low- and middle-income countries, many smokers may simply not know about these risks. In China in 1996, for example, 61 percent of smokers questioned thought that tobacco did them "little or no harm." In high-income countries, smokers know they face increased risks, but they judge the size of these risks to be lower and less well established than do nonsmokers, and they also minimize the personal relevance of these risks.

Second, smoking is usually started in adolescence or early adulthood. Even when they have been given information, young people do not always have the capacity to use it to make sound decisions. Young people may be less aware than adults of the risk to their health that smoking poses. Most new recruits and would-be smokers also underestimate the risk of becoming addicted to nicotine. As a result, they seriously underestimate the future costs of smoking— that is, the costs of being unable in later life to reverse a youthful decision to smoke. Societies generally recognize that adolescent decision-making capacity is limited, and restrict young people's freedom to make certain choices, for example, by denying them the right to vote or to marry until a certain age. Likewise, societies may consider it valid to restrict young people's freedom to choose to become addicted to smoking, a behavior that carries a much greater risk of eventual death than most other risky activities in which young people engage.

Third, smoking imposes costs on nonsmokers. With some of their costs borne by others, smokers may have an incentive to smoke more than they would if they were bearing all the costs themselves. The costs to nonsmokers clearly include health damage as well as nuisance and irritation from exposure to environmental tobacco smoke. In addition, smokers may impose financial costs on others. Such costs are more difficult to identify and quantify, and variable in place and time, so it is not yet possible to determine how they might affect individuals' incentives to smoke more or less. However, we briefly discuss two such costs, healthcare and pensions.

In high-income countries, smoking-related healthcare accounts for between 6 and 15 percent of all annual healthcare costs. These figures will not necessarily apply to low- and middle-income countries, whose epidemics of smoking-related diseases are at earlier stages and may have other qualitative differences. Annual costs are of great importance to governments but, for individual consumers, the key question is the extent to which the costs will be borne by themselves or by others.

In any given year, smokers' healthcare costs will on average exceed nonsmokers'. If healthcare is paid for to some extent by general public taxation, nonsmokers will thus bear a part of the smoking population's costs. However, some analysts have argued that, because smokers tend to die earlier than nonsmokers, their lifetime healthcare costs may be no greater, and possibly even smaller, than nonsmokers'. This issue is controversial, but recent reviews in high-income countries suggest that smokers' lifetime costs are, after all, somewhat higher than nonsmokers', despite their shorter lives. However, whether higher or lower, the extent to which smokers impose their costs on others will depend on many factors, such as from the existing level of cigarette taxes, and how much healthcare is provided by the public sector. In low- and middle-income countries, meanwhile, there have been no reliable studies of these issues.

The question of pensions is equally complex. Some analysts in high-income countries have argued that smokers "pay their way" by contributing to public pension schemes and then dying earlier, on average, than nonsmokers. However, this question is irrelevant to the low- and middle-income countries where most smokers live, because public pension coverage in these countries is low.

In sum, smokers certainly impose some physical costs, including health damage, nuisance, and irritation, on nonsmokers. They may also impose financial costs, but the scope of these is still unclear.

## Appropriate Responses

It appears unlikely, then, that most smokers either know their full risks or bear the full costs of their choice. Governments may consider that intervention is therefore justified, primarily to deter children and adolescents from smoking and to protect nonsmokers, but also to give adults all the information they need to make an informed choice.

Governments' interventions should ideally remedy each identified problem specifically. Thus, for example, children's imperfect judgments about the health effects of smoking would most specifically be addressed by improving their education and that of their parents, or by restricting their access to cigarettes. But adolescents respond poorly to health education, perfect parents are rare, and existing forms of restriction on cigarette sales to the young do not work, even in the high-income countries. In reality, the most effective way to deter children from taking up smoking is to increase taxes on tobacco. High prices prevent some children and adolescents from starting and encourage those who already smoke to reduce their consumption.

Taxation is a blunt instrument, however, and if taxes on cigarettes are raised, adult smokers will tend to smoke less and pay more for the cigarettes that they do purchase. In fulfilling the goal of protecting children and adolescents, taxation would thus also be imposing costs on adult smokers. These costs might, however, be considered acceptable, depending upon how much societies value curbing consumption in children. In any case, one long-term effect of reducing adult consumption may be to further discourage children and adolescents from smoking.

The problem of nicotine addiction would also need to be addressed. For established smokers who want to quit, the cost of withdrawal from nicotine is considerable. Governments might consider interventions to help reduce those costs as part of the overall tobacco control package.

## Measures to Reduce the Demand for Tobacco

We turn now to a discussion of measures for tobacco control, evaluating each in turn.

## Raising Taxes

Evidence from countries of all income levels shows that price increases on cigarettes are highly effective in reducing demand. Higher taxes induce some smokers to quit and prevent others individuals from starting. They also reduce the number of ex-smokers who return to cigarettes and reduce consumption among continuing smokers. On average, a price rise of 10 percent on a pack of cigarettes would be expected to reduce demand for cigarettes by about 4 percent in high-income countries and by about 8 percent in low- and middle-income countries, where lower incomes tend to make people more responsive to price changes. Children and adolescents are more responsive to price rises than older adults, so this intervention would have a significant impact on them.

Models for this report show that tax increases that would raise the real price of cigarettes by 10 percent worldwide would cause 40 million smokers alive in 1995 to quit, and prevent a minimum of 10 million tobacco-related deaths. The price rise would also deter others from taking up smoking in the first place. The assumptions on which the model is based are deliberately conservative, and these figures should therefore be regarded as minimum estimates.

As many policymakers are aware, the question of what the right level of tax should be is a complex one. The size of the tax depends in subtle ways on empirical facts that may not yet be available, such as the scale of the costs to nonsmokers and income levels. It also depends on varying societal values, such as the extent to which children should be protected, and on what a society hopes to achieve through the tax, such as a specific gain in revenue or a specific reduction in disease burden. The report concludes that, for the time being, policymakers who seek to reduce smoking should use as a yardstick the tax levels adopted as part of the comprehensive tobacco control policies of countries where cigarette consumption has fallen. In such countries, the tax component of the price of a pack of cigarettes is between two-thirds and four-fifths of the retail cost. Currently, in the high-income countries, taxes average about two-thirds or more of the retail price of a pack of cigarettes. In lower-income countries taxes amount to not more than half the retail price of a pack of cigarettes.

## Nonprice Measures to Reduce Demand

Beyond raising the price, governments have also employed a range of other effective measures. These include comprehensive bans on advertising and promotion of tobacco; information measures such as mass media counter-advertising, prominent health warning labels, the publication and dissemination of research findings on the health consequences of smoking as well as restrictions on smoking in work and public places.

This report provides evidence that each of these measures can reduce the demand for cigarettes. For example, "information shocks," such as the publication of research studies with significant new information on the health effects of smoking, reduce demand. Their effect appears to be greatest when a population has relatively little general awareness of the health risks. Comprehensive bans on advertising and promotion can reduce demand by around 7 percent, according to econometric studies in high-income countries. Smoking restrictions clearly benefit nonsmokers, and there is also some evidence that they can reduce the prevalence of smoking.

Models developed for this report suggest that, employed as a package, such nonprice measures used globally could persuade some 23 million smokers alive in 1995 to quit and avert the tobacco-attributable deaths of 5 million of them. As with the estimates for tax increases, these are conservative estimates.

### Nicotine Replacement and Other Cessation Therapies

A third intervention would be to help those who wish to quit by making it easier for them to obtain nicotine replacement therapy (NRT) and other cessation interventions. NRT markedly increases the effectiveness of cessation efforts and also reduces individuals' withdrawal costs. Yet in many countries, NRT is difficult to obtain. Models for this study suggest that if NRT were made more widely available, it could help to reduce demand substantially.

The combined effect of all these demand-reducing measures is not known, since smokers in most countries with tobacco control policies are exposed to a mixture of them and none can be studied strictly in isolation. However, there is evidence that the implementation of one intervention supports the success of others, underscoring the importance of implementing tobacco controls as a package. Together, in sum, these measures could avert many millions of deaths.

## Measures to Reduce the Supply of Tobacco

While interventions to reduce demand for tobacco are likely to succeed, measures to reduce its supply are less promising. This is because, if one supplier is shut down, an alternative supplier gains an incentive to enter the market.

The extreme measure of prohibiting tobacco is unwarranted on economic grounds as well as unrealistic and likely to fail. Crop substitution is often proposed as a means to reduce the tobacco supply, but there is scarcely any evidence that it reduces consumption, since the incentives to farmers to grow tobacco are currently much greater than for most other crops. While crop substitution is not an effective way to reduce consumption, it may be a useful strategy where needed to aid the poorest tobacco farmers in transition to other livelihoods, as part of a broader diversification program.

Similarly, the evidence so far suggests that trade restrictions, such as import bans, will have little impact on cigarette consumption worldwide. Instead, countries are more likely to succeed in curbing tobacco consumption by adopting measures that effectively reduce demand and applying those measures symmetrically to imported and domestically-produced cigarettes. Likewise, in a framework of sound trade and agriculture policies, the subsidies on tobacco production that are found mainly in high-income countries make little sense. In any case, their removal would have little impact on total retail price.

However, one supply-side measure is key to an effective strategy for tobacco control: action against smuggling. Effective measures include prominent tax stamps and local-language warnings on cigarette packs, as well as the aggressive enforcement and consistent application of tough penalties to deter smugglers. Tight controls on smuggling improve governments' revenue yields from tobacco tax increases.

### The Costs and Consequences of Tobacco Control

Policymakers traditionally raise several concerns about acting to control tobacco. The first of these concerns is that tobacco controls will cause permanent job losses in an economy. However, falling demand for tobacco does not mean a fall in a country's total employment level. Money that smokers once spent on cigarettes would instead be spent on other goods and services, generating other jobs to replace any lost from the tobacco industry. Studies for this report show that most countries would see no net job losses, and that a few would see net gains, if tobacco consumption fell.

There are however a very small number of countries, mostly in Sub-Saharan Africa, whose economies are heavily dependent on tobacco farming. For these countries, while reductions in domestic demand would have little impact, a global fall in demand would result in job losses. Policies to aid adjustment in such circumstances would be essential. However, it should be stressed that, even if demand were to fall significantly, it would occur slowly, over a generation or more.

A second concern is that higher tax rates will reduce government revenues. In fact, the empirical evidence shows that raised tobacco taxes bring greater tobacco tax revenues. This is in part because the proportionate reduction in demand does not match the proportionate size of the tax increase, since addicted consumers respond relatively slowly to price rises. A model developed for this study concludes that modest increases in cigarette excise taxes of 10 percent worldwide would increase tobacco tax revenues by about 7 percent overall, with the effects varying by country.

A third concern is that higher taxes will lead to massive increases in smuggling, thereby keeping cigarette consumption high but reducing government revenues. Smuggling is a serious problem, but the report concludes that, even where it occurs at high rates, tax increases bring greater revenues and reduce consumption. Therefore, rather than foregoing tax increases, the appropriate response to smuggling is to crack down on criminal activity.

A fourth concern is that increases in cigarette taxes will have a disproportionate impact on poor consumers. Existing tobacco taxes do consume a higher share of the income of poor consumers than of rich consumers. However, policymakers' main concern should be over the distributional impact of the entire tax and expenditure system, and less on particular taxes in isolation. It is important to note that poor consumers are usually more responsive to price increases than rich consumers, so their consumption of cigarettes will fall more sharply following a tax increase, and their relative financial burden may be correspondingly reduced. Nonetheless, their loss of perceived benefits of smoking may be comparatively greater.

### Is Tobacco Control Worth Paying for?

For governments considering intervention, an important further consideration is the cost-effectiveness of tobacco control measures relative to other health interventions. Preliminary estimates were performed for this report in which the public costs of implementing and administrating tobacco control programs were weighed against the potential number of healthy years of life saved. The results are consistent with earlier studies that suggest that tobacco control is highly cost-effective as part of a basic public health package in low- and middle-income countries.

Measured in terms of the cost per year of healthy life saved, tax increases would be cost-effective. Depending on various assumptions, this instrument could cost between US . . . $5 and $17 for each year of healthy life saved in low- and middle-income countries. [*Note:* All dollar amounts are in 1999 U.S. dollars.] This compares favorably with many health interventions commonly financed by governments, such as child immunization. Nonprice measures are also cost-effective in many settings. Measures to liberalize access to nicotine replacement therapy, for example, by changing the conditions for its sale, would probably also be cost-effective in most settings. However, individual countries would need to make careful assessments before deciding to provide subsidies for NRT and other cessation interventions for poor smokers.

The unique potential of tobacco taxation to raise revenues cannot be ignored. In China, for example, conservative estimates suggest that a 10 percent increase in cigarette tax would decrease consumption by 5 percent, increase revenue by 5 percent, and that the increase would be sufficient to finance a package of essential health services for one-third of China's poorest 100 million citizens.

## An Agenda for Action

Each society makes its own decisions about policies that concern individual choices. In reality, most policies would be based on a mix of criteria, not only economic ones. Most societies would wish to reduce the unquantifiable suffering and emotional losses wrought by tobacco's burden of disease and premature death. For the policymaker seeking to improve public health, too, tobacco control is an attractive option. Even modest reductions in a disease burden of such large size would bring highly significant health gains.

Some policymakers will consider that the strongest grounds for intervening are to deter children from smoking. However, a strategy aimed solely at deterring children is not practical and would bring no significant benefits to public health for several decades. Most of the tobacco-related deaths that are projected to occur in the next 50 years are among today's existing smokers. Governments concerned with health gains in the medium term may therefore consider adopting broader measures that help adults to quit.

The report has two recommendations:

1.  Where governments decide to take strong action to curb the tobacco epidemic, a multi-pronged strategy should be adopted. Its aims should be to deter children from smoking, to protect nonsmokers, and to provide all smokers with information about the health effects of tobacco. The strategy, tailored to individual country needs, would include (1) raising taxes using as a yardstick the rates adopted by countries with comprehensive tobacco control policies. In these countries, tax accounts for two-thirds to four-fifths of the retail price of cigarettes; (2) publishing and disseminating research results on the health effects of tobacco, adding prominent warning labels to cigarettes, adopting comprehensive bans on advertising and promotion, and restricting smoking in workplaces and public places, and (3) widening access to nicotine replacement and other cessation therapies.
2.  International agencies such as the UN agencies should review their existing programs and policies, to ensure that tobacco control is given due prominence; they should sponsor research into the causes, consequences and costs of smoking, and the cost-effectiveness of interventions at the local level; and they should address tobacco control issues that cross borders, including working with the WHO's new Framework Convention for Tobacco Control. Key areas for action include facilitating international agreements on smuggling control, discussions on tax harmonization to reduce the incentives for

smuggling, and bans on advertising and promotion involving the global communications media.

The threat posed by smoking to global health is unprecedented, but so is the potential for reducing smoking-related mortality with cost-effective policies. This report shows the scale of what might be achieved: moderate action could ensure substantial health gains for the 21st century.

# Excerpt from "The European Code against Cancer"

*Point number one of "The European Code against Cancer" includes the following: "Do Not Smoke. Smokers, stop as quickly as possible, and do not smoke in the presence of others. If you do not smoke, do not try it." After this beginning, the document goes on to discuss some of the evidence against smoking and the general situation in Europe is characterized as "particularly worrying."*

## [Point Number 1 of the Code's 10 Points]

1. Do not smoke. Smokers, stop as quickly as possible and do not smoke in the presence of others. If you do not smoke, do not try it. . . .

## [From the Annex to the Code]

It is estimated that between 25 and 30 percent of all cancers in developed countries are tobacco-related. From the results of studies conducted in Europe, Japan and North America, between 83 and 92 percent of lung cancers in men, and between 57 and 80 percent of lung cancers in women, are attributable to cigarette smoking. Between 80 and 90 percent of cancers arising in the esophagus, larynx and oral cavity are related to the effect of tobacco, both acting singly and jointly with alcohol consumption.

Cancers of the bladder, pancreas, kidney, stomach and cervix are causally related to tobacco smoking and there have been suggestions of an association with cigarette smoking and an increased risk of leukemia and colorectal cancer, although the causal nature of these latter associations has not been accepted.

Because of the length of the latency period, tobacco-related cancers observed today are related to cigarette smoking patterns over two decades ago. Consequently, following any decrease in smoking prevalence there will be a period of time which will elapse before any decrease in the incidence of tobacco-related cancers becomes apparent.

There is now strong evidence of the adverse health consequences of Environmental Tobacco Smoking (ETS) sometimes referred to as passive smoking. On the basis of the available epidemiological data, the United States Environmental Protection Agency declared in 1992 that ETS was a proven lung carcinogen in humans.

---

*Source:* European Communities, Directorate-General Health and Consumer Protection. 1995. "The European Code against Cancer." Reprinted with permission.

The risk of lung cancer is increased in non-smoking women who have husbands who smoke tobacco. There also appears to be an increased risk of myocardial infarction due to exposure to ETS and the adverse health consequences in children whose parents smoke includes an increase in the frequency and severity of asthma and of upper and lower respiratory tract infections.

Tobacco can kill in more than 20 different ways including causes such as lung cancer and other forms of cancer, heart disease, strokes and chronic bronchitis and other respiratory diseases. Smokers have three times the death rate in middle-age (between the ages of 35 and 69) than non-smokers and about half of regular cigarette smokers will eventually die from their habit.

Many of these are not particularly heavy smokers but they can be characterized by starting smoking in their teenage years. Half of the deaths from tobacco will take place in middle age (35–69). . . . there is clear and consistent evidence that stopping smoking before having cancer or some other serious disease avoids most of the later excess risk of death from tobacco even if smoking stops in middle age.

It is estimated that world-wide, smoking kills three million people each year: the second half of the 20th century was notable in that there was estimated to have been 60 million deaths caused by tobacco world-wide. In most countries the worst consequences of the Tobacco Epidemic are yet to come, particularly among women in developing countries and in populations of developing countries, since by the time the young smokers of today reach middle or old age there will be about 10 million deaths each year from tobacco.

Approximately 500 million of the world's population today can expect to be killed by tobacco, 250 million of these deaths being premature and occurring in middle age.

The situation in Europe is particularly worrying. The European Union is the second-largest producer of cigarettes (694 billion in 1993) after China (1.675 trillion) and the major exporter of cigarettes (218 billion). In Central and Eastern Europe there is a continual increase in the smoking habit. Of the six World Health Organization (WHO) regions, Europe has the highest per capita consumption levels of manufactured cigarettes and faces an immediate and major challenge in meeting the WHO target for a minimum of 80 percent of the population to be non-smoking.

Currently (spring 1994) in the European Union, 42 percent of men and 28 percent of women are regular smokers. The smoking prevalence in women is artificially lowered by the low rates reported in southern Europe where there is evidence that these rates are rising and seem set to continue to rise over the next decade. In addition, smoking prevalence in the age range 25–39 years is high (55 percent in men and 40 percent in women) and can be expected to have a profound influence on the future cancer pattern. It is especially concerning that the smoking prevalence among general practitioners, who play an exemplary role in health behavior, remains high in many parts of Europe. This should be a target for immediate action.

It has been demonstrated that changes in cigarette consumption are affected mainly at a sociological level rather than by actions, such as individual smoking cessation programs, targeted at individuals. Actions such as advertising bans and increases in the price of cigarettes influence cigarette sales particularly among adolescents. Therefore, a Tobacco Policy is necessary to reduce the health consequences of tobacco, and experience shows that this should be targeted via a variety of actions aimed to stop young people from starting smoking and to help smokers to quit.

To be efficient and successful, a tobacco policy has to be comprehensive and maintained over a long time period. Increased taxes on tobacco, total bans on direct and indirect advertising, smoke-free enclosed public areas, education, effective health warning labels on tobacco products, a policy of low maximum tar and nicotine levels in cigarettes, encouragement of stopping smoking and individual health interventions have to be implemented.

The importance of adequate intervention is demonstrated by the low lung cancer rates in Scandinavian countries which, since the early 1970s, have adopted integrated central and local policies and programs against smoking. In the United Kingdom, tobacco consumption has declined by 30 percent since 1970 and lung cancer mortality among men has been decreasing since 1980 although the rate remains high. In France, between 1992 and 1993 there has been a 3 percent reduction in tobacco consumption due to the implementation of anti-tobacco measures introduced by the Loi Evin.

Hence, the first point of the European Code Against Cancer is:

DO NOT SMOKE. Smoking is the largest single cause of premature death.

SMOKERS: STOP AS QUICKLY AS POSSIBLE. In terms of health improvement, stopping smoking before having cancer or some other serious disease avoids most of the later excess risk of death from tobacco even if smoking stops in middle age.

DO NOT SMOKE IN THE PRESENCE OF OTHERS. The health consequences of your smoking may affect the health of others around you.

IF YOU DO NOT SMOKE, DO NOT EXPERIMENT WITH TOBACCO. Most who experiment become regular smokers: it is difficult to stop once you have started.

# "African Americans and Tobacco"

*Although smoking rates among African Americans have declined in recent years, the CDC reports in "African Americans and Tobacco" that recent increases in smoking rates among African American young people underscore the importance of continuing prevention efforts.*

Smoking rates among African American adults historically have been higher than among the general U.S. population; however, in recent years smoking rates have been similar. Smoking among African American teens has declined dramatically since 1976; however, recent increases in teen smoking among African Americans document the need for continued prevention efforts. African Americans continue to suffer disproportionately from chronic and preventable disease compared to white Americans. Of the three leading causes of death in African Americans—heart disease, cancer, and stroke—smoking and other tobacco use are major contributors to these illnesses.[1]

- Each year, approximately 45,000 African Americans die from a smoking-related disease that could have been prevented.[2]
- If current patterns continue, an estimated 1.6 million African Americans who are now under the age of 18 will become regular smokers. About 500,000 of those smokers will die of a smoking-related disease.[2]
- Aggregated data from 1994 and 1995 show that current smoking prevalence rates were similar among African American adults (26.5%) and white adults (25.9%) in the United States.[3]
- In 1995, about 5.7 million African American adults smoked cigarettes, accounting for approximately 12% of the 47 million adult smokers in the United States.[3]
- In 1994 and 1995, African American men (31.4%) smoked at a higher rate than white men (27.6%), while African American women (22.7%) and white women (24.4%) smoked at a similar rate.[3]
- Among African Americans, as seen in other U.S. populations, the prevalence of smoking declines as education increases. Smoking rates were higher among African Americans who had less than a high school education (34.8%) compared to those with a college education (16.7%).[3]

---

*Source:* CDC and Prevention, Office on Smoking and Health. 1998. "African Americans and Tobacco." Fact Sheet. http://www.cdc.gov/tobacco/sgr/sgr_1998/sgr-min-fs-afr.ntm.

- Among African American high school seniors, cigarette smoking declined from 1977 (36.7%) to 1992 (8.7%). However, smoking prevalence rates increased from 1992 to 1997 (14.3%).[4]
- Among African American 10th-grade students, smoking prevalence increased by 94% from 1992 (6.6%) to 1997 (12.8%). For African American eighth-grade students, smoking prevalence increased by 106% from 1992 (5.3%) to 1997 (10.9%). Although smoking prevalence among African American students continues to be lower than for white and Hispanic students, the rate of increase was substantially higher among African American students than for white and Hispanic students.[4]
- The Centers for Disease Control and Prevention's 1997 Youth Risk Behavior Survey data also show that the rate of past month cigarette smoking among high school students in grades nine through 12 are on the rise—increasing by nearly a third from 27.5% in 1991 to 36.4% in 1997. The rate of cigarette smoking increased by 80% among African American students, climbing from 12.6% to 22.7% between 1991 and 1997. The most dramatic increase was observed among African American males, whose cigarette smoking prevalence doubled from 14.1% in 1991 to 28.2% in 1997.[5]
- In 1997, there was no significant difference in current cigar use among racial/ethnic groups of high school students— 22.5% of whites, 19.4% of African Americans, and 20.3% of Hispanics reported smoking cigars in the past month. Cigar prevalence was higher among males than females in all three racial/ethnic groups.[5]
- In 1997, African American male high school students (3.2%) were less likely to use smokeless tobacco products than white male (20.6%) and Hispanic male (5.1%) high school students.[5]
- Of current African American adult smokers, more than 70% indicated that they want to quit smoking completely.[6]
- African American smokers are more likely than white smokers to have quit for at least one day during the previous year (48.7% vs. 40.3%). African Americans (7.9%), however, are much less likely than whites (14.0%) to remain abstinent for one month or more.[7]
- A one-year study found that three major African American publications—*Ebony, Jet and Essence*—had 12% more cigarette advertisements than widespread publications—*Newsweek, Time, People* and *Mademoiselle*.[8]
- Studies have found a higher density of tobacco billboards in racial/ethnic communities. For example, a study conducted

in Los Angeles, Calif., found the highest density of tobacco billboards (the number of billboards per mile) in African American communities and the lowest billboard placement in white communities.[9]

- Approximately 90% of the billboards in African American communities featured an African American as the central character, while in other ethnic communities whites were portrayed as the central characters.[9]
- The tobacco industry attempts to maintain a positive image and public support among African Americans by supporting cultural events and by funding minority higher education institutions, elected officials, civic and community organizations, and scholarship programs.[10]

## References

1. CDC (Centers for Disease Control and Prevention), *Chronic Disease in Minority Populations* (1994): 2–16.

2. CDC, Office of Smoking and Health, unpublished data, 1995.

3. U.S. Department of Health and Human Services. *Tobacco Use Among U.S. Racial/Ethnic Groups — African Americans, American Indian and Alaska Natives, Asian Americans and Pacific Islanders, and Hispanics: A Report of the Surgeon General.* Atlanta: U.S. Department of Health and Human Services, CDC, 1998.

4. The University of Michigan. Cigarette Smoking Rates May Have Peaked Among Younger Teens 1997 (press release), Dec. 18, 1997.

5. CDC. "Tobacco Use Among High School Students—United States, 1997." *MMWR (Morbidity and Mortality Weekly Report)* 1998 (46): 433–440.

6. CDC. "Cigarette Smoking Among Adults—United States, 1993." *MMWR* 1994 (43): 925–929.

7. CDC. "Smoking Cessation During Previous Year Among Adults—United States, 1990 and 1991." *MMWR* 1993 (42): 504–507.

8. Cummings, K. M., Giovino, G., Mendicino, A. J. "Cigarette Advertising and Black-White Differences in Brand Preference." *Public Health Reports,* 1987 (102): 698–701.

9. Stoddard, J. L., Johnson, C. A., Boley-Cruz, T., Sussman, S. "Target Tobacco Markets: Outdoor Advertising in Los Angeles Minority Neighborhoods" (letter). *American Journal of Public Health,* 1997 (87): 1232–1233.

10. Freeman, H., Delgado, J. L., Douglas, C. E. *Minority Issues. Tobacco Use: An American Crisis. Final Report of the Conference* (January 1993): 43–47.

# "Facts You Should Know"

*According to a survey posted by the CDC, most teenagers hold negative opinions with regard to smoking. They say, for example, that seeing someone smoke turns them off, that they dislike being around smokers, and that they prefer to date nonsmokers. Most of them also recognize that using tobacco, even for a short time, may cause cancer.*

*The same document provides a list of facts about secondhand smoke, making the point that just being around a smoker may turn out to be fully dangerous as smoking. One fact the list omits is that smokers themselves are also vulnerable to all the risks associated with secondhand smoke. It pollutes their environment as much as it does the environment of everyone else. And when smokers congregate, they multiply the risks for themselves as well as for others.*

### Teen Opinions on Smoking

Way more young people don't smoke than do. And most consider it a foul, unattractive habit. In fact, smoking is about the least popular thing you can do if you want to hang out with other teenagers. Here's what teens across the USA said in response to these statements about tobacco [see Table 7]. . . .

### Secondhand Smoke Facts

Secondhand smoke is the name for the sickening, poisonous smoke given off by a burning cigarette, cigar, or pipe. Smokers may claim to have a right to smoke, but nonsmokers have a more important right to breathe safe air. So the next time one of your friends lights up in front of you, fire off these facts about secondhand smoke.

- Secondhand smoke can produce six times the pollution of a busy highway when in a crowded restaurant.
- Secondhand smoke causes 30 times as many lung cancer deaths as all regulated pollutants combined.
- Secondhand smoke makes clothes and hair stink.
- Secondhand smoke causes wheezing, coughing, colds, earaches, and asthma attacks.
- Secondhand smoke fills the air with many of the same poisons found in the air around toxic waste dumps.

*Source:* CDC, Office on Smoking and Health, HHS. 2000. "Facts You Should Know." TIPS Fact Sheet. Reviewed November 2. http://www.cdc.gov/tobacco/tips_4_youth/facts.htm.

**[Table 7]**
**[What Teens think about Smoking, Responses by Percentage]**

| [Statement] | Agree | Disagree | No Opinion or Don't Know |
|---|---|---|---|
| Seeing someone smoke turns me off. | 67 | 22 | 10 |
| I'd rather date people who don't smoke. | 86 | 8 | 6 |
| It's safe to smoke for only a year or two. | 7 | 92 | 1 |
| Smoking can help you when you're bored. | 7 | 92 | 1 |
| Smoking helps reduce stress. | 21 | 78 | 3 |
| Smoking helps keep your weight down. | 18 | 80 | 2 |
| Chewing tobacco and snuff cause cancer. | 95 | 2 | 3 |
| I strongly dislike being around smokers. | 65 | 22 | 13 |

- Secondhand smoke wrecks the smell and taste of food.
- Secondhand smoke causes reddening, itching, and watering of the eyes.
- Secondhand smoke kills about 3,000 nonsmokers each year from lung cancer.
- Secondhand smoke causes up to 300,000 lung infections (such as pneumonia and bronchitis) in infants and young children each year.

# "Environmental Tobacco Smoke Seriously Endangers Children's Health"

*The dangers of secondhand smoke as they apply specifically to children are addressed by WHO in "Environmental Tobacco Smoke Seriously Endangers Children's Health."*

Tobacco smoke seriously damages children's health, a new World Health Organization (WHO) report, entitled International Consultation on Environmental Tobacco Smoke (ETS) and Child Health, released today in London, concludes.

The research results, announced today by WHO Director-General Dr. Gro Harlem Brundtland at the Third Ministerial Conference on Environment and Health, show that environmental tobacco smoke causes a wide variety of adverse health effects in children, including pneumonia, bronchitis, coughing, wheezing, worsening of asthma and middle-ear infections. Children's exposure to environmental tobacco smoke may also contribute to cardiovascular disease in adulthood.

The report notes that:

> 700 million children—almost half of all children worldwide—live in a home of a smoker. The large number of exposed children, coupled with the evidence that ETS causes illness in children, constitutes a substantial public health threat.

> Children whose mothers smoke have an estimated 70% more respiratory problems, including croup, bronchitis and pneumonia as well as middle-ear infections; the prevalence is 30% higher if the father smokes.

> Infants of mothers who smoke have almost five times the risk of sudden infant death syndrome. There are also other well documented effects, including reduced birth weight and reduced lung functioning.

> Annual health costs attributed to environmental tobacco smoke in the United States alone amount to US $1 billion. If the problems related to reduced birth weight caused by maternal smoking are added to this, the figure doubles.

---

*Source:* WHO. 1999. "Environmental Tobacco Smoke Seriously Endangers Children's Health." Press Release WHO 35. June 16. All WHO press releases, fact sheets, and features as well as other information on this subject can be obtained on Internet on the WHO home page: http://www.who.int. Reprinted with permission.

"Swift action to highlight the need for strong public policies to protect children from exposure to tobacco smoke is essential," the report concludes. "These policies should aim to ensure the right of every child to grow up in an environment free of tobacco smoke. This can be achieved by two complementary strategies: eliminating children's contact with tobacco smoke *in utero* and in childhood, and reducing overall consumption of tobacco products."

## Secondhand Smoke: "How Big a Lung Cancer Risk for Adults?"

*In this excerpt from "Setting the Record Straight," the EPA estimates that each year at least 3,000 nonsmoking adults die of lung cancer resulting from secondhand smoke. An estimated 800 of these deaths result from exposure to ETS at home and 2,200 from exposure at work or in social situations.*

*The EPA stresses that although a person's risk of developing lung cancer from exposure to secondhand smoke is relatively small compared to that of a smoker, the person who breathes secondhand smoke often does so involuntarily, as is true of young children.*

The evidence is clear and consistent: secondhand smoke is a cause of lung cancer in adults who don't smoke. EPA has never claimed that minimal exposure to secondhand smoke poses a huge individual cancer risk. Even though the lung cancer risk from secondhand smoke is relatively small compared to the risk from direct smoking, unlike a smoker who chooses to smoke, the nonsmoker's risk is often involuntary. In addition, exposure to secondhand smoke varies tremendously among exposed individuals. For those who must live or work in close proximity to one or more smokers, the risk would certainly be greater than for those less exposed. EPA estimates that secondhand smoke is responsible for about 3,000 lung cancer deaths each year among nonsmokers in the U.S.; of these, the estimate is 800 from exposure to secondhand smoke at home and 2,200 from exposure in work or social situations.

---

*Source:* Excerpted from: EPA. 2000. "Setting the Record Straight: Secondhand Smoke Is a Preventable Health Risk." Last modified, June 26, 2000. Available online http://www.epa.gov/iaq/pubs/strsfs.html.

# Secondhand Smoke: "The Risks to Children Are Widely Acknowledged"

*In this excerpt from "Setting the Record Straight," the EPA estimates that every year, between 150,000 and 300,000 children under one and one-half years of age get bronchitis or pneumonia as a result of breathing secondhand smoke.*

The conclusion that secondhand smoke causes respiratory effects in children is widely shared and virtually undisputed. Even the tobacco industry does not contest these effects in its media and public relations campaign. EPA estimates that every year, between 150,000 and 300,000 children under 1½ years of age get bronchitis or pneumonia from breathing secondhand tobacco smoke, resulting in thousands of hospitalizations. In children under 18 years of age, secondhand smoke exposure also results in more coughing and wheezing, a small but significant decrease in lung function, and an increase in fluid in the middle ear. Children with asthma have more frequent and more severe asthma attacks because of exposure to secondhand smoke, which is also a risk factor for the onset of asthma in children who did not previously have symptoms.

*Source:* Excerpted from: EPA. 2000. "Setting the Record Straight: Secondhand Smoke Is a Preventable Health Risk." Last modified, June 26, 2000. Available from http://www.epa.gov/iaq/pubs/strsfs.html.

# "Tobacco Free Initiative"

*"Tobacco Free Initiative," a WHO document, explains the importance of tobacco control as a means of averting some of the millions of tobacco-related deaths predicted in underdeveloped countries in the coming decades.*

According to WHO estimates, there are currently 4 million deaths a year from tobacco, a figure expected to rise to about 10 million by 2030. By that date, based on current smoking trends, tobacco is predicted to be the leading cause of disease burden in the world, causing about one in eight deaths. 70% of those deaths will occur in developing countries. The sheer scale of tobacco's impact on global disease burden, and particularly what is likely to happen without appropriate intervention in developing countries, is often not fully appreciated. The extremely negative impact of tobacco on health now and in the future is the primary reason for giving explicit and strong support to tobacco control on a world-wide basis.

In response to these concerns the Director-General, Dr. Gro Harlem Brundtland, established a Cabinet project, the Tobacco Free Initiative (TFI), in July 1998 to coordinate an improved global strategic response to tobacco as an important public health issue. The long-term mission of global tobacco control is to reduce smoking prevalence and tobacco consumption in all countries and among all groups, and thereby reduce the burden of disease caused by tobacco. In support of this mission, the goals of the Tobacco Free Initiative are to:

- Galvanize global support for evidence-based tobacco control policies and actions
- Build new, and strengthen existing partnerships for action
- Heighten awareness of the social, human and economic harm of tobacco in all sectors of society, and the need to take comprehensive actions at all levels
- Accelerate national, regional and global strategic planning, implementation and evaluation
- Commission policy research to support rapid, sustained and innovative actions
- Mobilize adequate resources . . .
- Integrate tobacco into the broader agenda of health and development
- Facilitate the development of an effective Framework Convention for Tobacco Control and related protocols

In achieving these goals, the Tobacco Free Initiative will build strong internal and external partnerships "with a purpose" with each WHO Cluster and Regional and Country Offices, and with a range of organizations and institutions around the world. The purpose of these partnerships will reflect the unique and complementary roles of WHO's partners and of WHO at all levels of the organization. Success will be measured in terms of actions achieved at local, country and global levels that lead to better tobacco control.

The Tobacco Free Initiative will take a global leadership role in promoting effective policies and interventions that make a real difference to tobacco prevalence and associated health outcomes. Despite the seriousness of the problem, there is evidence to show that countries which undertake concerted and comprehensive actions to address tobacco control can bring about significant reductions in tobacco related harm. These success stories indicate the importance of considering the best mix of specific interventions required to achieve the same goal: increased cessation and lowered initiation. The specific mix of interventions in a broad policy framework will vary according to each country's political, social, cultural and economic reality.

Critical to the success of these global tobacco control actions, will be the ability to mobilize human, institutional and financial resources to support enhanced activity. Current allocations at regional and global levels are severely inadequate, especially when faced with a $400 billion industry which promotes these harmful tobacco products. Increased allocations will enable improved international research, policy development and action to address the massive public health impact of tobacco.

# "Tobacco Epidemic: Health Dimensions"

*In "Tobacco Epidemic: Health Dimensions," WHO provides a summary of the scope of tobacco use worldwide, pointing especially to the expected consequences in the developing countries and the increasing tobacco use among women.*

## Tobacco Is a Greater Cause of Death and Disability Than Any Single Disease

There is no longer any doubt that tobacco use worldwide has reached the proportion of a global epidemic approaching its peak among men in most developed countries and spreading now to men in developing countries and women in all countries.

- Today, according to WHO estimates, there are approximately 1.1 thousand million smokers in the world, which represents about one-third of the global population aged 15 years and over. Of these, 800 million are in developing countries.
- Since the mid 1980s, estimated global cigarette consumption has remained relatively steady at about 1600 cigarettes per adult per year.
- However, there has been a shift in the distribution of tobacco consumption in the last two decades. Declining consumption in developed countries has been counterbalanced by increasing consumption in developing countries.
- Available data suggest that, globally, approximately 47% of men and 12% of women smoke. In developing countries, 48% of men and 7% of women smoke, while in developed countries, 42% of men smoke as do 24% of women.
- Although life expectancy for both sexes is predicted to be on the rise, in many countries, the gap between them is growing significantly due to the larger number of men who smoke and die of tobacco-related diseases.

In certain regions, the health consequences of tobacco use are particularly devastating.

---

*Source:*WHO. 1998. "Tobacco Epidemic: Health Dimensions." Fact Sheet N° 154. Revised May 1998. Available online http://www.who.int/inf-fs/en/fact154.html. For further information, please contact Health Communications and Public Relations, WHO, Geneva. Telephone (41-22) 791-2532. Fax (41-22) 791-4858. E-Mail: rozovi@who.ch. Reprinted with permission.

- In the Former Socialist Economies (FSE), in 1990, around 14% of all deaths were due to tobacco use. This figure is predicted to increase so that in 2020, more than 22% of all deaths in the FSE region will be due to tobacco.
- In this region, smoking is likely to be a major factor underlying the 56% projected increase in male deaths from chronic disease between 1990 and 2020. In fact, the FSE region is projected in 2020 to have the highest adult male risk of death, even higher than that in sub-Saharan Africa.
- In absolute figures, the biggest and sharpest increases in disease burden are expected in India and China where the use of tobacco has grown most steeply. In China alone, where there are about 300 million smokers, and the cigarette consumption is estimated at around 1900 cigarettes per adult per year, around 50 million Chinese, who are now under 20 years of age, will eventually be killed by tobacco.

Health consequences of the tobacco epidemic in both developed and developing countries are devastating. By 2020, it is expected to kill more people than any single disease.

- Since the middle of the twentieth century, tobacco products have killed more than 60 million people in developed countries alone.
- Currently, tobacco is responsible for three and a half million deaths worldwide—or about 7% of all deaths—per year.
- Based on current trends, that figure is expected to grow to ten million deaths per year by the 2020s or early 2030s. It is estimated that half a billion people now alive will be killed by tobacco products.
- By 2020, tobacco use will cause 17.7% of all deaths in developed countries and 10.9% of all deaths in developing countries.
- The rise in tobacco mortality mirrors almost exactly the rise in smoking prevalence, three to four decades later.
- Tobacco is a known or probable cause of about 25 diseases, and the sheer scale of its impact on global disease burden is still not fully appreciated. For example, it is well known that tobacco is the most important cause of lung cancer. Less known is the fact that it kills even more people through many other diseases, including cancers at other sites, heart disease, stroke, emphysema and other chronic lung diseases.
- Studies in the United Kingdom have shown that smokers in

their 30s and 40s are five times more likely to have a heart attack than non-smokers.
- On average, lifetime smokers have a 50% chance of dying from tobacco. And half of these will die in middle age, before age seventy, losing 22 years of normal life expectancy. In 1990, smoking was responsible for 35% of all male deaths occurring in middle age (age 35–69) in developed countries.

Tobacco dependence has been classified as a behavioral disorder in the WHO International Classification of Diseases (ICD-10).

- Tobacco dependence is caused by nicotine, which is contained in all tobacco products in substantial quantities and which has been internationally recognized as a drug of addiction.
- Tobacco dependence is a real public health problem which warrants serious attention if the epidemic of tobacco-related mortality and morbidity is to be reduced.
- The revenues of the tobacco industry directly depend on the number of people addicted to smoking.

Environmental tobacco smoke (ETS) contains essentially all of the same carcinogens and toxic agents that are inhaled by the smoker. ETS is harmful to nonsmokers because it causes lung cancer and other diseases and aggravates allergies and asthma.

Maternal smoking is associated with a higher risk of miscarriage, lower birthweight of babies, and inhibited child development. Parental smoking is also a factor in sudden infant death syndrome and is associated with higher rates of respiratory illnesses, including bronchitis, colds, and pneumonia in children.

Smoking cessation has substantial health benefits and dramatically reduces the risk of most smoking-related diseases.

- One year after quitting, the risk of coronary heart disease (CHD) decreases by 50%, and within 15 years, the relative risk of dying from CHD for an ex-smoker approaches that of a long-time non-smoker.
- The relative risk of developing lung cancer, chronic obstructive lung diseases, and stroke also decreases, but more slowly.
- Ten to fourteen years after smoking cessation, the risk of mortality from cancer decreases to nearly that of those who have never smoked.
- Quitting smoking benefits health no matter at what age one quits.

How tobacco affects young people[:]

- Tobacco affects young people in an extraordinary number of ways. Due to environmental tobacco smoke (ETS) and maternal smoking, children's health may even be compromised from before the time they are born. In many countries, children may grow up in a haze of tobacco smoke, wreaking further havoc with their health.
- Household money that is spent on tobacco reduces the amount available for food, education and medical care. Children may also suffer the emotional pain and financial insecurity that comes for the loss of a parent or caretaker who dies an untimely death due to tobacco.
- On another level are the pervasive pressures for young people to use tobacco. People everywhere seem to be smoking. Attractive advertisements and exciting tobacco promotions are difficult to resist. Especially when the price is affordable, and it is not a problem for minors to buy tobacco.
- Even if the health risks are understood, the message that tobacco kills is not very relevant to young smokers, who believe themselves to be immortal. By the time they are ready to quit smoking, addiction has taken hold. These factors all contribute to the grim statistics. Based on current trends, about 250 million children alive in the world today will eventually be killed by tobacco.
- WHO believes that every child has the right to grow up without tobacco. This means without the rampant pressures to use tobacco, which in many countries emanates from all corners. There is a need to change the environment to one where non-smoking is considered normal social behaviour and where the choice not to smoke is the easier choice.

Children exposed to ETS

- get more coughs and colds and are more likely to suffer acute upper and lower respiratory tract infections. One study showed that children exposed to ETS during the first 18 months of life have a 60 per cent increase in the risk of developing lower respiratory illnesses such as croup, bronchitis, bronchiolitis and pneumonia.
- have an increased chance of developing asthma. If they already have asthma, second-hand smoke can bring on asthma attacks and make them worse.
- are at risk of impaired lung function, and may have breathing problems in the future.

- have an increased frequency of middle-ear infections, which can lead to reduced hearing.
- babies born to women who smoke during pregnancy, as well as those infants exposed to ETS have a significantly greater risk of dying of sudden infant death syndrome (SIDS).

# "Tobacco Epidemic: Much More Than a Health Issue"

*The worldwide tobacco epidemic must be seriously addressed, not only by ministries of health and WHO, but also by all current and potential partners. Only through concerted efforts and by pulling together all available resources on local, national, and international levels will this looming public health catastrophe be averted. In "Tobacco Epidemic: Much More Than a Health Issue" WHO presents another side to the phenomenal spread of tobacco use throughout the world. WHO says tobacco use "cause[s] a loss to the world economy that is so large that even a conservative estimate ranks it as an amount exceeding total current health expenditures in all developing countries combined."*

## Tobacco Use Is a Major Drain on the World's Financial Resources

The current tobacco epidemic of unprecedented proportion is obviously a public health problem. Yet, it is a complex issue which goes beyond the public health domain. Tobacco use is a major drain on the world's financial resources, and has been labeled a major threat to sustainable and equitable development.

- Tobacco products cause a loss to the world economy that is so large that even a conservative estimate ranks it as an amount exceeding total current health expenditures in all developing countries combined. A World Bank study entitled "The Economic Costs and Benefits of Investing in Tobacco" (March 1993) has estimated that the use of tobacco results in a global net loss of US$200 billion per year, with half of these losses occurring in developing countries.
- There are other costs resulting from the use of tobacco. Some of them are hard or impossible to quantify—for example, reduced quality of life of smokers and their families. . . .
- The same World Bank study also estimated that smoking

*Source:* WHO. 1998. "Tobacco Epidemic: Much More Than a Health Issue." Fact Sheet N° 155. May 1998. Geneva: WHO. Available online http://www.who.int/inf-fs/en/fact155.html. For further information, please contact Health Communications and Public Relations, WHO, Geneva. Telephone (41-22) 791-2532. Fax (41-22) 791-4858. E-Mail: rozovi@who.ch. All WHO press releases, fact sheets, and features can be obtained on Internet on the WHO home page http://www.who.ch. Reprinted with permission.

prevention is among the most cost-effective of all health interventions. Such measures are thus important components of a country's economic health. For example,

—In a developing country with a per capita gross domestic product of US$2000, effective smoking prevention costs approximately US$20 to US$40 per year of life gained.
—On the other hand, lung cancer treatment, which can prolong the lives of only about 10% of affected people, would cost US$18000 per year of life gained.

Sound economic measures can protect the public health while maximizing government revenues and reducing health costs: In the absence of effective government intervention, the tobacco industry will continue to aggressively market its products, and consequently tobacco use can be expected to increase with time. This is especially true in developing countries. However, successes in reducing consumption have been achieved when tobacco control programmes, which are truly comprehensive, have been implemented. In particular, economic measures, such as increased taxes on tobacco, have resulted in most impressive victories in public health campaigns to reduce smoking.

- Studies in many countries have shown that for every 10% increase in the real "inflation adjusted" price, there will be a 2% to 8% drop in tobacco consumption.
- Additional research suggests that teenagers are particularly affected by price, with a 10% increase in price reducing their consumption by more than 10%, and deterring many from ever starting to smoke. This is particularly important, because if people reach their 20s without becoming smokers, it is very unlikely that they will ever smoke.
- Higher tobacco taxes, complemented with sound implementation measures to discourage tobacco use, yield higher revenues and reduce tobacco consumption.
- Some countries have earmarked part of tobacco tax revenues to encourage people to stop smoking, or to sponsor sports, arts and other events

## The Smuggling Issue:

Concerns have been expressed that higher tobacco taxes will lead to smuggling.

- Tobacco interests use the smuggling issue to urge governments to reduce or not increase taxes. At the same time, tobacco companies benefit greatly from the illegal trade in cigarettes. First, they gain their normal profit by legally selling these cigarettes duty-free to distributors. These cigarettes make their way into the illegal market, and, since taxes have not been paid on these cigarettes, they can be sold at reduced prices, stimulating demand for these international brands.

- Governments are not powerless against smuggling. There are a range of measures that can be taken against smugglers and those who seek to supply them. For example, many countries are moving towards the use of prominently displayed "tax paid" markings on all tobacco products, in order to distinguish between legal and illegal goods. The contraband products become easier to detect and therefore the laws easier to enforce. WHO is also working with a number of governments in the development of an international framework convention on tobacco, which will address such issues as smuggling.

In most countries, tobacco production has a negative effect on national economy:

- In a number of countries, government programmes subsidize tobacco production. Yet, in many instances, tobacco subsidies do not even make economic sense. For example, studies have shown that considerable savings would be generated if tobacco farmers in the countries of the European Union were paid an amount equal to their net income and required not to grow tobacco.
- The enormous profits from tobacco go mostly to transnational tobacco companies, and only a small amount goes to the developing countries. The majority of tobacco farmers receive only a small percentage of the profits that tobacco generates.
- Particularly in developing countries, tobacco cultivation may have an adverse effect on food production and nutrition, while large amounts of firewood, needed for fuel and heating, are often used for tobacco curing.
- Tobacco creates a net loss to the balance of trade in the majority of developing countries. These countries should be wary of authorizing the use of scarce foreign exchange reserves for the purchase of tobacco machinery, tobacco leaf and other tobacco manufacturing inputs. Reduced demand in the United States, the European Union, and the Nordic countries will decrease the amount of foreign currency earned by developing countries that export tobacco. This loss of hard currency, combined with increased imports of foreign

cigarettes will impose additional burdens on the economies of countries already struggling with serious balance of payment problems.

- Efforts to slow the spread of tobacco-caused diseases sometimes run up against arguments about those who make a living from growing tobacco. However, even the most comprehensive tobacco control policies will result only in very slow declines in tobacco demand, leaving plenty of time for economic adjustment in the agricultural sector. By devoting sufficient resources towards developing economic alternatives to tobacco, national governments are likely to discover that tobacco agricultural and industrial workers are more likely to support comprehensive tobacco control strategies.

- Recent studies have shown that tobacco control policies do not result in less employment. In fact, some studies have suggested that as employment in the tobacco sector decreases, overall employment levels may increase. Simply put, as one section of economic activity declines, others open up.

The current tobacco epidemic is much more than a health issue. Ministries of Health alone are not in a position to curb it. Thousands of lives can be spared only through comprehensive concerted actions at the national and international levels.

# "The Tobacco Epidemic in Latin America"

*WHO predicts in "The Tobacco Epidemic in Latin America" that deaths resulting from tobacco use will almost triple in the next quarter century. "Of particular concern," WHO says, "is the projected escalation in the proportion of tobacco-caused deaths among women in the region." WHO also expects per-capita consumption of cigarettes to rise in many Latin American countries.*

## More Than 400 Latin Americans Are Killed Every Day

At present, there are an estimated 150,000 deaths per year from tobacco in Latin America. The numbers are rising steadily, and in the next quarter-century this toll will almost triple. By 2020, tobacco will be killing around 400,000 people every year. Of particular concern is the projected escalation in the proportion of tobacco-caused deaths occurring among women in the region.

The pace of epidemiological transition in Latin America is among the highest of any developing region. In Latin America, more people already die of non-communicable diseases, many of which are caused by tobacco, than of communicable diseases, maternal and perinatal conditions and nutritional deficiencies.

In Latin America, the predominance of non-communicable diseases, already apparent in 1990, will become even more evident over the next few decades. From 1990 to 2020, deaths from chronic diseases are expected to double, by which time they might well account for about three-fourths of all deaths in the region. By 2020, there will be seven times more deaths from non-communicable diseases than infectious diseases, compared to twice as many at present.

## Consumption:

In the early 1990s, per capita consumption of cigarettes for adults aged 15 and above averaged about 1300 annually. This ranged from around 350 to 450 in countries such as Peru and Guatemala to around

*Source:* WHO. 1998. "The Tobacco Epidemic in Latin America." Fact Sheet N° 196. May 1998. Geneva: WHO. Available online http://www.who.int/inf-fs/en/fact196.html. For further information, please contact Health Communications and Public Relations, WHO, Geneva. Telephone (41-22) 791-2532. Fax (41-22) 791-4858. E-mail:info@who.ch. All WHO press releases, fact sheets, and features can be obtained on Internet on the WHO home page http://www.who.org. Reprinted with permission.

2000 and above in Venezuela and Cuba. Today, an estimated average of 12 cigarettes are smoked per smoker per day in the region.

- After rapid growth in per capita tobacco consumption in Latin America during the 1960s and 1970s, a severe economic downturn in the 1980s led to a decline in tobacco consumption, which for many countries continued into the 1990s. However, there are strong indications that by the end of the decade, an increase in cigarette consumption will be experienced in many countries of the region.
- Predicted increases in consumption are attributed to such factors as improved economic conditions, a rise in disposable income, population growth, and an increase in smoking among women.
- According to WHO estimates, approximately 40% of men and 21% of women in Latin America and the Caribbean smoke. In general, smoking prevalence is highest in urban populations.
- The prevalence of smoking in Latin America is variable, but reaches 50% or more among young people in some urban areas. Significant numbers of women in the region have taken up smoking in recent years.
- Studies conducted in a number of Latin American countries indicate that three-fourths of smokers start smoking between the ages of 14 and 17. There appears to have been an increase in smoking prevalence among teenagers, mostly in urban areas. In contrast, rural populations, particularly indigenous or native populations record relatively low smoking prevalence.
- In Latin America, public awareness of the health risks of tobacco use is generally low, so are the levels of motivation to quit smoking.

## Tobacco Economics: Tobacco Is Grown in a Number of Countries in Latin America

The number of hectares devoted to tobacco cultivation ranges from 25,000 hectares in countries such as Peru and Colombia to more than 50,000 hectares in large producing countries such as Brazil, Argentina, and Cuba.

- Only a few countries of Latin America presently have economies that are largely dependent on tobacco production. The economic impact of the tobacco industry ranges from negative, due to a negative balance of trade for tobacco products and goods used in tobacco production and manufacture, to substantial, for countries such as Brazil.

Brazil is the largest producer of tobacco in Latin America, and the third largest producer of tobacco in the world, with over 700,000 hectares under cultivation.

- In the countries where tobacco production and marketing represent an important part of the national economies, this has often led to a conflict of interest concerning the implementation of effective tobacco control policies and programmes.
- The tobacco industry in Latin America is dominated by multinational companies. In recent years, multinational tobacco companies have been expanding rapidly in Latin America and their investments in the region appear to be rewarding. According to a trade journal, in 1996 a British multinational tobacco company sold 174 billion of its cigarettes in Latin America, earning it $390 million in profits.
- Cigarette smuggling remains a problem for many countries of the region.

## Tobacco Control Measures: They Are Badly Needed in Order to Reverse the Tobacco Epidemic in Latin America

- Tobacco advertising and promotions by multinational tobacco companies are prolific throughout the region. Multinational tobacco companies are frequent sponsors of sports and cultural events, many of which are popular with young people.
- In some countries children work selling single cigarettes, and are also employed in tobacco cultivation.
- In general, medical professionals are not widely informed about the risks of tobacco. There is also a lack of health promotion programmes. This results in a lack of public knowledge which serves to reinforce a culture where tobacco use is socially acceptable. This makes it difficult for tobacco control programmes to advance.
- Although many countries in Latin America have passed tobacco control legislation, the legislation tends to be weak and contain loopholes which serve to the advantage of tobacco companies. In recent years, there are some Latin American countries which have passed fairly strong tobacco control legislation. Yet, few countries have adopted comprehensive tobacco control programmes and policies as recommended by WHO.
- The Tobacco Control Coordinating Committee for Latin America (CLACCTA) has been actively involved in moving

countries towards the adoption of comprehensive tobacco control polices and programmes.

- An Interagency Action Plan has been developed for Latin America to provide assistance and technical support to the various countries involved in the development and/or strengthening of tobacco control groups at the country level. One goal is to facilitate the establishment of strategic alliances or coalitions which are multisectoral and involve both government and nongovernmental organizations. The plan provides an important framework for implementing and monitoring progress on tobacco control in Latin America.

# "The Tobacco Industry's Youth Anti-Tobacco Programs"

*In "The Tobacco Industry's Youth Anti-Tobacco Programs," the Campaign for Tobacco-Free Kids casts a skeptical eye over the tobacco industry's antismoking campaigns, both past and present.*

In early December, tobacco giant Philip Morris announced that it was launching a new $100 million campaign to discourage youth from smoking. It features television advertisements promoting the message "Think. Don't Smoke."

## [Background Information]

Given the urgency of the problem of tobacco use by youth, it would seem at first glance that those concerned about the well-being of America's children should welcome the Philip Morris campaign. But the unfortunate truth is that this is another in a long line of efforts by the tobacco companies to make it appear as though they are seriously addressing the problem of youth smoking. All of these programs have been launched at particularly sensitive political moments for the tobacco industry, and all have been designed more to relieve political pressure on the industry than actually to discourage tobacco use by kids.

This latest effort by Philip Morris should be regarded very skeptically, especially by organizations Philip Morris may try to enlist as partners. Philip Morris and the tobacco industry frequently have attempted to recruit mainstream organizations to give their programs, and thus their policies and reputations, a patina of credibility.

If Philip Morris were truly serious about reducing tobacco use by kids, it would greatly reduce and revise, or even eliminate its marketing and advertising practices such as the use of the Marlboro Man that have been so effective in attracting young smokers. As it stands, Philip Morris is promoting its youth smoking programs as an answer to reducing underage tobacco use, while at the same time spending millions every day on marketing efforts that affect kids and fighting real tobacco control programs at local, state and federal levels.

*Source:* Campaign for Tobacco-Free Kids. 1997. "The Tobacco Industry's Youth Anti-Tobacco Programs." Date accessed: January 29, 1999. www.tobaccofreekids.org. Reprinted with permission.

## I. Previous Tobacco Industry Youth Smoking Programs

In response to intense political pressure and in an effort to avoid government regulation, the tobacco industry repeatedly has offered voluntary restrictions and programs ostensibly designed to reduce tobacco use:

- In 1964, in response to growing public knowledge of the dangers of smoking, the industry adopted an Advertising Code that prohibited advertising that suggests smoking is essential to "social prominence, distinction, or sexual attraction." From the rugged Marlboro Cowboy to the fun-loving Newport Couple, this code has been regularly violated for over three decades.

- In the 1980s, the Tobacco Institute, in response to Congressional interest in restrictions on tobacco ads and the problem of youth smoking, launched several programs, including "Helping Youth Decide" and "Helping Youth Say No." These programs emphasized decision-making for kids rather than warning them of the health dangers of tobacco. A study in the Journal of Family Practice found that the "Helping Youth Say No" program could actually encourage youth smoking by its suggestion that tobacco use is an adult activity.

- In 1990, the tobacco industry launched a new program called "It's the Law," again in response to Congressional interest in reducing tobacco use among youth. "It's the Law" shifted focus from youth decision-making to providing retailers with educational materials about not selling to kids. Beyond sending decals and signage to retail stores, this program was never effectively implemented. A 1992 study in the *American Journal of Public Health* found that compliance with the program was extremely low.

- In the later 1990s, to combat growing Congressional interest in the behavior of the tobacco industry, Philip Morris and its allies launched several additional programs, including "We Card" and "Action Against Access." Like previous programs, these were half-efforts at best, a point illustrated in an audit of "Action Against Access" by former U.S. Senator Warren Rudman, who found that retailers did not take the program seriously and that it was not implemented completely. Two years after the program had been in place, Philip Morris had penalized only 16 out of more than 400,000 tobacco retailers for selling to kids.

While the industry used these programs to deflect criticism that it was encouraging youth smoking, it opposed virtually all efforts to enact effective policies to protect kids from tobacco. Moreover, it sharpened and expanded its marketing practices, that have been shown to influence children to begin smoking and also to influence brand selection among youth smokers. These are the "replacement smokers" of tomorrow, as they have been called in tobacco industry memos.

## II. Internal Industry Documents

Recently released internal tobacco industry documents show that the goal of these industry programs is to deflect political pressure and avoid government regulation rather than actually protect kids:

- A 1979 Tobacco Institute memo from then Executive Vice President Franklin Dryden recommended that the industry consider a "pre-adult education" program: "It seems to me our objective is . . . a 'media event' which in itself promises a lot but produces little."
- A 1981 Tobacco Institute memo stated: "In order to offset further erosion of the industry's image in this area, and to avoid further legislative forays, the tobacco industry should take two actions: Clearly and visibly announce our position on teenage smoking to the public generally and to leaders of all youth-oriented organizations [and] . . . A program to depict cigarette smoking as one of many activities some people choose to do as adults."
- The same memo shows how tobacco companies seek mainstream partners for these efforts. The Tobacco Institute recommended that the programs be conducted with "major national educational organizations and . . . be directly supportive of their existing 'responsible living' programs."
- A 1990 Tobacco Institute memo outlined the "Helping Youth Decide" program: "The industry has in the past and must continue to defend its marketing practices. To ensure that the industry is putting forth maximum effort to meet these growing challenges, I have asked Institute staff to identify opportunities to politically and publicly reaffirm the industry's continued commitment to address the issue of youth smoking. . . . In order for this program to achieve its legislative goal, we believe a multi-year commitment must be made up front."
- In 1995, Philip Morris Senior Vice President Ellen Merlo wrote a memo warning her colleagues that the industry still faced a hostile climate on Capitol Hill. She warned: " . . . If we don't do something fast to project the sense of industry responsibility regarding the youth access issue, we are going to be looking at severe marketing restrictions in a very short

time. Those restrictions will pave the way for equally severe legislation or regulation on where adults are allowed to smoke."

- A Philip Morris executive wrote in 1995: "If we can frame proactive legislation or other kinds of action on the Youth Access issue . . . we will be protecting our industry for decades to come."

These memos demonstrate that the motivation behind these programs has not been to reduce tobacco use among kids, but rather to gain the industry positive publicity and create the appearance of action. It is therefore not surprising that there is scarce evidence showing the effectiveness of any of the industry's programs.

## III. Alliances with Mainstream Organizations

The tobacco industry has repeatedly reached out to well-respected organizations in an effort to secure credibility for its programs and policies. Most recently, the industry has worked closely with the U.S. Junior Chamber of Commerce to develop its "JAYS" (Jaycees Against Youth Smoking) program. This program is intended to encourage retailers to enforce minimum-age sales laws and to work with communities to raise awareness of the problem of the illegal sale of tobacco to kids.

While these efforts are positive and the Jaycees undoubtedly have the best intentions, this program has done little to reduce smoking because it lacks the key components of effective youth access initiatives, such as mandated retailer-compliance checks using undercover youth buyers.

A hallmark of all industry-designed efforts is the absence of the most effective tools for combating youth tobacco use. The industry seeks collaboration with well-meaning and credible organizations, such as the Jaycees, in an attempt to hide these glaring policy omissions.

## IV. The New Philip Morris Program

Philip Morris' new $100 million advertising campaign bears the hallmarks of the company's previous failed efforts:

- It is timed to relieve pressure on the industry from encroaching regulation and public action to reduce smoking. More specifically, it is likely that a key motivation is to discourage Congress and state legislatures from earmarking money from the recent tobacco settlement towards hard-hitting counter-advertising campaigns and other measures.
- The program fails to use the tobacco control policies that

have been proven to be most effective. Although there is not one single message that works best to discourage kids from using tobacco, the results from Massachusetts and California, which have aggressive counter-advertising campaigns, are instructive. These programs show that the appeals that have the most resonance among youth clearly depict the health consequences of smoking and focus on the industry's marketing and advertising practices. Such messages are conspicuously absent from the Philip Morris ads.

- The industry continues to oppose efforts to protect youth from tobacco and is still impacting kids with its marketing. Approximately 85 percent of youth who smoke choose the three most heavily advertised brands, including nearly 60 percent who smoke Marlboro. Yet, Philip Morris refuses to end such marketing. If the company was truly serious about ending youth smoking, then it would send the Marlboro Man into retirement. This is precisely what Philip Morris and other tobacco companies agreed to do in the June 20, 1997 agreement with state Attorneys General: eliminate all human and cartoon characters from their marketing. Later, the tobacco industry opposed and helped defeat the McCain bill, which would have ratified the agreement. Thus, it was never implemented.

- The industry continues to spend far more on advertising and marketing that attracts kids than on its youth anti-smoking program. The companies spent approximately $5 billion last year marketing tobacco products. Although Philip Morris' $100 million youth campaign is a substantial amount of money, even if it paid for an effective program, the messages would be drowned out by images of the Marlboro Man in venues ranging from convenience stores to magazines read heavily by kids.

- Philip Morris benefits from TV exposure. Since the early 1970s, tobacco companies have not been on television, except for a joint campaign in 1998 to oppose Congressional action against tobacco. Now, with the only national anti-tobacco campaign on TV by any organization—government, corporate or non-profit—Philip Morris stands to gain exposure and potentially an enhanced reputation, despite the generally low regard in which the public holds cigarette companies.

Advertising critics also have chastised the Philip Morris campaign:

- *ADWEEK* columnist Barbara Lippert wrote: "[T]hese ads are too tepid and generic . . . they could sell anything from orange juice to toothpaste . . . PM has chosen to create a mellow, sensitive, 'rely on your good sense, son' picture. Are they serious?

This is advertising covering a life-and-death issue! So where is the big stick? The scare tactics? The hit 'em over your head with destroying life stuff?"

- *USA Today* advertising columnist Bruce Horovitz placed Philip Morris' new campaign on his "Worst Ads of 1998" list. He wrote: "This is Philip Morris' jaded attempt at PR. Three spots with kids who say smoking isn't cool. . . . Philip Morris says it wants kids to stop smoking. Right. Just like Bill Gates want kids to stop staring at computer screens."
- Fred Goldberg, chairman-CEO of Goldberg Moser O'Neill, an advertising agency in San Francisco, wrote in *Advertising Age:* "I call it unmitigated gall and hypocrisy; incredible and disheartening. It is another reflection of the distorted values and warped standards that exist today more than ever."

## V. Conclusion

If Philip Morris honestly wanted to reduce youth smoking, it would immediately do the following:

- Stop marketing its tobacco products to kids.
- Quit using the Marlboro Man, the most recognized and effective cigarette icon, in its advertising.
- Implement all other marketing restrictions it agreed to in the June, 1997 Attorneys General settlement, including:

  —a ban on vending machines;
  —a ban on tobacco internet advertising;
  —a limitation on all tobacco ads in magazines with significant youth audiences to black-and-white text only;
  —a ban on outdoor ads at retail outlets; a complete ban on all brand name sponsorships of teams, sports, entertainment and other events;
  —stronger and more visible warning labels on all tobacco packaging and ads;
  —a limit of two small tobacco ads in black-and-white text only at each retail outlet; and
  —a ban on all self-service displays for cigarettes.

The new Philip Morris campaign, like the company's previous efforts, does none of the above and should be seen for what it really is [,] . . . a paper tiger. It is not likely to be effective. Nor is it a substitute for a comprehensive program to reduce tobacco use among kids, and most certainly it is not a replacement for aggressive counter-advertising campaigns at state and national levels.

It will be unfortunate if credible organizations partner with Philip Morris and attach their names and reputations to this program, which may help enhance the company's image with certain members of Congress, with stockholders and perhaps with some of the public, including children. This new Philip Morris campaign most likely will have met its corporate goal if it succeeds in diverting or stopping serious efforts to reduce tobacco use among kids.

# "Tobacco Use by Children: A Paediatric Disease"

*Because almost all smokers begin smoking while they are underage, Dr. David Kessler, commissioner of the Food and Drug Administration (FDA), has called smoking a pediatric disease, and in "Tobacco Use by Children," WHO explores some of the aspects of tobacco as a "disease" of children, including onset, prevalence, and consequences.*

Studies carried out in different countries have invariably shown that the majority of smokers start using tobacco while in their teenage years, sometimes even earlier. Soon after initiation, smoking becomes an intractable habit because of tobacco's powerful addictive properties. This has led Dr. David Kessler, Commissioner of the United States' Food and Drug Administration to say: "Nicotine addiction begins when most tobacco users are teenagers, so let's call this what it really is: a paediatric disease."

Tobacco use is growing among young people while the age of smoking initiation is declining.

- Smoking prevalence among US high school students increased from 28% in 1991 to 36% in 1997. And smoking can be just as prevalent among youth in developing countries. A survey, whose results were published in 1996, in one region of Argentina estimated that 40% of adolescents aged 13–18 were smokers.
- More than 80% of American youth who smoke start smoking before the age of eighteen. In many Latin American countries, 75% or more of smoking initiation occurs between the ages of 14 and 17.
- Even trying cigarettes is dangerous. One-third to one-half of adolescents who experiment with cigarettes go on to become regular smokers. One prospective study found that among those who experimented with cigarettes, about one-half had become regular smokers within one year.

Studies carried out in many countries show that if young people do not begin to use tobacco before the age of 20, they are unlikely to start smoking as adults. This highlights the importance of preventing smoking among young people.

*Reasons:* There are a number of complex and interacting reasons

---

*Source:* WHO. 1998. "Tobacco Use by Children: A Paediatric Disease." Fact Sheet N° 197. May 1998. Geneva: WHO. http://www.who.int/inf-fs/en/. Reprinted with permission.

why children and adolescents "contract" this disease. They mistake smoking for an attribute of independence—an image they see in adults who smoke and skillfully built by tobacco advertising.

- Adults who smoke, such as family members, film stars and sports heroes, influence children and, especially, adolescents a great deal. In many countries, very high numbers of teachers, medical professionals, and politicians/government officials smoke.
- Tobacco advertising plays a key role in encouraging young people to smoke. In countries around the world, billions of dollars are being spent on sophisticated tobacco advertising and promotions, portraying tobacco use as "fun," "glamourous," "mature," "modern," and "Western."

*Children and Environmental Tobacco Smoke (ETS):* The tobacco smoke of others has serious adverse health effects on infants and children.

- Due to maternal smoking and ETS, children's health may be compromised from before the time they are born. Babies born to women who smoke during pregnancy, as well as those infants exposed to ETS have a significantly greater risk of dying of sudden infant death syndrome (SIDS).
- Children exposed to ETS are more likely to suffer from respiratory illnesses, are at risk of impaired lung function, and have an increased frequency of middle-ear infections.
- Children exposed to ETS also have an increased chance of developing asthma, and for those children who already have asthma, ETS can exacerbate the problem.

*Nicotine Addiction in Young Smokers:* What often starts out as an "act of independence" may rapidly become an addictive dependence on tobacco.

The younger people start smoking cigarettes, the more likely they are to become strongly addicted to nicotine. By the time teenagers have been smoking on a daily basis for a number of years, the smoking habit and addiction levels may well have become entrenched, and they are faced with the same difficulties in quitting as adult smokers. Although intentions to quit and quit attempts are common among teenagers, only small numbers of teenagers actually stop.

- Studies by health scientists in the United States have found that about three-fourths of young smokers consider themselves addicted, while a majority of adolescent smokers in Australia have tried to quit and found it very difficult. In another US study, about two-thirds of adolescent smokers indicated that they wanted to quit smoking, and 70% said that they would not have started if they could choose again.

*Tobacco Industry and Young Smokers:* Although the tobacco industry claims that it does not want young people to smoke, their own documents, recently released to the public, show a longstanding interest in young smokers. The results of the above-mentioned US studies are remarkably similar to the conclusions of studies conducted years earlier for a Canadian tobacco company.

- "However intriguing smoking was at 11, 12 or 13, by the age of 16 or 17 many regretted their use of cigarettes for health reasons, and because they feel unable to stop smoking when they want to."
- "The desire to quit seems to come earlier now than before, even prior to the end of high school. In fact it often seems to take hold as soon as the recent starter admits to himself that he is hooked on smoking. However, the desire to quit, and actually carrying it out are two quite different things, as the would be quitter soon learns."

*Public Policies and Tobacco Use by Children:* Public policies can have a strong influence on whether or not children smoke. In drafting such policies, one should take into consideration that:

- Children are likely to start smoking if they grow up in an environment where tobacco advertising is prolific, where smoking rates are high among adults (including those that serve as role models for young people), where tobacco products are cheap and easily accessible, and where smoking is unrestricted in public places.
- Educational programmes and health promotion campaigns can serve a useful role in tobacco control, particularly in countries where the harms of tobacco use are not widely known. However, unless they are backed up by strong public policies, which help young people refrain from using tobacco, educational programmes have only modest results. Such education programmes and health promotion campaigns should be placed in the overall context of strong and coherent tobacco control policies.
- Health promotion campaigns to persuade young people not to smoke will likely be far more successful when increased attention is also given to helping adults quit smoking.

# "Tobacco and Kids"

*"Tobacco and Kids," produced by the Campaign for Tobacco-Free Kids, http://tobaccofreekids.org/, makes clear that the tobacco companies do regard youngsters under 18 as appropriate targets of their advertising. Some internal documents speak of targeting children as young as 13.*

Tobacco companies spend over $5 billion each year (nearly $14 million every day) promoting their products in order to replace the thousands of customers who either die or quit using these products each day.(1)

Tobacco industry documents, research on the effect of marketing to kids, and the opinions of advertising experts combine to reveal the intent and the success of the industry's efforts to attract new smokers from the ranks of children.

## Industry Documents

Numerous tobacco industry documents make clear that the industry has viewed kids as young as 13 years of age as a key market, studied the smoking habits of kids, and developed products and marketing campaigns aimed at them:

- "Evidence is now available to indicate that the 14–18 year old group is an increasing segment of the smoking population. RJR-T must soon establish a successful new brand in this market if our position in the industry is to be maintained in the long term."—"Planned Assumptions and Forecast for the Period 1977–1986" for RJ Reynolds Tobacco Company, March 15, 1976
- "This young adult market, the 14–24 group, . . . represent[s] tomorrow's cigarette business. As this 14–24 age group matures, they will account for a key share of the total cigarette volume—for at least the next 25 years."—Presentation from C.A. Tucker, Vice President of Marketing, to the Board of Directors of RJR Industries, September 30, 1974
- "To ensure increased and longer-term growth for the Camel Filter, the brand must increase its share penetration among

*Source:* Campaign for Tobacco-Free Kids. 2000 (access date). "Tobacco and Kids." http://tobaccofreekids.org/. Reprinted with permission.

the 14–24 age group which have a new set of more liberal values and which represent tomorrow's cigarette business."—1975 Memo to C.A. Tucker, Vice President for Marketing, RJR
- "Cherry Skoal is for somebody who likes the taste of candy, if you know what I'm saying."—former UST sales representative, quoted in a 1994 *Wall Street Journal* article on UST's graduation strategy
- "Today's teenager is tomorrow's potential regular customer, and the overwhelming majority of smokers first begin to smoke while still in their teens. . . . The smoking patterns of teenagers are particularly important to Philip Morris."—1981 Philip Morris internal document

## Empirical Evidence

In addition to the industry's own statements, there is compelling evidence that much of their advertising and promotion is directed at kids and that these efforts are very successful in recruiting new tobacco users to years of addiction:

- 86 percent of kids who smoke prefer Marlboro, Camel and Newport—the three most heavily advertised brands; only about one-third of adult smokers choose these brands. Marlboro, the most heavily advertised brand, constitutes almost 60 percent of the youth market but only about 25 percent of the adult market.(2)
- Each day, more than 3,000 kids become regular smokers.(3) Since 1991, past-month smoking has increased by one-third among eighth graders and tenth graders. Smoking among high school seniors reached a 19-year high of 36.5 percent in 1997 and is currently at 35.1 percent.(4)
- Almost 90 percent of adults who have ever been regular smokers began smoking at or before age 18.(5)
- 30 percent of kids (12 to 17 years old), both smokers and nonsmokers, own at least one tobacco promotional item, such as T-shirts, backpacks, and CD players.(6)
- Between 1989 and 1993, when advertising for the new Joe Camel campaign jumped from $27 million to $43 million, Camel's share among youth increased by more than 50 percent, while its adult market share did not change at all.(7)
- A study published in the *Journal of the National Cancer Institute* found that teens are more likely to be influenced to smoke by cigarette advertising than they are by peer pressure.(8)
- A 1996 study in the *Journal of Marketing* found that teenagers are three times as sensitive as adults to cigarette advertising.(9)

- A 1994 article in the *Journal of the American Medical Association* documented a rapid and unprecedented increase in the smoking initiation rate of adolescent girls subsequent to the launch in the late 1960s of women's cigarette brands like Virginia Slims.(10)
- A new (1998) longitudinal study of teenagers in the *Journal of the American Medical Association* showed that tobacco industry promotional activities influenced previously non-susceptible non-smokers to become susceptible to or experiment with smoking.(11)
- The development and marketing of "starter products" with such features as pouches and cherry flavoring have resulted in smokeless tobacco going from a product used primarily by older men to one for which young men comprise the largest portion of the market.(12) Nearly 16 percent of high school boys are current smokeless tobacco users.(13)
- According to a 1998 study, cigarette advertising and promotions led to 3.6 million new experimenters between 1988 and 1997. Of these, 2.6 million can be attributed to Camel promotional activities and 1.4 million to Marlboro. Of these new experimenters, nearly 1 million will eventually die from smoking-related diseases: 0.4 million from Camel and 0.2 million from Marlboro.(14)

## Advertising Experts

Even advertising industry executives believe that tobacco marketing influences kids, and a clear majority think this is done intentionally. Commissioned by the New York advertising firm of Shepardson, Stern, and Kaminsky in December of 1996, a telephone survey of 300 advertising industry executives in agencies with billings of more than $10 million revealed the following:

- 82 percent believe advertising for cigarettes and tobacco products reaches children and teenagers in significant numbers.
- 78 percent believe current tobacco advertising makes smoking more appealing or socially acceptable to kids.
- 71 percent believe that tobacco advertising changes behavior and increases smoking among kids.
- 59 percent believe that a GOAL of tobacco advertising is marketing cigarettes to teenagers who do not already smoke.
- 79 percent favor limitations on the style and placement of advertising for cigarette and tobacco products to minimize impact on children and teenagers.

## Sources

1. Federal Trade Commission, *1998 Federal Trade Commission Report to Congress for 1996,* Pursuant to the Federal Cigarette Labeling and Advertising Act, 1998.

2. U.S. Centers for Disease Control and Prevention (CDC), "Changes in the Cigarette Brand Preference of Adolescent Smokers, U.S. 1989–1993," *Morbidity and Mortality Weekly Report (MMWR),* August 1994.

3. CDC. "Incidence of Initiation of Cigarette Smoking—United States, 1965–1996," *MMWR,* 9 October 1998, Vol. 47, No. 39.

4. University of Michigan, Institute for Social Research, *The Monitoring the Future Study,* 1998.

5. *Preventing Tobacco Use Among Young People: A Report of The Surgeon General,* 1994.

6. Gallup International Institute, "Teen-age Attitudes and Behaviors Concerning Tobacco," September 1992.

7. CDC. "Changes in the Cigarette Brand Preference of Adolescent Smokers, U.S. 1989–1993," *MMWR,* August, 1994.

8. "Influence of Tobacco Marketing and Exposure to Smokers on Adolescent Susceptibility to Smoking," *Journal of the National Cancer Institute,* October, 1995.

9. Pollay, et al., "The Last Straw? Cigarette Advertising and Realized Market Shares Among Youth and Adults," *Journal of Marketing,* Vol. 60, No. 2.

10. Pierce, J., Lee L., and Gilpin E. R., "Smoking Initiation by Adolescent Girls, 1944 Through 1988," *JAMA,* Vol. 271, No. 8, 1994.

11. Pierce, J., et al., " Tobacco Industry Promotion of Cigarettes and Adolescent Smoking," *JAMA,* Vol. 279, No. 7, 1998.

12. CDC. "Surveillance for Selected Tobacco-Use Behaviors—United States, 1900–1994," *MMWR,* 18 November 1994, Vol. 43, No. SS-03.

13. CDC, "Tobacco Use Among High School Students —United States, 1997," *MMWR,* 3 April 1998, Vol. 47, No. 12.

14. Pierce, J. P., et al., "Sharing the Blame: Smoking Experimentation and Future Smoking-Related Mortality Due to Joe Camel and Marlboro Advertising and Promotions," Cancer Prevention and Control Program, Cancer Center, University of California, San Diego, 1998.

# "Nicotine Addiction in Adolescence"

*"Nicotine Addiction in Adolescence" explores the risk of becoming addicted to nicotine in adolescence and provides a number of observations relating to early addiction.*

Nicotine dependency through cigarette smoking is the most common form of drug addiction and causes more death and disease than all other addictions combined.[1] Forty percent of teenagers who smoke daily have tried to quit and failed.[2] Although nicotine is not normally associated with intoxication, its ability to addict users is much higher than so-called "harder" drugs. The risk of becoming dependent on alcohol with regular use is one in nine. For crack or cocaine used intravenously, the chance is one in four. However, the risk of becoming addicted to nicotine is between one in four and one in three.[3] . . .

[*Note*: 70% of underage smokers consider themselves addicted. (Smokers are defined as those who smoked 100 or more cigarettes and smoked during the past month. *Source: 1994 Surgeon General's Report.*)]

- More than 80% of young people who smoke one pack or more of cigarettes per day report that they "need" or are dependent on cigarettes.[4]
- Nicotine is as addictive as heroin, cocaine, and alcohol. Moreover, because the typical tobacco user receives daily and repeated doses of nicotine, addiction is more common among all tobacco users than among other drug users.[4]
- Among addictive behaviors, cigarette smoking is the one most likely to take hold during adolescence.[5]
- The younger people are when they start smoking cigarettes, the more likely they are to become strongly addicted to nicotine.[5]
- Each year, only 3% of all smokers who try to quit smoking have long-term success.[4]
- 42% of young people who smoke as few as three cigarettes go on to become regular smokers.[4]
- 50% of all smokers who have lost a lung because of cancer or have undergone major heart surgery cannot quit for more than a few weeks.[4]
- Young people who try to quit smoking suffer the same nicotine withdrawal symptoms as adults who try to quit.[7]
- Among young people who are daily smokers, more than half

*Source:* CDC. 1995. "Nicotine Addiction in Adolescence." Part of the "Stop the Sale, Prevent the Addiction" materials.

smoke their first cigarette within 30 minutes of waking in the morning.[8]

- About two-thirds of adolescent smokers say they want to quit smoking, and 70% say they would not have started smoking if they could choose again.[9]
- Three-fourths of young people who use tobacco daily report that they use it because "it's really hard to quit." Findings were the same for cigarette smokers and for smokeless tobacco users.[10]
- Over 90% of young people who use tobacco daily (cigarettes or smokeless tobacco) experienced at least one symptom of nicotine withdrawal when they tried to quit. [10]

## [Sources]

1. *SGR (Surgeon General's Report), Preventing Tobacco Use Among Young People,* p. 30.

2. *SGR, Preventing Tobacco Use Among Young People,* p. 78.

3. *Comparative Epidemiology of Dependence on Tobacco, Alcohol, Controlled Substances, and Inhalants: Basic Findings from the National Comorbidity Survey,* Anthony, J. C., Warner, L. A., Kessler, R. C., 1994, 2:244–268.

4. *SGR, Preventing Tobacco Use Among Young People,* p. 31.

5. *SGR, Preventing Tobacco Use Among Young People,* p. 9.

6. OSH, unpublished data from TAPS-II, 1994.

7. *SGR, Preventing Tobacco Use Among Young People,* p. 33.

8. Epidemiology of Tobacco Use and Symptoms of Nicotine Addiction in the United States: A Compilation of Data from Large National Surveys, Presentation for the Food and Drug Administration, Drug Abuse Advisory Committee, Giovino, G. A., Zhu, B. P., Tomar, S. Aug. 2, 1994.

9. George H. Gallup International Institute, *Teen-age Attitudes and Behavior Concerning Tobacco: Report of the Findings,* Princeton, N.J., 1992.

10. CDC, Reasons for Tobacco Use and Symptoms of Nicotine Withdrawal Among Adolescent and Young Adult Tobacco Users, United States, 1993, *MMWR* 1994, 43:745–750.

# Table of Consumption Data

*Table 8, "Consumption Data" (on opposite page), shows the total num-ber of cigarettes consumed year by year since 1900 along with per capita consumption and the percentage of change from year to year. These data are especially interesting with regard to World War I, the publication of the* 1964 Surgeon General's Report on Smoking and Health, *and the growth of the antitobacco movement.*

*Source:* CDC TIPS. 2000. Consumption Data Section. Table on "Total and per capita manufactured cigarette consumption and percentage change in per capita consumption—United States. United States Department of Agriculture, 1900–1995." http://www.cdc.gov/.

**Table [8]**
**Consumption Data: Total and Per Capita Manufactured Cigarette Consumption* and Percentage Change in Per Capita Consumption—United States Department of Agriculture, 1900–1995**

| Year | Total (Billion) | Per Capita+ (>18 yrs) | Percentage change in per capita consumption from previous year | Year | Total (Billion) | Per Capita+ (>18 yrs) | Percentage change in per capita consumption from previous year |
|---|---|---|---|---|---|---|---|
| 1900 | 2.5 | 54 | | 1948 | 358.9 | 3,505 | +2.6 |
| 1901 | 2.5 | 53 | -1.9 | 1949 | 360.9 | 3,480 | -0.7 |
| 1902 | 2.8 | 60 | +13.2 | 1950 | 369.8 | 3,552 | +2.1 |
| 1903 | 3.1 | 64 | +6.7 | 1951 | 397.1 | 3,744 | +5.4 |
| 1904 | 3.3 | 66 | +3.1 | 1952 | 416.0 | 3,886 | +3.8 |
| 1905 | 3.6 | 70 | +6.1 | 1953 | 408.2 | 3,778 | -2.8 |
| 1906 | 4.5 | 86 | +22.9 | 1954 | 387.8 | 3,546 | -6.1 |
| 1907 | 5.3 | 99 | +15.1 | 1955 | 396.4 | 3,597 | +1.4 |
| 1908 | 5.7 | 105 | +6.1 | 1956 | 406.5 | 3,650 | +1.5 |
| 1909 | 7.0 | 125 | +19.0 | 1957 | 422.5 | 3,755 | +2.9 |
| 1910 | 8.6 | 151 | +20.8 | 1958 | 448.9 | 3,953 | +5.3 |
| 1911 | 10.1 | 173 | +14.6 | 1959 | 467.5 | 4,073 | +3.0 |
| 1912 | 13.2 | 223 | +28.9 | 1960 | 484.4 | 4,171 | +2.4 |
| 1913 | 15.8 | 260 | +16.6 | 1961 | 502.5 | 4,266 | +2.3 |
| 1914 | 16.5 | 267 | +2.7 | 1962 | 508.4 | 4,266 | 0.0 |
| 1915 | 17.9 | 285 | +6.7 | 1963 | 523.9 | 4,345 | +1.9 |
| 1916 | 25.2 | 395 | +38.6 | 1964 | 511.3 | 4,194 | -3.5 |
| 1917 | 35.7 | 551 | +39.5 | 1965 | 528.8 | 4,258 | +1.5 |
| 1918 | 45.6 | 697 | +26.5 | 1966 | 541.3 | 4,287 | +0.7 |
| 1919 | 48.0 | 727 | +4.3 | 1967 | 549.3 | 4,280 | -0.2 |
| 1920 | 44.6 | 665 | -8.5 | 1968 | 545.6 | 4,186 | -2.2 |
| 1921 | 50.7 | 742 | +11.6 | 1969 | 528.9 | 3,993 | -4.6 |
| 1922 | 53.4 | 770 | +3.8 | 1970 | 536.5 | 3,985 | -0.2 |
| 1923 | 64.4 | 911 | +18.3 | 1971 | 555.1 | 4,037 | +1.3 |
| 1924 | 71.0 | 982 | +7.8 | 1972 | 566.8 | 4,043 | +0.1 |
| 1925 | 79.8 | 1,085 | +10.5 | 1973 | 589.7 | 4,148 | +2.6 |
| 1926 | 89.1 | 1,191 | +9.8 | 1974 | 599.0 | 4,141 | -0.2 |
| 1927 | 97.5 | 1,279 | +7.4 | 1975 | 607.2 | 4,122 | -0.5 |
| 1928 | 106.0 | 1,366 | +6.8 | 1976 | 613.5 | 4,091 | -0.8 |
| 1929 | 118.6 | 1,504 | +10.1 | 1977 | 617.0 | 4,043 | -1.2 |
| 1930 | 119.3 | 1,485 | -1.3 | 1978 | 616.0 | 3,970 | -1.8 |
| 1931 | 114.0 | 1,399 | -5.8 | 1979 | 621.5 | 3,861 | -2.7 |
| 1932 | 102.8 | 1,245 | -11.0 | 1980 | 631.5 | 3,849 | -0.3 |
| 1933 | 111.6 | 1,334 | +7.1 | 1981 | 640.0 | 3,836 | -0.3 |
| 1934 | 125.7 | 1,483 | +11.2 | 1982 | 634.0 | 3,739 | -2.5 |
| 1935 | 134.4 | 1,564 | +5.5 | 1983 | 600.0 | 3,488 | -6.7 |
| 1936 | 152.7 | 1,754 | +12.1 | 1984 | 600.4 | 3,446 | -1.2 |
| 1937 | 162.8 | 1,847 | +5.3 | 1985 | 594.0 | 3,370 | -2.2 |
| 1938 | 163.4 | 1,830 | -0.9 | 1986 | 583.8 | 3,274 | -2.8 |
| 1939 | 172.1 | 1,900 | +3.8 | 1987 | 575.0 | 3,197 | -2.4 |
| 1940 | 181.9 | 1,976 | +4.0 | 1988 | 562.5 | 3,096 | -3.3 |
| 1941 | 208.9 | 2,236 | +13.2 | 1989 | 540.0 | 2,926 | -5.5 |
| 1942 | 245.0 | 2,585 | +15.6 | 1990 | 525.0 | 2,826 | -3.4 |
| 1943 | 284.3 | 2,956 | +14.4 | 1991 | 510.0 | 2,720 | -3.8 |
| 1944 | 296.3 | 3,039 | +2.8 | 1992 | 500.0 | 2,641 | -2.9 |
| 1945 | 340.3 | 3,449 | +13.5 | 1993 | 485.0 | 2,538 | -3.9 |
| 1946 | 344.3 | 3,446 | -0.1 | 1994 | 485.0 | 2,522 | -0.6 |
| 1947 | 345.4 | 3,416 | -0.9 | 1995 est | 487.0 | 2,515 | -0.3 |

*Includes overseas forces: "Total" consumption, 1917–1919 and 1940 to date, "Per Capita" consumption, 1930 to date.
+Ages 18 years and older.
est = Estimated.

*Sources: Tobacco Situation and Outlook Report,* U.S.D.A., April 1996 and September 1987. Miller, R. "U.S. cigarette consumption, 1900 to date." in Harr, W., ed. *Tobacco Yearbook, 1981– ,* p. 53.

## "Smokeless Tobacco: A Dangerous Alternative"

*"Smokeless Tobacco is not a safe alternative to cigarettes," says the CDC, and in "Smokeless Tobacco: A Dangerous Alternative" it provides documented facts about the health risks associated with smokeless tobacco.*

Smokeless tobacco is not a safe alternative to cigarettes. In 1977, when Sean Marsee was 12, a tobacco company representative handed him free samples of snuff in his hometown of Talihana, Okla. He soon began using chewing tobacco and became addicted to nicotine. Sean was a star athlete: he was named Talihana High School's Outstanding Athlete of 1983. But because of heavy smokeless tobacco use, Sean developed oral cancer and died in 1984. Contrary to what 60 percent of high school users think, smokeless tobacco is very harmful to their health. . . .[see Figure 4].

- Use of smokeless tobacco among youth is a growing problem. Between 1970 and 1986, the use of snuff increased 15 times and the use of chewing tobacco increased four times among male adolescents ages 17–19.[3]
- Smokeless tobacco use can cause gum disease and cancer of the mouth, pharynx, esophagus, and pancreas.[4]
- Animal studies suggest that the cancer-causing agents in smokeless tobacco can cause lung cancer, even though they do not enter the body through the lungs.[5]
- Smokeless tobacco use can lead to irreversible gum recession.[4]
- Smokeless tobacco might play a role in cardiovascular disease and stroke by increasing blood pressure and causing an irregular heart beat. One major study has shown that smokeless tobacco use doubles the risk of dying from cardiovascular disease.[4]
- About one-third of American high school seniors—and more than half of male high school seniors—have tried smokeless tobacco.[6]
- 40% of high school users believe that there is only slight risk in smokeless tobacco use.[2]
- In some states, nearly one out of three male high school students currently uses smokeless tobacco.[4]
- People who stop using smokeless tobacco have nicotine withdrawal symptoms that are the same as those for people

*Source:* CDC. 1999 (access date). "Smokeless Tobacco: A Dangerous Alternative." www.cdc.gov/tobacco/sgr/sgr4kids/smokless.htm.

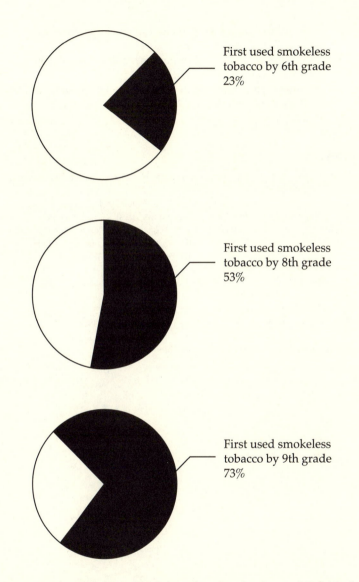

First used smokeless
tobacco by 6th grade
23%

First used smokeless
tobacco by 8th grade
53%

First used smokeless
tobacco by 9th grade
73%

**Figure 4  Pattern of First Use of Smokeless Tobacco Based on Survey of High School Seniors Who Use Smokeless Tobacco**

*Source: Surgeon General's 1994 Report*

who try to stop smoking, including cravings, irritability, distractibility, and hunger.[7]
- Adolescents who use smokeless tobacco are more likely to become cigarette smokers.[8]
- Among high school seniors who use smokeless tobacco, 23% had tried it by grade six, 53% by grade eight, and 73% by grade nine.[9]

## [Sources]

1. SGR (Surgeon General Report), Preventing Tobacco Use Among Young People, p. 97.

2. SGR, Preventing Tobacco Use Among Young People, p. 145.

3. U.S. Department of Health and Human Services, Reducing the Health Consequence of Smoking: 25 Years of Progress. A Report of the Surgeon General, 1989. Rockville, Md.: U.S. Department of Health and Human Services, Public Health Service, Centers for Disease Control, 1989, publication no. 89–8411.

4. SGR, Preventing Tobacco Use Among Young People, p. 39.

5. National Cancer Institute Monograph 2, Smokeless Tobacco or Health: An International Perspective, 1992, p. 114.

6. SGR, Preventing Tobacco Use Among Young People, p. 95.

7. SGR, Preventing Tobacco Use Among Young People, p. 230.

8. SGR, Preventing Tobacco Use Among Young People, p. 231.

9. SGR, Preventing Tobacco Use Among Young People, p. 101.

# "Young Women and Smoking"

*In "Young Women and Smoking," the Office on Women's Health reports that smoking by teenage girls is widespread and increasing and that females appear to be more susceptible both to peer pressure to smoke and to the addictive properties of tobacco. Worse, evidence indicates that women are 10 times more likely than men to develop lung cancer as a result of smoking.*

## The Facts

Smoking is the number one preventable cause of death in women in the United States. Of the more than 140,000 women who die prematurely from tobacco-related illnesses each year, 80 percent began smoking while they were adolescents. Evidence demonstrates that young people who begin to use tobacco do not understand the nature of the addiction and, as a result, believe they will be able to avoid the harmful consequences of tobacco use. These adolescents do not adequately appreciate the long-term effects of their actions.

## Smoking by Girls: Widespread and Increasing

Each day in the United Stated about 1,500 girls begin smoking. Nearly all first use of tobacco occurs before high school graduation.

Since 1991, cigarette smoking by adolescents has risen annually. The 1995 National Household Survey on Drug Abuse estimates that 20 percent of youths aged 12–17 (4.5 million adolescents) were current smokers in 1995. In 1994, the rate was 18.9 percent.

Approximately 1 of 5 teenage girls is now a smoker. The 1995 Centers for Disease Control and Prevention (CDC) Youth Risk Behavior Survey (YRBS) indicates that an increasing number of high school students are smoking on a regular basis, i.e., having smoked on one or more of the 30 days preceding the survey ("current" smokers) or having smoked on 20 or more of the 30 days ("frequent" smokers). Survey data reveal the following about high school girls and their smoking behavior:

- 39.8 percent of white, non-Hispanic girls are current smokers and 20.8 percent are frequent smokers.

*Source:* Office on Women's Health, U.S. Public Health Service, U.S. Department of Health and Human Services. 2000 (access date). "Young Women and Smoking." Fact Sheets on Women and Tobacco. http://www.inwat.org/young.htm.

- 32.9 percent of Hispanic girls are current smokers and 9.3 percent are frequent smokers.
- 12.2 percent of black, non-Hispanic girls are current smokers and 1.3 percent are frequent smokers.
- Overall, 34.3 percent of high school girls are current smokers and 5.9 percent are frequent smokers.

Similar findings were revealed by The Monitoring the Future Study, a survey of 8th, 10th, and 12th graders sponsored by the National Institute on Drug Abuse:

- Cigarette use by girls and boys combined increased from 28.3 percent in 1991 to 33.5 percent in 1995.
- The prevalence of smoking among 8th grade girls rose from 13.1 percent in 1991 to 19.0 percent in 1995. For 10th grade girls the increase during this time period was even higher— 20.7 percent to 27.9 percent—and for 12th grade girls it rose from 27.5 percent to 32 percent.

## Why Do Girls Smoke?

When most girls begin smoking, they are usually caught up in the moment, in the immediate experience of what appears to be a "cool," "adult," or even "glamorous" behavior. They are naive about the powerful addictive nature of nicotine, which, for some adolescents, takes hold after only a few cigarettes. For example:

- Most adolescents who have smoked as few as 100 cigarettes in their lifetime report that they would like to quit, but cannot. The Monitoring the Future Study found that 70 percent of high school seniors who smoked as few as one to five cigarettes a day were still smoking 5 years later, and most of those young people had increased the number of cigarettes they smoked.
- Combined 1991 and 1992 data from the National Health Interview Survey show that 76 percent of young women smokers ages 12 to 24 years say they feel dependent on cigarettes. Among those who had tried to quit smoking during the 12 months preceding the survey, 82 percent were unable to do so.

The initiation of cigarette smoking is influenced by several interrelated factors, including:

- Having friends who smoke and having a best friend who smokes.

- Parental smoking, which tends to establish smoking as a normative behavior.
- Low self-esteem, poor self-image, low perception of self-efficacy, and susceptibility to peer pressure.
- Sensation-seeking, rebelliousness, and a sense of invulnerability.
- Low knowledge level of the adverse effects of cigarette smoking.
- Anxiety or depression.
- Sociodemographic characteristics. Girls are more likely to smoke if they do not plan to complete 4 years of college, if their parents have a low number of years of education, or if they live in single-parent or unsupervised households.
- Pharmacologic response.
- Advertising and exposure to smoking in mass media outlets such as television, movies, and sports events which reinforces the idea that smoking is a normal, sophisticated, adult behavior and that it is glamorous.

Advertising specifically targeted to young women in the late 1960s and early 1970s correlates with smoking initiation by young women during the same period. Data from the National Health Interview Survey of more than 102,600 women show an abrupt increase in smoking initiation in girls under age 18 around 1967, when tobacco advertising introduced specific brands of cigarettes for women.

## Access to Tobacco Products

Acquiring cigarettes is currently not difficult for adolescents, even though every State has a law prohibiting the sale of cigarettes to minors. Over the past 4 years, three-fourths of surveyed 8th graders and more than 90 percent of 10th graders said they can get cigarettes fairly easily. Of girls who smoke, nearly one-fourth of 9th graders, one-third of 10th graders, and one-half of 11th graders and 12th graders buy their cigarettes in a convenience store, supermarket, or gas station. Of the 9th graders, only 17 percent were asked to show proof of age when buying cigarettes.

## Health Effects of Smoking

The short-term effects of smoking include:

- *Nicotine Addiction.* The younger an adolescent is when she begins to smoke, the more severe her level of nicotine addiction is likely to be.

- *Respiratory Problems.* Cigarette smoking during childhood and adolescence causes an increase in cough and phlegm production, an increase in the number and severity of respiratory illnesses, decreased physical fitness, and potential retardation in the rate of lung growth and in the level of maximum lung function.
- *Coronary Artery Disease.* Smokers have early development of coronary artery disease and abnormal lipid levels, possible precursors of heart disease.
- *Dental Problems.* Tobacco use by adolescents is associated with early signs of periodontal degeneration and with lesions in the mouth that can develop into oral cancers.
- *Mental Health Effects.* Many adolescent smokers report mental health effects, such as nervousness and depression, and tend to engage in more high-risk behaviors than adolescents who do not smoke.
- *Health-Damaging Behaviors.* Tobacco is associated with a range of health-damaging behaviors, including an increased risk of being involved in fights, engaging in high-risk sexual behavior, and using alcohol and other drugs.
- *Negative Effects on Quality of Life.* Smoking affects a young woman's quality of life—leading to bad breath, wrinkled skin, stained teeth, and other negative effects that influence how she looks and feels.

Long-term health effects of smoking include:

- *Cancer.* Women who smoke have at least a 10 times greater likelihood of developing lung cancer than nonsmoking women. The increase in lung cancer among women parallels the increase in smoking in women over the past six decades. Between 1960 and 1990, the death rate from lung cancer among women increased by more than 400 percent, and the rate is continuing to increase. In 1987, lung cancer surpassed breast cancer as the number one cause of cancer deaths among American women. In 1995, lung cancer killed 62,000 women; of those deaths, 47,182 (76.1 percent) are attributable to smoking. In addition to lung cancer, tobacco use is a major risk factor for cancers of the mouth, throat, esophagus, kidney, pancreas, bladder, and cervix.
- *Cardiovascular and Respiratory Diseases.* Cigarette smoking greatly increases a woman's chance of developing cardiovascular diseases. Smoking by women in the United States is associated with almost as many deaths from heart disease as from lung cancer, more than 61,000 each year. A woman who smokes is two to six times more likely to suffer a

heart attack than a nonsmoking woman, and the risk increases with the number of cigarettes smoked each day. The risk for cardiovascular disease also increases among young women who both smoke and use oral contraceptives. In addition, smoking increases the risk of having a stroke. Each year, about 8,000 women die from strokes attributable to smoking. The risks for emphysema, bronchitis, and pneumonia are also increased among women who smoke.

- *Reproductive Health.* Smoking may be damaging to women's reproductive health. It is associated with infertility, complications during pregnancy, and an earlier onset of menopause. The estimated 18 to 20 percent of pregnant women who smoke throughout their pregnancies subject themselves and their fetuses and newborns to significant health risks, including miscarriage, stillbirth, preterm delivery, low birth weight infants, and higher rates of infant mortality.
- *Children's Health.* Tobacco use by mothers can also adversely affect the health of their children. The risk for Sudden Infant Death Syndrome (SIDS) increases among infants who are exposed to intrauterine smoke and to secondhand smoke after pregnancy. A study from the Centers for Disease Control and Prevention (CDC) and Emory University reports that smoking during pregnancy also increases the risk by 50 percent of having a child with mental retardation; this increased risk rises up to 85 percent among those who smoke a pack or more of cigarettes each day. The health of as many as 1 million children with asthma is worsened by exposure to secondhand smoke.

## Gender Differences in the Effects of Tobacco Use

*Physiological differences.* Women appear to be more susceptible to the addictive properties of nicotine and have a slower metabolic clearance of nicotine from their bodies than do men.

Females appear to be more susceptible to the effects of tobacco carcinogens than males. Some studies have shown that smoking the same number of cigarettes, women have higher rates of lung cancer. Girls and women are significantly more likely than boys and men to feel dependent on cigarettes and more likely to report being unable to cut down on smoking.

## Gender Differences in Smoking Cessation

Several strategies are available to help young women stop smoking including cessation programs, behavioral/cognitive interventions, hypnosis, and medication.

- Clinical trials reveal that the same treatments benefit women and men.
- There are no gender differences in quit attempts and success rates.
- Few studies have examined programs specifically tailored to one gender.
- Interventions such as restricted access to cigarettes by minors, limiting cigarette advertising, and increasing cigarette taxes seem to affect men and women similarly.

While women appear to benefit from the same interventions as do men, women may face different stressors and barriers to quitting smoking that must be addressed:

- Greater likelihood of depression
- Weight control concerns
- Child care issues

## Tobacco Prevention and Control Programs of the U.S. Department of Health and Human Services: Preventing Tobacco Use by Girls—Public Health Approaches

To prevent the adverse health effects and deaths in women caused by tobacco use, the most effective approach is to deter smoking initiation by girls and adolescent women. Education, restriction of advertising to young people, reduced access, and restriction of smoking in public places have been shown to be effective techniques for smoking prevention.

Consistent with its mission to protect and advance the Nation's health, the U.S. Department of Health and Human Services (DHHS) has made prevention and control of tobacco use by children and adolescents a top priority. One of the most important objectives of the Healthy People 2000 initiative sponsored by the U.S. Public Health Service (PHS), DHHS, is to "Reduce the initiation of cigarette smoking by children and youth so that no more than 15 percent have become regular cigarette smokers by age 20."

# Warning Label Laws and Their Labels

*The following list is a collection of the various warning labels, past and present, for cigarettes, cigars, and smokeless tobacco. The first cigarette label appeared shortly after Surgeon General Luther Terry's 1964 Report on Smoking and Health. It was a weak statement of risk: "Cigarette Smoking May Be Hazardous to Your Health." Terry's advisory panel had been certain, but even "May Be" did not satisfy the tobacco companies. Among the several phrases to which they objected was "Your Health." The longtime chairman of the Scientific Advisory Board of the TIRC/CTR, Clarence Cook Little, had argued that some people were genetically more likely than others to develop cancer. Accordingly, the tobacco people wanted the warning amended to " . . . May Be Hazardous to the Health of Some People" or "of Susceptible People." But the legislators apparently believed they had already made enough compromises.*

*In 1969 the warning was strengthened to say that "[s]moking Is Dangerous," and in 1984 it was expanded to four more specific warnings, including reference to the benefits of quitting.*

*The fourth of the four warnings, incidentally, reflects a final small victory for tobacco. A tobacco representative is said to have asked that carbon monoxide not be identified as a poisonous gas, and the label says only that carbon monoxide is present in tobacco smoke.*

*Law:* The Federal Cigarette Labeling and Advertising Act of 1965 (Public Law 89–92).
*Label:* Caution: Cigarette Smoking May Be Hazardous to Your Health.

*Law:* 1969 Public Health Cigarette Smoking Act (Public Law 91–222).
*Label:* Warning: The Surgeon General Has Determined That Cigarette Smoking Is Dangerous to Your Health.

*Law:* Comprehensive Smoking Education Act of 1984 (which required four specific health warnings on all cigarette packages and advertisements).
*Labels:*
SURGEON GENERAL'S WARNING: Smoking Causes Lung Cancer, Heart Disease, Emphysema, and May Complicate Pregnancy.

---

*Source:* Text of labels drawn from various reports by the surgeon general.

SURGEON GENERAL'S WARNING: Quitting Smoking Now Greatly Reduces Serious Risks to Your Health.

SURGEON GENERAL'S WARNING: Smoking by Pregnant Women May Result in Fetal Injury, Premature Birth, and Low Birth Weight.

SURGEON GENERAL'S WARNING: Cigarette Smoke Contains Carbon Monoxide.

*Law:* Comprehensive Smokeless Tobacco Health Education Act of 1986.

*Labels:*

Warning: This Product May Cause Mouth Cancer

Warning: This Product May Cause Gum Disease and Tooth Loss

Warning: This Product is Not a Safe Alternative to Cigarettes

*Law:* In a settlement with the FTC on June 26, 2000, the U.S. cigar companies agreed to the following health warnings on cigar packaging:

*Labels:*

SURGEON GENERAL'S WARNING: Cigar Smoking Can Cause Cancers of the Mouth and Throat, Even If You Do Not Inhale.

SURGEON GENERAL'S WARNING: Cigar Smoking Can Cause Lung Cancer and Heart Disease.

SURGEON GENERAL'S WARNING: Tobacco Use Increases the Risk of Infertility, Stillbirth and Low Birth Weight.

SURGEON GENERAL'S WARNING: Cigars Are Not a Safe Alternative to Cigarettes.

SURGEON GENERAL'S WARNING: Tobacco Smoke Increases the Risk of Lung Cancer and Heart Disease, Even in Nonsmokers.

# "Framework Convention on Tobacco Control"

*Under the leadership of Director-General Gro Harlem Brundtland, WHO is spearheading worldwide opposition to tobacco. WHO describes the Framework Convention on Tobacco Control (FCTC) as the world's first set of multilaterally negotiated rules devoted entirely to a major health issue. It will be ready for signature no later than 2003. WHO says it is expected to address issues as diverse as tobacco advertising and promotion, agricultural diversification, regulation, smuggling, treatment of tobacco addiction, and smoke-free areas. The "FCTC Primer" also discusses the Tobacco Free Initiative (TFI), a WHO cabinet project designed to focus international attention and resources on the tobacco pandemic, which kills an estimated 4 million people a year, most in the developing world. The TFI's central message is that every one of these deaths is preventable.*

The spectacular rise and spread of tobacco consumption around the world is a challenge and an opportunity for the World Health Organization. The challenge comes in seeking global solutions for a problem that cuts across national boundaries, cultures, societies and socio-economic strata. The unique and massive public health impact of tobacco provides WHO an opportunity to propose to the world a first comprehensive response to deal with the silent epidemic as the tobacco menace has often been called. The Tobacco Free Initiative (TFI) has begun preliminary work in this direction.

On 24 May 1999, the World Health Assembly (WHA), the governing body of the World Health Organization (WHO), paved the way for multilateral negotiations to begin on a set of rules and regulations that will govern the global rise and spread of tobacco and tobacco products in the next century. The 191-member WHA unanimously backed a resolution calling for work to begin on the Framework Convention on Tobacco Control (FCTC)—a new legal instrument that could address issues as diverse as tobacco advertising and promotion, agricultural diversification, smuggling, taxes and subsidies. A record 50 nations took the floor to pledge financial and political support for the Convention. The list included the five permanent members of the United Nations Security Council, major tobacco growers and exporters as well as several countries in the developing and developed world which face the brunt of the tobacco

*Source:* Excerpted from: WHO. 2001 (access date). "Framework Convention on Tobacco Control: A Primer—Frequently Asked Questions." http://tobacco.who.int/en/fctc/index.html. Reprinted with permission.

industry's marketing and promotion pitch. The European Union and 5 NGOs also made statements in support of the Convention and the Director-General's leadership in global tobacco control.

The Working Group on the WHO Framework Convention on Tobacco Control held two meetings which, together, were attended by participants from a wide range of sectors and included representatives from 153 Member States (representing 95% of the world's population) and the European Community, as well as observers from the Holy See, Palestine, organizations of the United Nations system, other intergovernmental organizations and nongovernmental organizations.

In May 2000, the World Health Assembly unanimously adopted a resolution which formally launched the political negotiations which commenced the 16 to 21 October 2000 in Geneva, Switzerland. At the first session of negotiations, Member States elected Ambassador Amorim of Brazil Chairman of the Intergovernmental Negotiating Body, as well as vice chairs from Australia, India, Iran, South Africa, Turkey, and the United States. Substantive matters were addressed in the Plenary and three technical working groups were established. A President's Draft of the Convention will be available in January 2001. The second session of negotiations will be held 30 April–5 May 2001 in Geneva, Switzerland.

# 5

# Directory of Organizations and Agencies

Other or more specialized organizations may be found by searching DIRLINE (National Library of Medicine web site). DIRLINE allows a search by keyword, phrase, acronym, or initials.

## Federal Government

**Agency for Health Care Policy and Research (AHCPR)**
AHCPR Publications Clearinghouse
P.O. Box 8547
Silver Spring, MD 20907-8547
(800) 358-9295
http://www.ahcpr.gov/

Part of the U.S. Department of Health and Human Services, AHCPR was created in 1989 to provide information about health care and the health-care system. More specifically, it seeks to support and conduct research that creates a scientific base for improvements in clinical care and in the organization and financing of health care. It also seeks to develop databases and research tools for public and private decision makers; to encourage the development of public-private partnerships to identify research priorities; and to conduct studies, translate findings into clinical practice, and disseminate information for public use.

**Agricultural Research Service (USDA)**
1400 Independence Avenue, S.W.
Washington, DC 20250
(301) 504-1638
http://www.ars.usda.gov/

The Agricultural Research Service (ARS) is the main in-house research arm of the U.S. Department of Agriculture. In this capacity, according to its mission statement, it conducts research to develop solutions to agricultural problems of high national priority and provide information access and dissemination. The purpose of this research is to "ensure high-quality safe food and other agricultural products; assess the nutritional needs of Americans; sustain a competitive agricultural economy, enhance the natural resource base and the environment, and; provide economic opportunities for rural citizens, communities, and society as a whole." Traditionally, ARS research has been associated with increased production and higher quality produce.

**Bureau of Alcohol, Tobacco and Firearms (ATF)**
U.S. Department of Treasury
Bureau of Alcohol, Tobacco and Firearms
Regulations Branch
650 Massachusetts Avenue, N.W.
Washington, DC 20226
Director: (202) 927-8700
Fax: (202) 927-8876
General information: (202) 927-7777
http://www.atf.treas.gov/

The ATF is a law-enforcement organization within the U.S. Department of the Treasury. Among its responsibilities are reducing violent crime, collecting revenue, and protecting the public. It enforces federal laws relating to alcohol, tobacco, firearms, explosives, and arson. The ATF is a source of information about current tax rates and tax revenues pertaining to tobacco.

**Center for Substance Abuse Prevention (CSAP)**
5600 Fishers Lane
Rockwall II
Rockville, MD 20857
(301) 443-0365

E-mail: nnadal@samhsa.gov
http://www.samhsa.gov/csap/index.htm

CSAP says its mission is "to provide national leadership in the federal effort to prevent alcohol, tobacco, and illicit drug problems." As part of its effort to prevent such problems, CSAP "connects people and resources to innovative ideas and strategies"; "encourages efforts to reduce and eliminate alcohol, tobacco, and illicit drug problems"; and "fosters the development of comprehensive . . . prevention policies and systems" that "target both individuals and the environments in which they live." CSAP is part of the Substance Abuse and Mental Health Services Administration, a federal agency that seeks to improve the quality and availability of prevention, treatment, and rehabilitation services.

**Centers for Disease Control and Prevention (CDC)**
National Center for Chronic Disease Prevention and Health
    Promotion (NCCDPHP)
Office on Smoking and Health (OSH)
Mail Stop #K-50
4770 Buford Highway, N.E.
Atlanta, GA 30341-3724
General information and publication requests: (770) 488-5705
Media campaign response line and fax service: (800) CDC-1311
http://www.cdc.gov/tobacco/

With regard to tobacco, the CDC directs the U.S. government's tobacco and health activities; collects and distributes smoking and health information; and maintains a bibliographic database of smoking and health-related information that spans 30 years and contains more than 56,000 records. The database may be accessed through the OSH web site and is also available on a CD-ROM (CDP file), which is available for use at Federal Deposit libraries. Copies may be purchased from the Government Printing Office (GPO) by calling (202) 512-1800.

**Department of Agriculture (USDA)**
Tobacco and Peanut Division, USDA
1400 Independence Avenue, S.W.
Washington, DC 20250-0514
(202) 720-4318
http://www.usda.gov/

The USDA provides information related to tobacco price-support programs and other agricultural issues pertaining to tobacco.

**Department of Health and Human Services (HHS)**
Office of Secretary of HHS
Hubert H. Humphrey Building
200 Independence Avenue, S.W.
Washington, DC 20201
(202) 690-7000
Fax: (202) 690-7203
http://www.hhs.gov/

The HHS helps to formulate national policy on smoking and health. *See also* the list of state health departments, which along with local health departments provide health information relating to tobacco.

**Department of Labor** (*See* Occupational Safety and Health Administration)

**Department of Transportation** (*See* Federal Aviation Administration)

**Department of the Treasury**
Main Treasury
1500 Pennsylvania Avenue, N.W.
Washington, DC 20220
Secretary's Office: (202) 622-5300
Public information: (202) 622-2960
Fax: (202) 622-2599
http://www.treas.gov/

The Department of the Treasury is a source for information on tobacco tax policy. *See also* Bureau of Alcohol, Tobacco and Firearms.

**Economic Research Service (USDA)**
USDA
Economic Research Service
1800 M Street, N.W.
Washington, DC 20036-5831
Public Information: (202) 694-5050
Publications: (800) 999-6779
http://www.ers.usda.gov/

A division of the U.S. Department of Agriculture, the Economic Research Service was established in 1961 to provide economic analysis related to agriculture, food, the environment, and rural development to improve public and private decision-making.

**Environmental Protection Agency (EPA)**
Indoor Air Quality Information Clearinghouse
P.O. Box 37133
Washington, DC 20013-7133
(800) 438-4318
http://www.epa.gov/iaq/

The EPA serves as the U.S. government's lead agency on environmental issues. With regard to tobacco, it offers publications and information on the adverse effects of environmental tobacco smoke and indoor air pollution.

**Federal Aviation Administration (FAA)**
800 Independence Avenue, S.W.
Washington, DC 20591
(202) 267-3111
Fax: (202) 267-5047
Consumer Hotline: (800) 322-7873 and (202) 267-8592
Safety Hotline: (800) 255-1111 and (202) 267-8590
http://www.faa.gov/

The FAA has information about airline smoking regulations.

**Federal Communications Commission (FCC)**
1919 M Street, N.W.
Washington, DC 20554
Chairman: (202) 632-6600
Fax: (202) 632-0163
http://www.fcc.gov/

The FCC can provide information on the regulation of electronic media, including the federal ban on tobacco ads.

**Federal Election Commission**
Pepco Building
999 E Street
Washington, DC 20413
Commissioner: (202) 219-4110

Fax: (202) 219-8491
Information Services: (202) 219-3420
Fax: (202) 219-3880
Public Disclosure: (202) 219-4140
http://www.fec.gov/

The Federal Election Commission is the official source for information on tobacco company contributions to members of Congress.

**Federal Trade Commission (FTC)**
Public Reference Branch
600 Pennsylvania Avenue, N.W.
Washington, DC 20580
Public Affairs: (202) 326-2180
Publications: (202) 326-2222
Tobacco-related questions: (202) 326-3090
http://www.ftc.gov/

As the U.S. government's main authority on trade issues, the FTC provides publications and information related to trade policies and tobacco advertising, including health warning labels. The FTC also produces a report that contains data on the tar, nicotine, and carbon monoxide levels in domestic cigarettes.

**Food and Drug Administration (FDA)**
Office of Consumer Affairs
5600 Fishers Lane, HFE-50
Rockville, MD 20857
(301) 827-4420
Fax: (301) 443-9767
Information: (888) INFOFDA [(888) 463-6332]
http://www.fda.gov/

The FDA provides consumers with information on how to restrict the sale and distribution of cigarettes and smokeless tobacco to protect children and adolescents. FDA public affairs specialists with offices throughout the United States will respond to questions relating to tobacco. They also have printed materials that are available to the public. Names of public affairs specialists may be found in the U.S. government section of local telephone directories under the FDA listing (which is under the Department of Health and Human Services).

**Government Printing Office (GPO)**
GPO Building 3
732 North Capitol Street, N.W.
Washington, DC 20401
Public Printer's Office: (202) 512-2034
Fax: (202) 512-1347
Legislation and Public Affairs: (202) 512-1991
Fax: (202) 512-1293
Publications, subscriptions: (202) 783-3238
http://www.gpo.gov/

The GPO is the central source for obtaining U.S. government publications on smoking and health.

**Indian Health Service (IHS)**
Public Affairs Staff
Parklawn Building, Room 6-35
5600 Fishers Lane
Rockville, MD 20857
(301) 443-3593
Fax: (301) 443-0507
http://www.ihs.gov/

The IHS provides a comprehensive health services delivery system for American Indians and Alaska Natives. It helps to coordinate health planning and to obtain health resources available through federal, state, and local programs.

**National Cancer Institute (NCI)**
Office of Cancer Communications
31 Center Drive, MSC-2580
Building 31, Room 10A24
Bethesda, MD 20892-2580
(800) 4-CANCER
http://www.nci.nih.gov/

NCI develops and implements smoking intervention programs and produces publications on smoking. It provides telephone counseling services for smoking cessation. Programs and materials are available to the public as well as to health professionals.

**National Center for Health Statistics (NCHS)**
Data Dissemination Branch
6525 Belcrest Road
Room 1064
Hyattsville, MD 20782
(301) 436-8500
http://www.cdc.gov/nchs/

The NCHS seeks to make health information readily available to health professionals and ordinary citizens. It provides ordering information for publications and electronic products sold through the Government Printing Office and the National Technical Information Service. Specific statistical data collected by the National Center for Health Statistics are also available.

**National Clearinghouse for Alcohol and Drug Information (NCADI)**
Center for Substance Abuse Prevention
National Clearinghouse for Alcohol and Drug Information
P.O. Box 2345
Rockville, MD 20847-2345
(800) SAY-NOTO
http://www.health.org/

NCADI has been described as the nation's one-stop information shop for public access to the most current materials and information on alcohol, tobacco, and drug prevention. It has videos, fact sheets, and pamphlets, most of which are free.

**National Health Information Center (NHIC)**
P.O. Box 1133
Washington, DC 20013-1133
(800) 336-4797
(301) 565-4167
Fax: (301) 984-4256
http://nhic-nt.health.org/

The NHIC helps the public and health professionals locate information on tobacco and other topics through identification of resources, an information and referral system, and publications. It also prepares and distributes publications and directories on health promotion and disease prevention topics.

**National Heart, Lung, and Blood Institute (NHLBI)**
Information Center
P.O. Box 30105
Bethesda, MD 20824-0105
(301) 251-1222
Fax: (301) 251-1223
http://www.nhlbi.nih.gov/

The NHLBI is an especially good source of information relating to the health risks of tobacco use and to the prevention of tobacco-related disease. It provides educational activities and disseminates materials aimed at prevention and cessation.

**National Institute for Occupational Safety and Health (NIOSH)**
Information Retrieval and Analysis Team
4676 Columbia Parkway, MSC-13
Cincinnati, OH 45226
(800) 35-NIOSH
Fax: (513) 533–8573
http://www.cdc.gov/niosh/

With regard to tobacco, NIOSH's concern is environmental tobacco smoke. It maintains an automated database on the field of occupational safety and health and has a library open to the public.

**National Institute on Child Health and Human Development (NICHD)**
NICHD Clearinghouse
P.O. Box 3006
Rockville, MD 20847
Public Information: (301) 496-5133
Publications/Clearinghouse: (800) 370-2943
Fax: (301) 984-1473
E-mail: NICHDClearinghouse@iqsolutions.com
http://www.nichd.nih.gov/

Part of the National Institutes of Health, the NICHD conducts and supports research on the various processes "that determine and maintain the health of children, adults, families and populations." With regard to tobacco use, the NICHD's principal concern is pregnancy and smoking; its research focuses on pregnancy, reproduction, and infant mortality, as well as such areas as child growth and development and vaccinology. The NICHD Clearinghouse provides free information to professionals, researchers, educators, and the general public.

**National Library of Medicine (NLM)**
Office of Inquiries and Publications Management
8600 Rockville Pike
Bethesda, MD 20894
(800) 272-4787
Public information: (301) 496-6308
Reference: (301) 496-6095
Fax: (301) 402-1384
http://www.nlm.nih.gov/

The world's largest medical library, the NLM exists primarily to serve the information needs of U.S. health professionals, but its services are available throughout the world. The library's collection may be consulted in NLM's reading room, through interlibrary loan, or online through its website.

**National Oral Health Information Clearinghouse (NOHIC)**
1 NOHIC Way
Bethesda, MD 20892-3500
(301) 402-7364
Fax: (301) 907-8830
E-mail: nidr@aerie.com
http://www.aerie.com/nohicweb/

NOHIC seeks to identify the best sources of information and materials on specific special-care topics in oral health—i.e., care that is tailored to individual needs. It provides access to the Oral Health Database, which contains information on publications and audiovisuals, including information on the risks associated with smokeless tobacco.

**National Technical Information Service (NTIS)**
5285 Port Royal Road
Springfield, VA 22161
(703) 605-6000 (regular service); (800) 553-NTIS (rush service)
Fax: 703/321–8547
http://www.ntis.gov/

The NTIS describes itself as "the federal government's central source for the sale of scientific, technical, engineering, and related business information produced by or for the U.S. government and complementary material from international sources." Nearly 3 million products are available through NTIS. Among them are all materials formerly available through the National Audiovisual Center (NAC), which has been absorbed by the NTIS.

**National Women's Health Information Center (NWHIC)**
U.S. Department of Health and Human Services
200 Independence Avenue, S.W.
Washington, DC 20201
(800) 994-WOMAN (9662)
http://www.4woman.org/

NWHIC, a project of the Office on Women's Health (HHS), is the gateway to women's health-related materials developed by both federal agencies and private sources.

**Occupational Safety and Health Administration (OSHA)**
Department of Labor
200 Constitution Avenue, N.W.
Washington, DC 20210
(202) 219-8151
http://www.osha.gov/

OSHA, which is responsible for occupational safety and health, is a source for information on tobacco smoke as a workplace hazard.

**Office of Minority Health Resource Center (OMH-RC)**
P.O. Box 37337
Washington, DC 20013-7337
(800) 444-6472
Fax: (301) 589-0884
http://www.omhrc.gov/

The OMH-RC responds to questions from health professionals and consumers on minority health issues. It also provides referrals and distributes materials.

**Office on Smoking and Health** (*See* Centers for Disease Control and Prevention.)

**Office of U.S. Surgeon General**
Hubert H. Humphrey Building
200 Independence Ave., S.W.
Washington, DC 20201
(202) 690-6467
Fax: (202) 690-5810
http://www.surgeongeneral.gov/

The Office of the U.S. Surgeon General office responds to inquiries about the medical aspects of smoking and health and the surgeon general's reports.

# Nongovernment Organizations and Other Information Sources

**Action on Smoking and Health (ASH)**
2013 H Street, N.W.
Washington, DC 20006
(202) 659-4310
http://ash.org/

Action on Smoking and Health (UK)
102 Clifton Street
London EC2A 4HW
(0207) 613-0531
http://www.ash.org.uk

ASH is a thirty-one-year-old legal-action antismoking organization entirely supported by tax-deductible contributions. ASH works to protect the rights of nonsmokers and others concerned about smoking. It produces materials on a variety of smoking and health topics for the public, emphasizing legal action to protect the health of nonsmokers.

**Addiction Research Foundation (ARF)**
33 Russell Street
Toronto, Ontario
Canada M5S 2S1
(416) 595-6144
Fax: (416) 595-6601
E-mail: isd@arf.org
http://www.arf.org/

ARF is a nonprofit research center in Ontario, Canada. It provides access to a wide variety of materials for health professionals and the public, including videos and research reports.

**Advocacy Institute (AI)**
1730 Rhode Island Avenue, N.W., Suite 600
Washington, DC 20036-3118
(202) 659-8475
Fax: (202) 659-8484
E-mail: info@advocacy.org
http://www.advocacy.org/

AI defines its mission as supporting the development of advocacy skills on behalf of social and economic justice. It provides information on a variety of public interest topics, including tobacco, and supports antitobacco activism.

**American Cancer Society (ACS)**
American Cancer Society
1599 Clifton Road, N.E.
Atlanta, GA 30329-4251
(800) ACS-2345
http://www.cancer.org/

ACS describes itself as "the nationwide community-based voluntary health organization dedicated to eliminating cancer as a major health problem by preventing cancer, saving lives and diminishing suffering from cancer, through research, education, advocacy, and service." ACS devotes considerable attention to educating the public about the health risks associated with tobacco use, and it focuses on cessation as well as prevention. Publications, fact sheets, videos, and other materials are available from local chapters (see telephone directory) and from the national office (listing above).

**American Council on Science and Health (ACSH)**
1995 Broadway, 2nd Floor
New York, NY 10023-5860
(212) 362-7044
Fax: (212) 362-4919
http://www.acsh.org/

The American Council on Science and Health, founded in 1978, is a nonprofit, tax-exempt consumer education consortium concerned with issues related to food, nutrition, chemicals, pharmaceuticals, lifestyle, the environment, and health. A reliable source of objective information, ACSH is especially active in exposing the danger of tobacco use.

**American Heart Association (AHA)**
National Center
7272 Greenville Avenue
Dallas, TX 75231
(800) AHA-USA1
http://www.americanheart.org/

The American Heart Association, together with the American Stroke Association, a division of the AHA, is a central source of information about tobacco-related heart disease and stroke. It provides smoking cessation programs and intervention programs at schools, workplaces, and health-care sites. Fact sheets and brochures are available from the national headquarters (address above) and from local chapters.

**American Legacy Foundation**
1001 G Street NW, Suite 800
Washington, DC 20001
(202) 454-5555
Fax: (202) 454-5599
http://www.americanlegacy.org/

The Master Settlement Agreement of 1998 provided for the establishment of an organization dedicated to reducing tobacco use in the United States. As such, the American Legacy Foundation has four goals: "(1) Reduce youth tobacco use; (2) Reduce exposure to secondhand smoke among all ages and populations; (3) Increase successful quit rate among all ages and populations; and (4) Decrease tobacco consumption among all ages and populations." The organization promotes education, sponsors and conducts research, and serves as a conduit for information about tobacco.

**American Lung Association (ALA)**
1740 Broadway
New York, NY 10019-4374

(800) LUNG-USA; (212) 315-8700
http://www.lungusa.org/

The central purpose of the ALA, founded in 1904, is to fight lung disease "through education, community service, advocacy and research." In more recent years it has become increasingly involved in the campaign against smoking. The ALA provides a variety of educational materials for health professionals and the public. Like the American Heart Association and the American Cancer Society, the ALA has hundreds of local offices as well as the headquarters listed above.

**American Medical Association (AMA)**
515 N. State Street
Chicago, IL 60610
(312) 464-5000
http://www.ama-assn.org/

The "core purpose" of the AMA, the physician's professional organization, is "to promote the art and science of medicine and the betterment of public health." Its wide range of activities include continuing education and publication of the *Journal of the American Medical Association* (*JAMA*).

**American Public Health Association (APHA)**
800 I Street, NW
Washington, DC 20001-3710
(202) 777-APHA (2742)
(202) 777-2532
http://www.apha.org/

The APHA is the oldest and largest organization of public health professionals in the world. It focuses on influencing policies and setting priorities.

**Americans for Nonsmokers' Rights (ANR)/Americans for Nonsmokers' Rights Foundation (ANRF)**
2530 San Pablo Avenue, Suite J
Berkeley, CA 94702
(510) 841-3032
Fax: (510) 841-3060
E-mail: anr@no-smoke.org
http://www.no-smoke.org/

ANR's main concern is secondhand smoke, but it believes that establishing nonsmoking as the norm requires raising "a generation free from addiction to tobacco." Consequently, it provides information to organizations and individuals to assist in passing ordinances, implementing workplace regulations, and developing smoking policies in the workplace. Education is a high priority, and a number of useful publications for young people are available from ANR free of charge.

**Association of State and Territorial Health Officials (ASTHO)**
1275 K Street, N.W.
Suite 800
Washington, DC 20005
(202) 371-9090
http://www.astho.org/

ASTHO provides information about state health department activities related to tobacco and other health issues.

**Campaign for Tobacco-Free Kids**
440 Eye Street
Suite 1200
Washington, DC 20005
(800) 284-KIDS
E-mail: info@tobaccofreekids.org
http://www.tobaccofreekids.org/

The Campaign for Tobacco-Free Kids describes itself as "the country's largest nongovernment initiative ever launched to protect children from tobacco addiction and exposure to secondhand smoke." The Campaign works to alter the nation's social, political, and economic environment regarding tobacco; to change public policies at federal, state, and local levels; and to increase the number of organizations and individuals involved. The Campaign serves as "a resource and partner for more than 130 health, civic, corporate, youth and religious groups dedicated to reducing tobacco use among America's children," and "promotes youth advocacy and tobacco control efforts through its annual Kick Butts Day, a nationwide event that encourages activism among kids." Current funding, the Campaign reports, is from the Robert Wood Johnson Foundation, American Cancer Society, American Heart Association, Annie E. Casey Foundation, Everett Foundation, and the Thoracic Foundation.

### Cancer Research Foundation of America (CRFA)
1600 Duke Street, Suite 10
Alexandria, VA 22314
(800) 227-CRFA; (703) 836-4412
Fax: (703) 836-4413
http://www.preventcancer.org/

"When I lost my father to cancer in 1984," says Carolyn Aldige, founder of CRFA, "I was determined to do everything I could to help others fight cancer. So, in 1985, I opened the doors of CRFA to prevent cancer through scientific research and education programs. We believe the best way to defeat the disease is to attack it at the front end." The "front end" means prevention through research and education. CRFA provides funding for scientists researching the causes and treatment of cancer and sponsors public education programs that emphasize prevention and early detection.

### Competitive Enterprise Institute (CEI)
1001 Connecticut Avenue, N.W., Suite 1250
Washington, DC 20036
(202) 331-1010
Fax: (202) 331-0640
E-mail: info@cei.org
http://www.cei.org/

A nonprofit public policy organization, CEI is dedicated to the principles of free enterprise and limited government. CEI says it is not a traditional think tank. "We frequently produce ground-breaking research on regulatory issues," it says, "but . . . [i]t is not enough to simply identify and articulate solutions to public policy problems; it is also necessary to defend and promote those solutions. For that reason, we are actively engaged in many phases of the public policy debate." Tobacco and smoking are among the issues with which CEI is concerned—specifically, regulation of tobacco use; secondhand smoke and indoor air quality; legal liability of tobacco companies; and advertising.

### Doctors Ought to Care (DOC)

The addresses of two of the larger chapters are listed below:

### DOC Seattle Chapter
P.O. Box 20065
Seattle, WA 98102-1065

(206) 326-2894
http://kickbutt.org/

**DOC Houston Chapter**
5615 Kirby Drive, Suite 440
Houston, TX 77005
(713) 528-1487
Fax: (713) 528-2146
http://www.bcm.tmc.edu/doc/

Founded in 1977 "to challenge the growing use and promotion of tobacco and alcohol products among adolescents," DOC focuses its efforts on "the major preventable causes of poor health and high medical costs" and on combating "the promotion of lethal lifestyles in the mass media." Through more than 150 chapters in the United States, DOC generates information and antitobacco advertisements for use in schools, clinics, and communities.

**Economic Research Service (USDA)**
1800 M Street N.W.
Washington, DC 20036-5831
(202) 694-5050 (Information Center)

The Economic Research Service (ERS) describes its functions as providing economic analyses to support (1) a competitive agricultural system; (2) a safe food system; (3) a healthy, well-nourished population; (4) harmony between agriculture and the environment; and (5) enhanced quality of life for rural Americans. It provides, among other information, data on U.S. and world tobacco production, stocks, imports and exports, consumption, and prices. Its publications include *Agricultural Outlook* (published 10 times annually). The January-February 2001 issue contains good examples of the kind of information with which it is concerned: a feature titled "Cigarette Consumption Continues to Slip," with sidebars about tobacco types, quotas, and price supports; and news of President Clinton's establishment of a commission to improve economic opportunity in communities dependent on tobacco production.

**Fight Ordinances & Restrictions to Control and Eliminate Smoking (FORCES)**
P.O. Box 591257
San Francisco, CA 94159

(415) 824-4716
http://www.forces.org/

FORCES fights smoking ordinances and restrictions that it considers excessively strict and seeks to increase public awareness of smoking-related legislation. The organization defends the individual's right to smoke and maintains that smokers should be permitted to smoke provided they do not infringe the rights of nonsmokers.

### Foundation for Economic Education
30 S. Broadway
Irvington-on-Hudson, NY 10533
(914) 591-7230
Fax: (914) 591-8910
E-mail: freeman@westnet.com
http://www.fee.org/

Promoting private property rights, the free market economic system, and limited government, the Foundation for Economic Education also publishes a monthly journal, the *Freeman*.

### Group against Smokers' Pollution (GASP)
P.O. Box 632
College Park, MD 20741-0632
(301) 459-4791

GASP provides information about laws and policies relating to smoking and the health hazards of secondhand smoke.

### Indiana Prevention Resource Center (IPRC)
Indiana University
Creative Arts Bldg.
2735 E. 10th Street, Room 110
Bloomington, IN 47408-2606
(812) 855-1237; Indiana only: (800) 346-3077
Fax: (812) 855-4940
E-mail: drugprc@indiana.edu
http://www.drugs.indiana.edu/

The Indiana Prevention Resource Center at Indiana University is a statewide clearinghouse for prevention, technical assistance, and information about alcohol, tobacco, and other drugs. Indiana's officially designated RADAR (Regional Alcohol and

Drug Awareness Resource) Network State Center, it is operated by Indiana University's Department of Applied Health Science in the School of Health, Physical Education and Recreation and is affiliated with the Indiana University Institute for Drug Abuse Prevention.

The IPRC Library's audiovisual collection includes a broad selection of videotapes, curricula and leader's guides, and kits. The IPRC publishes a quarterly newsletter, *Prevention Newsline,* which is available to Indiana-based prevention programs without charge. This information also is published on the Web. A print subscription to this newsletter is available to out-of-state subscribers at a cost of $20 per year. IPRC also publishes occasional monographs and *Factlines,* a series of fact sheets about alcohol-, tobacco-, and other drug-related topics, all of which are available on the Web.

**INFACT**
256 Hanover Street
Boston, MA 02113
(617) 742-4583
Fax: (617) 367-0191
E-mail: infact@igc.apc.org
http://www.infact.org/

INFACT is a national grassroots organization founded in 1977 whose purpose is "to stop life-threatening abuses by transnational corporations and increase their accountability to people around the world." INFACT's Tobacco Industry Campaign, launched in 1993, is one of two of its major ongoing projects.

**March of Dimes Birth Defects Foundation**
1275 Mamaroneck Avenue
White Plains, NY 10605
(914) 428-7100
Fax: (914) 428-8203
http://www.modimes.org/

The major concerns of the March of Dimes Birth Defects Foundation are birth defects, infant mortality, low birthweight, and lack of parental care. The effects of smoking during pregnancy are among its priorities.

**Massachusetts Tobacco Education Clearinghouse (MTEC)**
JSI Research and Training Institute
44 Farnsworth Street
Boston, MA 02212-1211
(617) 482-9485
E-mail: mtec@jsi.com

MTEC was created in 1993 to distribute tobacco education materials to Massachusetts Tobacco Control Programs (MTCP). Its materials, including a large video library, are also available to persons nationwide.

**National Council for Reliable Health Information (NCRHI)**
P.O. Box 1276
Loma Linda, CA 92354-1276
Fax: 909/824-4838
http://www.ncahf.org

NCRHI describes itself as a private nonprofit, voluntary health agency that focuses upon health misinformation, fraud, and quackery as public health problems. It "unites consumers with health professionals, educators, researchers, attorneys, and others who believe that everyone has a stake in the quality of the health marketplace." NCRHI's positions on consumer health issues "are based upon principles of science that underlie consumer protection law. Required are: (1) adequate disclosure in labeling and other warranties to enable consumers to make proper choices; (2) pre-marketing proof of safety and efficacy for products and services that claim to prevent, alleviate, or cure any disease or disorder; and, (3) accountability for those who violate consumer laws."

**National Drug Strategy Network (NDSN)**
1225 I Street N.W., Suite 500
Washington, DC 20005
(202) 312-2015
Fax: (202) 842-2620
E-mail: ndsn@ndsn.org
http://www.ndsn.org/

The National Drug Strategy Network works to find effective ways to address the world's drug problems by sharing accurate and up-to-date information about developments that affect drug strategy.

NDSN is composed of individuals and organizations around the world. It is supported by the Criminal Justice Policy Foundation, a privately funded, nonprofit educational charity that promotes solutions to problems facing the criminal justice system. NDSN welcomes individuals and organizations concerned about the problems of drugs: critics of the war on drugs as well as public officials, law-enforcement officials, scholars, researchers, drug treatment professionals, judges, prosecutors, etc. NDSN is concerned about all aspects of the drug problem—illegal and legal drugs of all kinds; international, U.S., state, and local developments; law enforcement; drug treatment; legal developments; prison conditions; HIV and AIDS; medical marijuana; acupuncture—the entire spectrum of issues related to drug policy. The organization publishes a bimonthly newsletter, *NewsBriefs*, a comprehensive, accurate, up-to-date newsletter on drug policy.

**National Families in Action (NFIA)**
2296 Henderson Mill Road, Suite 300
Atlanta, GA 30345
(770) 934-6364
Fax: (770) 934-7137
http://www.emory.edu/NFIA/

National Families in Action works with other national organizations to rebuild the parent drug prevention movement.

**National Federation of State High School Associations (NFSHSA)**
P.O. Box 20626
Kansas City, MO 64195-0626
(816) 464-5400
Fax: (816) 464-5571
http://www.nfhs.org/

NFSHSA disseminates healthy lifestyle education/prevention information, primarily for high school athletic/activity associations.

**National Smokers Alliance (NSA)**
901 N. Washington Street, Suite 400
Alexandria, VA 22314
(800) 224-3322
Fax: (703) 739-1328
http://www.smokersalliance.org/

The NSA identifies itself as a nonprofit organization composed of adults who "support accommodation of smokers and non-smokers in public places and in the workplace." It opposes "discrimination against smokers," "excessive taxation or regulation of tobacco products," and "government-imposed smoking bans," and it believes "business owners should have the right to determine their own smoking policies."

**PICS, Inc.**
12007 Sunrise Valley Drive
Reston, VA 20191
(800) 543-3744; (703) 758-1400
Fax: (703) 758-1799
E-mail: Info@TobaccoWeek.com
http://www.tobaccoweek.org/

PICS, Inc., maintains the TobaccoWeek.org web site. The organization describes itself as "a 16-year-old company specializing in developing products that address major health issues, such as tobacco addiction, obesity, hypertension, diabetes, chronic headache and stress management." Its products are "targeted to the consumer directly and to the professional community."

**Public Citizen**
1600 20th Street, N.W.
Washington, DC 20009
(202) 588-1000
http://www.citizen.org/Tobacco/

Founded by consumer advocate Ralph Nader, Public Citizen is a watchdog group concerned with "protecting health, safety and democracy."

**Robert Wood Johnson Foundation (RWJF)**
Route 1 and College Road East
P.O. Box 2316
Princeton, NJ 08543-2316
(609) 452-8701
E-mail: mail@rwjf.org

Created by the founder of Johnson & Johnson and established as a national institution in 1972, the Robert Wood Johnson Foundation is the nation's largest philanthropy devoted exclusively to health and health care. RWJF defines its program goals as follows: to assure that all Americans have access to basic health care at reasonable cost; to improve care and support for people with chronic health conditions; and to promote health and prevent disease by reducing the harm caused by substance abuse—tobacco, alcohol, and illicit drugs.

**SmokeFree Educational Services, Inc.**
375 South End Avenue
Suite 32F
New York, NY 10280
(212) 912-0960
Fax: (212) 488-8911
http://www.smokescreen.org/

SmokeFree Education Services provides educational materials on smoking for schools and workplaces.

**Society for Research on Nicotine and Tobacco (SRNT)**
7611 Elmwood Avenue
Middleton, WI 53562
(608) 836-3787
Fax: (608) 831-5485
E-mail: SRNT1@aol.com
http://www.srnt.org/

SRNT's mission is "to stimulate the generation of new knowledge concerning nicotine in all its manifestations—from molecular to societal."

**Spit Tobacco Prevention Network (STOPN)**
1946 S. Interregional, Box 109
Austin, TX 78704
(512) 443-1064
http://www.flash.net/~stopn/

STOPN is a collaborative public and private effort "dedicated to diminishing and ultimately eliminating spit tobacco use in Texas through statewide, collaborative, and integrated research, education, and public policy initiatives."

**State of Minnesota Document Depository**
Hennepin Business Center

1201 Tenth Avenue, S.E.
Minneapolis, MN 55414
(612) 379-1936
http://documents.rjrt.com/minn.html

Philip Morris and other defendants in *State of Minnesota et al. v. Philip Morris, Inc., et al.* were ordered by the court to establish a document depository for internal documents turned over to the state in the course of the trial. As a result, the public is allowed to view the documents in the depository and to see copies of the documents that have been made available at the various company web sites.

### Stop Teenage Addiction to Tobacco (STAT)
511 E. Columbus Avenue
Springfield, MA 01105
(413) 732-STAT
Fax: (413) 732-4219
http://www.stat.org/

STAT provides information for health professionals and the public, emphasizing the need to stop tobacco companies from marketing to young people.

### Student Coalition Against Tobacco (SCAT)
P.O. Box 5995
Washington, DC 20016
(202) 828-3093

SCAT identifies itself as "a national student organization dedicated to reducing the use of tobacco by teens, reducing the tobacco industry's access to children and teens, and reducing exposure to secondhand smoke."

### Tobacco Control Archives (TCA)
University of California, San Francisco
San Francisco, CA 94143
(415) 476-2337
E-mail: tobacco-info@library.ucsf.edu
http://www.library.ucsf.edu/tobacco/

The Tobacco Control Archives (TCA) at the University of California at San Francisco is a major source of papers, unpublished documents, and electronic resources pertaining to tobacco-control issues.

**Tobacco Control Resource Center, Inc. (TCRC)** (*See also* Tobacco Products Liability Project)
102 The Fenway
117 Cushing Hall
Northeastern University
Boston, MA 02115
(617) 373-2026
Fax: (617) 373-3672
http://tobacco.neu.edu/tcu/

TCRC, parent organization of the Tobacco Products Liability Project (described in a following entry), works with Northeastern University School of Law to perform the legal research and analysis needed to help states, municipalities, health insurers, and public-interest groups develop innovative ways to reduce tobacco use.

**Tobacco Merchants Association (TMA)**
P.O. Box 8019
Princeton, NJ 08543-8019
(609) 275-4900
Fax: (609) 275-8379
E-mail: tma@tma.org
http://www.tma.org/

Founded in 1915, the Tobacco Merchants Association is the principal news source for the tobacco industry, both in the United States and abroad. It tracks statistics on the sale and distribution of tobacco and informs its members of this information through a number of newletters, including *Executive Summary; World Alert; U.S. Tobacco Weekly; Leaf Bulletin; Legislative Bulletin;* and *Issues Monitor.*

**Tobacco Products Liability Project (TPLP)** (*See also* Tobacco Control Resource Center, Inc.)
360 Huntington Avenue
117 Cushing Hall
Northeastern University
Boston, MA 02115
(617) 373-2026
Fax: (617) 373-3672
http://tobacco.neu.edu/

Founded in 1984, TPLP studies, encourages, and coordinates (1) product liability suits against the tobacco industry, and (2) legislative and regulatory initiatives to control the sale and use of tobacco as a public health strategy. The purpose of the product liability suits, according to TPLP, is to increase public awareness about the dangers of cigarette smoking and to offset the billions of dollars spent annually by the tobacco industry in promoting its products. "These suits also help to increase the cost of each pack of cigarettes," TPLP says, "thereby discouraging consumption and new addiction, particularly among the children and young adults who are the principal targets of tobacco advertising."

## Foreign and International Organizations

**European Bureau for Action on Smoking Prevention**
117, Rue des Atrebates
1040 Bruxelles, Belgium
32 (2) 732-24-68

This antismoking organization disseminates information about the European community's fight against tobacco.

**The International Network of Women against Tobacco (INWAT)**
P.O. Box 224
Metuchen, NJ 08840
(732) 549-9054
Fax: (732) 549-9056
E-mail: info@inwat.org

Women leaders in tobacco control founded INWAT in 1990 to address the complex issues of tobacco use among women and young girls. Specifically, the group "provides contacts, primarily women, to individuals and organizations working in tobacco control; collects and distributes information regarding global women and tobacco issues; shares strategies to counter tobacco advertising and promotion; supports the development of women-centered tobacco use prevention and cessation programs; assists in the organization and planning of conferences on tobacco control; collaborates on the development of publications regarding women and tobacco issues; and promotes female leadership."

**The International Union against Cancer (Union Internationale Contre le Cancer—UICC)**
3, Rue du Conseil-General
1205 Geneva, Switzerland
41 (22) 809-1811
Fax: 41 (22) 809-1810
http://www.globalink.org/tobacco/

The UICC carries out numerous programs around the world, including programs on tobacco and cancer. It developed and sponsors GLOBALink, which is an international tobacco control computer network providing in-depth and timely information.

**Pan American Health Organization (PAHO)**
525 23rd Street, N.W.
Washington, DC 20037
(202) 974-3000
Fax: (202) 974-3663
http://www.paho.org/

Seeking to prevent tobacco use in the Americas, PAHO develops policies and programs, disseminates information, conducts training and research, provides technical advisory services, and produces a variety of technical and scientific publications.

**The Panos Institute**
9 White Lion Street
London N1 9PD
UK
44 (0) 20-7278-1111
Fax: 44 (0) 20-7278-0345
E-mail: panos@panoslondon.org.uk
http://www.oneworld.org/panos

Founded in 1986 as a not-for-profit organization, the Panos Institute of London, according to its mission statement, "specialises in information for development, and stimulates public debate by providing accessible information on environmental and social development issues." It believes "that diversity, or 'pluralism,' in civil society underpins sustainable, people-centred development" and that "access to—and freedom of—information leads to informed and vigorous debate and allows people to play a constructive and often challenging role in public decision-making." Panos says its aim is "to stimulate debate by providing carefully researched, accessible, balanced information on neglected or poorly understood topics in the fields of environment, reproductive health and population, HIV / AIDS, poverty, gender, human rights and communications."

**World Health Organization (WHO)**
Avenue Appia 20
1211 Geneva 27
Switzerland
41 (22) 791-21-11
Fax: 41 (22) 791-31-11
Telex: 415 416
E-mail: info@who.ch (WHO has a number of specialized e-mail addresses, available on the Internet at http:/ /www.who.int/ home/hq.htm.)

Regional (U.S.) office:
World Health Organization
525 23rd Street, N.W.
Washington, DC 20037
(202) 974-3000
Fax: (202) 974-3663
Telex: 248338-440057-64152-892744
E-mail: postmaster@paho.org
http:/ /www.paho.org/

WHO is a specialized agency of the United Nations with 191 member states. It defines its main functions as follows: to give worldwide guidance in the field of health; to set global standards for health; to cooperate with governments in strengthening national health programs; and to develop and transfer appropriate health technology, information, and standards. WHO calls itself "a key player" not only in "fighting disease but in promoting primary health care, delivering essential drugs, making cities healthier, building partnerships for health, [and] promoting healthy lifestyles and environments," to achieve WHO's goal of health for all.

# State and Territorial Health Departments

Note that the departments' web sites are accessible from the web site of the Association of State and Territorial Health Officials (http://www.astho.org).

**Alabama Department of Public Health**
Tobacco Branch
RSA Tower, P.O. Box 303017
Montgomery, AL 36130-3017
(334) 206-5300
http://www.alapubhealth.org/

**Alaska Department of Health and Social Services**
P.O. Box 110610
Juneau, AK 99811-0610
(907) 465-3090
http://health.hss.state.ak.us/

**Arizona Department of Health Services**
1740 W. Adams Street
Phoenix, AZ 85007
602/542-1024
http://www.hs.state.az.us/

**Arkansas Department of Health**
5800 W. 10th Street
Little Rock, AR 72204
(501) 661-2000
http://health.state.ar.us/

**California Department of Health Services**
714 P Street
Sacramento, CA 95814
(916) 445-4171
http://www.dhs.cahwnet.gov/

**Colorado Department of Public Health and Environment**
4300 Cherry Creek Drive South
Denver, CO 80246-1530
(303) 692-2035
http://www.state.co.us/

**Connecticut Department of Public Health**
P.O. Box 340308
Hartford, CT 06134-0308
(860) 509-8000
http://www.state.ct.us/dph/

**Delaware Health and Social Services**
Division of Public Health
P.O. Box 637
Dover, DE 19903
http://www.state.de.us/govern/agencies/dhss/irm/dph/
dphhome.htm

**District of Columbia Department of Human Services**
Commission of Public Health
1660 L Street, N.W.
Washington, DC 20036
(202) 673-7700
http://www.dchealth.com/

**Florida Department of Health**
2020 Capital Circle SE
Tallahassee, FL 32399-1700
(904) 467-2705
http://www.doh.state.fl.us/

**Guam Department of Public Health and Social Services**
P.O. Box 2816
Agana, Guam 96910
(671) 734-2083
http://168.123.2.104/pubhealth/

**Hawaii Department of Health**
P.O. Box 3378
Honolulu, HI 96801
(808) 586-4410
http://www.state.hi.us/health/

**Idaho Department of Health and Welfare**
450 W. State Street
Boise, ID 83720-0036
(208) 334-5500
http://www.state.id.us/dhw/hwgd_www/

**Illinois Department of Public Health**
535 W. Jefferson Street
Springfield, IL 62761
(217) 782-4977
http://www.idph.state.il.us/

**Indiana State Department of Health**
2 N. Meridian Street
Indianapolis, IN 46204
(317) 233-1325
http://www.state.in.us/isdh/

**Iowa Department of Public Health**
Lucas State Office Building
Des Moines, IA 50319-0075
(515) 281-5787
http://www.idph.state.ia.us/

**Kansas Department of Health and Environment**
400 SW Eighth Street, 2nd Floor
Topeka, KS 66603-3930
(785) 368-6368
http://www.kdhe.state.ks.us/

**Kentucky Department of Public Health**
275 E. Main Street
Frankfort, KY 40621
(502) 564-3970
http://cfc-chs.chr.state.ky.us/

**Louisiana Department of Health and Hospitals**
1201 Capitol Access Road, P.O. Box 629
Baton Rouge, LA 70821-0629
(225) 342-9500
http://www.dhh.state.la.us/

**Maine Department of Human Services**
221 State Street
Augusta, ME 04333
(207) 287-3707
http://janus.state.me.us/dhs/

**Maryland Department of Health and Mental Hygiene**
201 W. Preston Street
Baltimore, MD 21201

(410) 767-6860
http://www.dhmh.state.md.us/

**Massachusetts Department of Public Health**
250 Washington Street
Boston, MA 02108-4619
(617) 624-6000
http://www.magnet.state.ma.us/dph/

**Michigan Department of Community Health**
Lewis Cass Building, 6th Floor
320 S. Walnut Street
Lansing, MI 48913
(517) 373-3500
http://www.mdch.state.mi.us/

**Minnesota Department of Health**
85 E. Seventh Place
Saint Paul, MN 55101
(651) 215-5800
http://www.health.state.mn.us/

**Mississippi State Department of Health**
Office of Community Health
2423 N. State Street
P.O. Box 1700
Jackson, MS 39215-1700
(601) 576-7725
http://www.msdh.state.ms.us/

**Missouri State Department of Health**
920–930 Wildwood
P.O. Box 570
Jefferson City, MO 65102-0570
(573) 751-6001
http://www.health.state.mo.us/

**Montana Department of Public Health and Human Services**
Tobacco Use Prevention Program
1400 Broadway
P.O. Box 202951
Helena, MT 59620-2951
(406) 444-2555
http://www.dphhs.state.mt.us/

**Nebraska Health and Human Services System**
301 Centennial Mall South
P.O. Box 95044
Lincoln, NE 68509-5044
(402) 471-2101
http://www.hhs.state.ne.us/

**Nevada State Health Division**
Bureau of Disease Control and Intervention Services
505 E. King Street, Rm. 103
Carson City, NV 89701
(775) 684-5900
http://www.state.nv.us/health/

**New Hampshire Department of Health and Human Services**
6 Hazen Drive
Concord, NH 03301-6505
(800) 852-3345
http://www.state.nh.us/

**New Jersey Department of Health and Senior Services**
P.O. Box 360
John Fitch Plaza
Trenton, NJ 08625-0360
(609) 633-9597
http://www.state.nj.us/health/

**New Mexico Department of Health**
P.O. Box 26110
1190 S. St. Francis Drive
Santa Fe, NM 87502-6110
(505) 827-2613
http://www.health.state.nm.us/

**New York State Department of Health**
Corning Tower, Empire State Plaza
Albany, NY 12237
(518) 474-5370
http://www.ogs.state.ny.us/

**North Carolina Department of Health Services**
512 N. Salisbury Street
P.O. Box 27687
Raleigh, NC 27611

(919) 733-4984
http://www.dhhs.state.nc.us/

**North Dakota Department of Health**
600 E. Boulevard Avenue
Bismarck, ND 58505-0200
(701) 328-2372
http://www.health.state.nd.us/ndhd/

**Ohio Department of Health**
246 N. High Street
Columbus, OH 43266-0588
(614) 466-3543
http://www.odh.state.oh.us/

**Oklahoma State Department of Health**
1000 NE 10th Street
Oklahoma City, OK 73117
(405) 271-5600
http://www.health.state.ok.us/

**Oregon State Health Division**
800 NE Oregon Street
Portland, OR 97232
(503) 731-4000
http://www.ohd.hr.state.or.us/

**Pennsylvania Department of Health**
P.O. Box 90
Health and Welfare Building
Harrisburg, PA 17108
(800) 692-7254
http://www.health.state.pa.us/

**Puerto Rico Department of Health**
Building A, Call Box 70184
San Juan, PR 00936
(809) 766-1616
http://fortaleza.govpr.org/

**Rhode Island Department of Health**
3 Capitol Hill
Providence, RI 02908
(401) 222-2231
http://www.health.state.ri.us/

**South Carolina Department of Health and Human Services**
P.O. Box 8206
Columbia, SC 29202-8206
(803) 898-2500
http://www.dhhs.state.sc.us/

**South Dakota Department of Health**
Health Building
600 E. Capitol
Pierre, SD 57501-2536
http://www.state.sd.us/executive/doh.html

**Tennessee Department of Health**
344 Cordell Hull Building
Nashville, TN 37247-0101
(615) 741-3111
http://www.state.tn.us/health/

**Texas Department of Health**
1100 W. 49th Street
Austin, TX 78756-3199
(512) 458-7111
http://www.tdh.state.tx.us/

**Utah Department of Health**
P.O. Box 1010
Salt Lake City, UT 84114-1010
(801) 538-6101
http://hlunix.hl.state.ut.us/

**Vermont Department of Health**
108 Cherry Street
Burlington, VT 05402-0070
(800) 464-4343
http://www.state.vt.us/health/

**Virgin Islands Department of Health**
St. Thomas, VI 00802
(809) 774-0117
http://www.gov.vi/health/

**Virginia Department of Health**
Main Street Station
1500 E. Main Street
Richmond, VA 23219

(804) 786-3561
http://www.vdh.state.va.us/

**Washington State Department of Health**
1112 SE Quince Street
P.O. Box 47890
Olympia, WA 98504-7890
(360) 236-4010
http://www.doh.wa.gov/

**West Virginia Department of Health and Human Resources**
Bureau for Public Health
Capitol Complex
Bldg. 3, Rm. 206
Charleston, WV 25305
(304) 558-1035
http://www.wvdhhr.org/bph

**Wisconsin Department of Health and Family Services**
Division of Public Health
P.O. Box 309
Madison, WI 53701-0309
(608) 266-1511
http://www.dhfs.state.wi.us/

**Wyoming Department of Health**
117 Hathaway Building
Cheyenne, WY 82002
(307) 777-7657
http://wdhfs.state.wy.us/WDH/

# Tobacco Companies

Information about these tobacco companies is available at Hoover's Online (http://www.hoovers.com/).

**British American Tobacco p.l.c.**
Globe House, 4 Temple Place
London WC2R 2PG
United Kingdom
Ph.: +44-171-845-1000
Fax: +44-171-240-0555

**Brown & Williamson Tobacco Corp.**
200 Brown & Williamson Tower
401 S. Fourth Street
Louisville, KY 40202
(800) 341-5211; (502) 568-7000
Fax: (502) 568-7107
http://www.bw.com/

**Imperial Tobacco Group PLC**
Upton Road
Bristol BS99 7UJ
UK
+44-117-963-6636
Fax: +44-117-966-7405
http://www.imperial-tobacco.com

**Lorillard Tobacco Company**
714 Green Valley Road
Greensboro, NC 27408-7018
(336) 335-7000
Fax: (336) 335-7414

**Philip Morris U.S.A.**
120 Park Avenue
New York, NY 10017-5592
(917) 663-5000
Fax: (917) 663-2167

**R. J. Reynolds Tobacco Holdings Inc.**
401 N. Main Street
Winston-Salem, NC 27101
(336) 741-5000
Fax: (336) 741-4238
http://www.rjrt.com/

**UST Inc.**
100 W. Putnam Avenue
Greenwich, CT 06830
(203) 661-1100
Fax: (203) 622-3493
http://www.ustshareholder.com

**Vector Group Ltd.**
100 SE Second Street
32nd Floor
Miami, FL 33131
(305) 579-8000
Fax: (305) 579-8001
http://www.brookegroup.com

# 6

# Selected Print Resources

## Bibliographies and Databases

The CDC's Office on Smoking and Health publishes an annual *Bibliography of Smoking and Health*. It also maintains the Smoking and Health Database, consisting of about 60,000 records. The bibliography and a CD-ROM version of the database are both available from the Government Printing Office, Superintendent of Documents, Washington, DC 20402.

## Periodicals

The best advice for anyone researching the topic of tobacco as it relates to health is to search ULM's MEDLINE using either of two retrieval systems provided by the National Library of Medicine— PubMed or Internet Grateful Med. Both are free and provide links to about 400 journals for full-text articles.

**Journal of the American Medical Association (JAMA)**
A nonspecialized weekly, *JAMA* is a useful and authoritative source of information. It contains articles, news and analysis, editorials, and commentary. Much of the material is sufficiently "low-tech" that persons outside the world of health care and research can fully understand it. Examples of tobacco-related article topics include a survey of smoking in China, a study of

tobacco and alcohol use in G-rated animated films, and a survey of smoking among high school students.

**Morbidity and Mortality Weekly Report (MMWR)**
The reports in this CDC publication are compiled from information submitted weekly by state health departments. Researchers can access the CDC web site or http://www2.cdc.gov/mmwr/mmwrsrch.htm. E-mail subscriptions, which are free, may be requested at http://www.cdc.gov/subscribe.html.

**Priorities for Long Life and Good Health**
*Priorities*, a quarterly magazine published by the American Council on Science and Health, focuses on nutrition, chemicals, the environment, lifestyle, and human health. Many of its issues contain articles about tobacco. *Priorities* is available at the ACSH web site, http://www.acsh.org.

**Tobacco Control Update**
This quarterly newsmagazine covers news events in Massachusetts relating to tobacco regulation, legal policy, and legislation. Issues of the magazine are available online at http://tobacco.neu.edu/tcu/.

# Books, Reports, and Pamphlets

Additional print sources may be found by using the National Library of Medicine's LOCATORplus search engine. LOCATORplus will identify periodicals as well as books. Users may search by title, subject, author, or keyword. LOCATORplus may be accessed at http://www.nlm.nih.gov/locatorplus/locatorplus.html.

American Council on Science and Health (ACSH). **Environmental Tobacco Smoke: Health Risk or Health Hype?** New York: American Council on Science and Health, 1999. 38p. $5.

ACSH reviews the case against environmental tobacco smoke and identifies which health risks have been established and which ones have not.

American Tobacco Company. **'Sold American!'—The First Fifty Years.** The American Tobacco Company, 1954. 144p.

This is an official history of the American Tobacco Company, produced at a time when tobacco companies were not on the defensive. Its sections on tobacco history and advertising are especially interesting.

Apperson, G. L. **The Social History of Smoking.** London: Martin Secker, 1914. 255p.

Apperson's subject is huge (though he limits it to England) and his coverage of its history is relatively thin. For example, when he says that the popularity of tobacco use declined, he does not cite any survey data in support. What he does offer is a fascinating collection of colorful and telling anecdotes. Some of them are of dubious significance or are otherwise problematical—e.g., when he writes about the belief that smoking would protect one from the plague, he quotes "a certain Tom Rogers," who recalled that as a student at Eton he was whipped for not smoking.

Brigham, Janet. **Dying to Quit: Why We Smoke and How We Stop.** National Academy Press, 1998. 289p. $29.95. ISBN 0-309-06409-0.

Janet Brigham is a former science journalist who is now a research psychologist. In **Dying to Quit,** she examines the sociological and psychological factors involved in beginning to smoke, smoking, and quitting. As she makes clear, there is much more to smoking than meets the eye, much more to quitting than simply not lighting up.

Buckley, Christopher. **Thank You for Smoking.** New York: Random House, 1995. 288p. $13. ISBN 0-060-97662-4.

**Thank You for Smoking** is fiction, not fact, but the line between the two seems indistinguishable at times. Buckley writes about ethics and political correctness, framing his discussion around the character of Nick Naylor, chief propagandist for the tobacco industry—a spin doctor who says he is just trying to pay off his mortgage.

Burnham, John C. **Bad Habits: Drinking, Smoking, Taking Drugs, Gambling, Sexual Misbehavior, and Swearing in American History.** New York: New York University Press, 1993. 385p. ISBN 0-8147-1187-1.

Only one chapter of John Burnham's informative book deals with smoking, but in that chapter he writes entertainingly about the taboos against smoking and the role of advertising in overcoming them. As Burnham explains, World War I both popularized and "masculinized" the cigarette. It also shifted the focus of cigarette advertising to the younger segment of the population—especially to young men in the armed services. As smoking became increasingly acceptable, the next logical step was to make it more acceptable for women. Opposition to this effort, Burnham contends, only made the cigarette more appealing to women and also to young people.

Den Uyl, Douglas J., and Tibor R. Machan. "Should Cigarette Advertising Be Banned?" *The Freeman*, December 1987.

The authors argue that attempts to ban tobacco advertising confuse basic rights with what is morally or ethically right.

Doron, Gideon. **The Smoking Paradox: Public Regulation in the Cigarette Industry.** Cambridge, MA: Abt Books, 1979. ISBN 0-89011-531-1.

Though relatively old in the context of today's tobacco controversy, this book is nevertheless useful, especially in its analysis of the effects of regulation on the tobacco industry.

Food and Drug Administration. **Nicotine in Cigarettes and Smokeless Tobacco Products Is a Drug.** Washington, D.C.: Food and Drug Administration, Department of Health and Human Services, 1995. 313p. $21. GPO S/N 017-012-00373-7.

This is a compilation of reports on smoking that includes sections on nicotine; tobacco marketing; FDA letters to tobacco manufacturers; and statements by Dr. David Kessler, commissioner of the FDA. It also includes a bibliography of industry-funded research studies.

Glantz, Stanton A., John Slade, Lisa A. Bero, Peter Hanauer, and Deborah E. Barnes. **The Cigarette Papers.** Berkeley: University of California Press, 1996. 560p. $19.95. ISBN 0-520-20572-3.

The title of **The Cigarette Papers** refers to the 8,000 pages of Brown & Williamson documents—confidential memos, proposals, notes, and research reports—stolen by Merrell Williams. In a review of the book in *The New Yorker*, Jonathan Franzen said: "[*The Cigarette Papers*] [m]akes it clear that Big Tobacco has known for decades that cigarettes are lethal and addictive and has done everything in its power to suppress and deny that knowledge. . . . [A] shocking collection."

Goodman, Jordan. **Tobacco in History: The Cultures of Dependence.** London: Routledge, 1993. 280p. ISBN 0-415-04963-6.

This British writer begins in the Americas, where tobacco had its beginnings, and then concentrates on the spread of its popularity in England. **Tobacco in History** is an impressively researched book with considerable detail (e.g., the number of pipemakers in England in each decade of the 1600s).

Greaves, Lorraine. **Smoke Screen: Women's Smoking and Social Control.** Halifax, Canada: Fernwood Publishing, 1996. 144p. ISBN 1-895686-57-1.

The chapter titles in *Smoke Screen* are intriguing—for example, "The Meanings of Smoking to Women," "Women's Experiences with Tobacco," and "How Society Benefits from Women's Smoking." Arguing for a woman-centered approach to smoking prevention, Greaves focuses on the complexities of an act (smoking) that is personal and social on the one hand and has serious medical and economic consequences on the other.

Hilts, Philip J. **Smoke Screen: The Truth Behind the Tobacco Industry Cover-Up.** Reading, MA.: Addison-Wesley Publishing, 1996. 253p. ISBN 0-201-48836-1.

This is an outstanding book detailing the tobacco industry's cover-up of evidence linking tobacco use to cancer and other diseases. A former health and science reporter for the *New York Times,* Hilts writes clearly and with considerable expertise, beginning with a dramatic description of a secret December 1953 meeting at which tobacco's top executives devised a strategy to combat news of tobacco's ill effects. The remainder of the book chronicles the industry's gradual decline.

Hutchison, William G. **Lyra Nicotiana.** London: Walter Scott, Ltd., 1898. 262p.

This book is a collection of old poetry and verse praising tobacco. One poet calls it the "sweetest enchantment of my solitude," a "sublime delight"; another dedicates his poem to "a young lady who desired that Tobacco might be planted over her grave."

Included is one Charles Lamb quote about quitting, in which he says, "For thy sake, tobacco, I / Would do anything but die."

Jacobson, Bobbie. **The Ladykillers: Why Smoking Is a Feminist Issue.** New York: Continuum, 1982. 136p. ISBN 0-8264-0185-6.

Jacobson discusses why women smoke and examines ways in which advertisers try to make smoking appealing to them.

Kessler, David. **A Question of Intent: A Great American Battle with a Deadly Industry.** New York: Public Affairs Press, 2001. 400p.

Published only recently, this book by David Kessler, former head of the Food and Drug Administration, will undoubtedly prove an invaluable reference source for anyone writing about the tobacco controversy. A prepublication news release described it as the inside story of Kessler's unsuccessful effort to bring cigarettes under FDA control.

Kiernan, V. G. **Tobacco: A History.** London: Hutchinson Radius, 1991. 249p. ISBN 0-09-174216-1.

This is a highly entertaining history of tobacco written by a man to whom smoking was an almost heavenly delight. He at last gave it up, acknowledging that the risks outweighed the benefits.

Kilbourne, Jean. **Deadly Persuasion: Why Women and Girls Must Fight the Addictive Power of Advertising.** New York: Free Press, 1999. 272p. $26. ISBN 0-684-86599-8.

As Jean Kilbourne makes clear, the imagery and highly sophisticated techniques of advertising, including tobacco advertising, are sometimes targeted at women, influencing not only their tastes but also their most deeply held values and concepts of self.

Kluger, Richard. **Ashes to Ashes: America's Hundred-Year Cigarette War, the Public Health, and the Unabashed Triumph of Philip Morris.** New York: Alfred A. Knopf, 1996. 807p. $23.95. ISBN 0-394-57076-6.

Well-written and highly readable, Kluger's book is an essential source for anyone seeking to understand the history of the tobacco industry.

Laufer, Berthold. **Introduction of Tobacco into Europe.** Chicago: Field Museum of Natural History, 1924. 66p. Anthropology Leaflet 19.

This pamphlet is a concise and carefully researched study of tobacco use in England, with brief sections at the end describing tobacco use in France, Portugal, Spain, Italy, Russia, and Turkey.

Lewine, Harris. **Good-Bye to All That.** New York: McGraw-Hill, 1970. 128p. ISBN 07- 037454–6.

Lewine provides a nostalgic look at cigarettes in the early years of the twentieth century, with an emphasis on cigarette advertising.

Lewis, Charles. **The Buying of the Congress: How Special Interests Have Stolen Your Right to Life, Liberty, and the Pursuit of Happiness.** New York: Harper, 1998. 400p. $25. ISBN 0-380-97596-3.

Reporting on an investigation he conducted with researchers from the Center for Public Integrity, Charles Lewis reveals the extent to which corporate money influences votes in Congress.

Males, Mike A. **Smoked: Why Joe Camel Is Still Smiling.** Monroe, Maine: Common Courage Press, 1999. 150p. $10. ISBN 1-567-51172-4.

Dr. C. Everett Koop, U.S. surgeon general from 1981 to 1989, described **Smoked** as follows: "If you think you know why kids start to smoke and what efforts are effective in preventing them, . . . you need to read this book. . . . This politically incorrect, enjoyable read could spark the debate that leads to a better understanding and possibly to success in preventing kids from smoking."

Mollenkamp, Carrick, Adam Levn, Joseph Menn, and Jeffrey Rothfeder. **The People Vs. Big Tobacco: How the States Took on the Cigarette Giants.** Princeton, NJ: Bloomberg Press, 1998. 335p. $23.95. ISBN 1-57660-057-2.

Armed with thousands of documents stolen from the Brown & Williamson Tobacco Corp., private lawyers and state attorneys general launched a two-pronged campaign against the tobacco industry, representing individual plaintiffs and state Medicaid plans, respectively. This book is a blow-by-blow account of how the state attorneys general finally won a $368 billion settlement.

Napier, Kristine, and William M. London, Elizabeth M. Whelan, and Andrea Golaine Case, eds. **What the Warning Label Doesn't Tell You.** New York: American Council on Science and Health, 1996. 186p. $19.95.LCCC 96-86418.

Published in 1996, this book is already out of date because so much has been learned in the past few years about cigarette smoking. However, **What the Label Doesn't Tell You** is a well-written, highly authoritative source and may be used confidently as a guide to the basic health risks of smoking.

Orey, Michael. **Assuming the Risk: The Mavericks, the Lawyers and the Whistleblowers Who Beat Big Tobacco.** Boston: Little, Brown & Company, 1999. 352p. $24.95. ISBN 0-316-66489-8.

Michael Orey is a graduate of the University of Michigan Law School who covered the "tobacco wars" for *The American Lawyer.* He is an editor at the *Wall Street Journal.*

Pringle, Peter. **Cornered: Big Tobacco at the Bar of Justice.** New York: Henry Holt, 1998. 352p. $27.50. ISBN 0-8050-4292-X.

While Carrick Mollenkamp's *The People Vs. Big Tobacco* examines the states' legal efforts against the tobacco industry, *Cornered* follows the progress of the trial and personal-injury lawyers who took on cases for individuals.

Reynolds, Patrick, and Tom Shachtman. **The Gilded Leaf: Triumph, Tragedy, and Tobacco.** Boston: Little, Brown & Company, 1989. 353p. ISBN 0-316-74121-3.

Patrick Reynolds, now an antismoking activist, tells the story of three generations of his family—the Reynolds of the R. J. Reynolds tobacco dynasty.

Schaler, Jeffrey. **Addiction Is a Choice.** Chicago: Open Court, 2000. 256p. $19.95. ISBN 0-812-69404-X.

In Schaler's view, tobacco addiction is a choice: smokers choose to be addicted; and they are therefore responsible for their addiction, not simply victims of it. He then proceeds to analyze current public policies and to suggest how they might be revised to deal with addiction more successfully.

Schaler, Jeffrey, and Magda E. Schaler, eds. **Smoking: Who Has the Right?** Amherst, N.Y.: Prometheus Books, 1998. 388p. $17.95. ISBN 1-573-92254-4.

In a review of this book, Dr. Ernst Wynder, president of the American Health Foundation, noted: "In a democracy, everyone has personal rights, in particular, where such choice does not affect the well-being of others. In this regard, smoking behavior has both public and private health implications. This compilation features significant authors who express their views and prejudices on both sides of the issue . . . [and] will make us think comprehensively about the medical, social, financial and political problems surrounding tobacco use."

Sobel, Robert. **They Satisfy: The Cigarette in American Life**. Garden City, NJ: Anchor Books, 1978. 255p. ISBN 0-385-12956-4.

Robert Sobel wrote this book, he says, as "an effort at history, not propaganda." In fact, though, **They Satisfy** was published in 1978, long after highly persuasive evidence of smoking's dangers was made public, Sobel expresses doubts as to the health risks of tobacco use. As he remarks in the Preface, "Perhaps there is no causal link between tobacco and cancer," but, "then again, one might exist." The book is a nonargumentative and pleasantly readable account of tobacco's popularity in the early and middle years of the twentieth century, concluding with a straightforward report of the campaign against smoking begun by Sen. Maurine Neuberger.

Sullum, Jacob. **For Your Own Good: The Anti-Smoking Crusade and the Tyranny of Public Health.** New York: The Free Press, 1998. 338p. $25. ISBN 0-684-82736-0.

Jacob Sullum is a drug policy expert and senior editor of *Reason* magazine. He stands on the "other" side of the tobacco controversy, insisting that many claims of the antismoking activists are simply not true. Sullum also argues that the government has no right to protect people from themselves, only from others.

Tate, Cassandra. **Cigarette Wars: The Triumph of 'The Little White Slaver.'** New York: Oxford University Press, 1999. 204p. $29.95. ISBN 0-19-511851-0.

Here is the story of the first major crusade against the cigarette, in the late nineteenth and early twentieth centuries, when Lucy Page Gaston and others attacked the cigarette as a moral blight. Gaston's followers denounced smoking as the first step on a path that would lead to criminality and degeneracy. Cassandra Tate writes entertainingly and well.

Taylor, Peter. **Smoke Ring: The Politics of Tobacco.** London: The Bodley Head, 1984. 329p. ISBN 0-370-30513-2.

Taylor's concern when he wrote this book was the political and economic interests that formed a protective ring around the tobacco industry. That ring no longer exists—at least, not as it did in 1984, when the book was published—but tobacco still has powerful friends. This book provides the background for understanding what is happening today.

Tollison, Robert D., ed. **Smoking and Society: Toward a More Balanced Assessment.** Lexington, MA: D. C. Heath and Company, 1986.

Parts of Tollison's book are outdated, but it is nevertheless worth consulting. Especially valuable are Chapter 3, "Psychological Determinants of Smoking Behavior"; Chapter 6, "Smoking, Human Rights, and Civil Liberties"; and Chapter 12, "Tobacco Advertising in a Free Society."

Tollison, Robert D., and Richard E. Wagner. **Smoking and the State: Social Costs, Rent Seeking, and Public Policy.** Lexington, MA: D. C. Heath and Company, 1988.

Like *Smoking and Society,* **Smoking and the State** is somewhat outdated, but the issues discussed in the last two chapters—pertaining to constitutional and individual rights—are at the forefront of the current controversy.

U.S. Congress, House Committee on Commerce. **The Tobacco Settlement: Views of Tobacco Industry Executives.** Hearing Before the Committee on Commerce, House of Representatives, Jan. 29, 1998. Washington, D.C.: Government Printing Office, Superintendent of Documents. GPO S/N 1019-A-01; 1019-B-01 (MF).

This document records the hearing at which seven industry CEOs swore they did not believe that nicotine was addictive.

U.S. Department of Agriculture. **Agriculture Fact Book 1998.** Washington, D.C.: Government Printing Office, Superintendent of Documents. GPO S/N 001-000-04661-6.

Downloadable at the USDA web site. This book is the source to use in determining how much tobacco was produced in the United States on a year-by-year basis and how much was exported.

U.S. Department of Education. **Youth & Tobacco: Preventing Tobacco Use among Young People.** Washington, D.C.: Government Printing Office, 1994.

Excerpts from the 1994 report of the surgeon general.

U.S. Department of Health and Human Services. **Preventing Tobacco Use among Young People: A Report of the Surgeon General.** Atlanta, GA: U.S. Department of Health and Human Services, Centers for Disease Control and Prevention, National Center for Chronic Disease Prevention and Health Promotion, Office on Smoking and Health, 1998. 323p. $19. S/N 017-001-00491-0.

This is the first surgeon general's report to focus on the problem of tobacco use by young people. Among its six major conclusions is the following: Almost all adult tobacco users took up the habit in adolescence.

U.S. Department of Health and Human Services. **Tobacco Use among U.S. Racial/Ethnic Minority Groups—African Americans, American Indians and Alaska Natives, Asian Americans and Pacific Islanders, Hispanics: A Report of the Surgeon General.** Atlanta, Ga.: U.S. Department of Health and Human Services, for Disease Control and Prevention, National Center for Chronic Disease Prevention and Health Promotion, Office on Smoking and Health, 1998. 332p. $20. S/N 017-001-00527.

Surveying tobacco use by subgroups in the population, this report warns that the rapid increases in smoking by minority teenagers threaten to reverse the progress against lung cancer.

Viscusi, W. Kip. **Smoking: Making the Risky Decision.** New York: Oxford University Press, 1992. 170p. ISBN 0-19-507486-6.

There is much talk in this book of "risk perception," "risk regulation," and "risk communication"—a complex differentiation that makes it more appealing to a scholarly audience than the average reader. It is, however, an interesting study of why people smoke despite the evidence of its dangers.

Wagner, Susan. **Cigarette Country: Tobacco in American History and Politics.** New York: Praeger Publishers, 1971. 248p. LC 72-134768.

**Cigarette Country,** according to the author, is "not a book with a cause." She wrote it, she says, simply because she became interested in smoking as "a sociopolitical phenomenon," because it is so much a part of American life and mythology. Filled with anecdotes and entertainingly written, **Cigarette Country,** tells the story of tobacco in America from the beginnings to 1970, when tobacco farmers the author interviewed in Kentucky were beginning to worry about their future.

Whelan, Elizabeth M. **Cigarettes: What the Warning Label Doesn't Tell You: The First Comprehensive Guide to the Health Consequences of Smoking.** Amherst, NY: Prometheus Books, 1997. 212p. $9.95. ISBN 1-573-92158-0.

For those who want to know precisely what smoking will do to them, Elizabeth Whelan, cofounder and executive director of the American Council on Science and Health, and 20 specialists provide the answers. The chapter titles make clear her purpose—e.g., "Smoking and Lung Disease," "Smoking and Heart Disease," "Smoking and Cancer Risk," "Smoking and the Skin," "Smoking and the Eyes," and so on. This is an "everything you ever wanted to know" book, and it may be especially useful to persons who are trying to quit.

Whelan, Elizabeth M. **A Smoking Gun: How the Tobacco Industry Gets Away with Murder.** Philadelphia: George F. Stickley, 1984. 244p. ISBN 0-89313-039-7.

Whelan calls this book "a chronicle of the politics of the cigarette." In it she examines the cigarette as a phenomenon, a "spectacular marketing and advertising success." She also describes "the floundering attempts of medical professionals, the media, advertisers, tobacco men, Congress, and the general public to deal with the newly discovered hazards of smoking."

White, Larry C. **Merchants of Death: The American Tobacco Industry.** New York: William Morrow, 1988. 240p. ISBN 0-688-06706-9.

This book focuses on the tobacco industry, describing how it handled the growing evidence of tobacco's dangers, its efforts to stand together behind "The Big Lie," and how it sought to preserve itself from destruction, largely through diversification and expanding markets.

Whiteside, Thomas. **Selling Death: Cigarette Advertising and Public Health.** New York: Liveright, 1971. 150p. ISBN 087-140-5415.

Radio and especially television continued to portray cigarette smoking as glamorous and sophisticated long after publication of the Surgeon General's 1964 report identifying smoking as a leading cause of lung cancer. Thomas Whiteside describes the infighting between the tobacco industry and its opponents, which eventually led to a total ban of broadcast advertising.

Zegart, Dan. **Civil Warriors: The Legal Siege of the Tobacco Industry.** New York: Delacorte, 2000. 358p. $25.95 ISBN 0-385-31935-5

A veteran journalist, Dan Zegart provides a behind-the-scenes look at the big-time personal-injury lawyers who have driven tobacco companies against the wall, beating them at their own game. Zegart spent five years traveling with Ron Motley, a leading product liability lawyer who set his sights on the tobacco industry, and his legal team. Dialogue, color, detail, and insider information, combined with Zegart's knowledge of his subject, make this book a fascinating and authoritative source, probably the most readable of the several books dealing with antitobacco litigation.

# Publications Available from Organizations and Agencies

## Surgeon General's Reports on Smoking and Health

The surgeon general's reports on the health consequences of tobacco use are listed by year of publication and title. They are available from the following sources, as indicated:

- IRP—Information Resources Press, 1110 North Glebe Road, Suite 550, Arlington, VA 22201, (703) 558-8270, (703) 558-4979 (fax).
- GPO—Government Printing Office, Superintendent of Documents, Publication Customer Service, Stop SSOS, Washington, DC 20402, (202) 512-1803, (202) 512-2168 (fax).
- NTIS—National Technical Information Service, 5285 Port Royal Road, Springfield, VA 22161, (703) 487-4650 (regular service), 1-800-553-NTIS (rush service), (703) 321-8547 (fax).
- OSH—Office on Smoking and Health, National Center for Chronic Disease Prevention and Health Promotion, Centers for Disease Control and Prevention, Mailstop K-50, 4770 Buford Highway, N.E., Atlanta, GA 30341-3724, (770) 488-5705.

The following are surgeon general reports that deal with tobacco use. They may be obtained through Information Resources Press (IRP) in Arlington, Va., the Government Printing Office, or online through the Centers for Disease Control web site, http://www.cdc.gov/tobacco. Some may also be available through the National Technical Information Service (NTIS) or the Office on Smoking and Health (OSH).

- 1964—**Smoking and Health: Report of the Advisory Committee to the Surgeon General of the Public Health Service.** Washington, D.C.: Government Printing Office. 387p.
- 1967—**The Health Consequences of Smoking: A Public Health Service Review.** Washington, D.C.: Government Printing Office. 227p.

- 1968—**The Health Consequences of Smoking: 1968 Supplement to the 1967 Public Health Service Review.** Washington, D.C.: Government Printing Office. 117p.
- 1969—**The Health Consequences of Smoking: 1969 Supplement to the 1967 Public Health Service Review.** Washington, D.C.: Government Printing Office. 98p.
- 1971—**The Health Consequences of Smoking: A Report of the Surgeon General.** Washington, D.C.: Government Printing Office. 458p.
- 1972—**The Health Consequences of Smoking: A Report of the Surgeon General.** Washington, D.C.: Government Printing Office. 150p.
- 1973—**The Health Consequences of Smoking, 1973.** Washington, D.C.: Government Printing Office. 261p.
- 1974—**The Health Consequences of Smoking, 1974.** Washington, D.C.: Government Printing Office. 124p.
- 1975—**The Health Consequences of Smoking, 1975.** Washington, D.C.: Government Printing Office. 235p. Also available through NTIS.
- 1976—**The Health Consequences of Smoking: Selected Chapters from 1971 through 1975 Reports.** Washington, D.C.: Government Printing Office. 633p.
- 1978—**The Health Consequences of Smoking, 1977–1978.** Washington, D.C.: Government Printing Office. 56p.
- 1979—**Smoking and Health: A Report of the Surgeon General.** Washington, D.C.: Government Printing Office. 587p. Also available through NTIS.
- 1980—**The Health Consequences of Smoking for Women: A Report of the Surgeon General.** Washington, D.C.: Government Printing Office. 360p. Also available through NTIS and OSH (single copy free to nonprofit organizations).
- 1981—**The Health Consequences of Smoking—The Changing Cigarette: A Report of the Surgeon General.** Washington, D.C.: Government Printing Office. 237p.
- 1982—**The Health Consequences of Smoking—Cancer: A Report of the Surgeon General.** Washington, D.C.: Government Printing Office. 304p.
- 1983—**The Health Consequences of Smoking—Cardiovascular Disease: A Report of the Surgeon General.** Washington, D.C.: Government Printing

Office. 384p. Also available through OSH (single copy
free to nonprofit organizations).

- 1984—**The Health Consequences of Smoking—Chronic
Obstructive Lung Disease: A Report of the Surgeon
General.** Washington, D.C.: Government Printing
Office. 545p.
- 1985—**The Health Consequences of Smoking—Cancer
and Chronic Lung Disease in the Workplace: A Report
of the Surgeon General.** Washington, D.C.: Government
Printing Office. 542p. Also available through OSH
(single copy free to nonprofit organizations).
- 1986—**The Health Consequences of Using Smokeless
Tobacco: A Report of the Advisory Committee to the
Surgeon General.** Washington, D.C.: Government
Printing Office. 221p.
- 1986—**The Health Consequences of Involuntary
Smoking: A Report of the Surgeon General.**
Washington, D.C.: Government Printing Office. 359p.
Also available through OSH (single copy free to
nonprofit organizations).
- 1988—**The Health Consequences of Smoking—Nicotine
Addiction: A Report of the Surgeon General.**
Washington, D.C.: Government Printing Office. 639p.
Also available through OSH (single copy free to
nonprofit organizations).
- 1989—**Reducing the Health Consequences of
Smoking—25 Years of Progress: A Report of the
Surgeon General.** Washington, D.C.: Government
Printing Office. 703p. Also available through OSH
(single copy free to nonprofit organizations).
- 1990—**The Health Benefits of Smoking Cessation: A
Report of the Surgeon General.** Washington, D.C.:
Government Printing Office. 628p. Also available
through OSH (single copy free to nonprofit
organizations).
- 1992—**Smoking and Health in the Americas: A Report
of the Surgeon General.** Washington, D.C.: Government
Printing Office. 213p. Also available through OSH
(single copy free to nonprofit organizations).
- 1994—**Preventing Tobacco Use among Young People: A
Report of the Surgeon General.** Washington, D.C.:
Government Printing Office. 314p. Also available

through OSH (single copy free to nonprofit organizations).

- 1998—**Tobacco Use among U.S. Racial/Ethnic Minority Groups.** Washington, D.C.: Government Printing Office.
- 2000—**Treating Tobacco Use and Dependence: A Clinical Practice Guideline.** Washington, D.C.: Government Printing Office.

# Centers for Disease Control (CDC)

Print materials may be ordered on the CDC's Tobacco Information and Prevention Source (TIPS) web site. Printed copies may be requested by clicking on the box beside the title and filling out the order form at the end of the list.

## General Information, CDC

**Targeting Tobacco Use: The Nation's Leading Cause of Death, at-a-Glance.** 1999. 6p.

This brochure documents the efforts of the Centers for Disease Control.

"Office on Smoking and Health's Information Resources." 1996. 3p.

This document details the information and resources provided by the Office on Smoking and Health, including published documents, voice recording and facsimile service, and an Internet homepage.

"Surgeon General's Report Listing, 1964–Present." 1994. 2p.

This document is a listing of reports by the surgeon general relating to smoking and health issues. This listing also includes year of publication and ordering information.

**The 1964 Surgeon General's Report on Smoking and Health—a Historical Review.** 1994. 3p.

This review documents the first surgeon general's report on smoking and health, which was released in 1964. Also included in the review are details of surgeon general reports that followed the landmark document.

"Significant Developments Related to Smoking and Health: 1964–1996." 6p.

This document outlines in chronological order the significant developments related to smoking and health from 1964 to 1996.

"Tobacco Control Information Sources." 1996. 4p.

This document lists government agencies and nonprofit organizations that provide information about smoking and health.

### Fact Sheets, CDC

"Cigarette Smoking-Related Mortality." 1991. 2p.

This fact sheet provides statistics for smoking-related deaths in 1990.

"Nicotine Addiction." 1995. 2p.

This fact sheet describes indicators of nicotine addiction, the action of nicotine, and treatments for nicotine addiction.

"Smoking Prevalence among U.S. Adults." 1995. 1p.

This fact sheet consists of a chart describing the smoking population from 1955 to 1993. The chart details the percentages of smoking adults in the United States by sex and race.

"Women and Tobacco." 1995. 2p.

This fact sheet reviews the prevalence of smoking among women and the special smoking-related health risks that women face.

### Fact Sheets on Youth, CDC

"Health Effects of Smoking among Young People."1995. 2p.

This fact sheet outlines the health consequences associated with smoking for young people.

"Nicotine Addiction in Adolescence." 1995.

This fact sheet describes the risks of nicotine addiction and its effect on adolescence.

"Smokeless Tobacco: A Dangerous Alternative." 1995. 2p.

This fact sheet describes how smokeless tobacco is not a safe alternative to cigarettes, especially for young people. It includes statistics on the health consequences of using smokeless tobacco and documents its addictive nature.

"Tobacco Industry Advertising and Promotion." 1995. 2p.

This fact sheet shows how the tobacco industry uses advertising and promotional campaigns to appeal to young people.

"Tobacco Sales to Youth." 1995. 2p.

It is illegal throughout the United States for persons under the age of 18 to purchase tobacco. This fact sheet presents statistics for tobacco sales to children and adolescents and describes the public's opinion of the tobacco sale laws.

"Trends in Tobacco Use among Youth." 1995. 2p.

This fact sheet describes trends in tobacco use by teenagers from 1983 through 1993. It details the factors encouraging youth to smoke—smoking by peers and family members, tobacco advertising and promotion, and easy availability of tobacco products.

### Cessation (Quitting) Materials, CDC

"'I Quit'—What to Do When You're Sick of Smoking, Chewing, or Dipping." 1997. 7p.

This cessation guide is targeted to teens who are trying to quit smoking cigarettes or using smokeless tobacco. It includes tips for dealing with nicotine withdrawal and for handling situations that may lead to relapse.

**Clearing the Air.** 1988. 24p.

This booklet by the National Cancer Institute (NCI) provides tips for smoking cessation. Limited quantities are available through CDC. For bulk orders contact the NCI at 1-800-4-CANCER.

"Don't Let Another Year Go Up in Smoke: Quit Tips." 1994. 1p.

Suggestions on how to quit smoking.

"Good News for Smokers 50 and Older." 1990. 2p.

This fact sheet for smokers age 50 and older outlines the health benefits of quitting smoking.

**Out of Ashes** 1990. 16p.

This booklet outlines and discusses various methods for quitting smoking.

**Pathways to Freedom.** 1992. 35p.

A colorful smoking cessation guide, produced in conjunction with the American Cancer Society (ACS), that is culturally appropriate for African Americans.

### Environmental (Secondhand) Tobacco Smoke, CDC
**Making Your Workplace Smokefree—A Decision Maker's Guide.** 1996. 50p.

Provides worksite decision makers with information on how to design, implement, and evaluate Environmental Tobacco Smoke (ETS) policies and related activities.

"No Sea Victima Pasiva Del Humo De Segunda Mano" [It's Time to Stop Being a Passive Victim: Action Guide]. Available in Spanish only. 1994. 10p.

A guide for effective action against secondhand smoke at home, in restaurants, in the workplace, and in other public places.

**Reducing the Health Risks of Secondhand Smoke.** 1992. 6p.

A pamphlet by the American Lung Association and the CDC that describes ways to avoid secondhand smoke at home, at work, and in public places.

"Respiratory Health Effects of Passive Smoking: EPA Fact Sheet." 1993. 4p.

A fact sheet by the Environmental Protection Agency that highlights key findings about environmental tobacco smoke.

**What You Can Do about Secondhand Smoke.** 1993. 4p.

This glossy pamphlet defines the health risks of secondhand smoke for children and adults. It also describes ways to reduce these risks.

### Smokeless (Spit) Tobacco, CDC
**Health Consequences of Using Smokeless Tobacco.** 1986. 18p.

This report provides a comprehensive review of the available scientific literature to determine whether using smokeless tobacco increases the risk of cancer and noncancerous oral diseases, leads to addiction and dependence, and contributes to other health problems.

"Smokeless Tobacco: An International Perspective." 1991. 4p.

A fact sheet by the National Cancer Institute that reports important findings from experts around the world about smokeless tobacco.

**Spit Tobacco and Youth.** 1992. 70p.

This study describes the present status of use of spit tobacco in six areas: prevalence and patterns of use, health effects, environmental influences on use, product promotion and sales, regulation and enforcement, and educational efforts.

## Office on Smoking and Health (OSH)

The Office on Smoking and Health (OSH), part of the National Center for Chronic Disease Prevention and Health Promotion, has prepared information on smoking, tobacco, and health. Most of the information is available in published documents, by voice recording or facsimile, and through the OSH Internet home page, http://www.healthy.net/pan/cso/cioi/OSHCDCP.htm.

### OSH Smoking and Health Database
Available on a CD-ROM for use at Federal Depository libraries. For Internet users with the Netscape browser, the database (called the CDP File) is accessible on the web through the CDC data service called WONDER. The web address is http://wonder.cdc.gov/. The CDP File may also be purchased from the Government Printing Office by calling (202) 512-1800.

The OSH Smoking and Health Database covers more than 30 years of information and contains more than 60,000 abstracts of scientific and technical literature related to smoking and tobacco use.

## OSH *Publications Catalog*

The Office on Smoking and Health continually updates its catalog of free publications. Allow 3 to 6 weeks for delivery of the catalog as well as any publications/materials ordered from it.

> Centers for Disease Control and Prevention
> National Center for Chronic Disease Prevention and Health Promotion
> Office on Smoking and Health
> Publications Catalog, Mail Stop K-50
> 4770 Buford Highway, N.
> Atlanta, GA 30341-3724
> (770) 488-5705
> Fax: (800) CDC-1311

### Ordering OSH Publications and Information

The Office on Smoking and Health's toll-free telephone number provides a convenient method to order publications. The user may select commands spoken in English or Spanish. During the phone ordering process, the user presses his or her telephone numeric keypad to respond to questions generated by the service. The answers are recorded and played back for the user's verification. This ordering process can be completed in minutes and provides a timely method for obtaining the latest publications on smoking, tobacco, and health.

If you are interested in receiving current information about smoking, tobacco, and health by recording or facsimile (FAX) call 1-800-CDC-1311. Please follow the prompts that direct you to the Smoking and Health prepared information. To request an up-to-date directory on smoking, tobacco, and health information call either 1-800-CDC-1311 or dial directly to the FAX information directory at (770) 332-2552. This automated service is available 24 hours a day.

# National Institutes of Health (NIH)

All of these publications are available at the NIH web site, http://www.nih.gov.

**Check Your Smoking I.Q.** (NHLBI).

**Clearing the Air: A Guide to Quitting Smoking** (NCI).

**I Mind Very Much If You Smoke** (NCI).

**Smoking Facts and Tips for Quitting** (NCI).

**Why Do You Smoke?** (NCI).

**Smoking and Your Digestive System** (NIDDK).

# National Center for Health Statistics (NCHS)

NCHS has a wide variety of news releases, fact sheets, and publications, many relating to tobacco available from the following address:

National Center for Health Statistics
Division of Data Services
6525 Belcrest Road
Hyattsville, MD 20782-2003
(301) 458-4636
http://www.cdc.gov/nchs/releases/releases.htm

# American Cancer Society (ACS)

These publications are free and may be ordered at the ACS web site or by calling 1-800-ACS-2345.

**Cancer Risk Report: 1998.**

This report is a useful reference for statistics and other data on tobacco control, nutrition, physical activity, and cancer screening.

**The Cold Hard Facts about Dip.**

This brochure gives young people straight facts about the dangers of smokeless tobacco and points out the deceptive nature of tobacco company advertising.

**Quitting Spitting.**

This pamphlet provides young dippers with more than enough reasons to stop using spit tobacco. Startling descriptions of the harmful health effects and other drawbacks of chewing tobacco are designed to help preteens and teens to kick the habit.

**Questions about Smoking, Tobacco and Health.**

Honest answers to the most frequently asked questions about tobacco.

**Smokeless Tobacco: A Medical Perspective.**

Photos of carcinoma of the mouth graphically show the health risks of using smokeless tobacco.

## American Council on Science and Health (ACSH)

All of the following print materials may be ordered from ACSH and most are available at the ACSH web site, http://www.acsh.org.

### Selected News Releases, ACSH

**Cigarette Deal Unparalleled Setback for Public Health.** April 28, 1997.

**Public Health Group Rejects Closed Door Deal between Tobacco Industry and State AGs.** November 18, 1998.

**Public Health Scientists Warn about the Irreversible Effects of Smoking.** June 17, 1998.

**Public-Health Scientist Urges Attorneys General: Don't Sign 'Global Settlement' Granting Cigarette Companies Immunity from Lawsuits.** May 27, 1997.

**Science Panel Asserts: Minnesota Tobacco Deal Is Clear Evidence That a National Settlement Is Ill-Advised.** May 12, 1998.

**Scientific Panel Rejects Clinton Anti-Smoking Plan as Ineffectual.** August 22, 1996.

**Scientist Deplores Philip Morris's 'Woman Thing' Music Campaign as Latest Enticement to Young Girls.** May 22, 1997.

**Shattering the Smoke Screen of Silence: Health Group Honors Vogue for Spotlighting the Devastating Health Effects of Smoking.** March 30, 1999.

### Selected Publications, ACSH
Cigarettes: What The Warning Label Doesn't Tell You: The First Comprehensive Guide to the Health Consequences of Smoking. n.d.

Environmental Tobacco Smoke: Health Risk or Health Hype? n.d.

The Irreversible Health Effects of Cigarette Smoking. n.d.

Is a Deal with the Cigarette Companies in the Interest of Public Health? n.d.

Levy, Robert, and Rosalind Marimont. 1998. "A Critical Assessment of 'Lies, Damned Lies, and 400,000 Smoking-Related Deaths.'" *Regulation.* Fall.

The Tobacco Industry's Use of Tobacco as a Drug. n.d.

### Selected Editorials, ACSH *(Priorities)*
The following articles are all accessible on the ASCH web site under "Editorials."

Lukachko, Alicia. "Breast Cancer Fears." Accessed 1999.

Ross, Gilbert L. "Assault on a Behemoth Anything but Frivolous." Accessed 1999.

Ross, Gilbert L. "Big Tobacco Wants to Pay Congress to Allow Them to Keep Addicting Our Children." May 29, 1998.

Ross, Gilbert L. "Death and Disease, Up in Smoke." Accessed 1999.

Whelan, Elizabeth. "Bird Droppings or Cigarette Smoking . . . Which Causes Lung Cancer?" Vol. 5, No. 4, 1993.

Whelan, Elizabeth. "Cigarettes and Blurred Vision among 'Right' Minded People." Vol. 6, No. 3, 1994.

Whelan, Elizabeth. "Dangers of Smoking." Accessed 1999.

Whelan, Elizabeth. "Hear Ye! Hear Ye! The End of Cigarette Advertising Is Near." Vol. 4, No. 1, 1992.

Whelan, Elizabeth. "Introducing Virginia Slims V-Wear: Clothes Any Woman Would Die For!" Vol. 5, No. 2, 1993.

Whelan, Elizabeth. "Selling Death: Tobacco's Strategy for Survival." Vol. 6, No. 2, 1994.

Whelan, Elizabeth, and Alan Blum. "An Exchange between Two Veterans in the War against Smoking." Vol. 7, No. 3, 1995.

Whelan, Elizabeth, and Alan Blum. "The Tobacco Cartel's Most Valuable Asset: Societal Complacency." Vol. 7, No. 2, 1995.

### Selected Articles, ACSH *(Priorities)*

Douglas, Clifford E. "What Do the Recent Revelations Mean for Tobacco Control?" Accessed 1999.

Mayer, Debra A. "The Ties That Bind Smoking to Depression." Accessed 1999.

Napier, Kristine. "Inhaling More Than They Bargained for: More Bad News for Smokers." Accessed 1999.

Peck, Robert. "Point/Counterpoint: Is Cigarette Advertising Protected by the First Amendment?—Yes." Accessed 1999.

Rodu, Brad, and Philip Cole. "Point/Counterpoint: Would a Switch from Cigarettes to Smokeless Tobacco Benefit Public Health?—Yes." Accessed 1999.

Tomar, Scott L. "Point/Counterpoint: Would a Switch from Cigarettes to Smokeless Tobacco Benefit Public Health?—No." Accessed 1999.

Whelan, Elizabeth. "Health Advice in Women's Magazines: Up in Smoke?" Accessed 1999.

Whelan, Elizabeth. "Health Hazards in Women's Magazines." Accessed 1999.

Whelan, Elizabeth. "Is a Deal with the Cigarette Industry in the Interest of Public Health?" Accessed 1999.

White, Larry C. "Point/Counterpoint: Is Cigarette Advertising Protected by the First Amendment?—No." Accessed 1999.

White, Larry C. "A Sweet Deal for Big Tobacco." Accessed 1999.

White, Larry C. "The Tobacco Settlement: Who Will Win? Who Will Lose?" Accessed 1999.

### Selected Letters, ACSH *(Priorities)*
Ginzel, K. H. "How the Cigarette Industry Teaches Children Not to Smoke." Vol. 3, No. 3, 1991.

Ginzel, K. H. "What's in a Cigarette?" Vol. 2, No. 4, 1990.

Napier, Kristine. "Alcohol and Tobacco: A Deadly Duo." Vol. 2, No. 2, 1990.

Whelan, Elizabeth M. "Cigarettes, Lawsuits and the United States Supreme Court." Vol. 3, No. 4, 1991.

Whelan, Elizabeth M. "The March of the Anti-Anti-Smoking Brigade." Vol. 3, No. 2, 1991.

White, Larry C. "Cigarettes on Trial: The Public Health Balancing Act." Vol. 3, No. 4, 1991.

# Selected Tobacco Industry Documents

## Tobacco Industry Document Sites

Millions of industry documents have been released as a result of suits on behalf of states and individual plaintiffs. The documents are stored in several places and may be accessed on the Internet. The following list of sites is provided by the CDC. The CDC provides a guide to searching the sites at http://www.cdc.gov/tobacco/industrydocs/searchtips.htm. The CDC also provides links to these sites at http://www.cdc.gov/tobacco/industrydocs/index.htm.

American Tobacco Company (www.cdc.gov/tobacco/industry-docs/docsites.html)

Site produced by Brown & Williamson Tobacco Company containing American Tobacco Company and B&W tobacco documents released as part of Minnesota Blue Cross's litigation against the tobacco industry (for short, the Minnesota tobacco trial).

Anne Landman's Daily Document Newsletter

A "Daily Document Newsletter," or "Doc Alert," is available at no charge from Anne Landman, regional program coordinator of the American Lung Association of Colorado. Her analysis of a selected document, along with quotations, is sent to subscribers by e-mail. The subscription form is at http://www.smokescreen.org/list/det.cfm?listid=66&menuitem=message.

Brown & Williamson Document Web Site (http://www.bw.aalatg.com)

Same as site produced by American Tobacco Company.

Centers for Disease Control and Prevention, http://www.cdc.gov/tobacco/industrydocs/index.htm

This CDC page provides a good launch pad for examining industry documents. It consists of (1) an introduction, "About Tobacco Industry Documents"; (2) a glossary of terms used in the database; (3) "Industry Document Web Sites," which lists, describes briefly, and links to the various sites; (4) a link to the 4B Index, the citation index to documents stored at the Minnesota Depository; (5) a link to searching the Minnesota Select Set, documents used in the Minnesota tobacco trial; and (6) a search link for the Guildford-British American Tobacco documents, which are stored in Minnesota as part of the Minnesota Select Set.

The Council for Tobacco Research—U.S.A., Inc. (http://www.ctr-usa.org/ctr/ctr.wm?tab+home)

Contains documents released in state attorneys general reimbursement lawsuits.

Lorillard Tobacco Company Document Site (http://www.lorillarddocs.com/)

Contains Lorillard tobacco documents released as part of the Minnesota tobacco trial.

Minnesota Blue Cross/Blue Shield Tobacco Litigation (www.cdc.gov/tobacco/industrydocs/docsites.html)

Contains internal tobacco industry documents used as exhibits in Minnesota Blue Cross's litigation against the tobacco companies.

Philip Morris Incorporated Document Site (http://www. philipmorris.com/)

Contains Philip Morris tobacco documents released as part of the Minnesota tobacco trial.

R. J. Reynolds Tobacco Company Online Litigation Document Web Site (www.cdc.gov/tobacco/industrydocs/docsites.html)

Contains RJR tobacco documents released as part of the Minnesota tobacco trial.

Smokescreen Action Network (http://www.smokescreen.org/)

A private web site, requiring a password, that was developed by and is maintained by Smokescreen Action Network. *Requests for passwords must be approved by the site's moderator, who looks for good references to guard against infiltration by industry or pro-tobacco people.* The site contains a searchable collection of a subset of documents found on the U.S. House Documents site and a number of databases containing tobacco industry documents.

TobaccoArchives.com (http://www.tobaccoarchives.com/)

Provides public links to four major tobacco industry document sites—Philip Morris, R. J. Reynolds, Lorillard, and B&W—plus a link to Tobacco Resolutions.com. The site also provides information about the Minnesota Tobacco Documents Depository.

The Tobacco Institute (http://www.tobaccoinstitute.com/)

Contains documents released as part of the Minnesota tobacco trial.

University of California San Francisco Tobacco Control Archives (www.cdc.gov/tobacco/industrydocs/docsites.html)

Documents in this collection include the following: B&W documents released as part of the Minnesota tobacco trial; the *Mangini v. R. J. Reynolds Tobacco Company* collection; and California documents from the Minnesota Tobacco Document Depository. UCSF staff have categorized the contents and added abstracts and reviews.

U.S. House Committee on Commerce Tobacco Documents (http://www.house.gov/commerce/TobaccoDocs/documents.html)

Contains documents obtained from Lorillard, Philip Morris, B&W, R. J. Reynolds, the Council for Tobacco Research, and the Tobacco Institute.

## Tobacco Industry Documents

For exceptionally useful sources of other relevant documents, see Anne Landman's "Daily Document Newsletter," reprinted and collected, at http://www.tobaccofreedom.org and **The Cigarette Papers,** by Stanton Glantz et al.

A note about Bates numbers: Bates numbers (e.g., 1000123662/3666) are used to identify some documents in some of the depositories listed earlier and appear with many of the following document entries. A Bates number appears as nine digits followed by a slash and then four more digits. The first nine digits identify the first page of the document. The last four digits, after the slash, indicate the Bates number on the last page of the document, without repeating the first part of the original number. In other words, if the number of the first page is 503969238 and the four-digit number after the slash is 9242, this means the number of the final page is 503969242 and that the document is five pages long.

"Agrees to Use B&W Products in 5 Films for $500,000." B&W letter. April 28, 1983. 1p. UCSF document I.D. number: 2404.02.

Site: UCSF Tobacco Control Archive, www.cdc.gov/tobacco/industrydocs/docsites.html

Sylvester Stallone letter in which he agrees to use B&W tobacco products in "no less than five feature films" for a fee of $500,000.

"Beneficial Additive Cigarette." Philip Morris internal memo. March 19, 1981. 5p. Bates No. 1000123662/3666.

Site: Philip Morris Incorporated Document Site, http://www. pmdocs.com/getallimg.asp?DOCID=1000123662/3666

This memo discusses a number of ideas, among them adding beneficial ingredients to cigarettes and then having "experts" outside the industry point out the health benefits of smoking.

"The Benefits of Cigarettes: Exploratory Research." RJR study. August 1981. 49p. Bates No. 503725059/25108.

Site: UCSF Tobacco Control Archive, www.cdc.gov/tobacco/ industrydocs/docsites.html

This report identifies "15 major personal benefits that smokers derive from their smoking" as well as "seven underlying aspects of the smoking experience." The writers recommend further research into "the variety and subtlety of the deeply expressive gestures that smokers make with their cigarettes." They suggest that "an increased understanding of this 'language' could lead directly to more accurate and potent uses of symbolism within RJR's brand advertising."

"Biological Effects of Smokeless Tobacco Products." PM interoffice memo. April 8, 1982. 1p. Bates No. 2001207640.

Site: Philip Morris Incorporated Document Site, http://www. pmdocs.com/getallimg.asp?DOCID=2001207640

A Philip Morris scientist reports that the correlation between the use of smokeless tobacco and cancer is "quite strong."

"Briefing Book: R. J. Reynolds Youth Non-Smoking Programs." RJR report. 1992. 10p. Bates No. 512690138/0147.

Site: R. J. Reynolds Online Litigation Document Archive, www. cdc.gov/tobacco/industrydocs/docsites.html

This briefing book describes RJR's position on youth smoking and provides guidance in "handling the media."

"Camel: New Advertising Campaign Developments." RJR marketing plan. March 12, 1986. 5p. Bates No. 503969238/9242.

Site: R. J. Reynolds Online Litigation Document Archive, http://www.rjrtdocs.com/. (Click on "Basic Search." After the search page opens, scroll down to "Document ID." Type in all except the last digit of the beginning Bates number—50396923—and then, without spacing, type an asterisk [*], and hit "Search." Another document will appear, so simply scroll down to "Camel: New Advertising … [etc.]." Click on the title to open the document.)

Defining the target of RJR's advertising campaign as eighteen- to twenty-four-year-old male smokers, the writer goes on to say that ads will be designed with the goal of "convincing target smokers that by selecting Camel . . . they will project an image that will enhance their acceptance among their peers." The underlying approach is to suggest that by smoking Camels, young men will convey to others that they are masculine, nonconformist, and self-confident.

"The Chemistry of Kool and a Recommendation." PM interoffice memo. May 24, 1972. 1p.

Site: Smokescreen Action Network (Anne Landman), http://tobaccofreedom.globalink.org/issues/documents/landman (Scroll down to "Philip Morris: Chemistry of Kool Cigarettes—Why They're Popular with Marijuana Smokers.")

Company research, the writer says, shows that "Kool is considered to be good for 'after marijuana' to maintain the 'high' or for mixing with marijuana, or 'instead.'" He suggests that a Philip Morris product could compete if it had high nicotine and less tar but high menthol or other added flavors to mask the reduction in tar.

"Cigarette Market History and Interpretation." PM report. December 12, 1984. 46p. Bates No. 2001265000/5045.

Site: Philip Morris Incorporated Document Site, www.cdc.gov/tobacco/industrydocs/docsites.html

A brand loses smokers in three ways, the writer says—smokers switch to another brand, they quit, or they die. Also discussed in this document: the impact of the 1954 report of the Royal College of Physicians and Surgeons and the surgeon general's report of 1964, as well as the fact that health-conscious women smokers apparently liked menthol cigarettes because the menthol seemed medicinal.

"Community Relations Kit (Pilot Study) Part I." PM report. 1959. 6p. Bates No. 1002405165/5170.

Site: Philip Morris Incorporated Document Site, http://www. pmdocs.com/gettallimg.asp?DOCID=1002405165/5170

The writer discusses the need to gather information about anti-tobacco activities and pass it along to the Tobacco Institute so that the institute can be more effective in fighting local public health efforts.

"Corporate Affairs Plan." PM draft report. November 25, 1987. 9p. Bates No. 2501254715/4723.

Site: Philip Morris Incorporated Document Site, http://www. pmdocs.com/gettallimg.asp?DOCID=2501254715/4723

A discussion of strategies for developing markets in the Middle East and Northern Europe, this document emphasizes the impor-tance of being "proactive," of taking the offensive. Among the possible methods suggested are recruiting "whitecoats" (medical scientists) to dispute harmful findings, developing relationships with influential officials, maintaining control of the ETS issue, and communicating directly with consumers.

"Data on Aggregate Annual Nicotine Consumption." RJR letter; August 22, 1975. 1p. Bates No. 500484119/4119.

Site: R. J. Reynolds Online Litigation Document Archive, http:// www.rjrtdocs.com/

An RJR scientist suggests reducing the nicotine content of ciga-rettes so that persons addicted to nicotine would have to buy more cigarettes to maintain their level of addiction.

**Dependence on Cigarette Smoking: A Review.** BAT report; December 15, 1977. 190p. Bates No. 105458896/9086.

Site: CDC, http://outside.cdc.gov:8080/BASIS/ncctld/web/ mnimages/DDW?W=DETA ILSID=541

Researchers working for British American Tobacco report on the role of nicotine in making people want to smoke; the effects of nicotine; and differences between smokers and nonsmokers. Among their findings: 99 percent of heroin addicts at an addiction treatment center rated nicotine as their most "needed" drug.

"Description of the Constitutional Hypothesis." PM interoffice memo. July 20, 1972. 1p. Bates No. 1005136046.

Site: Philip Morris Incorporated Document Site, http://www.pmdocs.com/getallimg.asp?DOCID=1005136046

In response to statements about a supposed "genetic predisposition to smoking," a Philip Morris scientist suggests that the genetic disposition leads not to smoking but to difficulty in adapting to "the problems of existence." It is this difficulty of adapting, he says, that leads to smoking, and thus there is no direct genetic link.

"Established Brands' Strategic Planning Meeting: Less Educated Smokers." RJR report. April 23, 1985. 11p. Bates No. 505640927/0937.

Site: R. J. Reynolds Online Litigation Document Archive, http://www.rjrtdocs.com/ (Click "Basic Search" and search "Combined Text" for "less educated smokers," without the quotation marks.)

In the context of this report, "less educated" means "young people." The report discusses the characteristics of young people and what they want from a cigarette.

"Face the Nation: Interview with Joseph Cullman." PM transcript. January 3, 1971. 19p. Bates No. 1005081714/1732.

Site: Philip Morris Incorporated Document Site, http://www.pmdocs.com/getallimg.asp?DOCID=1005081714/1732

Cullman, then chairman of the board of Philip Morris, responds to reporters' questions and touches on a number of issues central to the smoking controversy.

"The Functional Significance of Smoking in Everyday Life." BAT "restricted" report. April 24, 1984. 300p. Bates No. 105538876/9175.

Site: CDC, http://outside.cdc.gov:8080/BASIS/ncctld/web/mnimages/DDW?W%3DDETAILSID%3D580%26M%3D4%26K%3D580%26R%3DY%26U%3D1

Although industry documents in general speak of the cigarette as a nicotine delivery system, a scientist at BAT's Group Research and Development Centre explains that smoking "has a functional value in acting as a personal tool by which the smoker adjusts his psychological responses to the world at large." This study focuses on smoking as behavior, "as a process embedded within every-day life."

"ICOSI [International Committee on Smoking Issues] Task Force Coverage of Fourth World Conference on Smoking and Health—June 1979 in Stockholm." PM report. September 1978. 7p. Bates No. 2024260650/0656.

Site: Philip Morris Incorporated Document Site, http://www.pmdocs.com/getallimg.asp?DOCID=2024260650/0656

Recognizing that "ICOSI constitutes the first initiative on a worldwide scale to counter the actions of antismoking groups," the writer suggests ways of frustrating ICOSI's efforts.

"Lorillard Sales Position." Lorillard memo. September 15, 1964. 9p.

Site: Smokescreen Action Network (Anne Landman), http://tobaccofreedom.globalink.org/issues/documents/landman (Scroll down to "LORILLARD: KENT Cigarettes—the Myth Behind the 'Safer Cigarette.'")

A market researcher talks about the success of Kent as a "safer" cigarette. He recommends a new ad campaign that would be more effective in the wake of the surgeon general's report of 1964.

"Motives and Incentives in Cigarette Smoking." PM report. November 1981. 18p. Bates No. 2056121547/1564.

Site: Philip Morris Incorporated Document Site, http://www.pmdocs.com/getallimg.asp?DOCID=2056121547/1564

This document looks at why smokers smoke, but also interesting is its bluntness in speaking of nicotine. For example: "The ciga-rette should be conceived not as a product but as a package. The product is nicotine. The cigarette is but one of many package lay-ers." Also: "Think of the cigarette pack as a storage container for a day's supply of nicotine . . ." and "[t]hink of the cigarette as a dispenser for a dose unit of nicotine."

"Nicotine Augmentation Project." Lorillard memo. May 4, 1976. 6p.

Site: Smokescreen Action Network (Anne Landman), http://tobaccofreedom.globalink.org/issues/documents/landman (Scroll down to "Project to . . . Augment . . . the Nicotine in Cigarettes")

A Lorillard scientist discusses the goal of developing "a flavorful cigarette delivering lower tar while at the same time delivering a level of nicotine higher" than that obtainable by conventional cigarette construction.

"Nicotine Review." BAT report. n.d. 120p. Bates No. 110168659/8784.

Site: CDC, http://outside.cdc.gov:8080/BASIS/ncctld/web/mnimages/DDW?W=DETA ILSID=26903

A highly detailed analysis of nicotine and its effects.

"Note for the Tobacco Strategy Review Team: Transdermal Nicotine." BAT report. May 19, 1992. 10p. Bates No. 500872815/5008728.

Site: CDC, http://outside.cdc.gov:8080/BASIS/ncctld/web/mnimages/DDW?W=DETA ILSID=26384

Although the purpose of nicotine patches is to help smokers quit, this report by a BAT researcher discusses the pros and cons of BAT itself becoming a manufacturer of patches. He points out that the patches are, after all, only another system of nicotine delivery, like cigarettes, and that they would be cheaper to produce than cigarettes. On the other hand, he says, selling patches as a drug-delivery device might lead the FDA to consider tobacco companies as pharmaceutical companies—and cigarettes themselves as drug-delivery devices. Further, he says, selling patches to help people quit smoking would undercut the tobacco industry's argument that smoking is not addictive and that people can quit on their own.

"Note to Mr. Crawford." BAT letter. December 18, 1986. 3p. Bates No. 101432831/2833.

Site: CDC, http://outside.cdc.gov:8080/BASIS/ncctld/web/mnimages/EDW?W=DETA ILSID=26849

This letter written to a scientist who had suggested that BAT try to produce a safer cigarette summarizes BAT's reasons for disagreeing. "[I]n attempting to develop a 'safe' cigarette you are, by implication, . . . in danger of being interpreted as accepting that the current product is 'unsafe,' and this is not a position that I think we should take."

"Operation Rainmaker." PM report. March 20, 1990. 4p.

Site: Smokescreen Action Network (Anne Landman), http://tobaccofreedom.globalink.org/issues/documents/landman (Scroll down to "Philip Morris: Top Secret Operation Rainmaker.")

"Document moles" consider "Operation Rainmaker" a classic, says antitobacco activist Anne Landman. It proposes ways of reversing the decline in smoking.

"Other Ways to Reach the Target." RJR marketing report. January 2, 1989. 18p. Bates No. 507176999/7016.

Site: R. J. Reynolds Online Litigation Document Archive, http://www.rjrtdocs.com/ (Click on "New Search," then "Combined Text," and enter "Other Ways to Reach the Target" [but without using quotation marks].)

The "target," as the report makes clear, is the youth market.

"Perhaps Nicotine Is the Least Guilty." BAT report. October 30, 1978. 3p. Bates No. 100428869/8871.

Site: CDC, http://outside.cdc.gov:8080/BASIS/ncctld/web/mnimages/DDW?W=DETA ILSID=758

Low-nicotine cigarettes are "even more harmful" than regular cigarettes, the writer says, because the nicotine actually counteracts the effect of the carbon monoxide. He explains that while nicotine increases blood flow, carbon monoxide "extracts oxygen from the heart," so decreasing nicotine intensifies the harmful effects of carbon monoxide.

Philip Morris confidential memo. February 25, 1975. 2p. Bates No. 1000016677/6678.

Site: Philip Morris Incorporated Document Site, http://www.pmdocs.com/getallimg.asp?DOCID=1000016677/6678

The writer talks about controlling the release of information regarding a chemical present in tobacco smoke.

Philip Morris handwritten letter. March 30, 1980. 3p.

Site: tobaccofreedom.org (Anne Landman), http://tobaccofreedom.globalink.org/issues/documents/landman (Scroll down to "Philip Morris: Dispute Findings of Scientific Papers 'Damaging to Our Business.'")

Having read an article relating to ETS (White, J. R., and H. F. Froeb, "Small-Airways Dysfunction in Nonsmokers Chronically Exposed to Tobacco Smoke," *New England Journal of Medicine*, Vol. 302, No. 13, March 27, 1980), the writer remarks that it is "an excellent piece of work" that "could be very damaging to our business" and goes on to discuss ways of disputing the findings.

"Pilferage Presentation: Core Presentation." RJR report with graphics. September 12, 1985. 33p. Bates No. 514348983/9015.

Site: R. J. Reynolds Online Litigation Document Archive, http://www.rjrtdocs.com/

This is a guide for marketing representatives, designed to help them persuade retailers to display cigarettes in places where they may be easily stolen.

"A Presentation by ARIA." BAT record. October 31, 1988. 3p. Bates No. 400974548/4550.

Site: CDC, http://outside.cdc.gov:8080/BASIS/ncctld/web/mnimages/DDW?W=DETA ILSID=2295

At a meeting in a London restaurant, three members of the Association for Research on Indoor Air (ARIA) tell tobacco company representatives about their new organization, which is funded by Philip Morris. One says that ARIA is "totally independent" of PM and that "there has to be no formal contact between individuals [members] and the industry." The person reporting on the meeting says, "It is still being discussed as to whether the group will undertake some research (as might be suggested by their title)," and he states the "concept" of ARIA as being that of a group that can "speak up in learned societies or at meetings."

"Profiles of Prominent Anti-Tobacco Organizations." RJR report. 1991. 26p. Bates No. 511992643/2668.

Site: R. J. Reynolds Online Litigation Document Archive, http://www.rjrtdocs.com/

Basic information about opponents of big tobacco—e.g., the American Public Health Association, Action on Smoking and Health, and Californians for Non-Smokers' Rights.

"Project Brass: A Plan of Action for the ETS Issue." PM report. March 23, 1993. 47p. Bates No. 2023329411/9457.

Site: Philip Morris Incorporated Document Site, http://www. pmdocs.com/getallimg.asp?DOCID=2023329411/9457

Philip Morris's public relations agency wrote this report in response to a 1993 EPA report that classified ETS as a "Group 'A' carcinogen"—i.e., as a substance that increased the risk of lung cancer for anyone breathing it. Among the agency's suggestions in this document is that the public be led to believe that "[t]he research may have made a bigger deal out of this than it really is," and that people should not be "overly concerned" about the effects of secondhand smoke.

"Project Coumarin—Top Secret." PM letter. March 16, 1987. 4p. Bates No. 2501046314/6317.

Site: Philip Morris Incorporated Document Site, http://www. pmdocs.com/getallimg.asp?DOCID=2501046314/6317

The writer expresses concern that health officials in Norway will discover that B&W puts coumarin, which causes lung cancer, into its cigarettes. The letter includes a discussion of ways to prevent their finding out.

"Project Kestrel." BAT memorandum. n.d. 2p.

Site: Tobacco Industry Information (Jack Cannon), http:// gate.net/ ~jcannon/tobacco.html (Scroll down to "Project Kestrel," or access the document directly at http://www.gate. net/~jcannon/documents/kestrel.txt.)

The BAT memorandum that became known as the Project Kestrel

memo has been dismissed by an industry lawyer, who is quoted as saying, "There's no indication [that the ideas contained in the memo were] even close to being commercialized." The memo proposes cigarettes flavored with root beer and Brazilian fruit juice, which would appeal to "the younger generation while being rejected by their parents."

"Reverse Hypothesis." PM internal memorandum. May 29, 1974. 1p. Bates No. 1005081339.

Site: Philip Morris Incorporated Document Site, http://www. pmdocs.com/getallimg.asp?DOCID=1005081339

A PM scientist suggests that the company counter arguments that smoking causes lung disease by arguing that lung disease causes smoking. He suggests that people who are likely to develop cancer are likely to find smoking pleasurable.

"The Roper Proposal." Lorillard memo. May 1, 1972. 3p.

Site: Smokescreen Action Network (Anne Landman), http:// tobaccofreedom.globalink.org/issues/documents/landman (Scroll down to "Lorillard: Creating Doubt about the Health Charge without Actually Denying It.")

The writer of this memo begins by summarizing the strategy used by tobacco companies to defend themselves against the charge that smoking is dangerous. Pointing out that their strategy of denial only delays their ultimate defeat, he argues that tobacco companies ought to acknowledge that tobacco may be a cause of health problems among smokers but that it is "only one of many causes." Examples of other causes, he says, include air pollution, viruses, and food additives.

"Share of Smokers by Age Group." RJR report. October 30, 1975. 5p. Bates No. 500769032/9036.

Site: Smokescreen Action Network (Anne Landman), http:// tobaccofreedom.globalink.org/issues/documents/landman (Scroll down to "R. J. Reynolds: CONFIDENTIAL Product Research Report—Share of Smokers by Age Group.")

The annual update of market trends and RJR brands' market shares. The writer expresses concern about declining use among "younger smokers," ages 14 through 17.

"Smoking and Health: The Present Position in the U.K. and How It Came About." PM report. June 20, 1969. 23p. Bates No. 1000215062/5085.

Site: Philip Morris Incorporated Document Site, http://www.pmdocs.com/getallimg.asp?DOCID=1000215062/5085

This is apparently a transcription of an oral presentation in which the speaker calls on his colleagues to face certain "unpleasant" facts—i.e., statistics linking cigarettes and lung cancer. "These vital statistics are really vital," he says. "They threaten the life of the tobacco industry in every country in the world."

"Still More on Trends in Cigarette Smoking Prevalence." PM interoffice memo. February 18, 1983. 1p. Bates No. 2001255628.

Site: Philip Morris Incorporated Document Site, http://www.pmdocs.com/getallimg.asp?DOCID=2001255628

Reporting an "encouraging upward trend in smoking prevalence among 18- to 29-year-olds," the writer comments on a relationship between cigarette smoking and the use of amphetamines or marijuana. "What I find intriguing," he says, "is that marijuana and stimulant use increased as cigarette smoking declined, and that stimulant use is virtually a mirror image of cigarette usage. It almost looks as though stimulants and cigarettes are interchangeable to these kids."

"Structured Creativity Group Presentation." BAT report. n.d. 15p. Bates No. 102690336/0350.

Site: CDC, http://outside.cdc.gov:8080/BASIS/ncctld/web/mnimages/DDW?W=DETA ILSID=1137

Looking to the future, the writer expresses fears that cigarettes will have to compete with marijuana, glue sniffing, and hard drugs such as heroin and cocaine. He says the tobacco industry must find ways to appeal to the young, to satisfy their need to protest. He worries that cigarettes will follow cigars and pipes as "something 'My father and grandfather did' unless we are careful," and that nicotine may one day be classified officially as a poison and be available by prescription only.

"Summary: Operation Down Under Conference." PM report. June 1987. 5p. Bates No. 2021502679/2683.

Site: Philip Morris Incorporated Document Site, http://www. pmdocs.com/getallimg.asp?DOCID=2021502679/2683

This document summarizes methods of altering "public perception of ETS in terms of perceived risk and annoyance."

"Summary Report on Public Affairs Components of SOSAS [Studies on the Social Acceptability of Smoking] Research. Section 1. Target Goal #1. Reversing Steadily Unfavorable Trends in Public Opinion Regarding the Social Acceptability of Smoking." RJR report. December 22, 1978. 42p. Bates No. 500851221/1262.

Site: R. J. Reynolds Online Litigation Document Archive, http:// www.rjrtdocs.com/ (Click on "Basic Search." In the "Document ID" field, enter the first eight digits of the opening Bates number followed by an asterisk: 50085122*. After page 1 opens, click on the star to see and scroll through all 42 pages rather than having to bring them up one at a time.)

The authors of this report touch on a number of interesting issues—such as smokers' rights, their concern about the effects of ETS, and their lowered self-esteem—all related to the company's goal of making smoking more socially acceptable. The report acknowledges the difficulty of achieving "Target Goal #1": "Public suicide and voluntary spreading of diseases to innocent victims are never going to be social[ly] acceptable or regarded as a characteristic of first-class citizenship."

"Survey of Cancer Research with Emphasis upon Possible Carcinogens from Tobacco." RJR report. February 2, 1953. 22p. Bates No. 501932947/2968.

Site: R. J. Reynolds Online Litigation Document Archive, http:// www.rjrtdocs.com/ (Click on "Basic Search." Then, in the title field, enter "Survey of Cancer Research" [without the quotation marks].)

After summarizing the findings of studies linking smoking to cancer, the writer recommends that RJR begin looking more closely at such research and that it carefully examine all of the additives used in its products. What makes this document especially interesting is the date—1953.

"The Toxicity of Nicotine: Cancer." BAT report. n.d. [after 1986]. 19p. Bates No. 401020821/0839.

Site: CDC, http://outside.cdc.gov:8080/BASIS/ncctid/web/mnimages/EDW?W=DETA ILSID=2133

The author concludes that nicotine itself probably does not cause cancer but says it may do so by combining with other chemicals.

"What Causes Smokers to Select Their First Brand of Cigarette?" RJR memorandum. July 3, 1974. 10p. Bates No. 508453908/3917.

Site: R. J. Reynolds Online Litigation Document Archive, http://www.rjrtdocs.com/

This memo from RJR's marketing research department not only addresses the question in the title but also reports on findings of research aimed at identifying "reasons for selecting a first 'usual' brand." The writer includes results of a study of characteristics associated with several brands of cigarettes—e.g., brave, tough, manly, daring, adventurous, aggressive, and ambitious.

"Youth Smoking/Youth Anti-Smoking Education." B&W report. December 2, 1977. 4p. Bates No. 680262936/2939.

Site: B&W Document Site, www.cdc.gov/tobacco/industry-docs/docsites.html

Arguments against school-based efforts to prevent students from smoking.

# 7

# Selected Nonprint Resources

## Videos

Videos and films dealing with tobacco are available on request from various state agencies such as departments of health. For example, the web site of the Oklahoma State Department of Health lists 21 videos, including *Death in the West,* which Oklahoma residents may borrow free of charge (paying only return postage).

Videotapes may also be obtained from local libraries and through local offices of the American Cancer Society, the American Heart Association, and similar organizations. Feature films relating to tobacco—notably *Bright Leaf* and *The Hucksters*—are available from video rental stores.

The National Library of Medicine (NLM) audiovisual collection consists of approximately 32,000 titles, which are available through interlibrary loan. Persons interested in finding a specific title or a listing of videos dealing with tobacco may use LOCATOR*plus* at the NLM web site to search an online catalog. Libraries are charged $9 for each interlibrary loan request that is filled. NLM pays postage for outgoing loans; the borrowing library is responsible for return postage.

Following is a selection of videos on various aspects of tobacco and tobacco use. Various information in the listings is adapted from "A List of Tobacco Movies, Documentaries, Films, Videos" at http://www.tobacco.org/Resources/tob_movies.html.

**Ad Libbing It**
*Type:* VHS videocassette
*Length:* 17 minutes
*Date:* 1991
*Cost:* $250.00
*Source:* Washington Department of Commerce
http://www.washdoc@win.com/

Designed for sixth- through eighth-graders, this video provides insights into how advertising seeks to make cigarettes appealing to young people.

**And Down Will Come Baby**
*Type:* VHS videocassette
*Length:* 17 minutes
*Date:* 1994
*Source:* U.S. Department of Education
Safe and Drug-Free Schools Program, Room 604
600 Independence Avenue, S.W.
Washington, DC 20202
(202) 260-3954

Teenage narrators warn of the consequences of smoking, drinking, and using illegal drugs during pregnancy. Interviews with young mothers reveal their deep sense of guilt and regret about having used potentially harmful substances during their pregnancies.

**Are You Up to Snuff?**
*Type:* VHS videocassette
*Length:* 12 minutes
*Date:* (n.d.)
*Source:* Department of Health and Welfare, Boise, Idaho

Aimed at high school students, this video identifies the negative social factors associated with using smokeless tobacco.

**Big Dipper**
*Type:* VHS videocassette
*Length:* 19 minutes
*Date:* 1986
*Cost:* $195.00
*Source:* Independent Video Services
401 E. 10th Avenue, Suite 160
Eugene, OR 97401

Through interviews with young people who use chew and snuff tobacco, *Big Dipper* examines the question of why they started. It provides information about tobacco's adverse effects on health, especially oral health.

**Bilal's Dream**
*Type:* VHS videocassette
*Length:* 12 minutes
*Date:* 1990
*Cost:* $200.00
*Source:* California Instructional Technology Clearinghouse
http://clearinghouse.k12.ca.us

*Bilal's Dream* combines rap music and real-life scenarios to help young viewers make an important decision—to smoke or not to smoke.

**Bright Leaf**
*Type:* VHS videocassette (feature film)
*Length:* 110 minutes
*Date:* 1950
*Source:* Video rental stores

Chronicle of nineteenth-century tobacco farmer building a cigarette empire. Directed by Michael Curtiz and starring Gary Cooper, Lauren Bacall, Patricia Neal, Jack Carson, and Donald Crisp.

**Butt Out!: The Proven Quit Smoking Method**
*Type:* VHS videocassette
*Length:* 35 minutes
*Date:* 1992
*Cost:* $24.95
*Source:*Library Video Company
P.O. Box 580
Wynnewood, PA 19096
(800) 843-3620
Fax: (610) 645- 4040
http://www.videolibrary.com/

Actor Ed Asner examines various methods of quitting smoking. He also explains what kinds of situations cause cravings and how to avoid them. The video features interviews with former smokers who tell about the methods they used to kick the habit.

### Chains of Smoke
*Type:* VHS videocassette
*Length:* 10 minutes
*Cost:* $295.00
*Source:* AGC Educational Media
1560 Sherman Avenue, Suite 100
Evanston, IL 60201
(800) 323-9084
Fax: (847) 328-6706
E-mail: agc@mcs.net

Featuring dramatic interviews with smokers, both young and old, the video makes the point that people smoke not because they want to but because they cannot stop.

### The Chews Blues
*Type:* VHS videocassette
*Length:* 23 minutes
*Date:* 1987
*Cost:* $115.00
*Source:* Balance Productions
11108 Stillwater Avenue
Kensington, MD 20895
(301) 942-7505

A high school student and the school's custodian look at the risks of smokeless tobacco.

### Cigarettes: Who Profits, Who Dies?
*Type:* VHS videocassette
*Length:* 50 minutes
*Date:* 1993
*Cost:* $149.00
*Source:* Films for the Humanities and Sciences

A look at how tobacco companies attract new smokers through advertising, emphasizing the difference between image and reality. The video features Wayne McLaren, the original Marlboro Man, who was dying of cancer when the video was made. Also featured is a Lucky Strike model who teaches her fellow laryngectomy patients how to talk again.

### Confessions of a Simple Surgeon
*Type:* VHS videocassette
*Length:* 18 minutes
*Date:* 1988
*Cost:* $225.00
*Source:* Pyramid Film and Video
2801 Colorado Avenue
Santa Monica, CA 90404
(213) 828-7577

Antismoking activist Dr. Arthur Evans explains how tobacco companies target youth and discusses the problem of addiction. He also talks about how the average citizen can fight back.

### Dangerous Game
*Type:* VHS videocassette
*Length:* 6 minutes
*Date:* 1995
*Source:* Cancer Information Service
National Cancer Institute
Bethesda, MD 20892-0001
(800) 4-CANCER

Primarily a series of interviews with professional baseball players. Some chose not to use chewing tobacco and explain why; others explain why they quit. One interview features a former player who used smokeless tobacco for a number of years and lost a large part of his jaw to oral cancer. He says that he regarded smokeless tobacco as a safe alternative to cigarettes.

### Death in the West: The Marlboro Story
*Type:* VHS videocassette
*Length:* 32 minutes
*Date:* 1983
*Cost:* $29.95
*Source:* Pyramid Film and Video
Box 1048
Santa Monica, CA 90406-1048
(800) 421-2304
Facets Multimedia, Inc.
1517 W. Fullerton Avenue

Chicago, IL 60614
(773) 281-9075
Fax: (773) 929-5437
E-mail: sales@facets.org

Juxtaposes interviews of physicians, researchers, and a tobacco industry executive with personal narratives of present-day cowboys dying from smoking-related lung diseases. A powerful exposé of the most successful cigarette advertising campaign in American history, which featured the Marlboro Man.

**Diary of a Teenage Smoker**
*Type:* VHS videocassette
*Length:* 26 minutes
*Date:* 1993
*Source:* Minister of Supply and Services, Canada; distributed by East West Media.

Commentaries from teenage girls designed to entertain, startle, and inspire commitment to being smoke-free. Explores the images that induce young girls to start smoking. Is accompanied by a facilitator's guide.

**Dirty Business**
*Type:* VHS videocassette
*Length:* 24 minutes
*Date:* 1988
*Source:* Varied Directions, Inc.
Camden, ME

Media producer Tony Schwartz tells about his efforts to counter the tobacco industry's $2.5 billion advertising campaign. He created ads and commercials that reveal the truth about tobacco's destructive and lethal effects.

**Dying for a Smoke**
*Type:* VHS videocassette
*Length:* 39 minutes
*Date:* 1994
*Cost:* $29.95
*Source:* Library Video Company
P.O. Box 580
Wynnewood, PA 19096

(800) 843-3620
Fax: (610) 645-4040
http://www.libraryvideo.com/

Former CBS journalist Bill Riead assembles a group of celebrities from across the political spectrum—among them actors Chuck Norris and Gregory Hines—and records their reflections on tobacco regulation and its effect on the tobacco industry. This debate-style program explores both sides of the issue, looking at it from the perspective of the industry titans and that of the anti-smoking lobby. Features medical facts about cigarette smoking and a look at the effects of ad campaigns on children.

### The Feminine Mistake
*Type:* VHS videocassette
*Length:* 24 minutes
*Date:* 1977
*Cost:* $125.00
*Source:* Pyramid Film and Video
Box 1048
Santa Monica, CA 90406-1048
(800) 421-2304

Cigarette advertising depicts smoking as liberating, sexually attractive, and glamorous. This video warns of the unique risks smoking poses for women by presenting women whose lives have been disrupted by smoking-related health problems.

### The Feminine Mistake: The Next Generation
*Type:* VHS videocassette
*Length:* 32 minutes
*Date:* 1989
*Cost:* $295.00
*Source:* Pyramid Film and Video
Box 1048
Santa Monica, CA 90406-1048
(800) 421-2304

This updated version of the preceding video describes ways in which teenage girls are enticed by their peers and by the tobacco industry to begin smoking. It includes a discussion of smoking's adverse effects, from early skin wrinkles to cancer.

**A Fight for Breath: Emphysema**
*Type:* VHS videocassette
*Length:* 12 minutes
*Date:* 1974
*Source:* CRM Films
Carlsbad, CA

Graphically illustrates the hard facts about emphysema.

**Fire without Smoke**
*Type:* VHS videocassette
*Length:* 17 minutes
*Date:* 1989
*Source:* School of Health
Loma Linda University
Loma Linda, CA

Traces the history of smokeless tobacco and examines its current popularity, which is based in part, it says, on the mistaken belief that smokeless tobacco is less dangerous than cigarettes.

**"Freshstart": 21 Days to Stop Smoking**
*Type:* VHS videocassette
*Length:*  75 minutes
*Date:* 1986
*Cost:* Purchase $29.95
*Source:* Library, American Cancer Society

The ACS describes this video as follows: "If you're a smoker who has resolved—whether firmly or a bit nervously—to quit, you'll find no one better qualified to help you succeed than the American Cancer Society. No one can match their unique insight into the needs, fears and discomforts which the budding nonsmoker experiences during the most critical time of quitting—the first three weeks."

This program consists of 21 short segments that address a different issue every day, taking viewers over each hurdle in the process of giving up cigarettes. Hosted by comedian and ex-smoker Robert Klein, *Freshstart* brings together expert advice from physicians, psychologists, and former smokers. They explain smoking's three "hooks"—physical dependency, habit, and psychological addiction—and present ways to cope with each, including strategies to handle stress, depression, sudden cravings, and even the temptation to overeat.

**Getting the Message . . . about Tobacco**
*Type:* VHS videocassette
*Length:* 15 minutes
*Date:* 1998
*Cost:* $295.00
*Source:* AGC Educational Media
1560 Sherman Avenue, Suite 100
Evanston, IL 60201
(800) 323-9084
Fax: (847) 328-6706
E-mail: agc@mcs.net

A follow-up to a broader video, *Getting the Message,* which describes advertising tactics and principles to apply in evaluating ads, this video focuses specifically on the various forms of tobacco advertising. It makes clear that there is more to such messages than meets the eye, explains how the brain processes them, and equips students with some fundamental tools to use in challenging them.

**Growing up in Smoke**
*Type:* VHS videocassette
*Length:* 15 minutes
*Date:* 1984
*Cost:* $149.00
*Source:* Durrin Productions, Inc.
4926 Sedgwick Street, N.W.
Washington, DC 20016-2326
(800) 536-6843
Fax: (202) 237-6738
E-mail: durrinprod@aol.com

Focusing on the tactics used to induce children to smoke, this video explains the thinking behind commercials and tobacco advertising in general.

**The Hucksters**
*Type:* VHS videocassette (feature film)
*Length:* 115 minutes
*Date:* 1947
*Source:* video rental store

Based on a 1946 bestseller written by Frederick Wakeman, who once worked at one of the biggest advertising agencies in the country, *The*

*Hucksters* exposes and satirizes Madison Avenue. The Sidney Greenstreet character is patterned after George Washington Hill, long-time head of advertising for American Tobacco Co.

**Hugh McCabe: The Coach's Final Lesson**
*Type:* VHS videocassette
*Length:* 17 minutes
*Date:* 1988
*Source:* American Lung Association

Hugh McCabe is a high school teacher, counselor, and coach who has lung cancer as a result of smoking but continues to smoke. He argues that the harm is already done, but the truth is that he is addicted and does not have the will to quit.

**The Insider**
*Type:* VHS videocassette (feature film)
*Length:* 160 minutes
*Date:* 1999
*Source:* Video rental store

A dramatization based on the revolt of Jeffrey Wigand, a tobacco industry scientist who became a whistleblower.

**Larry Hagman's Stop Smoking for Life**
*Type:* VHS videocassette
*Length:* 60 minutes
*Date:* 1987
*Source:* Karl-Lorimar Home Video
17942 Cowan
Irvine, CA 92714

Recommended by the American Cancer Society, *Stop Smoking for Life* offers a seven-day program using motivational and behavior-modification techniques. The strategy is based on a system developed by Elizabeth A. LaScala of the UCLA School of Public Health. Actor Larry Hagman, who had been unable to quit smoking until he tried La Scala's program, produced this video to share the benefits of the Stop Smoking for Life program.

**Leaves of Gold**
*Type:* VHS videocassette
*Length:* 50 minutes

*Date:* 1998
*Cost:* $19.95
*Source:* Library Video Company
P.O. Box 580
Wynnewood, PA 19096
(800) 843-3620
Fax: (610) 645-4040
http://www.libraryvideo.com/

Surveys the tobacco industry from the colonial era to the present day. Historians, politicians, health professionals, and industry insiders provide a comprehensive look at the issues that surround tobacco, the ultimate cash crop. Topics discussed include individual liberty versus the health of others, the welfare of farmers versus the interests of the medical industry, and more. Part of the "Empires of American Industry" series.

### Live Better Longer: The No Smoking Zone
*Type:* VHS videocassette
*Length:* 12 minutes
*Date:* 1987
*Source:* Education Associates
Frankfort, KY

### Lorne's Big Decision
*Type:* VHS videocassette
*Length:* 14 minutes
*Date:* 1997
*Cost:* $135.00

Young students have created a video to alert other young adults about the hazards of cigarettes and to counter the pressure of peers who encourage them to try smoking. The video tells the story of a young man named Lorne, who is trying to decide whether or not he should try smoking. Some of his friends have told him that smoking is cool. In an effort to make an informed decision, Lorne learns about the physiology of his lungs and how nicotine and smoke can affect his health. Lorne learns how to combat peer pressure in an assertive and effective manner. The video shows the viewer how to say "no" to cigarettes without being mean or causing anger. Curiosity about smoking is okay, but knowing the facts about smoking's effects is more important.

**Mara's Breathtaking Story**
*Type:* VHS videocassette
*Length:* 22 minutes
*Date:* 1994
*Source:* Gerald T Rogers Productions, Inc.
Skokie, IL

After Mara discovers she was in denial about the hazards of smoking, she recognizes she must break away from her friends and see new possibilities for herself. This video dramatizes the consequences of tobacco addiction and demonstrates the value in quitting. It also identifies the forces that lead to tobacco use and addiction, including peer pressure and exposure at home.

**Marketing Disease to Hispanics: The Selling of Alcohol and Tobacco**
*Type:* VHS videocassette
*Length:* 16 minutes
*Date:* 1992
*Cost:* $29.95
*Source:* UMDNJ-Robert Wood Johnson Medical School
Department of Environmental and Community Medicine
675 Hoes Lane
Piscataway, NJ 08854
(908) 463-5041

For a number of years Hispanics have been among the subgroups targeted by tobacco and alcohol advertising. This video explains some of the marketing tactics used to entice Hispanics to smoke and urges them to fight back.

**Nicotine: An Old-Fashioned Addiction**
*Type:* VHS videocassette
*Length:* 35 minutes
*Date:* 1991
*Cost:* Purchase $39.95
*Source:* Library Video Company
P.O. Box 580
Wynnewood, PA 19096
(800) 843-3620
Fax: 610/645–4040
http://www.libraryvideo.com/

This video goes to the heart of the matter by examining the chemistry of the tobacco plant and the nature of tar and nicotine. It explores the similarities between smoking and other forms of substance abuse, and explains the various ways in which it can damage or destroy the health of smokers.

### No Butts
*Type:* VHS videocassette
*Length:* 29 minutes
*Date:* 1987
*Cost:* $59.00
*Source:* MTI Film and Video
Northbrook, IL

*No Butts* explains why people smoke, discusses the dangers of smoking, and evaluates strategies for quitting.

### Pack of Lies: The Advertising of Tobacco
*Type:* VHS videocassette
*Length:* 35 minutes
*Date:* 1992
*Source:* Foundation for Media Education
Northampton, MA

A hard-hitting exposé of the tobacco industry's advertising strategies, this video reveals the cynical and manipulative way in which the industry seeks to create new generations of nicotine addicts by spreading a "pack of lies." Jean Kilboume and Rick Polay discuss tobacco industry advertising and how it creates new cigarette smokers.

### Paul's Fix
*Type:* VHS videocassette
*Length:* 12 minutes
*Date:* 1994
*Source:* BEST Foundation for a Drug-Free Tomorrow
1307 Riverside Drive, Suite 700
Sherman Oaks, CA 91423-2449
(800) 382-3860

Part of the Nancy Reagan "Afterschool" series, *Paul's Fix* is intended for thirteen- to fifteen-year-olds. This segment focuses on how to say "no" to cigarettes.

**The Performance Edge**
*Type:* VHS videocassette
*Length:* 15 minutes
*Date:* 1990
*Source:* Centers for Disease Control
(800) CDC-1311 or (800) 729-6686

The theme of this video is that young people can experience natural highs through healthful athletic activities, without the negative results of highs from using alcohol or tobacco.

**The Performance Edge (Revised)**
*Type:* VHS videocassette
*Length:* 9 minutes
*Date:* 1995
*Source:* Centers for Disease Control
(800) CDC-1311 or (800) 729-6686

This new version of *The Performance Edge* includes a football coach talking to his team about the adverse effects of alcohol and tobacco, stressing that their use decreases performance potential.

**Poisoning Your Children: The Perils of Secondhand Smoke**
*Type:* VHS videocassette
*Length:* 12 minutes
*Date:* 1993
*Source:* Pyramid Film and Video
Santa Monica, CA

Interviews with experts make clear how secondhand smoke harms health, especially the health of children. Animated segments show how tobacco smoke affects the body.

**Quitting Smoking**
*Type:* VHS videocassette
*Length:* 23 minutes
*Date:* 1999
*Cost:* $39.95
*Source:* Library Video Company
P.O. Box 580
Wynnewood, PA 19096
(800) 843-3620
Fax: (610) 645- 4040
http://www.videolibrary.com/

*Quitting Smoking* features interviews with teenagers who were addicted to tobacco but managed to quit. It addresses the critical problem of postponing quitting, explaining that putting it off only makes it harder.

### Secondhand Smoke (Revised)
*Type:* VHS videocassette
*Length:* 15 minutes
*Date:* 1995
*Source:* Pyramid Film and Video
Santa Monica, CA

*Secondhand Smoke* opens with a mad scientist trying to invent the perfect poison—but he finds that he cannot improve on second-hand smoke from cigarettes. The video is narrated by actor Jack Klugman, a survivor of throat cancer, who discusses smoking's health risks for nonsmokers, including unborn babies, and emphasizes that there are no safe levels of exposure.

### Showdown on Tobacco Road
*Type:* VHS videocassette
*Length:* 58 minutes
*Date:* 1987
*Source:* PBS Video
Alexandria, VA

This video examines what happens when one of the most popular and successful products in the history of America is found to be one of the most serious health risks.

### 60 Minutes to a Smoke-Free Life
*Type:* VHS videocassette
*Length:* 60 minutes
*Date:* 1990
*Cost:* $29.95
*Source:* Library Video Company
P.O. Box 580
Wynnewood, PA 19096
(800) 843-3620
Fax: (610) 645-4040
http://www.libraryvideo.com/

Psychotherapist Jonathan Robinson combines one-on-one counseling and scenes from his stop-smoking seminars that enable smokers to easily and quickly stop smoking. Robinson develops these effective techniques through revolutionary research, which explores the psychological aspects of smoking addictions. The video includes a booklet about Robinson's program and techniques.

**Smart Women Don't Smoke**
*Type:* VHS videocassette
*Length: 12 minutes*
Date: 1989
*Source:* WHO/OMS Media Service

The narrator is the daughter of actor Yul Brynner, a smoker who died of lung cancer. She discusses the increased health risks faced by women who smoke, especially in combination with birth-control pills and during pregnancy.

**Smokeless Tobacco: A Spittin' Image**
*Type:* VHS videocassette
*Length:* 15 minutes
*Date:* 1994
*Cost:* $110.00
*Source:* California Instructional Technology Clearinghouse
http://clearinghouse.k12.ca.us

Smokeless tobacco, spit tobacco, dip, chew, or snuff—all are addictive, expensive, and deadly. This video refutes tobacco industry advertising that smokeless tobacco is a harmless alternative to smoking.

**Smokeless Tobacco: Basic Facts**
*Type:* VHS videocassette
*Length:* 18 minutes
*Date:* 1999
*Cost:* $59.95
*Source:* Educational Video Network
1401 19th Street
Huntsville, TX 77340
Fax: (409) 294-0233
http://www.evn@edvidnet.com/

This hard-hitting video graphically depicts the terrible damage caused by smokeless tobacco, which is still harmful even though it is not inhaled.

**Smokeless Tobacco: Is It Worth the Risk?**
*Type:* VHS videocassette
*Length:* 15 minutes
*Date: 1998*
Cost: $19.95
*Source:* American Academy of Otolaryngology
(703) 836-4444

This video features testimonials by baseball players who have chewed tobacco.

**Smokeless Tobacco: It Can Snuff You Out**
*Type:* VHS videocassette
*Length:* 13 minutes
*Date:* 1986
*Cost:* Purchase $265.00
*Source:* Alfred Higgins Productions
Los Angeles, CA

Contrasting medical photos of oral cancer with advertising claims that smokeless tobacco is harmless, this video features interviews with users who tell why they started and describe the difficulty of quitting. Among the interviewees is a female user.

**Smokeless Tobacco: The Sean Marsee Story**
*Type:* VHS videocassette
*Length:* 17 minutes
*Date:* 1986
*Source:* Walt Disney Educational Media Co.
Burbank, CA

Tells the true story of Sean Marsee, a track star who died at the age of 19 after habitually using smokeless tobacco. Offers advice, suggestions, and opinions on the smokeless tobacco habit.

**Smoke Screen**
*Type:* VHS videocassette
*Length:* 26 minutes
*Date:* 1993
*Cost:* $199.00
*Source:* Intermedia
Seattle, WA

A former Winston model offers a behind-the-scenes look at cigarette advertising. He also talks about the harmful consequences of smoking and reveals facts that the tobacco companies "don't want you to know."

**Smoke That Cigarette**
*Type:* VHS videocassette
*Length:* 51 minutes
*Date:* 1987
*Cost:* $16.98
*Source:* BigStar Entertainment, Inc.
http://www.bigstar.com/

*Smoke That Cigarette* examines the changing image of smoking, beginning with the music, the ads, the movies, and the stars who glamorized smoking and working its way to the present.

**Smokeless Tobacco**
*Type:* VHS videocassette (music video)
*Length:* 11 minutes
*Date:* 1986
*Cost:* $68.00
*Source:* American Dental Association
Chicago, IL

A teenage girl is disgusted by the bad breath and stained teeth of a boy who uses smokeless tobacco. The video goes on to examine smokeless tobacco's more serious health risks and uses photos to illustrate the possible consequences.

**Smokeless Tobacco: It Can Snuff You Out (Revised)**
*Type:* VHS videocassette
*Length:* 13 minutes
*Date:* 1986
*Source:* Alfred Higgins Productions
Los Angeles, CA

This video discusses the health risks associated with smokeless tobacco, explaining why it is not a safe alternative to cigarettes.

**Smoking: Every Breath You Take**
*Type:* VHS videocassette
*Length:* 50 minutes

*Date:(n.d.)*
Cost: $39.95
*Source:* Educational Video Network
1401 19th Street
Huntsville, TX 77340
Fax: 9409) 294-0233
http://www.evn@edvidnet.com/

This video is about lung disease, which debilitates millions of Americans each year. It discusses the destruction wrought by tuberculosis and asthma and shows what happens during a lung transplant operation. The video also offers some strategies that work for people who want to stop smoking.

**Smokin': Somebody Stop Me!**
**(Part 1) Teen Smoking**
*Type:* VHS videocassette
*Length:* 23 minutes
*Date:* 1999
*Cost:* $39.95
*Source:* P.O. Box 580
Wynnewood, PA 19096
(800) 843-3620
Fax: (610) 645-4040
http://www.libraryvideo.com/

Part 1 of this video features candid interviews and debates about why teenagers smoke.

**Smokin': Somebody Stop Me!**
**(Part 2) Quitting Smoking**
*Type:* VHS videocassette
*Length:* 23 minutes
*Date:* 1999
*Cost:* $39.95
*Source:* P.O. Box 580
Wynnewood, PA 19096
(800) 843-3620
Fax: (610) 645-4040
http://www.libraryvideo.com/

Part 2 of this video examines the negative effects of smoking and offers techniques for quitting.

### Smoking against Your Will
*Type:* VHS videocassette
*Length:* 29 minutes
*Date:* 1985

Health-care professionals discuss the hazards of secondhand smoke for children and spouses of smokers and for people with allergies. Ultrasound images show a fetus responding to the presence of tobacco smoke, and before and after testing shows high levels of carbon monoxide in the blood of people who work in proximity to smokers. Smokers and nonsmokers discuss their concerns.

### Smoking: Time to Quit
*Type:* VHS videocassette
*Length:* 17 minutes
*Date:* 1994
*Source:* Films for the Humanities, Inc.
P.O. Box 2053
Princeton, NJ 08543-2053
(800) 257-5126
Fax: (609) 275-3767

Before smokers quit for good, this video explains, they may have to go through the withdrawal process four or five times. The message is that the only way to fail is to give up, to let the frustration of repeatedly quitting and relapsing overwhelm the desire to quit. *Smoking: Time to Quit* explains the various ways of quitting and emphasizes the importance of support groups in helping smokers cope with the setbacks and push on to success.

### Smoking's Not for Winners
*Type:* VHS videocassette
*Length:* 25 minutes
*Date:* 1990
*Source:* Educational Activities Video
Freeport, NY

Discusses the hazards of tobacco, smoke, "sidestream" smoke, and how tobacco advertising affects young people and smoking today.

### Some Traditions Should Be Broken
*Type:* VHS videocassette
*Length:* 30 minutes
*Date:* 1990

*Source:* National Clearinghouse for Drug and Alcohol Information
(800) 729-6686

A drama about a Korean immigrant family facing culture conflict
and a generation gap. The father's smoking habit affects his family, and the question is whether the son will smoke also. This
video is part of a project to reduce tobacco use among youth.

### Stop Before You Drop
*Type:* VHS videocassette
*Length:* 12 minutes
*Date:* 1989
*Source:* Durrin Productions, Inc.
4926 Sedgwick Street, N.W.
Washington, DC 20016-2326
(800) 536-6843
Fax: (202) 237-6738
E-mail: durrinprod@aol.com

Uses song, dance, and rap to convey the message to teens that
smoking is not healthy, glamorous, or fashionable. Offers realistic
alternatives to smoking and tips for quitting, and discusses how
peers can support each other in resisting the temptation. This fast-
paced, high energy, and entertaining video was created by and
for young people to celebrate life without cigarettes. It follows the
exploits of a young rapper, Larry Plummer, as he passes through
Richmond, California, on his way to audition for the "Stop Before
You Drop" music video.

### Stop the Sale: Prevent the Addiction
*Type:* VHS videocassette
*Length:* 26 minutes
*Date:* 1995
*Cost:* $8.50
*Source:* NCADI
Washington, DC

Addresses the problem of tobacco use among young people and
the importance of stopping the sale of tobacco to minors.

### Stop Smoking in 7 Days
*Type:* VHS videocassette
*Date:* 1997
*Cost:* $26.95

*Source:* Library Video Company
P.O. Box 580
Wynnewood, PA 19096
(800) 843-3620
Fax: (610) 645-4040
http://www.libraryvideo.com/

This program helps smokers control their smoking habits by using focused imaging and deep relaxation—techniques common to hypnosis, meditation, and other clinically proven methods of behavior modification. It is hosted by Nancy Siegrist, certified clinical hypnotherapist, member of the American Board of Hypnotherapy, and leader of many smoking cessation and weight-loss seminars across the country.

**Teens and Tobacco**
*Type:* VHS videocassette
*Length:* 19 minutes
*Date:* 1996
*Source:* California Instructional Technology Clearinghouse
http://clearinghouse.k12.ca.us/

*Teens and Tobacco* explores the dangers of smoking or chewing tobacco through interviews with teenagers, adult smokers, and physicians. Segments focus on (1) experiences of individuals who have suffered from tobacco use; (2) the reasons young people start using tobacco; (3) the harmful effects of tobacco use; (4) addiction to nicotine; and (5) the importance of resisting the pressure to start smoking. This video promotes wise decisions about avoiding tobacco use based on knowledge of tobacco's harmful effects on one's physical and mental well-being.

**Teen Smoking: Smoke Now, Lung Cancer Later**
*Type:* VHS videocassette
*Length:* 22 minutes
*Date:* 1997
*Cost:* $79.95
*Source:* Educational Video Network
1401 19th Street
Huntsville, TX 77340
Fax: 409/294–0233
http://www.evn@edvidnet.com/

A humorous look at a serious subject—the 4 million teenagers who smoke and the health consequences they ignore. Blending live interviews with computer animation and the antics of the Factoid Wizard and his friend Bonehead, a smoker, this program will hold the interest of teens and show them things they probably did not know about smoking.

### Teen Smoking: You Don't Have to Start
*Type:* VHS videocassette
*Length:* 19 minutes
*Date:* 1998
*Source:* Lucerne Media
37 Ground Pine Road
Morris Plains, NJ 07950
(800) 341-2293
Fax: (973) 538-0855

*Teen Smoking* is part of Promedion Productions' Teens-at-Risk series, which dramatizes situations in which young people find themselves and challenges them to make responsible decisions. Included are interviews with medical experts and teen counselors.

### Thanks, but No Thanks: Good Practice Today!
*Type:* VHS videocassette
*Length:* 30 minutes
*Date:* 1994
*Source:* BEST Foundation for a Drug-Free Tomorrow
13701 Riverside Drive, Suite 700
Sherman Oaks, CA 91423

Two short dramatizations in which young people are tempted by others to engage in undesirable behavior—in one case, shoplifting; in another, using spit tobacco.

### Think about It: Be Smart, Don't Start
*Type:* VHS videocassette
*Length:* 14 minutes
*Date:* 1991
*Source:* Center for Substance Abuse Prevention

Public service announcements aimed at preventing drug use in youths.

**Tobacco Abuse**
*Type:* VHS videocassette
*Length:* 15 minutes
*Date:(n.d.)*
*Cost:* $59.95
*Source:* Educational Video Network
1401 19th Street
Huntsville, TX 77340
Fax: 409/294–0233
http://www.evn@edvidnet.com/

Addressing influences that affect a teenager's decision to start using tobacco, this program examines the addictive nature of nicotine, the health risks of tobacco use, and the contents of tobacco products. It also shows the possible legal ramifications for minors who use tobacco products and offers tips on how to kick the habit.

**Tobacco: A Gift of Choice**
*Type:* VHS videocassette
*Length:* 16 minutes
*Date:* (n.d.)
*Source:* Shenandoah Film Productions
538 G Street
Arcata, CA 95521
(707) 822-1030
Fax: (707) 822-5334

A video directed at Native-American youth, *Tobacco: A Gift of Choice* depicts an elder telling his grandson about the traditional ceremonial use of tobacco and contrasting it with the use of cigarettes and chewing tobacco.

**Tobacco and Health: You Decide**
*Type:* VHS videocassette
*Length:* 25 minutes
*Date:* 1995
*Source:* Centers for Disease Control
Atlanta, GA

This video contains 1994 testimony heard by the House Subcommittee on Health and the Environment from CEOs of the leading tobacco manufacturers. How should a viewer respond to the tobacco industry's position on tobacco health effects, addiction, advertising policies, accommodation and prohibition? Should the facts speak for themselves? The viewer is left to decide.

### Tobacco and Smoking: Debate the Issues
*Type:* audio cassette (and brochure)
*Source:* NPR Outreach
Washington, DC

Part of National Public Radio's ongoing effort to educate and inform the public and promote discussion about the issues affecting our nation.

### Tobacco: Behind the Smoke and Mirrors
### (Part 1) Teens: Through the Eyes of Big Tobacco
*Type:* VHS videocassette
*Length:* 17 minutes
*Date:* 1998
*Cost:* $99.95
*Source:* Visual Mentor
40 Trace Lane
Half Moon Bay, CA 94019
(650) 726-9152
Fax: 650/726-2756
http://www.info@visual-mentor.com/

*Tobacco: Behind the Smoke and Mirrors* is a two-part set of tobacco-use prevention videos. It addresses the same social needs of adolescents that are addressed by tobacco advertising—the need to fit in, to exert independence from parental control, to develop physically, and to be sexually attractive. Reversing the thrust of tobacco advertising, the videos show not how smoking makes a teen belong, but how it causes social scorn and ostracism. Rather than liberating adolescents from adult control, smoking makes them dependent customers of tobacco companies. Instead of enhancing their physical and sexual identity, smoking affects teenagers' sexual prowess and physical appearance immediately, not just as they age.

Part 1 uses internal tobacco company documents to show how tobacco companies view teens as a source of long-term profits. It portrays tobacco executives at work, developing brand names and ad campaigns that promote nicotine addiction. It views tobacco executives buying influence in Congress and shows how the media compromises the truth about tobacco because of their reliance on tobacco advertising revenue. Finally, the video depicts teens evaluating the facts on the exaggerated representation of tobacco use in movies.

**Tobacco: Behind the Smoke and Mirrors**
**(Part 2) Smoking: Through the Eyes of Teens**
*Type:* VHS videocassette
*Length:* 18 minutes
*Date:* 1998
*Cost:* $99.95
*Source:* Visual Mentor
40 Trace Lane
Half Moon Bay, CA 94019
(650) 726-9152
Fax: 650/726-2756
http://www.info@visual-mentor.com/

*Tobacco: Behind the Smoke and Mirrors* is a two-part set of tobacco-use prevention videos. It addresses the same social needs of adolescents that are addressed by tobacco advertising—the need to fit in, to exert independence from parental control, to develop physically, and to be sexually attractive. Reversing the thrust of tobacco advertising, the videos show not how smoking makes a teen belong, but how it causes social scorn and ostracism. Rather than liberating adolescents from adult control, smoking makes them dependent customers of tobacco companies. Instead of enhancing their physical and sexual identity, smoking affects teenagers' sexual prowess and physical appearance immediately, not just as they age.

In Part 2, five teens make a video highlighting the realities of being a smoker, trying to combat the influence tobacco companies have on their peers. Interviewing both smokers and nonsmokers, the teens explore why smokers wish they had never started; what it is like living with nicotine addiction; how smoking makes a person less attractive; and why secondhand smoke is deeply resented. Finally, they document the reactions of young people to being the targets of big tobacco.

**Tobacco Horror Picture Show**
*Type:* VHS videocassette
*Length:* 25 minutes

*Date:* 1997
*Source:* California Instructional Technology Clearinghouse
http://clearinghouse.k12.ca.us/

This video examines the effects tobacco use and secondhand smoke have on the body. Cancer victims and emphysema sufferers join health care professionals in urging young people not to smoke.

### Tobacco: The Complete Story
*Type:* VHS videocassette
*Date:* 1981

This video is "complete" in that it presents a fairly objective view of the facts about smoking and the social and economic impact of tobacco. It touches briefly on production, pricing, legislation, and health issues. Published in 1981, the video may provide an interesting basis for discussion if members of the viewing group are aware of the developments in tobacco litigation in the late 1990s.

### Tobacco on Trial (Court TV: Landmark Cases)
*Type:* VHS videocassette
*Length:* 60 minutes
*Date:* 1997
*Cost:* $9.98
*Source:* BigStar Entertainment, Inc.
http://www.bigstar.com/

A report on the successful court case brought by lung cancer victim Grady Carter against the Brown & Williamson tobacco company.

### Tobacco: Smoking and Chewing
*Type:* 1/2 inch diskette
*Date:* 1995
*Source:* SAE Software, Inc.
670 S. Fourth Street
Edwardsville, KS 66113

A computer-assisted instruction program. The tobacco disk is included in a package of 15 disks dealing with different aspects of substance abuse. Among the other titles: "Introduction to Psychoactive Drugs," "Marijuana: Keep off the Grass," "Growing Up in a Drinking World," and "Cocaine and Crack."

**Tobacco: The Pushers and Their Victims**
*Type:* VHS videocassette
*Length:* 37 minutes
*Date:* 1990
*Source:* Doctors Ought to Care
University of Massachusetts
47 Ashby State Road
Fitchburg, MA 01420

This video examines the social causes of smoking, the strategies used by tobacco companies in marketing tobacco products to teenagers, and the reasons teenagers succumb to their appeal. In interviews, teens explain why they started smoking, how smoking has affected them, and the difficulties they have in trying to quit.

**Tobacco: The Winnable War**
*Type:* VHS videocassette
*Length:* 28 minutes
*Date:* 1988
*Cost:* $10.00
*Source:* Public Communications Department Resource Room
50 E. North Temple Street, 25th Fl.
Salt Lake City, UT 84150
(800) 453-3860, ext. 3229

Some of the statistics and information in this video regarding tobacco industry advertising are somewhat outdated, but its history of tobacco and information about the development of the tobacco industry is useful and informative.

**Up in Smoke: The Extreme Danger of Smoking Tobacco**
*Type:* VHS videocassette
*Length:* 28 minutes
*Date:* 1996
*Source:* Human Relations Media
175 Tompkins Avenue
Pleasantville, NY 10570

A group of students in a smoking cessation class in a California high school learn about the consequences of tobacco use. Students watch a surgeon remove a tumor from a patient's face, and they see another patient die as a result of spreading cancer. A patient whose voice box has been removed tells of the difficulties he faces.

**War against Tobacco**
*Type:* VHS videocassette
*Length:* 45 minutes
*Date:* 1997
*Cost:* $19.95
*Source:* Library Video Company
P.O. Box 580
Wynnewood, PA 19096
(800) 843-3620
Fax: (610) 645-4040
http://www.libraryvideo.com/

"Tobacco has been an important American crop since the days of the early colonists. Learn about the struggle to convince people of the dangers of tobacco use, understand why tobacco is such an addictive product, and see how regulation of a powerful industry is being achieved."

A&E (Arts and Entertainment Network) surveys 400 years of tobacco history to put the current debate into perspective. The video shows how the industry's arrogance (e.g., tobacco company executives testifying as recently as the mid-1990s that they think tobacco is not addictive) helps justify the current assault on smoking. This A&E investigation raises questions about business ethics and the tension between the government's role in protecting public health and people's right to enjoy something that has adverse effects. Part of the *20th Century with Mike Wallace* series.

**We Pray with Tobacco**
*Type:* VHS videocassette
*Length:* 60 minutes
*Date:* 1998
*Cost:* $30.00
*Source:* Coyote Press
http://www.dedot.com/coyote/video.html

Told entirely from a Native American perspective, this documentary focuses on the cultural and ritual uses of tobacco among Native Americans. Coyote Press summarizes the video: "For thousands of years the original peoples of this land have cherished tobacco as the most sacred of all gifts given by the Creator. It is holy, is sanctifies life and keeps everything in balance. Here we are at the end of the 20th century and Native American and mainstream populations are suffering, in various degrees, from nicotine addiction. What happened? It's all about the nature of one's relationship to the world and to life itself. There is very little that is, in and of itself, harmful, it is only how we choose to interact and relate with it that makes it so. It is precisely the critical importance of being in the 'right relationship' with all of life and how that relationship is expressed in the social, cultural, and ceremonial life of Native Americans, that this documentary explores." Among the participants are actor-singer Floyd "Red Crow" Westerman and singer-songwriter Elizabeth Hill.

## Internet Resources

Searching the Internet for "tobacco" (or "smoking" or "cigarettes") will produce a list of results that could take weeks to scroll through. Some sites are, without doubt, authoritative and reliable, some are not, and some might be. Using the Internet as a main research source is extremely time-consuming, because it requires comparing sites and the information they provide.

The list that follows contains names and addresses of some major tobacco-related web sites that not only offer reliable information but also provide links to other reliable sites. Some of them have e-mail portals through which visitors may ask questions or submit requests for informational materials.

*Note:* Typographical errors, misspellings, omission of lines, and other mistakes are not uncommon on some sites. Even material that has been scanned may have such mistakes, so it is important to be cautious when using information found on the Internet.

### ABC News

http://more.abcnews.com/sections/us/DailyNews/tobacco_index.html#top/

Numerous tobacco stories are accessible here. The special "Tobacco Under Fire" (July 31, 1998) contains a major article about the state suits against the tobacco industry, a series of pieces about the industry's contributions to members of Congress (including an interactive chart that matches congressional votes with money taken from the tobacco industry), and a collection of articles of related interest. There are also links to many major tobacco sites.

### Action on Smoking and Health (ASH)

http://ash.org/

This is a first-rate site, one of the best. It contains news articles, fact sheets, reports, excerpts from "secret" tobacco documents, and links to other antismoking groups, as well as links to Congress and state and federal agencies. Highly recommended.

### Advertising Law Resource Center

http://www.lawpublish.com/

Maintained by JLCom Publishing Co., LLC, the site contains two areas pertaining to tobacco, "Children and Tobacco Ads" and "Tobacco Advertising," as well as links to a number of useful sources.

### Agency for Health Care Policy and Research (AHCPR)

http://www.ahcpr.gov/

This is a wide-ranging but searchable site containing articles written for health professionals but with some interesting material relating to tobacco (especially to quitting smoking), such as "First Time Quitters: Winning Tips from Over One Million Quitters" and "You Can Quit Smoking."

### Agricultural Research Service (USDA)

http://www.ars.usda.gov/

This is the main in-house research arm of the Department of Agriculture. The entire site is searchable, but the search terms must be highly specific.

*See also* Economic Research Service (USDA).

### American Cancer Society (ACS)

http://www.cancer.org/

The ACS site is a first-rate source for information regarding the health risks involved in using tobacco, information on quitting, and statistics, among other material. Highly recommended.

### American Council on Science and Health (ACSH)

http://www.acsh.org/about/index.html

A valuable source, with clickable headlines and titles under four headings: "Press Releases," "Publications," "Editorials," and "*Priorities* Articles."

### American Legacy Foundation

http://www.americanlegacy.org/index2.html

The foundation's site provides tobacco-related news and information about research, education, and programs.

### American Lung Association (ALA)

http://www.lungusa.org/

Two areas of the site are pertinent to tobacco, "Data and Statistics" and "Tobacco Control," both of which are accessible through the menu on the left side of the home page. "Tobacco Control" contains six subsections: "Quitting Smoking," "Smoking and Women," "Tobacco Control," "Smoking and Teens," "Targeted Populations," and "General Smoking Information." Another valuable feature allows the user to search for contact information for all local branches of the ALA. Highly recommended.

*See also* http://www.smokescreen.org/alac/Index.html, ALA of Colorado's "Shoplifting Project: How Big Tobacco Encourages Shoplifting by Kids."

### American Smokers Alliance (ASA)

http://www.smokers.org/

ASA defends the rights of smokers and organizes opposition to actions that infringe on those rights.

### Americans for Nonsmokers' Rights (ANR) / Americans for Nonsmokers' Rights Foundation (ANRF)

http://www.no-smoke.org/

With its focus on the rights of nonsmokers, ANR/ANRF's site emphasizes areas in which those rights conflict with the rights of smokers, notably environmental tobacco smoke. It is also concerned with legislation to prohibit smoking in areas where non-smokers might find themselves, such as airports and restaurants. Free fact sheets, position papers, and other information are available at its linked pages: "Secondhand Smoke," "Smokefree Advocacy," and "Youth."

### Arizona Tobacco Education and Prevention Program (AzTEPP or TEPP)

http://www.nicnet.org/

One of the top sites, this site is also known as "Nicotine on the Net" or "NicNet." It is an appealing, user-friendly, well-designed site, with page-one links to various collections of useful articles. The links to collections are listed under the headings "Prevention," "Cessation," "Policy," "Kids," "ETS," "Cigar Smoke," "Pipe Smoke," "Chew," and "Tobacco News." NicNet also offers links to two closely related sites, those of the Arizona Program for Nicotine and Tobacco Research (APNTR), at the University of Arizona, and the Society for Research on Nicotine and Tobacco (SRNT).

### The Ashtray: Smoking and Tobacco Abuse (Boston University Medical Center)

http://www.bu.edu/cohis/smoking/smoke.htm

The Ashtray is part of a large site developed by the BU Medical Center's Community Outreach Health Information System (COHIS). It contains a wide range of reliable health information presented clearly and simply.

### Association of State and Territorial Health Officials (ASTHO)

http://www.astho.org/

This site has a "Subject Menu" on the opening page, a very good list of links under "Public Health Resources," and—especially useful—links to every state (and territorial) health department. These departments, of course, can provide information about tobacco use within their specific areas.

### BioSites

http://www.library.ucsf.edu/biosites/

Maintained by the Digital Library of the University of California at San Francisco, BioSites is "a virtual catalog of selected internet resources in the biomedical sciences."

### Blair's Quitting Smoking Resource Pages

http://www.quitsmokingsupport.com/

Useful information for persons who want to quit smoking and more than 50 links.

### Breed's Tobacco Web Sites Update

http://www.tobacco.org/Resources/9806breedupdate.html

A large collection of annotated links to a wide variety of sites, pro and con, with no issue overlooked. The web site organizer is Dr. Larry Breed of the Community Health Education Institute, whose other sites—Tobacco Activism Guide, Parts 1 and 2; Tobacco Activism Guide, Part 3; and Collection of Tobacco History Sites— are also accessible from www.tobacco.org. The "Tobacco Documents" section (http://www.tobacco.org/Documents/documents.html#aa) is especially good. Highly recommended.

### Brown and Williamson Document Web Site

www.cdc.gov/tobacco/industrydocs/docsites.html

More than 1 million documents produced by B & W and the former American Tobacco Company in various lawsuits and proceedings are accessible here.

### Bureau of Alcohol, Tobacco and Firearms (ATF)

http://www.atf.treas.gov/

The best way to find tobacco information on the ATF site is to click on the site map (on the home page) and then click on "Tobacco," which contains four subsections: "Information," "Permits," "Statistics," and "Federal Regulations."

### Campaign for Tobacco-Free Kids

http://www.tobaccofreekids.org/

This is a newsy site with numerous information options—"Factsheets"; "Press Releases" in a searchable archive; "Today's News"; background; quotes from industry documents; tobacco advertising; and "Global Efforts." It also has links to the sites of similar organizations, including Effective National Action to Control Tobacco (ENACT), of which the Campaign for Tobacco-Free Kids is a member. Highly recommended.

### Canadian Cancer Society—British Columbia and Yukon Division

http://www.bc.cancer.ca/ccs/

Clicking on "Information" will take the user to "Info/Prevention," which includes "Education and Awareness," "Research," "Cancer Information Service," and "Cancer Information Database."

### Center for Responsive Politics

http://www.opensecrets.org/

Described as "the online source for money in politics data," this site has information about contributions for every election campaign at the federal level, including congressional campaigns. The information can be accessed in various ways, making it possible, for example, to determine how much money specific members of Congress received from the tobacco industry.

### Centers for Disease Control and Prevention (CDC)

http://www.cdc.gov/

This is a primary source. Home page features include "Data and Statistics," "Health Topics A-Z," "In the News," "Publications, Software, Products," and the *Morbidity and Mortality Weekly Report* (*MMWR*). The Tobacco Information and Prevention Source (TIPS) can be accessed through this site also. Highly recommended.

http://www.cdc.gov/tobacco/industrydocs/index.htm

This CDC page provides a good launch pad for examining industry documents. It consists of (1) an introductory "About Tobacco Industry Documents"; (2) a glossary of terms used in the database; (3) "Industry Document Web Sites," which lists, describes briefly, and links to the various sites; (4) a link to the 4B Index, the citation index to documents stored at the Minnesota Depository; (5) a link to searching the Minnesota Select Set, documents used in the Minnesota tobacco trial; and (6) a search link for the Guildford-British American Tobacco documents, which are stored in Minnesota as part of the Minnesota Select Set.

### CNN Interactive

http://www.cnn.com/

The search option is in the top right corner. A general search ("tobacco") will produce more than a thousand hits, so it is necessary to be specific.

The URL http://www.cnn.com/US/9705/tobacco/ will open "Focus: Tobacco under Fire."

### Common Cause

http://www.commoncause.org/publications/tobaccotoc.htm

Material available here has to do mainly with political contributions and campaign finance reform.

### Community Outreach Health Information System (COHIS) (Boston University Medical Center)

Boston University Medical Center
Boston University
Community Outreach Health Information System
E-mail: cohis@bu.edu
http://web.bu.edu/COHIS

COHIS was formed in 1994. It offered the first comprehensive medical information site on the Internet. Among its goals are the following:

1. To provide health promotion and disease prevention information through the Internet—to make learning interactive.
2. To set up access to this system for community centers, health clinics, schools, hospitals, and all other public Internet access providers.

"Our primary focus," COHIS says, "is on children in their preteen or teenage years." By using current technology, COHIS intends to stimulate interest in disease prevention education among children in this age group.

### Congressional Record

http://www.access.gpo.gov/su_docs/aces/aces150.html

The database of the daily record of the U.S. House and Senate may be searched by keyword, with or without limitations of day, month, and year.

### Court TV Online

http://www.courttv.com/

Find information about current or recent cases by clicking "Trials" or "Verdicts" on the left side of the home page or use the search option at the bottom of the page.

### drkoop.com (Tackling Tobacco)

http://www.drkoop.com/

Open the site and search for "tobacco." This opens the "Tackling Tobacco" section, five pages of headings and summaries of articles on nicotine addiction, health risks, quitting, and smokeless tobacco. This is one of the all-around best sites. Highly recommended.

### Economic Research Service (USDA)

http://www.ers.usda.gov/

The opening page has two search options: (1) "Briefing Rooms," one of which provides information about tobacco, and (2) "Search This Site," through which the user may seek information on specific subjects, such as "tobacco imports," "tobacco consumption," and "tobacco farming trends." The Tobacco Briefing Room, which allows the user to scroll through its contents and see what kind of information is available, is probably the better place to begin.

*See also* Agricultural Research Service (USDA).

**Essential Action**

http://www.essentialaction.org/

Tobacco is only one of Essential Action's many concerns. Someone looking for information about secondhand smoke or spit tobacco, for example, might think that a site concerned only with tobacco would be more useful than Essential Action but that would be a mistake. There is much of value here. Besides a "Taking on Tobacco" page, there is a list of organizations using the site's "Essential Information" web server. The sites of all of these organizations, some fairly obscure, can be searched for tobacco-related information—with a likelihood of turning up something not available at the more heavily traveled places, which all interconnect.

**Facts on File World News CD-ROM—Issues and Controversies: Tobacco and Health**

http://www.facts.com/cd/i00003.htm

The Facts on File tobacco site contains a concise overview of developments from January 1980 through September 1998, as well as reports such as "Health Risks of Tobacco," "Who Smokes?" and "The Costs of Tobacco Use."

**Federal Trade Commission (FTC)**

http://www.ftc.gov/

There is a tobacco section at this site, accessible through the site map, but there are also sections such as "Formal Actions, Opinions and Activities" and "News Releases, Publications and Speeches," so a search is probably the most efficient way of finding specific information.

**FedStats**

http://www.fedstats.gov/

Linked to more than 70 federal agencies, this site provides quick access to statistics "of interest to the public." By means of a site map, users may access information by agency, by topic, or by keyword.

### Food and Drug Administration (FDA)

http://www.fda.gov/opacom/campaigns/tobacco.html

The FDA home page opens at www.fda.gov/, but the above URL opens the "Children and Tobacco" section. Among the options available are recent news releases, information for both consumers and retailers, and tobacco regulations.

### FORCES (Fight Ordinances and Restrictions to Control and Eliminate Smoking)

http://www.forces.org/

FORCES' smoking-rights site, described as "the largest tobacco resource Internet site that is funded entirely by private individuals, . . . presents an alternative to the information distributed by the government-funded anti-tobacco interests and the tobacco industry." It provides documents, articles, and links to sites maintained by FORCES chapters around the world.

### Foundation for a Smokefree America

http://www.notobacco.org/foundatn.html

A youth-oriented site, this is the home page of Patrick Reynolds, a grandson of the founder of the R. J. Reynolds Tobacco Company. Near the bottom of the page are links to "Message to Youth," "Cool Links," "Photo Gallery," "Quitting Tips for Youth," and "A Five-Minute Plan for You to Initiate a Live Talk in Your City." A click on "Advanced Stuff" takes the user to "tobaccofree.org," which features comments by Reynolds and information on current topics relating to tobacco.

### Frontline: The Cigarette Papers

http://www2.pbs.org/wgbh/pages/frontline/smoke/

"The Trail of the Secret Brown and Williamson Documents . . . those too-hot-to-handle internal papers. Who got them and what they did with them." This PBS site provides readings ("a full-text selection of background material and analyses on the ABC and CBS run-ins with tobacco companies") and interviews ("with journalists, First Amendment lawyers, media analysts, and others, talking newsroom policies, practices, and ethics"), as well as tapes, transcripts, and links.

### Frontline: Inside the Tobacco Deal

http://www.pbs.org/wgbh/pages/frontline/shows/settlement/

This is "the inside story of how two small-town Mississippi lawyers declared war on Big Tobacco and skillfully pursued a daring new litigation strategy that ultimately brought the industry to the negotiating table." Included are tapes, transcripts, timelines, interviews, and links.

### GASP (Group to Alleviate Smoking Pollution) of Colorado

http://www.gaspforair.org/top.html

GASP focuses on secondhand smoke. The Colorado site includes news articles and an educational section.

### Government Information Resources

http://voxlibris.claremont.edu/govdocs/federal/federal.html

This is a springboard providing quick access to government sites at federal, state, and local levels.

### GPO (Government Printing Office) Access

https://orders.access.gpo.gov/su_docs/index.html

Clicking "Site Search" retrieves web pages that relate to the search topic but does not retrieve material from within the various federal databases. A list of accessible databases appears under "What's Available." Clicking "Legislative," for example, will bring up a menu of congressional publications, including bills, transcripts of hearings, and congressional reports.

### healthfinder (U.S. Department of Health and Human Services)

http://www.healthfinder.gov/

Thorough list of links to state and federal health resources. Highly recommended.

### Health Statistics Sources: Internet Resources (National Library of Medicine)

http://www.nlm.nih.gov/nichsr/stats/internet.html

About 30 sites are listed here, with knowledgeable descriptions to

guide the user. One strength is the range and variety of the sites—
e.g., Consumer Product Safety Commission, Breast Cancer
Information Clearinghouse, Center for Assessment and Demographic Studies, and Health Care Financing Administration.

### Hoover's Online

http://www.hoovers.com/

The Hoover's search engine retrieves basic information about
tobacco companies. Nonsubscribers may access "company cap-
sules," stock market quotations, sales figures, and lists of company
executives, as well as press releases and news articles—under
headings such as "Business News," "News and Wire Services,"
and "General News." Also available here is a glossary of tobacco
terms, accessible through Hoover's "Library."

### Indiana Prevention Resource Center

http://www.drugs.indiana.edu/

This site, a primary source for any tobacco researcher, contains a
wide range of information, including a statistics section, both
Indiana and national news, discussion of current issues, legal and
legislative updates, and a long list of resources and links. Highly
recommended.

### INFACT

http://www.infact.org/

INFACT's site features fact sheets on the tobacco industry,
research findings on campaign donations by tobacco companies,
and information regarding the companies' efforts to attract young
smokers.

### International Personnel Management Association (IPMA)

http://www.ipma-hr.org/public/pubs_index.cfm

A list titled "Contacts for Further Information on Smoking
Issues" includes some sources not mentioned elsewhere: three in
the insurance industry and several relating specifically to the
workplace.

## Journal of the American Medical Association (JAMA)

http://jama.ama-assn.org/

The opening page of this web site contains the table of contents of the current issue of *JAMA*. Clicking on a title will open the article. After it opens, clicking on "Results" will scroll to the findings of the study and clicking on "Comment" will scroll to a paragraph in which its significance is explained. The site also allows a search of the archives of *JAMA* and 10 other specialized journals. (The "Search" button is on a thin bar across the top of the page.)

## Joe Camel Campaign Collection

*See* University of California at San Francisco Archives (Tobacco Control Archives), which links the user to more than 4,000 industry documents related to the Joe Camel campaign.

## kickbutt.org (Washington Doctors Ought to Care [DOC])

http://www.kickbutt.org/

A service of the Seattle, Washington, chapter of DOC (Doctors Ought to Care), the site features daily headline stories, archived news stories, action alerts, links, and a section on youth advocacy and activism. The most developed part of the site—and the most useful, from a researcher's point of view—is the links page, with links categorized under 20 subheadings. Highly recommended.

## LibertySearch

http://www.libertysearch.com/

This is a libertarian site with commentary on a wide range of topics, including the antismoking "crusade," tobacco regulation, and advertising.

## lorillarddocs.com

http://www.lorillarddocs.com/

Another industry site containing documents released to the public in accordance with the settlement provisions of suits against the major tobacco companies.

**Mangini v. R. J. Reynolds Tobacco Company Collection**

*See* University of California at San Francisco Archives (Tobacco Control Archives), which links the user to more than 4,000 industry documents related to the Joe Camel campaign.

**Massachusetts Tobacco Education Clearinghouse**

http://www.jsi.com/health/mtec/home.htm

Massachusetts Tobacco Education Clearinghouse (MTEC) offers a variety of services to support tobacco education efforts, including distribution of educational materials and tobacco videos.

**MedicineNet.com**

http://www.medicinenet.com/

Clicking the "dictionary" tab opens a user-friendly, easy-to-read medical dictionary.

**MedWeb**

http://www.medweb.emory.edu/MedWeb/

MedWeb, maintained by the Emory University Health Sciences Center Library, is a catalog of health-related web sites.

**Minnesota Tobacco Trial Quotes**

http://www.ama-assn.org/special/aos/tobacco/minnesot.htm

This is an AMA page containing a collection of excerpts from material made public in Minnesota's suit against the tobacco industry. The quotations were provided by the Minnesota Attorney General's Office.

**National Center for Health Statistics (NCHS)**

http://www.cdc.gov/nchs/releases/releases.htm

The URL above opens the "News Releases and Fact Sheets" page, which also has search options for NCHS and for "Health Topics A-Z."

### National Clearinghouse for Alcohol and Drug Information (NCADI)

http://www.health.org/

The home page connects to health information and a health resource directory. There is also a search option and a page of links to other databases, including the National Substance Abuse Web Index.

### National Clearinghouse on Tobacco and Health (NCTH)

http://www.cctc.ca/NCTHweb.nsf/

A Canadian site, the home page links to "Public Info," "Databases," "Publications," "Statistics," "Key Sites," "What's New," and "Ontario: Tobacco Free Times." Among the options on the database page are Canada's most comprehensive bibliographic database on tobacco and health literature, as well as a directory of organizations and public agencies. Especially useful is "Key Sites," which has links to a wide variety of sites worldwide, including nearly 100 in the United States.

### National Drug Strategy Network (NDSN)

http://www.ndsn.org/

Access to information from a variety of federal agencies is the main attraction here. "FedStats," for example, offers statistics on the national, state, and county level, in such topic areas as crime, education, health, and income. A link to the Center for Substance Abuse Prevention reports on antismoking programs in cities around the country.

### National Institute of Child Health and Human Development (NICHD)

http://www.nichd.nih.gov/

Among the clickable features are statistics and prevention, a publications clearinghouse, and recent news releases.

### National Institutes of Health (NIH)

http://www.nih.gov/

The "Health Information" option links to a variety of information sources, including health hotlines. The site also features a web search engine. (Note: A search for "teen smoking," on October 18, 1999, resulted in 115,427 hits, so search terms should be highly specific.)

### National Library of Medicine (NLM)

http://nlm.nih.gov

Among the features of the NLM site are the following: MED-LINE—references and abstracts from 4,300 biomedical journals; MEDLINE*plus*—answers to health questions; DIRLINE—directory of health organizations; and LOCATOR*plus*—a catalog of books, journals, and audiovisuals in the NLM collections. The web address for NLM's online catalog is http://www.nlm.nih.gov/locatorplus/.

*See also* National Network of Libraries of Medicine.

### National Network of Libraries of Medicine (NN/LM)

http://www.nnlm.gov/

Like the NLM site, this one offers a variety of databases and search engines.

### National Smokers Alliance

http://www.speakup.org/

A site "dedicated to fostering a society in which adult Americans will continue to have the freedom to make personal choices and business owners will continue to have the freedom to serve the needs of their customers," it provides a wide array of essays, articles, and transcripts presenting "the other side" of the tobacco controversy.

### National Women's Health Information Center (NWHIC)

http://www.4woman.gov/

The Office of Women's Health manages this site, which specializes in health information for women. Users can call up information by topic or keyword. More than a dozen specialized medical dictionaries and glossaries are also accessible, as well as news related to women's health.

**New York Times**

http://www.nytimes.com/

A major source for news, the *Times* site has a searchable archive of articles published within the past year. Articles may be downloaded and printed for a fee of $2.50.

*See also Washington Post.*

**NicNet**

*See* Arizona Tobacco Education and Prevention Program.

**NoTobacco.org**

*See* Foundation for a Smokefree America.

**opensecrets.org**

*See* Center for Responsive Politics.

**Office of Smoking and Health (OSH)**

http://www.cdc.gov/nccdphp/osh

The Office of Smoking and Health is a division of the Centers for Disease Control and Prevention, National Center for Chronic Disease Prevention and Health Promotion. It recommends two pages on the CDC site: (1) Overview, CDC's Tobacco Information and Prevention Sourcepage (TIPS), and (2) http://www.cdc.gov/nccdphp/osh/issue.htm. Several significant TIPS pages available through the OSH site are the following:

- **Tobacco Information and Prevention Sourcepage: Tobacco Use in the United States—CDC,**
  http://www.cdc.gov/nccdphp/osh/tobus_us.htm

- **Tobacco Information and Prevention Sourcepage: In the 30 Years Since the Release of the First Surgeon General's Report, CDC,**
  http://www.cdc.gov/nccdphp/osh/30yrs2t.htm

- Tobacco Information and Prevention Sourcepage: Significant Developments Related to Smoking and Health, 1964–1996—CDC, http://www.cdc.gov/nccdphp/osh/chron96.htm

- Surgeon General's Report for Kids about Smoking: 6 Facts about Kids and Smoking, http://www.cdc.gov/tobacco/sgr/sgr4kids/6facts.htm

- Tobacco Information and Prevention Sourcepage (TIPS): News Page—CDC, http://www.cdc.gov/nccdphp/osh/news.htm

- Tobacco Information and Prevention Sourcepage: History of the 1964 Surgeon General's Report, http://www.cdc.gov/nccdphp/osh/30yrsgen.htm

- Tobacco Information and Prevention Sourcepage: Surgeon General's Reports—CDC, http://www.cdc.gov/nccdphp/osh/sgrpage.htm

- Tobacco Information and Prevention Sourcepage: Smoking Quit Tips—CDC, http://www.cdc.gov/nccdphp/osh/quittip.htm

- Tobacco Information and Prevention Sourcepage: Educational Materials—CDC, http://www.cdc.gov/nccdphp/osh/edumat.htm

- Tobacco Information and Prevention Sourcepage: Publications Page—CDC, http://www.cdc.gov/nccdphp/osh/pubs.htm

- Surgeon General's Report for Kids about Smoking: The Real Deal about Tobacco, http://www.cdc.gov/tobacco/sgr/sgr4kids/realdeal.htm

- Tobacco Information and Prevention Sourcepage: Tobacco Use in the United States—CDC, http://www.cdc.gov/nccdphp/osh/tobus_us.htm

- **Surgeon General's Report for Kids about Smoking: Up in Smoke!**
  http://www.cdc.gov/tobacco/sgr/sgr4kids/upsmoke.htm

- **Surgeon General's Report for Kids about Smoking: Is Smokeless Tobacco Safer Than Cigarettes?**
  http://www.cdc.gov/tobacco/sgr/sgr4kids/smokless.htm

- **Surgeon General's Report for Kids about Smoking: Be an Ad Buster,**
  http://www.cdc.gov/tobacco/sgr/sgr4kids/adbust.htm

- **Surgeon General's Report for Kids about Smoking: Smoke-Free from Coast to Coast,**
  http://www.cdc.gov/tobacco/sgr/sgr4kids/coast.htm

- **Surgeon General's Report for Kids about Smoking: 10 Things You Can Do to Make Your World Smoke-Free,**
  http://www.cdc.gov/tobacco/sgr/sgr4kids/backpage.htm

### Philadelphia Inquirer

http://www.philly.com/packages/smoking/

The "packages/smoking" address opens the *Inquirer's* "Big Tobacco" section, a collection of articles about various aspects of the settlement worked out with Congress in 1997.

### Philip Morris Companies, Inc.

http://www.philipmorris.com/

News releases and policy statements are available here, as well as a fairly extensive discussion of tobacco issues. A section called "Our Tobacco Business" (most easily accessible through the site map) contains the following subsections: "Youth Smoking Prevention," "Cigarette Marketing Practices," "Health Issues for Smokers," "Quitting Smoking," "Ingredients in Cigarettes," "Understanding Tar and Nicotine," "Numbers," and "Second-hand Smoke." The site also provides links to other sites substantiating company statements or offering additional details.

### Physicians for a Smoke-Free Canada (PSC)

http://www.smoke-free.ca/

This is a site with special emphasis on advertising directed at children.

### Policy.com (Policy and News Information Service)

http://www.policy.com/

Links to reports, studies, and articles on various tobacco issues. The "Issues Library" is searchable.

### PREVLINE (NCADI)

*See* National Clearinghouse for Alcohol and Drug Information.

### Public Citizen

http://www.citizen.org/Tobacco/

Another outstanding site. Use the directory to go to "Tobacco Deal," which contains a wide variety of fact sheets, editorials, news releases, and documents, as well as links to other tobacco sites.

### Public Interest Research Group (PIRG)

http://www.pirg.org/

As the name suggests, the site has a public-interest orientation. The home page contains clickable news headlines, action alerts, and reports, as well as a search option.

### Quit 4 Life (Canada)

http://www.quit4life.com/html/splash.html

A youth-oriented site, Quit 4 Life opens with photos of four teenagers. "Choose any character," the user is told, "and follow their story from beginning to end. Stop at each of the five interactive steps along the way for help in kicking the habit and staying smoke-free. Your life could change forever, too."

### QuitNet (Massachusetts Tobacco Control Program)

http://www.quitnet.org/

An excellent site for would-be quitters, QuitNet provides expert advice, news, a library of resources, links to other helpful sites, and supportive chat rooms.

### R. J. Reynolds Tobacco Holdings, Inc.

http://www.rjrt.com/

From the home page one may access "Tobacco Issues," which contains information about RJR settlements and litigation, youth smoking, taxes and legislation, and smokers' rights.

### S.A.F.E. (SmokeFree Air for Everyone)

http://www.pacificnet.net/~safe/

S.A.F.E. is a network of persons injured or disabled by second-hand smoke. The site includes their newsletter, news stories, and links.

### Saskatchewan Lung Association (Canada)

http://www.sk.lung.ca/education/student/student.html

This is a youth-oriented site with basic information about the lungs ("Why We Need Them," "How They Work," etc.), tobacco ("Why Cigarettes Are Bad for Your Health," "Other Forms of Tobacco (Besides Cigarettes)," and "Why People Use Tobacco"), and other related topics.

### Smoking Control Advocacy Resource Center Network (SCARCNet)

This once-valuable activist site was discontinued as of September 30, 1999. Many of its resources can now be found at the Tobacco Control Project. *See* Tobacco Control Project.

### SmokeScreen Action Network (Michael Tacelosky)

http://www.smokescreen.org/

An "EZ-Action" search option on the home page makes it possible to call up news at the state level. Among other resources are searchable databases of tobacco-control organizations, activists, legislators, and attorneys general. (SmokeScreen's news summaries and news archives are now at Tobacco BBS.) Highly recommended.

### Society for Research on Nicotine and Tobacco (SRNT)

http://www.srnt.org/

Most of the material here is more scholarly than material found on other tobacco-related web sites. However, searching the SRNT newsletters (dating from fall 1994) might produce helpful results. For example, a search for "cigars" turns up "The Cigar Resurgence," which contains information about the increase in cigar smoking (100 million sold in 1992, more than 2 billion sold in 1995) and discusses, in plain language, the health risks.

### State Tobacco Information Center (STIC), Northeastern University

http://stic.neu.edu/

Searchable archives of documents related to tobacco litigation. STIC was created as a service to state attorneys general and the public to help them follow the progress of state litigation against the tobacco industry. With the litigation settled, STIC now serves as an archive of documents made public as a result of various lawsuits. A list of STIC libraries is available at http://www.stic.neu.edu/Libraries.html. The data on the STIC site are administered by the Library and Center for Knowledge Management at UCSF.

### Stop Teenage Addiction to Tobacco (STAT), Northeastern University

http://www.stat.org/

STAT's site contains fact sheets to be printed and distributed, "DOs and DON'Ts for Parents," and a description of training and educational materials designed to discourage children from using tobacco products.

### Substance Abuse and Mental Health Services Administration (SAMHSA)

http://www.samhsa.gov/

Besides a search option, the most important features of this site are statistics, news releases, and links to SAMHSA clearinghouses, including the National Clearinghouse on Alcohol and Drug Information.

### Surgeon General

http://www.surgeongeneral.gov/

Speeches and reports are accessible from the home page.

### Surgeon General's Report for Kids about Smoking

http://www.cdc.gov/tobacco/sgr/sgr4kids/sgrmenu.htm

Clearly organized and easily navigated, this is an online "smoke-free magazine" containing authoritative information about smoking and smokeless tobacco. The material is presented on a level intended for adolescents.

### Tips for Teens about Smoking

http://www.mninter.net/~publish/Ttsmoke.htm

Basic facts about smoking, presented clearly and concisely.

### TobaccoArchives.com

http://www.tobaccoarchives.com/

A launch site for accessing industry documents, Tobacco Archives.com has a search engine and links to the Minnesota Document Depository and the web sites of various tobacco companies.

### A Tobacco Anthology on the Web

http://shift.merriweb.com.au/books/tobacco/index.html

This is an offbeat site, but it contains a large collection of early verse relating to smoking, tobacco, nicotine, snuff, and pipes.

### Tobacco BBS (Gene Borio)

http://www.tobacco.org/

One of the best sites, covering industry news and litigation as well as tobacco issues in general. Among its features are "Tobacco Daily" ("used to fill in on stories the press may have missed"); an activism guide; advice for responsible investing; help for smokers who are trying to quit; alerts for tobacco-control activists; a section on the history of tobacco; documents; health news; and links to related sites.

Going to Adding News/news_archives.html will open "The News Archives," from which news stories elsewhere on the Web may be accessed by month and year of publication. This feature is especially useful in research relating to specific trials or events. Students may also join in chat groups with activists and health professionals. Highly recommended.

**Tobacco Briefing Room**

*See* Economic Research Service (USDA).

**Tobacco Control Archives (TCA)**

http://galen.library.ucsf.edu/tobacco/

Sponsored by the University of California at San Francisco, these archives of tobacco documents include the Brown & Williamson Collection, documents relating to the Joe Camel Campaign, and various Philip Morris documents.

**Tobacco Control Issues by Subject (University of Sydney, Australia)**

http://www.health.usyd.edu.au/tobacco/subject.html

Some of the topics discussed in this site—such as endangered ecological systems in the Third World and the tobacco industry's role in tropical deforestation—do not get much coverage in the United States.

**Tobacco Control Project (Advocacy Institute)**

http://www.advocacy.org/tobacco.htm

The main purpose of this site is to provide antitobacco activists with the resources needed to work for tobacco control on all levels, e.g., local, federal, and international. The site contains basic information, news of developments in the fight against tobacco, and links to other important sites.

**Tobacco Control Resource Center (TCRC)/Tobacco Products Liability Project (Northeastern University Law School)**

http://www.tobacco.neu.edu/index.html

Good source of information about tobacco lawsuits and tobacco control. The site features "Tobacco Control Update," a quarterly newsmagazine containing news (from Massachusetts and elsewhere) about tobacco control, legal policy, and legislative affairs. This site also has a good selection of links to other resources on the Internet. Especially useful is "Recent Major Tobacco Trials," which provides an up-to-date survey of ongoing and recent litigation. The web site address is http://www.tobacco.neu.edu/Upcoming.html.

### Tobacco Control Supersite

http://www.health.usyd.edu.au/tobacco/

This is an Australian site with information about all aspects of tobacco use and numerous links to information about tobacco use in other countries, among them England, Brazil, Canada, China, France, Italy, Malaysia, Poland, and Switzerland.

### Tobacco Documents Online

http://tobaccodocuments.org/

The site contains various public and private collections of industry documents that can be browsed and searched. An e-mail address is required for access and to subscribe to a daily newsletter that highlights interesting findings in tobacco industry documents.

### TobaccoFree.org

*See* Foundation for a Smokefree America.

### Tobacco Industry Information (Jack Cannon)

http://www.gate.net/~jcannon/tobacco.html

The main features here are industry-related news and documents.

### Tobacco Industry Documents Web Site (HHS)

http://www.cdc.gov/tobacco/

The U.S. Department of Health and Human Services built this site in response to an executive memo from President Clinton. It provides access to more than 27 million pages of tobacco industry documents, including everything housed at the Minnesota Tobacco Document Depository.

### Tobacco Information and Prevention Source (TIPS), CDC

http://www.cdc.gov/nccdphp/osh/

Another primary source, this site includes news articles; surgeon general's reports; research, data and reports; help on quitting; "Tips4Teens"; educational materials; information on tobacco control; a smoking and health database; and a "State Tobacco Activities Tracking and Evaluation System"; as well as many other features. Highly recommended.

### Tobacco Institute

http://www.tobaccoinstitute.com/

There are 19 searchable fields of information in this collection of documents. The settlement provisions of lawsuits by state attorneys general and other civil actions required that these documents be released.

### Tobacco Litigation

http://www.tobacco-litigation.com/index.html-ssi

Providing information about tobacco lawsuits and trials is the main purpose of this site, which is sponsored by the Wilmington Institute, a litigation research firm. Among its useful features is a state-by-state summary of tobacco suits.

### Tobacco Prevention Project

http://wdhfs.state.wy.us/tobacco

The theme at this Wyoming site is telling the truth about tobacco. Categories include "Addiction," "Teen Smoking Data," "Teen Smokeless Data," "Smokeless Tobacco Facts," and "Product Access."

### TobaccoResolution.com

http://www.tobaccoresolution.com/

An industry site providing information about the tobacco industry. A section called "Industry Facts" contains an industry profile broken up into a number of subsections: "Consumption," "Expenditures," "World Production," "U.S. Tobacco Production," "Manufacturing," "Supply Network," "Government Receipts from Taxes," "Government Tobacco Programs," and "Tobacco's Contribution to America's National Economy." Until recently this site provided access to industry documents, but now it redirects the user to TobaccoArchive.com.

### TSOnline

http://www.tsonline.co.uk/

The United Kingdom's counterpart to the U.S. Government Printing Office, the Stationery Office maintains this site. Thousands of government documents may be purchased or viewed, among them *Smoking Kills: A White Paper on Tobacco* (1998).

### USA Today

http://www.usatoday.com/

With regard to tobacco research, the strength of the *USA Today* site lies in its large and easily accessible files of stories relating to lawsuits against the tobacco industry.

### Tobacco Settlement

http://www.usatoday.com/news/smoke/smoke00.htm

Among the features at the USA Today site is a collection of links to USA Today's articles chronicling progress toward the Master Settlement Agreement and developments in the ongoing anti-tobacco litigation. In fact, these links provide what is probably the easiest means of documenting the downfall of the tobacco industry. To be sure, similar articles may be found at other newspaper sites, but nowhere are the links arranged so conveniently

### USDA (U.S. Department of Agriculture): How to Get Information from the USDA

http://www.usda.gov/news/howto/howto.htm

The USDA's "How to" site is a good place to begin looking for anything having to do with the agricultural side of tobacco. Among the links the site provides are the Agricultural Research Service, the National Agriculture Library, the Economic Research Service, and the National Agricultural Statistics Service.

### Virtual Clearinghouse on Alcohol, Tobacco and Other Drugs

http://www.atod.org/

This site, a collaborative effort by a number of organizations to provide "high-quality information about the nature, extent and consequences of alcohol, tobacco and other drug use," features full-text documents, searchable by author or title, and numerous links, searchable by topic.

### Washington Post

http://www.washingtonpost.com/

Besides being a good source to check for daily news in general, the *Post* web site has a searchable feature called "Tobacco Special Report," now several years old, to which new articles are added as events unfold. Clickable search keys within the tobacco section are "Top Story," "Overview," "Politics and Policy," "Lawsuits," "Health Issues," "Teen Smoking," "Industry News," and "Opinion." The site also has a search key for Associated Press articles relating to tobacco, arranged according to date.

# Abbreviations and Acronyms

This list includes many abbreviations that are not used in this book but that readers are likely to encounter on the Internet and in other sources.

AAO-HNS       American Academy of Otolaryngology-Head and Neck Surgery

AAP           American Academy of Pediatrics

ACOSH         Australian Council on Smoking and Health

ACP           attorney-client privilege
(A/CPRIV)

ACS           American Cancer Society

ACSH          American Council on Science and Health

ADAMHA        Synar Amendment to the Alcohol, Drug Abuse, and Mental Health Administration Reorganization Act of 1992; Alcohol, Drug Abuse, and Mental Health Administration

ADI           acceptable daily intake

ADL           Arthur D. Little, Inc.

AHA           American Heart Association

AHCPR         Agency for Health Care Policy and Research

AHF           American Health Foundation

| | |
|---|---|
| AI | Advocacy Institute |
| ALA | American Lung Association |
| ALAC | American Lung Association of Colorado |
| AMA | American Medical Association |
| AMWA | American Medical Women's Association |
| ANR | Americans for Nonsmokers' Rights |
| ANRF | Americans for Nonsmokers' Rights Foundation |
| APACT | Asian Pacific Association for the Control of Tobacco |
| APHA | American Public Health Association |
| APITEN | Asian Pacific Islander Tobacco Education Network |
| ARF | Addiction Research Foundation |
| ARIA | Associates for Research on Indoor Air |
| ARISE | Associates for Research in Substance Enjoyment |
| ASH | Action on Smoking and Health |
| ASH (UK) | Action on Smoking and Health (United Kingdom) |
| ASSIST | American Stop Smoking Intervention Study |
| ASTHO | Association of State and Territorial Health Officials |
| AT Co. | American Tobacco Company |
| ATF | (Bureau of) Alcohol, Tobacco and Firearms (also BATF) |

| | |
|---|---|
| ATLA | American Trial Lawyers Association |
| ATOD | alcohol, tobacco and other drugs |
| AzTEPP | Arizona Tobacco Education and Prevention Program |
| B&W (or BW) | Brown & Williamson Tobacco Corp. |
| BAP (BaP) | benzo(a)pyrene |
| BATF | Bureau of Alcohol, Tobacco and Firearms (also ATF) |
| BAT | British American Tobacco (Industries) |
| BATUS | U.S. division of BAT |
| BBS | bulletin board system |
| BEA | Bureau of Economic Analysis (Department of Commerce) |
| BIBRA | British Industry Biological Research Association |
| *BJC* | *British Journal of Cancer* |
| BM | Bursom Marstellar |
| BMA | British Medical Association |
| *BMJ* | *British Medical Journal* |
| BRFSS | Behavioral Risk Factor Surveillance System |
| BW | *See* B&W. |
| CAB | Civil Aeronautics Board |
| CAIS | Cancer Awareness in Scotland |
| CARE | Californians against Regulatory Excess |

CATS            Citizens against Tobacco Smoke

CCS             Canadian Cancer Society

CCSA            Canadian Centre on Substance Abuse

CCSH            Canadian Council on Smoking and Health

CCTC            Canadian Council for Tobacco Control
                (formerly CCSH, Canadian Council on
                Smoking and Health)

CDC             Centers for Disease Control and Prevention

*CDQ*           *Chronic Disease Quarterly*

CDR             Chronic Disease Reports (*MMWR*)

CEI             Competitive Enterprise Institute

CHD             coronary heart disease

CIAR            Center for Indoor Air Research

CIS             Congressional Information Service

CLAIR           clean air (CAIS program)

CNTC            China National Tobacco Corporation

CO              carbon monoxide

COHIS           Community Outreach Health Information
                System

COLD            chronic obstructive lung disease

COPD            chronic obstructive pulmonary disease

COTS            cotton, oilseeds, tobacco, and seeds

CPS             Current Population Surveys

| | |
|---|---|
| CRC | Consumer Response Center (FTC) |
| CRFA | Cancer Research Foundation of America |
| CRS | cut, rolled stem; Congressional Research Service |
| CSAP | Center for Substance Abuse Prevention |
| CSC | cigarette smoke condensate |
| CTAC | Counter-Drug Technology Assessment Center |
| CTFO | Council for a Tobacco-Free Ontario |
| CTR | Council for Tobacco Research |
| CVD | cardiovascular disease |
| DEG | diethylene glycol |
| DHHS | Department of Health and Human Services |
| DOC | Doctors Ought to Care; Department of Commerce |
| DOH | Department of Health |
| Dr. P.H. | doctor of public health |
| ELISAD | European Association of Libraries and Information Services on Alcohol and Other Drugs |
| ENACT | Effective National Action to Control Tobacco |
| EPA | Environmental Protection Agency (U.S.) |
| ERIC | Educational Resources Information Center |
| ERS | Economic Research Service (USDA) |
| ETS | environmental tobacco smoke (*See also* SHS [secondhand smoke].) |

| | |
|---|---|
| EU | European Union |
| FAA | Federal Aviation Administration |
| FAIR | Floridans against Increased Regulation |
| FAO | United Nations Food and Agriculture Organization |
| FAS | Foreign Agricultural Service (USDA) |
| FCC | Federal Communications Commission |
| FCTC | Framework Convention on Tobacco Control |
| FDA | Food and Drug Administration |
| FDCA | Food, Drug, and Cosmetic Act |
| FEC | Federal Election Commission |
| FEMA | Flavor and Extracts Manufacturers Association |
| FFDCA | Federal Food, Drug, and Cosmetic Act of 1938 |
| FHSA | Federal Hazardous Substances Labeling Act of 1960 |
| FORCES | Fight Ordinances and Restrictions to Control and Eliminate Smoking |
| FOREST | Freedom Organization for the Right to Enjoy Smoking Tobacco |
| FT | filter |
| FTC | Federal Trade Commission |
| FUBYAS | first usual brand young(er) adult smoker(s) |
| GASO | Great American Smokeout |

GASP            Group against Smokers' Pollution

GILS            Government Information Locator Service

GPO             Government Printing Office

GRAS            generally recognized as safe

HBI             Healthy Buildings International

HEW             U.S. Department of Health, Education and
                Welfare (now the Department of Health and
                Human Services)

HFA             Health for All

HHS             U.S. Department of Health and Human Services

HIS             Health Interview Survey (NCHS)

IAQ             indoor air quality

IARC            International Agency for Research on Cancer
                (WHO)

ICDRA           International Conference of Drug Regulatory
                Authorities

ICI             Imperial Chemical Industries (UK)

ICOSI           International Committee on Smoking Issues
                (succeeded by INFOTAB)

ICPA            International Commission for the Prevention of
                Alcoholism and Drug Dependency

ICPSR           Inter-university Consortium for Political and
                Social Research

IDA             Information about Drugs and Alcohol

IG              Inspector General (FTC)

| | |
|---|---|
| IGM | Internet Grateful Med |
| IHS | Indian Health Service |
| INFOTAB | International Tobacco Information Center/Centre International d'Information du Tabac |
| INWAT | International Network of Women against Tobacco |
| IPRC | Indiana Prevention Resource Center |
| IRP | Information Resources Press |
| ISR | Institute for Social Research (University of Michigan) |
| ITGA | International Tobacco Growers Association |
| *JAH* | *Journal of Adolescent Health* |
| *JAMA* | *Journal of the American Medical Association* |
| *JAMWA* | *Journal of the American Medical Women's Association* |
| KS | king-size |
| KSL | Kool Super Light |
| L&M | Liggett & Myers, Inc. |
| LCDC | Laboratory Centre for Disease Control (Canada) |
| MeSH | Medical Subject Headings |
| *MMWR* | *Morbidity and Mortality Weekly Report* |
| MPH | master of public health (degree) |
| MRD | marketing research department |

| | |
|---|---|
| MRFIT | Multiple Risk Fact Intervention Trial |
| MS | mainstream smoke |
| MSA | Multistate [or Master] Settlement Agreement |
| MTEC | Massachusetts Tobacco Education Clearinghouse |
| MTF | Monitoring the Future |
| NAAG | National Association of Attorneys General |
| NAC | National Audiovisual Center (NTIS) |
| NAP | Nicotine Augmentation Project (Lorillard) |
| NASS | National Agricultural Statistics Service (USDA) |
| NCADI | National Clearinghouse for Alcohol and Drug Information |
| NCBI | National Center for Biotechnology Information |
| NCCDPHP | National Center for Chronic Disease Prevention and Health Promotion |
| NCHS | National Center for Health Statistics |
| NCI | National Cancer Institute |
| NCRHI | National Council for Reliable Health Information |
| NCSH | National Clearinghouse for Smoking and Health |
| NCTH | National Clearinghouse on Tobacco and Health (Canada) |
| NCVHS | National Committee on Vital and Health Statistics |

| | |
|---|---|
| n.d. | no date |
| NDSN | National Drug Strategy Network |
| NFIA | National Families in Action |
| NGO(s) | nongovernmental organization(s) |
| NHANES | National Health and Nutrition Examination Survey |
| NHIC | National Health Information Center |
| NHIS | National Health Interview Survey |
| NHLBI | National Heart, Lung and Blood Institute |
| NHS | National Health Service (UK) |
| NICHD | National Institute of Child Health and Human Development |
| nicnet | Nicotine on the Net (web site of the Arizona Program for Nicotine and Tobacco Research) |
| NIDA | National Institute on Drug Abuse |
| NIDDK | National Digestive Diseases Information Clearinghouse |
| NIH | National Institutes of Health |
| NIOSH | National Institute for Occupational Safety and Health |
| NLM | National Library of Medicine |
| NMA(s) | national manufacturers' association(s) |
| NOHIC | National Oral Health Information Clearinghouse |

| | |
|---|---|
| N-O-T | Not on Tobacco (ALA) |
| NRT | nicotine replacement therapy |
| NSAWI | National Substance Abuse Web Index |
| NSCEP | National Service Center for Environmental Publications |
| NSM | new smoking material |
| NSTRTU | National Strategy to Reduce Tobacco Use in Canada |
| NTE | nicotine transfer efficiency |
| NTIS | National Technical Information Service |
| NWHIC | National Women's Health Information Center |
| NYSPP | National Youth Smoking Prevention Program |
| NYTS | National Youth Tobacco Survey |
| OAR | Office of Air and Radiation (EPA) |
| OCHP | Office of Children's Health Protection (EPA) |
| ODPHP | Office of Disease Prevention and Health Promotion |
| OIG | Office of Inspector General (FTC) |
| ONDCP | Office of National Drug Control Policy |
| OPHS | Office of Public Health and Science |
| OSH | Office on Smoking and Health (CDC) |
| OSHA | Occupational Safety and Health Administration |
| OTC | Office of Tobacco Control (Canada) |

| | |
|---|---|
| OTRU | Ontario Tobacco Research Unit |
| OTS | Ontario Tobacco Strategy |
| OWH | Office on Women's Health (PHS) |
| PAC(s) | political action committee(s) |
| PAH(s) | polycyclic aromatic hydrocarbon(s) |
| PAR | population-attributable risks |
| PATCH | Program against Teen Chewing |
| PCL | processed cigarette leaves |
| PEG | polyethylene glycol |
| PEI | polyethyleneimine |
| PEPS | Prevention Enhancement Protocols System |
| PHS | Public Health Service |
| PIRG(s) | public interest research group(s) |
| PM | Philip Morris |
| PME | Philip Morris Europe |
| PMI | Philip Morris International |
| *PNAS* | *Proceedings of the National Academy of Sciences* |
| PSC | Physicians for a Smoke Free Canada |
| PTCC | Program Training and Resource Center (Canada) |
| R&D | research and development |
| RADAR | Regional Alcohol and Drug Awareness |

Resource Center

RCP          Royal College of Physicians (England)

RITC         Research for International Tobacco Control

RJR          R. J. Reynolds Tobacco Holdings, Inc.

RJRT        R. J. Reynolds Tobacco Company (also simply RJR when context makes the meaning clear)

RPCI        Roswell Park Cancer Institute, Buffalo, New York

RTD         resistance to draw

RYO         roll-your-own

SAB         Scientific Advisory Board (CTR)

SALIS      Substance Abuse Librarians and Information Specialists

SAMHDA  Substance Abuse and Mental Health Data Archive, ICPSR

SAMHSA   Substance Abuse and Mental Health Services Administration

SAMMEC  Smoking-Attributable Mortality, Morbidity, and Economic Costs

S&T PME  Science and Technology, Philip Morris Europe

S and H    smoking and health

SCARC    Smoking Control Advocacy Resource Center

SCARCNet  Smoking Control Advocacy Resource Center Network

SCAT       Student Coalition against Tobacco

| | |
|---|---|
| SG | surgeon general |
| SGAC | Surgeon General's Advisory Committee |
| *SGR*(s) | *Surgeon General's Report*(s) |
| SH&B | Shook, Hardy & Bacon |
| SHS | secondhand smoke (*See also* ETS [environmental tobacco smoke].) |
| SLT | smokeless tobacco |
| SOSAS | Studies on the Social Acceptability of Smoking |
| SRNT | Society for Research on Nicotine and Tobacco |
| SS | sidestream smoke |
| ST | spit tobacco |
| STAT | Stop Teenage Addiction to Tobacco |
| STATE System | State Tobacco Activities Tracking and Evaluation System |
| STIC | State Tobacco Information Center |
| STMSA | Smokeless Tobacco Master Settlement Agreement |
| STOPN | Spit Tobacco Prevention Network |
| TACT | Trans-Atlantic Conference on Tobacco |
| TAEP | Tobacco Awareness Exhibits Program |
| TAPS | Teenage Attitudes and Practices Survey |
| TASSC | The Advancement of Sound Science Coalition |
| TATU | Teens against Tobacco Use |

| | |
|---|---|
| TCA | Tobacco Control Archives |
| TCRC | Tobacco Control Resource Center, Inc. |
| TDRS | Tobacco Demand Reduction Strategy (Canada) |
| TEPP | Tobacco Education and Prevention Program |
| TFI | Tobacco Free Initiative |
| TI | Tobacco Institute; tobacco industry |
| TIPS | Tobacco Information and Prevention Source (CDC) |
| TIRC | Tobacco Industry Research Committee (later the Council for Tobacco Research) |
| *TJI* | *Tobacco Journal International Magazine* |
| TMA | Tobacco Merchants Association |
| TMSC | Tobacco Manufacturers' Standing Committee |
| T/N ratio | tar-and-nicotine ratio |
| TPLP | Tobacco Products Liability Project |
| TPM | total particulate matter |
| TSNA(s) | tobacco-specific nitrosamine(s) |
| TTC(s) | transnational tobacco company(-ies) |
| UCSF | University of California at San Francisco |
| UICC | Union Internationale Contre le Cancer (International Union Against Cancer) |
| UMICH | University of Michigan |
| UMLS | Unified Medical Language System |

| | |
|---|---|
| UNCTAD | United Nations Conference on Trade and Development |
| USDA | U.S. Department of Agriculture |
| USDHHS | U.S. Department of Health and Human Services |
| USTC | United States Tobacco Company |
| WCTOH | World Conference on Tobacco OR Health |
| WHO | World Health Organization |
| YAS | young adult smoker(s) (*See also* FUBYAS.) |
| YMN | Youth Media Network |

# Index

Foundation for Economic Education, 261
"Framework Convention on Tobacco Control" (WHO), 241–42
"Frank Statement," 88
Franzen, Jonathan: on Big Tobacco, 286
Frontline: Inside the Tobacco Deal, site of, 366
Frontline: The Cigarette Papers, site of, 365
FTC. See Federal Trade Commission
"Functional Significance of Smoking in Everyday Life, The," 316–17

Gable, Clark, 5
GASP (Group to Alleviate Smoking Pollution) of Colorado, site of, 366
Gaston, Lucy Page
    Anti-Cigarette League and, 80, 83
    biographical sketch of, 126–27
    birth of, 78
    death of, 84
    on smoking, 292
General Foods, PM and, 97
Ginzel, K. H.: carcinogens and, 33
Glantz, Stanton
    B&W documents and, 102, 104
    biographical sketch of, 127
    on movies/smoking, 46, 112
Goldstone, Steven, 107
    on McCain bill, 112
    MSA and, 22
    national settlement and, 109
    RJR Nabisco Holdings Corp. and, 105
Goodman, Ellen: on Congress/big tobacco, 62
Gottlieb, Mark, 25
Government Information Resources, site of, 366
Government Printing Office (GPO), 249
GPO (Government Printing Office) Access, site of, 366
Grace, Edwin: on lung cancer/smoking, 86
Graham, Evarts A., 6, 16, 58
    biographical sketch of, 138
    study by, 87, 88
Great American Smokeout, 94
Great Forswearing, 13
Great Relapse, 13
Green, Harold: biographical sketch of, 127–28
Group against Smokers' Pollution (GASP), 261
Guam Department of Public Health

and Social Services, 273
"Guidelines for Controlling and Monitoring the Tobacco Epidemic" (WHO) 106
"Guidelines for School Health Programs to Prevent Tobacco Use and Addiction" (CDC), 51

Hahn, Paul D.: Plaza meeting and, 7
Haines case (1992), 100–101
Hammond, E. Cuyler, 6
Hariot, Thomas, 74
Harrison, William, 74
Hawaii Department of Health, 273
Hawkins, John, 73
Health, 26–32, 74, 112, 290
    smoking and, 15, 23, 25, 27, 60, 90, 290, 291, 299, 300
"Health Effects of Smoking among Young People" (CDC), 155–56
healthfinder (HHS), site of, 366
Health Statistics Sources: Internet Resources (National Library of Medicine), site of, 366–67
Heart attacks, 54, 104
Heart disease, 29
Hecht, Stephen, 34
Heim, Robert: defense by, 60
Hill & Knowlton (H&K), 7
Hill, A. Bradford, 6, 88, 89
Hill, John, 7, 77
Hilts, Philip J., 8, 287
Hoover's Online, site of, 367
Horn, Daniel, 6
Horton, Nathan, 61
Howard, Leslie, 5
Howard A. Engle, M.D., et al. v. R. J. Reynolds Tobacco et al. (1994), 24, 25
Humphrey, Hubert III: Medicaid suit by, 21, 103

"ICOSI Task Force Coverage of the Fourth World Conference on Smoking and Health—June 1979 in Stockholm," 317
Idaho Department of Health and Welfare, 273
Illinois Department of Public Health, 274
I Mind Very Much If You Smoke (NCI), 305
Imperial Cancer Research Fund, 37
Imperial Tobacco Group PLC, 280
Independent Scientific Committee on Smoking and Health, tar levels and, 96

# About the Author

D r. Harold V. Cordry is a graduate of the University of Kansas, where he received a B.A. in English, political science, and international relations, and a B.S. and M.A. in English and education. After working several years at *The Kansas City Star* and *The Times*, he earned a Ph.D. from the University of Missouri-Columbia in international and intercultural communication and Soviet studies. Before returning to daily journalism, he taught several years at MU School of Journalism and reviewed books and wrote commentary for numerous U.S. and Canadian newspapers. Throughout his subsequent career in university teaching, he has remained active in journalism, chiefly as an editorial writer and commentator. He has also published several books about language and etymology.